A 17, 19

Legal Concerns

ap. 4   A 12

ap. 6   A 13
               A 14

Education

2nd Edition

Education
An Introduction

DAVID G. ARMSTRONG
TEXAS A&M UNIVERSITY

KENNETH T. HENSON
UNIVERSITY OF ALABAMA

TOM V. SAVAGE
TEXAS A&M UNIVERSITY

MACMILLAN PUBLISHING COMPANY
NEW YORK
COLLIER MACMILLAN PUBLISHERS
LONDON

Acknowledgments

We would like to acknowledge Juliann Barbato for providing most of the photos that decorate our part and chapter openings. Also we acknowledge the Clover Park School District, Tacoma, WA, who provided the photo on p. 24, Sue Anderson and Gary Gerhard, Monroe School District, Monroe, WA, for the photo on p. 256, and the Tacoma School District, Tacoma, WA, for the photo on p. 418.

Copyright © 1985, Macmillan Publishing Company, a division of Macmillan, Inc.

PRINTED IN THE UNITED STATES OF AMERICA

Earlier edition copyright © 1981 by Macmillan Publishing Company

Macmillan Publishing Company
866 Third Avenue, New York, New York 10022

Collier Macmillan Canada, Inc.

Library of Congress Cataloging in Publication Data

Armstrong, David G.
   Education, an introduction.

   Includes bibliographical references and index.
   1. Public schools—United States.   I. Henson, Kenneth T.   II. Savage, Tom V.   III. Title.
LA217.A86 1985   371'.01'0973   84-4972
ISBN 0-02-304100-5

Printing: 6 7 8   Year: 6 7 8 9 0 1 2 3

ISBN 0-02-304100-5

Preface

Today, education is very much in the national spotlight. Schools are viewed as nurturers of the nation's intellectual capital. As such, there is an expectation that they provide youngsters with the kinds of capabilities they will need to survive in a postindustrial society that increasingly is characterized by an emphasis on high technology. There are concerns that American schools have not been "keeping up" in terms of their ability to produce young people with the kinds of intellectual skills needed for the nation to survive in a world where, increasingly, technological talent is being prized.

These concerns, in the early and middle 1980s, spawned a number of national efforts to study the condition of American education. Such groups as the Task Force on Education for Economic Growth and the National Commission on Excellence in Education produced reports highly critical of many present school practices. These reports have generated a tremendous amount of public interest and much political debate.

Escalation of public interest in education, from the perspective of professional educators, has had both positive and negative points. Certainly those who have worked in the field for years are heartened by a clear public appreciation for the importance of education. On the other hand, the popularity of the issue, at times, has prompted some people to speak out on the issue who have not been as knowledgeable about the complexities of the problems facing schools and teachers as professional educators would have hoped. To be blunt, much misinformation and incomplete information continue to circulate in discussions about the quality of American education. This situation challenges prospective teachers to become knowledgeable professionals who have a secure command of issues and who can communicate them intelligently to the general public. This new edition of *Education: An Introduction* strives to provide individuals interested in education with the kind of information needed to discuss educational issues intelligently and to make reasoned judgments about the advisability of committing themselves to a career in this field.

The first part of the book, entitled "Schools," contains six chapters that focus generally on schools as institutions. The first two chapters place public schools in their appropriate cultural and historical contexts. The third and fourth chapters examine issues related to control of public education and organization of school programs. The fifth chapter introduces information about the new area of computers and public school programs. The last chapter in the section briefly sketches the dimensions of a number of critical current educational issues.

Most users of this text probably are giving some thought to the possibility of becoming a classroom teacher. The chapters in Part II of the book, entitled "Teachers," examine issues associated with the people who teach and their roles in the schools today. The first two chapters in the section explore alternative motives for teaching and take note of statistical data profiling the kinds of individuals attracted to the profession. Subsequent chapters deal with such diverse topics as philosophical differences among teachers, teachers' roles, classroom management and discipline, teachers and the law, teachers' professional groups, and teachers' relationships with other professional groups who work in the schools.

The third part of the book, "Learners," introduces content related to characteristics of youngsters in public school classrooms. The first chapter in the section outlines some statistical profiles of today's learners. The second chapter focuses on exceptional learners in the school and provides particular insights regarding implications of important federal mainstreaming legislation. Other chapters introduce legal rights and responsibilities of learners and the role of extracurricular programming in the school.

The final part of the text, "Professional Considerations," focuses on issues associated with teachers' employment. The first chapter in the section details specific procedures followed in locating teacher vacancies and making applications. The final chapter in both the section and the book provides readers with an opportunity to engage in analysis of personal strengths and weaknesses as they wrestle with the decision "to teach or not to teach." The chapter also provides opportunities for reflection regarding how to achieve a "good fit" between the teacher and the age level or grade level with which he or she aspires to work.

This book could not have been published without the assistance of many considerate and caring people. We particularly extend our thanks to members of our families, who tolerated our frequent absences from home while we worked on this revision. We also greatly appreciate the assistance with manuscript preparation provided by Gay DeRouen. Finally, our thanks go out to our faithful and tolerant Macmillan editor and friend, Lloyd C. Chilton, for his thoughtful counsel on this project.

David G. Armstrong

Kenneth T. Henson

Tom V. Savage

Contents

PART I   Schools

CHAPTER 1 The Role of the School in Society   3

    Objectives 4
    Pretest 4
    Introduction 5
    Education's Importance: Perspectives from History 6
    Status of Education and Educators 10
    Education and Schooling 11
    Expectations of Schooling 11
    School Purposes: A Selection of Perspectives 14
    Recapitulation of Major Ideas 20
    Posttest 20
    Summary 21
    References 22

CHAPTER 2 History of American Education   24

    Objectives 25
    Pretest 25
    Introduction 26
    Education in the Early Colonial Period 28
    Education in the Late Colonial and the Revolutionary War Period 31
    Education from 1800 to the Civil War 32
    Education from the Civil War to 1900 34
    Twentieth Century Education to World War II 35
    American Education After World War II 39
    Recapitulation of Major Ideas 42
    Posttest 43
    Summary 44
    References 45

CHAPTER 3 Who Controls?   46

  Objectives   47
  Pretest   47
  Introduction   48
  Local Influences on the Schools   50
  State Influences on the Schools   55
  Federal Influences on the Schools   61
  Local, State, and Federal Influences: Some Final Thoughts   66
  Recapitulation of Major Ideas   67
  Posttest   68
  Summary   69
  References   70

CHAPTER 4 How Curricula Are Organized   71

  Objectives   72
  Pretest   72
  Introduction   73
  Nature of the Subject Matter   76
  Needs of Society   81
  Characteristics of Learners   84
  Curricula Today: State of Present Practices   88
  Recapitulation of Major Ideas   88
  Posttest   90
  Summary   90
  References   91

CHAPTER 5 Computers and Schools   92

  Objectives   93
  Pretest   93
  Introduction   94
  Computer Use in Schools: Some Alleged Advantages   95
  Computer Use in Schools: Some Concerns   99
  Academic Program Applications of Computers   101
  New Computer Applications for School Program Management   103
  Learning About Computers: Suggestions for Prospective Teachers   106
  Recapitulation of Major Ideas   110
  Posttest   111
  Summary   112
  References   113
  Glossary of Computer Terms   113

CHAPTER 6 Current Issues in Education   116

    Objectives   117
    Pretest   117
    Introduction   118
    Civil Rights   119
    Disenchantment with Public Institutions   129
    Quality of Education   130
    The Revolt of the Taxpayers   133
    Competency Testing   135
    Recapitulation of Major Ideas   137
    Posttest   138
    Summary   139
    References   139

PART II   Teachers

CHAPTER 7 Reasons for Teaching   143

    Objectives   144
    Pretest   144
    Introduction   145
    Nice Working Conditions   150
    Lack of Routine   152
    Importance of Teaching   157
    Excitement of Learning   160
    Why Teach? Some Final Thoughts   162
    Recapitulation of Major Ideas   162
    Posttest   163
    Summary   164
    References   165

CHAPTER 8 Who Are the Teachers?   166

    Objectives   167
    Pretest   167
    Introduction   168
    Personal and Family Backgrounds of Teachers   168
    Employment Situations of Teachers   172
    Teacher Supply and Demand   179
    Recapitulation of Major Ideas   183
    Posttest   184

Summary   185
References   185

CHAPTER 9 The Teacher's Philosophy   187

Objectives   188
Pretest   188
Introduction   188
Metaphysics   192
Epistemology   193
Axiology   196
Logic   197
Philosophies of Education   198
Teachers' Philosophies and Educational Issues   204
Recapitulation of Major Ideas   205
Posttest   207
Summary   207
References   208

CHAPTER 10 The Roles of the Teacher   209

Objectives   210
Pretest   210
Introduction   211
Teachers' Instructional Responsibilities   213
Teachers' Counseling Responsibilities   219
Teachers' Administrative and Supervisory Responsibilities   221
Curriculum Development Responsibilities   223
Teachers' Responsibilities for Professional Growth   224
Teachers' Public Relations Responsibilities   226
Teachers' Roles: Some Reflections   229
Recapitulation of Major Ideas   230
Posttest   232
Summary   232
References   233

CHAPTER 11 Classroom Management and Discipline   234

Objectives   235
Pretest   235
Introduction   236
Classroom Management   237
Discipline   242

Classroom Management and Discipline: Some Final Thoughts   251
Recapitulation of Major Ideas   252
Posttest   253
Summary   254
References   254

CHAPTER 12   Legal Concerns of Teachers   **256**

Objectives   257
Pretest   257
Introduction   258
Conditions of Employment   258
Teachers' Rights   269
Teachers' Legal Liability   275
Recapitulation of Major Ideas   280
Posttest   281
Summary   282
References   282

CHAPTER 13   Teachers' Professional Groups   **284**

Objectives   285
Pretest   285
Introduction   286
The National Education Association   288
The American Federation of Teachers   295
What's Ahead for Teachers' Organizations?   299
Recapitulation of Major Ideas   300
Posttest   301
Summary   302
References   303

CHAPTER 14   Teachers and Other Professionals   **304**

Objectives   305
Pretest   305
Introduction   306
Education Professors and Teachers   307
Teachers and Administrators   311
Teachers and Counselors   314
Teachers and School Psychologists   317
Teachers and District Curriculum Specialists   318
Teachers and Selected Other Nonteaching Professionals   321

Recapitulation of Major Ideas   322

Posttest   323

Summary   324

References   324

PART III   Learners

CHAPTER 15   Learner Characteristics   329

Objectives   330

Pretest   330

Introduction   331

Changing Patterns in School Classrooms   331

Patterns of Children's Development   336

The Work of Jean Piaget   337

Physical Characteristics of Youngsters of Different Ages   340

Recapitulation of Major Ideas   349

Posttest   349

Summary   350

References   351

CHAPTER 16   The Exceptional Learner   352

Objectives   353

Pretest   353

Introduction   354

Public Law 94-142: Basic Provisions   356

The Nature of Handicapping Conditions   359

School District Administrations and Public Law 94-142   368

Recapitulation of Major Ideas   370

Posttest   371

Summary   372

References   373

CHAPTER 17   Learners' Rights and Responsibilities   374

Objectives   375

Pretest   375

Introduction   376

Historical Changes in Society's View of the Child in School   376

Disciplining Learners   380

Due Process   383
Marriage and Pregnancy   384
Freedom of Speech and Expression   386
Search and Seizure   387
Grades, Diplomas, and Graduation   389
Family Educational Rights and Privacy   389
Curriculum and Instruction   390
Recapitulation of Major Ideas   392
Posttest   393
Summary   394
References   394

CHAPTER 18 The Extracurricular/Cocurricular Program   396

Objectives   397
Pretest   397
Introduction   398
Kinds of Extracurricular/Cocurricular Programs   399
Criticisms of the Extracurricular/Cocurricular Program   402
How Are Activities Programs Supposed to Benefit Students?   406
Why Do Students Participate in School Activities?   408
The Numbers of Learners in Activities Programs   409
What Keeps Learners from Participating in the Activities Program?   410
The Question of Teachers' Pay for Extracurricular/Cocurricular Work   412
Recapitulation of Major Ideas   414
Posttest   415
Summary   416
References   416

PART IV: Professional Considerations

CHAPTER 19 Getting a Job   421

Objectives   422
Pretest   422
Introduction   423
Finding Out About Teaching Vacancies   424
The Letter of Inquiry   427
The Résumé   431
Applications   434
Placement Centers   435

The Interview   438
Recapitulation of Major Ideas   442
Posttest   445
Summary   445
References   446

CHAPTER 20 Teaching and You   **447**

Objectives   448
Values Inventory   448
Do You Really Want to Teach?   449
"I Don't Know What Else to Do!"   450
"Teaching Isn't Intellectually Demanding!"   451
"Several of My Relatives Are Teachers . . . ."   453
"I Like the Autonomy of Teachers."   454
"I Like Working with Youngsters."   454
"I Want to Make a Contribution to Society."   456
Where Can You Make Your Best Contribution?   457
Some Final Thoughts   461
Recapitulation of Major Ideas   461
Postexercise   462
Summary   463
References   464

APPENDIX Answers to Pretest/Posttest Questions   **465**

Name Index   **469**

Subject Index   **473**

1
The Role of the
School in Society

Objectives

This chapter provides information to help the reader to

1. Identify basic assumptions concerning the role of schools in society.
2. Define the differences between education and schooling.
3. Identify the differing expectations that people hold regarding desired outcomes of schooling.
4. Identify a number of different and potentially contradictory purposes of education.

Pretest

DIRECTIONS: Using your own paper, answer each of the following true/false questions. For each correct statement, write the word *true* on your paper. For each incorrect statement, write the word *false* on your paper.

1. *Education* and *schooling* are identical terms that can be used interchangeably.
2. American society generally has placed little faith in the public school system.
3. The American educational system has few concrete accomplishments to its credit.
4. Nearly three fourths of the young people of the United States attain reading levels that are attained only by much smaller percentages of young people in many other countries.
5. United States' students, in terms of their knowledge of rights and responsibilities associated with their roles as citizens, rank higher than students in any other nation.
6. Schools are institutions that are particularly well-suited for solving serious social problems.
7. Only in relatively recent times has citizenship education been recognized as an important responsibility of the public schools.
8. Some opponents of vocational programs in the schools oppose them on the grounds that they may tend to perpetuate class differences in our society.
9. There is general agreement about which subjects should be taught to produce maximum intellectual growth in young people.
10. Proposed changes in education almost always enjoy nearly unanimous public support.

Introduction

Spring comes late to the Centennial Valley. In this high western Montana basin country, snow sometimes lingers until April or even May. Nights remain cool throughout the summer. Hard, killing frosts come in late August or early September. With a growing season that is too short for wheat or even barley, this spectacular landscape is home to a small number of hardy cattle ranchers. Roads are few. Neighbors are distant. Department stores, pharmacies, and most other kinds of business do not exist. Yet, even here, there are schools. And in these schools, there are teachers.

Far to the southeast of the tranquil Centennial Valley, bulldozers scrape earth, cranes lift steel, and commuters dodge thick traffic on crowded freeways. Another morning breaks in the bustling Houston area. In the city's center, youngsters who are black, brown, yellow, white, and every intermediate shade head off to their schools in the urban core. In the suburbs, other groups of youngsters, predominantly white, wait for buses to carry them to well-manicured school campuses. These schools represent a tremendous diversity. And in each of them, dedicated teachers are at work.

Well to the east of Houston, not far from where the Atlantic brushes against the continent's easternmost reaches, lies Snow Hill, Maryland. Nestled in the rural landscapes of Maryland's Eastern Shore, Snow Hill is far removed from the maintstream hubs of the nation's east-coast metropolises. There are no large museums. There are no operas. No resident symphony claims the area as home. But there are schools. And teachers go forth pridefully each day in Snow Hill much as they do in Houston and in the Centennial Valley.

Even in the middle 1980s, the United States contains hundreds of isolated fastnesses like Montana's Centennial Valley. Today, Houston is but one of the many major urban centers found in the East, the West, the North, and the South. Still, too, pleasant rural communities such as Snow Hill continue to exist in surprising numbers. Each of these places boasts unique features. Each exudes a special quality that says to the native daughter or son, "Here I am home." Yet, for all that is unique among American places, each shares access to a unifying American institution: the public school.

Public schools are everywhere. They provide a common set of experiences through which the vast majority of Americans pass. They are bearers and transmitters of many important cultural values and traditions. In short, they provide much of the social glue that binds together millions of people scattered in diverse physical settings across the breadth of a continent.

Given the importance of schools in American society, not surprisingly the institution has had a long history as a focal point for discussion and debate. In the sections that follow, attention is directed to issues associated with the place of the school in our society and to how this place has led to a continuing argument over what schools should and should not do.

Education's Importance: Perspectives from History

Throughout history, the importance of education has been widely recognized. Aristotle, the Greek philosopher, believed that the success of governments depended on the quality of education provided to young people. He saw education as charged with the obligation of saving society by providing educated citizens capable of assuming responsibilities of governance.

A similar political purpose for education was reflected in the thought of some of the founders of the United States. Thomas Jefferson noted that, "If a nation expects to be ignorant and free, in a state of civilization, it expects what never was and never will be" (Jefferson, reported in Ford, 1893, p. 221). To Jefferson, education was fundamental to the preservation of a free society.

From its beginnings as a nation, the United States was seen as a land of opportunity by people living elsewhere. As American schools developed, access to schooling came to be seen as one of the opportunities available to those who came to America's shores. As opposed to the situation existing in many other lands, potential immigrants to the United States soon recognized that in this new country children could attain, through education, a higher status in the society than that accorded their parents. For many, the American educational system came to be recognized as a ladder to both economic and social success.

Some scholars viewed education not simply as a mechanism for improving the lot of individual students but as an ingredient essential to the health of the entire society. In a long career spanning the late nineteenth and the first half of the twentieth century, John Dewey, one of the most influential figures in the development of educational thought, suggested that education was vital to the maintenance of the core values of the society (Dewey, 1916). H. G. Wells made this point perhaps as dramatically as it has ever been made. He wrote, "Human history becomes more and more a race between education and catastrophe" (Lean, 1976, p. 138).

President John F. Kennedy continued this theme in a message to Congress. He said:

> Education is the keystone and the arch of freedom and progress. Nothing has contributed more to the enlargement of this nation's strength and opportunities than our traditional system of free, universal elementary and secondary education coupled with widespread availability of college education. (Kennedy, 1963, p. 103)

Education's Accomplishments

The accomplishments of public education in the United States have been impressive. Jarolimek (1981) cites, as examples of how schools have served

Box 1-1
Limitations of Education in a Society without Schools

In times long past, societies had no formal institutions known as schools. Young people were taught by parents, other relatives, and occasionally, by friends. Knowledge useful in one generation automatically was presumed to be useful for the next.

LET'S PONDER

Consider how you personally might have been affected had you been raised in a society without a formal system of schools. Then, respond to the following questions.

1. Consider your own parents. What kinds of occupations might they follow today if their only source of education had been their parents?
2. What do you think would happen to our rate of economic development were all schools to close and youngsters to become dependent on their parents, relatives, and friends for all of their education?
3. Americans pride themselves on the social mobility made possible by their society. Would this be possible without a school system? Why, or why not?
4. Do you think people had a larger sense of personal security before school systems developed and they were taught primarily by family members? Do people feel comfortable when they are exposed to information and attitudes unknown to their parents? Why, or why not?
5. Some have said schools are basic to human progress. Progress implies change. Do people really like change? Have schools and the changes they have made possible made people more psychologically uncomfortable than they would be otherwise? Why, or why not?

society, advances in medicine and allied health, responses to the space race, diminished rates of illiteracy, and the flowering of American agriculture. He points out that in 1930 only 5 percent of Nobel Prizes had been claimed by Americans. Today, that figure has risen to more than 40 percent.

Other authorities have emphasized the impact of the educational system on the overall economic growth of the country. Hodgkinson (1982) states that economists now estimate that between one fourth and one half of the growth in the value of goods and services produced in the United States over the past twenty years can be attributed to an increasingly educated work force.

Benefits that have come to the society from education in large measure derive from an important historical trend. Simply stated, this trend has witnessed a pattern of increasing availability of educational opportunity over time. To illustrate how far we have come, some historical statistics are revealing. In the spring of 1890, there were only 203,000 students enrolled in high schools in the entire country. For the most part, these were academically talented youngsters who were preparing themselves for college (*Historical Statistics of the United States: Colonial Times to 1970*, 1975, p. 368). These students represented only a small fraction of all the fifteen- to nineteen-year-old youngsters in the country. Today, about 75 percent of such young people are full-time students. Similar figures for France and Germany are 51 percent, for Great Britain 44 percent, and for Italy 40 percent (Hodgkinson, 1982).

Access to education has improved dramatically for minorities seeking the benefits of schooling in the United States. In 1950, only 38 percent of black students who started high school graduated. By 1982, this figure had increased to 75 percent (Hodgkinson, 1982).

The Educational Quality Issue

Some people have argued that increased access to educational opportunities has resulted in a decline in the quality of educational experiences. Let us for a moment examine an assumption that frequently accompanies charges that education today is not what it used to be. This assumption is that at some unspecified time in the past, schools were better and, hence, people as a whole were better educated. This assumption simply will not stand up to close examination.

Consider, for example, that historically the period 1540 to 1640 is viewed as a time of educational boom in England. At the *end* of this "boom," the literacy rate for London had increased to only about 60 percent and the literacy rate for England as a whole to only about 30 percent. (It is between 95 and 100 percent in the United States today.) In the years before this "boom," educational attainment was restricted to much smaller numbers of people. For example, between the sixth and eleventh centuries, only three English kings were able to sign their names (Brandt, 1982).

Statistics from earlier in the United States history suggest that our nation in former times definitely was not an educational utopia. In 1839, for example, Governor Campbell of Virginia lamented that in many cities and counties only about one fourth of the men applying for marriage licenses could sign their own names. Somewhat later in the nineteenth century, the United States Commissioner of Education reported that illiteracy had grown faster than the population as a whole during the years from 1840 to 1850 (*Report of the Commissioner of Education*, 1870). There was a fear that the nation was rushing headlong toward total illiteracy.

In our own century, rapid increases in school enrollments during the 1920s and 1930s led many people to declare that educational standards were falling. Krug has commented on these concerns:

> Today's older people would not be flattered by what was said about them then. According to the pedagogical rhetoric of the 1920s, the academic quality of the

students then in high school represented a calamitous decline from the heights of excellence . . . occupied by their predecessors before the war (Krug, 1972, pp. 107–108).

Somewhat similar concerns have been voiced in more recent times as efforts have been mounted to provide educational services to virtually the entire age-eligible population.

Though some may differ, the preponderance of evidence suggests that there never has been a "golden age" when average educational levels were better than they are today. But what about today? Is there evidence that our educational system has gone "soft?" How do the performance levels of American students compare with those of youngsters elsewhere? Generally, the answer is that graduates of American schools have little to hang their heads about.

Tyler (1981) reported on a broad-ranging international assessment of educational performance. He found that the average scores of American fourteen-your-olds on a test of reading comprehension was third highest of the fifteen nations tested. American students were outperformed only by students of New Zealand and Finland. These results, as Tyler noted, are remarkable given that the American school system admits virtually all comers, whereas those of many other countries serve only a much narrower group of intellectually talented young people.

In the field of mathematics, Tyler noted that in the area of applying mathematics to everyday problems, students from the United States were outscored only by students from Japan. Hodgkinson (1982) reported that at the 1981 International Mathematics Olympiad, the United States team placed first among teams fielded by 27 nations. He concluded that even though public education in the United States is designed to serve every student, still the top 5 percent of students in the United States are as skillful as the top 5 percent of the school population anywhere in the world.

A number of standardized tests reveal improvement in some important curricular areas. A study of Indiana youngsters revealed that students in the fourth grade and the tenth grade in 1944 did not read as well as similar groups of students in 1976 (Hodgkinson, 1982).

There are some areas where test scores have not revealed such positive results. Certainly there has been continuing concern over declines of Scholastic Aptitude Test scores over the past decade. Recent evidence has suggested that this decline may have been arrested. In another area, in his report of international assessment of educational performance Tyler (1981) noted that students in the United States did not compare favorably with youngsters from other countries in terms of their grasp of their political system and their rights and responsibilities as citizens. This study also revealed that the United States education system possibly may be deficient in providing for a smooth transition from the world of the school to the world of work.

Box 1-2
Criticism of the Schools

There are frequent articles and reports in the news media criticizing the public schools. They are usually accompanied by some proposals to improve the schools or return them to some previous status.

LET'S PONDER

1. Based on your own experience, what do you think needs to be improved in the schools?
2. Does your experience support or contradict the picture painted by contemporary critics?
3. Do you believe your experience with the schools was common or unique? What leads you to that conclusion?
4. What evidence is presented by contemporary critics of education to prove that schools are worse now than in the past?
5. It has been stated that the decade of the 1980s will go down in history as the decade when America turned its back on the public schools. What indications do you see that this might be the case? What evidence would you cite that might refute this conclusion?

Status of Education and Educators

Education and educators have statuses that seem to wobble unpredictably between the extremes of high and low. As Lortie (1975) has noted, the profession of education is both honored and disdained. Teachers, for example, may be praised for doing good and important work, but parents, in the main, seem anxious to advise their children to seek "higher" status and better paying occupations. In general, teachers' work is widely esteemed for its importance, but teachers themselves generally are not given the kind of regard reserved for those who achieve success in business, government, or the so-called "learned professions" such as medicine and the law.

Curiosities abound as one attempts to pin down the relative standing of education in the United States today. Duea (1982) reports that a recent Gallup poll ranked the schools second only to churches as institutions in which the public has confidence. Schools ranked well ahead of governmental agencies, the legal profession, and professional journalism. It is amusing to speculate what to make of journalists, whose profession apparently appears less credible to the public than that of educators, writing articles suggesting that the schools have lost their credibility. Where *does* the truth lie? That is an imponderable at this point, but certainly the search for it provides abundant potentials for debate and discussion.

While there are certainly important arguments to be made on many sides of the issue of the status of education, present trends do suggest that many people feel that all is not right with education. This concern increasingly is being observed in state capitals as legislators reflect constituents' beliefs that "something should be done" to upgrade the quality of school programs. Efforts to establish tougher minimum graduation requirements and to do a more thorough job of screening would-be teachers are symptomatic of a present concern for educational quality. Indications are that this general concern will be with us for some time to come.

Education and Schooling

As topics in this text are considered, it might be well to keep in mind the distinction between *education* and *schooling*. Education refers to the totality of experiences individuals go through in learning to cope with their physical and social environments. It is a lifelong process that may involve contacts with many people and institutions. Individuals learn from their families, from the media, from friends, and from institutions and experiences of all kinds. Education does not begin or end with the school. Ultimately, responsibility for education resides with each person. Every one of us must decide what is important about a given experience and what might be learned from it.

Different societies have developed different procedures to promote the educational process. In some cultures, nearly all responsibility is borne by the family. In technically advanced societies such as ours, a special institution has evolved that has been assigned the responsibility for a large share of the educational function. This is the school. Schooling consists of that part of education that results from an individual's contact with schools. Though schooling is important, it alone is never the only contributor to the total education of a given individual. Other influences also continue to play a role.

In technical societies, schooling generally plays a larger part in the total education of an individual than in nontechnical societies. Advancing technology has made the overall goals of education so complex that they really require the kind of organization and specialization that can be found in the school. Parental knowledge generally is not broad enough to equip a young person for the kinds of roles demanded by a technically advanced society. Most parents recognize this point, and they willingly turn over their youngsters at an early age to the schools out of a recognition that to do otherwise would place youngsters at a severe disadvantage in their later years.

Expectations of Schooling

Concerns parents and others might have about schools are to a large degree associated with expectations regarding what schooling can do. Throughout American history, there has been a tradition of placing great expectations on schooling. The colonial Puritans went so far as to link schooling, education,

Box 1-3
Are the Schools Oppressors?

The following long letter recently appeared on an editorial page of a leading newspaper.

America the land of the free???? Now that's just baloney. Let me explain myself. For six years, I've been in the courts trying to keep my youngster out of public schools. And, for six years, I've been threatened with jail if I don't see to it my son arrives to become part of the "official herd" on the first day of classes.

Now, what I want to do is educate my son at home. I'm well read, so is my wife. Furthermore, I know what kind of attitudes I want my son to have when he's 16 or 17. *And,* I know these attitudes are different from those he'll pick up in school. (I feel he's already been damaged.)

Public schools are nothing but a factory for state-approved indoctrination. The real purpose is to convince kids that "more is better," "mass produced is superior," and that "accepting what the government says is 'god-like.'" The way my wife and I see it, those attitudes build an air-tight case for future disaster. We don't buy it. And, we don't think the school has the right to impose these assumptions on an impressionable youngster. We believe in freedom of choice. The schools say they do too, but obviously this is a concept valued more as a vacuous verbalism than as a principle to live by.

I urge all of you to write your state legislator to urge *immediate repeal* of all existing mandatory attendance laws."

LET'S PONDER

1. Suppose you decided to write a letter opposing this view. What would you say?
2. What do you find to be the strongest points in the letter?
3. What points in the letter do you find hardest to accept? Why?
4. Overall, what is your personal reaction to the position taken by the letter writer?
5. What changes might you expect if his campaign to repeal mandatory attendance laws was successful?

and salvation. While perhaps limiting the Puritan feeling that there might be some afterlife benefit from good education, the founding fathers of the United States and those who came after them still had extraordinarily high expectations of schooling. Many saw it as a vehicle for overcoming class distinctions and for building a commitment to broadly held values. Later, schools were seen as places where immigrants could be transformed into "real" Americans, where prejudice could be erased, and where vocational training of every kind could provide a skilled work force for the nation's employers. This tradition of high expectation continues today.

In particular, the view is widespread that schools ought to be leaders in efforts to overcome serious social problems of all kinds. If drug abuse is an important problem, then the schools should help solve it. If there are too many highway fatalities, then some courses in the schools are believed, by many, to be realistic reponses to the problem. Some critics of this approach suggest that the schools may have become convenient "dumping grounds" for social problems. The idea appears to be—so allege the critics—to assign the schools to "solve" whatever social problems become troublesome. Perkinson (1977) has argued that such practices represent escapist thinking. He contends that converting social problems into educational problems may be simply a way for the adult world to avoid facing up to these issues.

How well equipped are schools to remedy deeply rooted social problems? Not very. Schools are part of society. Thus, when problems such as racism affect the larger society, the schools too are affected. It is too much to assume that schools, alone, can change attitudes and values and overcome problems without a similar change in attitudes and values in the larger society of which the school is a part. As Jarolimek (1981) points out, much of the decision-making required to attack serious social problems is influenced by social, political, and economic forces that the school is powerless to control.

Arguments over the possible role of schools as social-problem solvers represent only one area of debate regarding what schools, properly, should do. A number of additional issues are raised in the next section.

Box 1-4
The School as a Solver of Deep-seated Social Problems

Some have argued that schools properly should assume reponsibility for such thorny problems as pollution, racism, sexism, and poverty. They allege that a "good education" will cure these ills. By implication, presence of these problems seems to suggest that today education may not be "good."

LET'S PONDER

Read the paragraph above and respond to the following questions:

1. How do you react to the paragraph above? What is the basis for your reaction?
2. Have educators been too willing to assume responsibility for problems beyond their capacity to solve? Why, or why not?
3. Is there a need for educators to feel guilty because the school, apparently, has been unable to solve certain major social problems? Why, or why not?
4. Is the school a social leader or a social follower? Why do you think so?
5. Would social problems disappear if everybody had a "good" education? Why, or why not?
6. Twenty years from now would you expect schools to be under more pressure or less pressure to solve serious social problems? Why?

School Purposes: A Selection of Perspectives

Conceptions about the purposes of schools have been sources of debate in education for years, and such debates range over a tremendous variety of topics. Today, for example, there are ongoing discussions focusing on such important themes as "back to the basics," educating youngsters to ensure that they have certain "minimum competencies," and adequately preparing youngsters for the demands of the "world of work."

In thinking about alternative views of what schooling should accomplish, sometimes it is tempting to suggest that virtually all stated purposes have some merit. Indeed, some people do argue that schools should take on such diverse responsibilities as (1) ensuring the preservation of the social order, (2) preparing youngsters for effective citizenship, (3) imparting sound intellectual knowledge, (4) preparing youngsters for vocations, and (5) helping young people realize their individual potentials. The problem with the "schools-can-do-all-of-these-things-and-more" approach is that time is limited. In fact, schools must make choices and must allocate more time to some purposes than to others. The necessity to choose, given time constraints, suggests that schools in reality do not have the option of giving equal attention to a number of purposes. Any attempt to do that likely will result in no purpose being well served. Given that choices will have to be made, it makes sense for individuals contemplating careers in teaching to become familiar with issues associated with several alternative school purposes. Such knowledge can contribute to sound decision-making when choices have to be made. A number of program perspectives are briefly described in the subsections that follow.

Education for Citizenship

Education for citizenship has been a purpose of schooling that has enjoyed a long history. The perspective derives from the idea that there is a unique American world view. This world view is thought to require citizens who accept democratic decision-making as a core value and who willingly assume active roles in the self-governance process. Given this understanding, schools are viewed as agencies that properly encourage youngsters to commit to these deeply held values. This perspective sometimes is viewed as placing special obligations on such courses as United States History and American Government where, it is assumed, a "good citizenship" orientation flows quite naturally from the content of the subject matter.

In practice, the education-for-citizenship approach has spawned much debate. A basic problem is that of defining the term *good citizenship*. Some see the term as providing a framework for school programs that will teach an appreciation for existing social patterns. Others, critical of existing patterns, believe that good citizenship involves social activism designed to challenge existing social patterns. Clearly teachers who are committed to the education-for-citizenship approach vary in terms of what they think such programs should accomplish. Even more importantly, there are tremendous differences in the community as a whole regarding the appropriate ends of good citizenship programs. Consequently, teachers must be prepared for something less than 100-percent community support for education-for-citizenship program in the schools. Conceptions regarding what constitutes "good and appropriate" instruction vary too much within the community for such programs ever to please everyone.

Box 1-5
Let's Educate those Radicals Away

The following "guest editorial" recently appeared in a newspaper.

They said Johnny couldn't read, and rightly they were concerned. They said Johnny couldn't compute, and rightly they were concerned. They said Johnny couldn't write grammatical sentences, and rightly they were concerned. But they never asked whether Johnny could put it all together in a *responsible* way, and that's why we should all be concerned.

Today, voting rates among the under-25 age group are at historic lows. Volunteer agencies complain that they cannot find any help and that young people are the most reluctant volunteers of all. The caliber of people presenting themselves as candidates for public office is at an all-time low. Signs pointing to a social Apocalypse are all about us. Unless we do something, we shall reap a bitter harvest indeed.

Let us begin with the programs our youngsters are exposed to in the schools. Let us reemphasize the old values or responsibility, of mutual caring, of respect for constituted authority. Let us put to rest negativism, challenge-for-the-sake-of-challenge, unbridled cynicism about our institutions, and an irresponsible commitment to unproductive "me-ism." Let education for good citizenship become the rallying cry of our schools. Let us again produce the kinds of people proud to be Americans, dedicated to our institutions, and proud of our present social order.

LET'S PONDER

1. What kind of a school program might be implied by this editorial?
2. How would this program be regarded by the teaching staff? Would you expect all teachers to support it? Why, or why not?
3. What assumptions does the writer make about traditional social institutions? Do all people share these assumptions?
4. What kind of public reaction might you expect if a program similar to that described in the editorial were installed in the schools?
5. What is your personal reaction to proposals made in the editorial?

Education for Vocational Preparation

Vocational education as an appropriate purpose of schooling has had a relatively long history. Certainly it is an orientation that continues to enjoy broad support today. Indeed, many citizens would argue that the best measure of a school's effectiveness is its ability to turn out students who are well-prepared for the world of work.

For people strongly committed to the education-for-vocational-preparation view, the most "basic" school subjects are those most obviously needed by adults in the workplace. Reading and writing, for example, receive high marks as "important" school subjects. On the other hand, courses in such areas as art and music might be regarded as "nice to have" but certainly not "essential."

The vocational preparation view of schooling is not without its critics. Critics attack the perspective on several grounds. Some contend that a school program heavily oriented toward vocational preparation has the potential to perpetuate social class distinctions. These critics fear that students may be channeled into a narrow vocational stream that will restrict their career options to only a few alternatives. It is argued that such restrictions may unnecessarily restrict individual freedom and social mobility.

Other critics point out that the vocational needs of the society change in an unpredictable fashion. Hence, there is a danger that vocationally oriented programs may turn out students with skills that are obsolete. Critics with these kinds of concerns contend that the best vocational preparation may be that provided after school graduation by individual employers who know exactly what kinds of skills their employees need. Some of these critics suggest that the best preparation the schools can provide for the world of work is a broad-based program that produces students who are flexible, capable of thinking, and adaptable to a variety of world-of-work circumstances.

In summary, the vocational-preparation perspective shares with the citizenship-education perspective a capacity to generate a good deal of controversy. Beginning teachers are unlikely to find complete agreement either within the school or outside the school about the appropriateness of vocational preparation as a proper purpose of schooling.

Education for Intellectual Attainment

Almost no one argues against the view that schools have an important responsibility to develop students' intellects. Controversy centers, rather, on the degree to which this responsibility should supersede all other responsibilities or potential responsibilities.

Some strong supporters of intellectual attainment as the primary objective of schools suggest that this purpose really is what schooling is all about and that other outcomes should receive only minimal emphasis. One proponent of this view, Robert Hutchins, has commented: "If education is rightly understood, it will be understood as the cultivator of intellect" (Butts, 1975, p. 5).

This position has a long history in American education. In general, the view suggests that school programs should not tackle citizenship education or vocational preparation directly. Rather, programs should focus on intellectual attainment. Once intellectual attainment has been achieved, good citizenship and an ability to handle work-related responsibilities will be natural by-products.

Critics of this purpose of education raise a number of objections. Some question the assumption that without direct instruction in the schools, students automatically will acquire good citizenship and vocational competence as a result of their exposure to programs emphasizing intellectual competence. There is some feeling that it is too much to expect young people to bridge the gap between intellectual knowledge and the kinds of citizenship skills and job-related knowledge they will need in the "real world."

Other critics take issue with suggestions of some proponents of a heavy emphasis on intellectual attainment that school programs be strongly centered on such subjects as foreign languages, mathematics, history, literature, and the hard sciences—subjects thought capable of "challenging" the intellect. Critics allege that such subjects really are directed at a narrow, college-bound, intellectual elite. When schools serve the entire population of young people, it is not appropriate, these critics argue, to place such a heavy emphasis on an orientation that, in reality, is of benefit only to a small percentage of the total school population.

Other arguments, too, have been raised against the intellectual-attainment orientation. Certainly it appears to be an issue that will continue to be debated in the years ahead.

Education for Individual Development

"Consider individual differences" is an admonition so ingrained in the psyche of American educators as to rank almost as an unquestioned article of faith. The statement flows logically from a core value of American society: the worth and dignity of the individual human being. There is an American bias that great human achievement, in the main, results from individual rather than collective effort. Hence, it is not surprising that nurturing the development of individual differences has been an oft-expressed expectation of American schools.

As is true with other statements of expectation, the view that schools should place a heavy emphasis on individual development has critics as well as supporters. Some critics suggest that overemphasis on individualism reflects an ignorance of the cooperative nature of our society. Human beings, critics point out, are social creatures who benefit from living together and exchanging skills. Our society could not exist as it does today and people would certainly be less well off if people really acted as if they had responsibility to no one other than themselves. Youngsters may be damaged, some critics feel, if school programs hold individualism up as the only value worth pursuing. Young people live in a social world, and the school program must prepare them for the reality of working with and accepting others.

Supporters of the individualism perspective claim that critics misunderstand their position. They are not suggesting, so they say, that individuals be taught that they exist in a vacuum and that they need have no interactions with others. Rather, proponents suggest that the individualism emphasis merely is designed to help youngsters establish a strong sense of personal identity and purpose in a world in which, necessarily, they must work closely with others.

The debate between critics and supporters of the individual development perspective seems destined to go on for a good many years to come. In preparing to deal with this issue, prospective teachers should demand a clear explanation of terms when words like *individualism* and *individualized programs* are used. They also should expect controversy to flow from any programs incorporating these very emotive terms.

The Role of Schools Today

As information presented in the preceding subsections has suggested, there is no consensus today in support of a single "purpose" of schooling. Intense

---

Box 1-6
Emphases of the School Program

In general, it is fair to say that school programs emphasize citizenship, vocational preparation, intellectual attainment, and individual development. Relative attention given to each of these emphases varies from place to place:

LET'S PONDER

Consider your own public school experience. What kind of emphasis characterized the schools you attended?

1. What would be the specific course or experience that was designed to emphasize citizenship? Vocational preparation? Intellectual attainment? Individual development?
2. What seemed to be the major purpose of the schools you attended?
3. What do you see as the major purpose of the schools? Why do you think this should be the major purpose?
4. If you were designing a school program, how would you accommodate the various purposes of education?
5. As you view the contemporary scene, what do you see emerging as the primary purposes of education?

debates rage from a number of perspectives regarding what schools should be doing. There is a general thread of agreement joining partisans of many views to the effect that schools should "do better." But what tends to be "better" for one group may well be viewed as "worse" by another group.

This point is an important one for prospective teachers to grasp. Because of the multiplicity of perspectives regarding what constitutes "good" schooling, it is almost impossible for any existing program to satisfy everyone. Indeed, attempts to appease each of the many constituencies with firm ideas about what "quality" schooling means are likely to result in a confusing array of practices that may well please no one at all. The bottom line, then, is that controversy is a constant within American education. It is unlikely that a solid consensus will ever be built behind a single view of the purpose of schooling. Educators should not expect such a consensus but should develop positions they can defend and learn to articulate them effectively in the kind of give-and-take debate that prefaces decision-making in a democratic society.

"Education's okay, but I'm not crazy about school as a delivery system."

Recapitulation of Major Ideas

1. Education is one of the most important functions in any society. Its importance accounts, in large measure, for the controversy with which it frequently is surrounded.

2. Americans traditionally have placed great faith in the capacity of their educational system for attaining a large number of objectives. Among other things, schools have been expected to develop youngsters' appreciation for democratic values, to overcome deep-seated social problems, to provide for social mobility, to prepare young people for the world of work, to facilitate individual pursuit of happiness, and to develop learners' intellectual powers.

3. Accomplishments of the American educational system have been impressive. For example, never before in history has such a populous and diverse nation raised such a high percentage of its citizens to literacy. In spite of accomplishments that are very real, American education still is not regarded by some people as being as good as it might be.

4. Teaching is not a profession that has been accorded extremely high status in the United States. Americans tend to view education and teachers in contradictory ways. The teachers' mission tends to be admired, but many parents urge their children to prepare for occupations enjoying high social status.

5. *Education* and *schooling* are not synonymous terms. *Education* includes virtually all life experiences that educate. *Schooling* encompasses those experiences provided by institutions called schools.

6. Contemporary criticisms of the school are best understood in the light of conflicting conceptions about the "proper" purposes of the school. Proponents of various positions apply quite different criteria in judging school program quality. The differences in these criteria and the different conceptions of quality schooling suggest that it is unlikely that any school program or orientation will enjoy the support of all of the people. Controversy, hence, is a constant of life in public education. Prospective teachers need to grasp this point and to be prepared for a world of work in which some will find fault with what they do.

Posttest

DIRECTIONS: Using your own paper, answer each of the following true/false questions. For each correct statement, write the word *true* on your paper. For each incorrect statement, write the word *false* on your paper.

1. *Education* and *schooling* are identical terms that can be used interchangeably.
2. American society generally has placed little faith in the public school system.
3. The American educational system has few concrete accomplishments to its credit.
4. Nearly three fourths of the young people of the United States attain reading levels that are attained only by much smaller percentages of young people in many other countries.
5. United States students, in terms of their knowledge of rights and responsibilities associated with their roles as citizens, rank higher than students in any other nation.
6. Schools are institutions that are particularly well-suited for solving serious social problems.
7. Only in relatively recent times has citizenship education been recognized as an important responsibility of public schools.
8. Some opponents of vocational programs in the schools oppose them on the grounds that they may tend to perpetuate class differences in our society.
9. There is general agreement about which subjects should be taught to produce maximum intellectual growth in young people.
10. Proposed changes in education almost always enjoy nearly unanimous public support.

Summary

American schools, by many measures, have achieved notable successes. Certainly few would argue that they have brought high levels of general education to a large and diverse population. In spite of what, in many respects, is an enviable record, many critics today charge that schools in the United States are not as good as they should be.

Part of the difficulty in assessing the quality of public education in the United States is that there is not a common set of criteria that is applied in determining whether performance levels are good or bad. This is true because of the very different conceptions of school purposes held by different individuals and groups of individuals. Kinds of school programs seen as "promising" and "good" by one group may well be seen as "disheartening" and "bad" by another group. The diversity of opinion regarding what, properly, schools should do ensures that controversy is a constant companion of public school people everywhere. There is little likelihood that any configuration of school programs or experiences could be devised that would satisfy everyone.

In contemplating a career in education, prospective teachers must recognize that they will be entering a profession characterized by ongoing controversy rather than national consensus. The profession demands knowledgeable, well-grounded individuals who are willing to defend what they are doing in the free marketplace of ideas that characterizes decision-making in a democratic society.

References

BIEHLER, ROBERT, T. *Psychology Applied to Teaching*, 2nd ed. Boston: Houghton Mifflin, 1974.

BRANDT, ANTHONY. "Do We Care if Johnny Can Read?" In Fred Schultz (Ed). *Annual Editions: Education, 82/83,* Guilford, Connecticut: Dasking Publishing Co., 1982: 4–11.

BUTTS, FREEMAN. "The Search for Purpose in American Education." *The College Board Review* (Winter 1975–1976): 3–19.

DEWEY, JOHN. *Democracy and Education: An Introduction to the Philosophy of of Education.* New York: The Macmillan Company, 1916.

DUEA, JERRY. "School Officials and the Public Hold Disparate Views on Education." *Phi Delta Kappan* (March, 1982): 477–479.

ELKIND, DAVID. *Children and Adolescents: Interpretive Essays on Jean Piaget.* New York: Oxford University Press, 1970.

ERIKSON, ERIK H. *Identity: Youth and Crisis.* New York: Norton, 1968.

GALLUP, GEORGE, H. "Gallup Poll of the Public's Attitudes Toward the Public Schools." *Phi Delta Kappan* (Sept., 1982): 37–50.

HENSON, KENNETH T. *Secondary Teaching Methods.* Lexington, Massachusetts: D. C. Heath and Co., 1981.

Historical Statistics of the United States: Colonial Times to 1970; pt. 1. Washington, D.C.: United States Department of Commerce, Bureau of the Census, 1975.

HODGKINSON, HAROLD. "What's Still Right in Education?" *Phi Delta Kappan* (Dec., 1982): 231–235.

JAROLIMEK, JOHN. *The Schools in Contemporary Society: An Analysis of Social Currents, Issues, and Forces.* New York: Macmillan Publishing Co., 1981.

JEFFERSON, THOMAS. "A Bill for the More General Diffusion of Knowledge." In Paul L. Ford, (Ed.). *The Writings of Thomas Jefferson,* vol. 2. New York: G. P. Putnam's, 1893: 221.

KENNEDY, JOHN F. "Special Messages to the Congress on Education." Document 43, January 29, 1963, *Public Papers* (1963): 105–116.

KRUG, EDWARD A. *The Shaping of the American High School,* vol. 2, 1920–1941. Madison, Wisc.: University of Wisconsin Press, 1972.

LEAN, ARTHUR F. *And Merely Teach: Irreverent Essays on the Methodology of Education,* 2nd ed. Carbondale, Ill.: Southern Illinois University Press, 1976.

LORTIE, DAN C. *School Teacher: A Sociological Study.* Chicago: University of Chicago Press, 1975.

PERKINSON, HENRY J. *The Imperfect Panacea: American Faith in Education, 1865–1976,* 2nd ed. New York: Random House, 1977.

Report of the Commissioner of Education. Washington, D.C., United States Government Printing Office, 1870.

Sprinthall, Richard C. and Sprinthall, Norman A. *Educational Psychology: A Developmental Approach,* 2nd ed. Menlo Park, Calif.: Addison-Wesley, 1977.

Tyler, Ralph W. "The U.S. vs. The World: A Comparison of Educational Performance." *Phi Delta Kappan* (Jan. 1981): 307–310.

Wadsworth, Barry J. *Piaget for the Classroom Teacher.* New York: Longmans, 1978.

2
History of American Education

Objectives

This chapter provides information to help the reader to

1. State a rationale for studying the history of education.
2. Identify several major educational precedents set in the seventeenth century.
3. Point out several weaknesses of the Boston Latin Grammar School.
4. Cite several strengths and weaknesses of the Franklin Academy.
5. Describe how important societal events have influenced the development of education.
6. Explain several contributions to public education made by Horace Mann.
7. Point out examples of John Dewey's influence on education.
8. Explain the significance of the Seven Cardinal Principles of American education.

Pretest

DIRECTIONS: Using your own paper, answer each of the following true/false questions. For each correct statement, write the word *true* on your paper. For each incorrect statement, write the word *false* on your paper.

1. Involvement of lay citizens in educational policy-making is a characteristic of the American public school system.
2. Many present school practices that were originally developed in response to real needs are maintained by tradition today.
3. There is general agreement about what goes on in a school where teachers are thought to be doing a "good job."
4. "Local control of schooling" is an idea that sprang from biblical interpretations made by the New England Puritans.
5. In general, the curriculum of the Boston Latin Grammar School was more "practical" and "vocationally oriented" than the curriculum of the academy.
6. Thomas Jefferson strongly opposed the idea that schools should lead children to place high value on democratic principles.
7. Horace Mann was strongly committed to the "common school," a school for the average person.
8. The decision in the "Kalamazoo case" supported the right of a state legislature to pass laws allowing local communities to collect taxes for secondary schools as well as for elementary schools.
9. Intelligence testing was first developed in the United States and is

regarded widely as one of the most important American contributions to public education.

10. The Cardinal Principles constitute a set of goals for American schools that suggest that schools have responsibilities going beyond the transmission of academic content.

Introduction

Not long ago, an American educator was escorting an English educator on a tour of several American schools. During the day, the topic of control and policy making arose. The English educator had some difficulty in understanding how Americans can vest so much authority in the hands of local school boards composed of individuals with little formal training in educational theory or practice. Indeed, it is not only to the English that this arrangement appears strange. In many parts of the world, control of the schools is centralized in the hands of relatively small numbers of specialists. The American practice of distributing this authority widely and encouraging participation by a broad cross section of the population is a special feature of our system.

The involvement of lay citizens in educational policy making has a long history. To Americans, who may live out their lives without ever experiencing an alternative way of organizing school management, it might appear that citizen involvement in schools at the local level "just happened." Although the reasons may not be readily apparent to us now, the involvement of lay citizens in roles of power in education developed initially to meet a very real and specific need.

Other educational practices as well developed for very good reasons, though today, some of these reasons are not easily recalled. Why, for example, are certain subjects placed at one grade level? (Is there something magical about teaching American history to eleventh-graders?) Why, too, are youngsters in the schools still generally segregated into groups according to their chronological age? Why are letter grades so firmly entrenched? Why do schools have such a long summer vacation?

Answers to these questions are not quickly apparent to the casual observer. Indeed, suspicions that these school practices may not be sound have led to dozens of proposals for changes. But for a case to be made for abandoning these traditional ways of doing things, it is necessary to understand the nature of the need that prompted their adoption in the first place. When the need can be identified, we are then in a position to look around us and respond to two critical questions: (1) Is the need that led to the practice in the first place still important? (2) If so, is the traditional practice still the best way to respond to the need?

A study of educational history can bring to light needs that today may be forgotten but that initially prompted the adoption of many familiar educational practices. History reveals that these practices tend to be maintained by

" . . . and the reason we have summer vacation is so you can go home to help with the crops."

the force of tradition long after people have lost sight of the original need. Consider, for example, the school calendar and, more particularly, the typical long summer vacation featured as part of this calendar. Initially the calendar developed in response to some very real needs of rural Americans. Youngsters in these areas were needed at home to help with planting and harvesting crops. Today, though the calendar with its long summer vacation remains intact, it can hardly be argued that most youngsters in schools need released time to help out on the farm. A study of educational history reveals the potency of tradition as a shaper and maintainer of school practices.

In addition to tradition, many school practices have resulted as responses to important public events. Education tends to reflect perceptions of the society of which it is a part. When events change these perceptions, then the schools, too, are affected. A study of educational history can suggest relevant patterns from the past that can provide a useful context for us as we try to understand the impact or potential impact on the schools of those large issues and events that capture the collective interest of the society.

Finally, a study of history reveals that the traditional expectations people have of the schools influence their responses to the question "Are the schools doing an adequate job?" Answers to this question tend to vary in terms of the kinds of experiences the respondents had when they were in school. For example, many of today's parents were in school when school practices reflected quite different sets of social problems and priorities than those that concern us today. Today's educators must respond with programs and practices reasonably consistent with the issues that are of consuming interest now. Because of the need to provide learning experiences that are not hopelessly at odds with the demands of the 1980s, educators may find themselves with very different expectations of the schools than those of parents and other adults, whose expectations were shaped by their own schooling in the 1940s, 1950s, and 1960s.

Patterns of educational development over time prompt the consideration of responses to four basic questions: (1) What was the perceived purpose of education? (2) Who was to be educated? (3) What were learners expected to derive from their school experience? (4) How were learners to be educated? In the sections that follow, think about responses to these key questions. An understanding of how these queries were answered at different points in our history can provide a foundation for understanding the bases of positions taken by contending parties in present-day debates over educational policies and procedures.

Education in the Early Colonial Period

To understand education in the Colonial period, one must have some familiarity with conditions in the English homeland of early settlers. In sixteenth-century England and on into the seventeenth century, there was little room for open discussion of alternatives to the established church, the Church of England. The roots of this problem can be traced back to the official role played by the Church of England.

Briefly stated, the Church of England was created as a state church to supplant the influence of Rome. The church became a political entity as well as a religious entity. Because it was a state church, those who espoused religious views inconsistent with the teachings of the Church of England tended to be seen by those in power as disloyal, not only to the church but also to the state. In effect, the church was a simple extension of the legal authority of the state. Consequently, there was a tendency to deal harshly with religious dissidents, who tended to be regarded as potentially subversive to the power of the crown.

While political problems in England for groups such as the Puritans, who wished to reform practices of the Church of England, prompted an interest in the New World, probably equally important was their fear of exposing their children to what they perceived to be religious error. The Puritans who came to Massachusetts were no civil libertarians. Witness, for example, their persecution of nonconforming Roger Williams. Their purpose was not to provide for religious freedom. Rather, they sought to establish a church and

Box 2-1
School Practices and Tradition

LET'S PONDER

Respond to the following questions:

1. Other than some of the things mentioned in the chapter, what examples can you think of regarding school practices that are maintained by tradition?
2. Were there any "real" reasons for these practices when they were first introduced? What were they?
3. If the original "need" for certain school practices has disappeared, why then is it so difficult to change these practices?
4. Do you have any expectations about schools that seem perfectly "right" to you now but in twenty years might seem hopelessly out of step to your children?
5. As a teacher, how can you strike a balance between concerns of parents and other adults for maintaining certain traditions and for some learners for changing school practices to meet more contemporary needs?
6. Suppose as a leader of a professional educational programs group you convinced your people to propose to the community each of the following changes:
   a. Football shall be a spring sport rather than a fall sport.
   b. Learners shall start school at age 7 and graduate at age 19.
   c. All interschool athletic competition shall be abolished. Instead, a massive program of intramural sports shall be instituted.
   d. Schools shall be run for 12 months of the year. In addition to the traditional December–January holidays, learners shall have a two-week vacation during the summer months.
   e. U.S. history shall be required of 9th graders, and World history shall be required of 12th graders.

How would people in the community react to these proposals? What traditions would have to be abandoned to install this program? Why were these traditional practices first introduced?

a government different from those in England and in their view, more consistent with their interpretation of the Bible's teachings. The concern for establishing a church and a government consistent with the Bible had important educational implications.

The Puritans believed the Bible to be the source of all wisdom. Consequently they placed high importance on people's developing reading skills that would enable them to read "God's Holy Word." The particular form that efforts to encourage literacy took was a reflection of the Puritans' reaction against conditions in England. Their reading of the scriptures led the Puritans to believe that the kind of church described in the Bible was one in which a great deal of autonomy was given to local congregations. In England, authority in the Church of England was highly centralized, and few decisions were left to the discretion of local congregations. When the Massachusetts Bay Colony was settled, the Puritans insisted on observing the biblical principle of local congregational autonomy in many matters. This principle set a pattern for local control in civil matters as well as religious matters. It was out of this context that a tradition of local control of education sprang.

Concern for education in Massachuetts was reflected in the Massachusetts School Law of 1642. This law charged local magistrates with the responsibility of ensuring that parents would not neglect the education of their children. Though the law did not itself set up schools, it did require that children attend schools. This law represents the first attempt to make school attendance compulsory. Reflecting the local-control tradition, this law placed the responsibility for enforcement at the local level rather than at the state level.

The law of 1642 was extended by the famous "Old Deluder Satan Act" of 1647. The name derives from a rationale for education as a buffer against Satan's wiles. The law required every town of fifty or more families to hire a teacher of reading and writing. This teacher was to be paid by the community or by the parents of the students. The law represents an early legislative attempt to establish the principle of public responsiblity for education.

It must be remembered, however, that during the seventeenth century concern for publicly supported education was really concern for only the very basic education of young children. Very few students went to secondary schools. Secondary schools, however, did exist in very limited numbers in the seventeenth century. One of the most famous of these was the Boston Latin Grammar School, founded in 1635. It had a very specific purpose: the preparation of boys for Harvard. The curriculum consisted of difficult academic subjects, including Latin, Greek, and theology. The purpose of the Latin Grammar School was to prepare the sons of the upper classes for positions of political leadership and for the ministry.

In summary, the early Colonial period in New England did witness the establishment of some schools for all. But the obligation to educate all young people was restricted to a relatively few years' instruction in basic skills. Little thought was given to the provision of advanced instruction in "practical" or "useful" subjects. Education beyond the basic levels tended to be restricted to the sons of upper-class families. Such education, largely classical in nature, was designed to prepare these boys for roles of leadership. Reflecting the Puritans' abhorrence of concentrated authority, patterns of control tended to be local rather than central. This practice established a precedent for the tradition of local control of public schools.

Education in the Late Colonial and the Revolutionary War Period

In the middle and late 1700s, some ideas began taking root that prompted questions about the view that intermediate and advanced education should be reserved for a select few. Intellectual leaders such as Thomas Jefferson argued that political stability was enhanced when knowledge was widespread across the population. The idea that education in more than a few simple survival skills ought to be open to children from all economic and social classes began to spread.

During this time, too, middle-class merchants and other people of the "practical world" were becoming more vocal and politically influential. They began to press for intermediate education of a more practical bent than that offered by the Boston Latin Grammar School. They argued that the study of the classics was of little value to young people who would be challenged to conquer a frontier and to earn a living.

Benjamin Franklin made one of the first moves to give American education a more practical orientation. In 1749, in a publication entitled *Proposals Relating to the Youth of Pennsylvania,* Franklin suggested a new school, oriented to the "real world," that was to be free of all religious ties. Two years later, he established the Franklin Academy, an institution that was nonsectarian and that offered such practical subjects as mathematics, astronomy, navigation, and bookkeeping. By the end of the Revolutionary War, the Franklin Academy had replaced the Boston Latin Grammar School as the most important secondary school in America. Students in the Franklin Academy were able to make some choices about their course of study, thus setting the pattern for the system of elective courses common in high schools today.

For all its strengths, relatively few youngsters could attend the Franklin Academy. It was a private school. Tuition was beyond the means of many families. But the Franklin Academy sowed the seed that ultimately flowered in the establishment of free public secondary schools, which resulted from the tremendous public interest in the Franklin Academy's work. This interest soon translated into the establishment of a number of other private academies, including, among others, such institutions as Phillips Academy at Andover, Massachusetts (established in 1778), and Phillips Exeter Academy at Exeter, New Hampshire (established in 1783). These academies popularized the idea that secondary education had something important to offer and laid the foundation for public support of secondary education. Collectively the academies set the following precedents for American education:

1. American education would have a more practical orientation than other world educational systems.
2. American education would be nonsectarian.
3. American education would be diverse in terms of course offerings.

In summary, two primary strands in present-day American education can be traced to the late Colonial and Revolutionary War period. On the one hand, Jefferson and others planted the suggestion that schools have a political mission to train children to value the democratic principles of the society. On the other hand, the academies promoted the idea that schools should provide youngsters with practical training. Today, the ideals of "education for citizenship" and "education for work" are very much with us.

Education from 1800 to the Civil War

During the first twenty years of the nineteenth century, there were few innovations in educational practices. The society was consumed with settling the nation and providing workers for burgeoning industries. There was more interest in providing youngsters to perform jobs than in providing learners for schools. Schooling, of any but a very rudimentary kind, tended to remain available only to those children of families able to pay for the privilege. Thoughts of an education system that was universal and free were just beginning to surface.

In 1821, a precedent-shattering event occurred in Boston. In that year, the Boston English Classical School was established. The name was changed shortly thereafter to the English High School. This was the first high school in the country, and more importantly, it was the first secondary school supported with public funds. The curriculum emphasized a host of practical subjects. Though other high schools were established after this time, the innovation was not at first very popular, and growth was slow.

During the 1820s, Horace Mann, a figure who was to exert tremendous influence on American education, began to make his views known. Elected to the Massachusetts legislature in 1827, Mann was an eloquent speaker who took up the cause of the "common school," a school for the average person. His mission was to convince taxpayers that it was in their best interest to support the establishment of a system of public education. Mann pointed out that an educated citizenry developed through a system of public schools would have skills that would result in an improved standard of living for all. To those who would attend the schools, Mann suggested that the education would give them tremendous social and economic mobility. The school, in Mann's view, was the springboard for opportunity and for equalizing differences among people coming from different social classes.

Mann's arguments were persuasive. In 1837, Massachusetts established a state board of education. Horace Mann gave up his career in politics to become the first secretary of the Massachusetts State Board of Education. In time, Mann's views attracted audiences all across the country.

Beyond the need to establish publicly supported schools, Mann recognized the importance of improving teachers' qualifications. In response to this con-

Box 2-2
Early Schools: Some "What If's"

The Latin Grammar School was oriented toward teaching sons of well-to-do parents traditional classical knowledge. Latin, Greek, and theological studies constituted a good deal of the curriculum. There was no emphasis on subjects of a "practical" nature. These were not viewed as a proper function for the school. They were not necessary for an "educated" person.

LET'S PONDER

Suppose American education had taken quite a different direction than it did. Suppose that education had become free and public, but that the model for public schools had been the Latin Grammar School. Consider this situation as you respond to the following questions:

1. What kinds of courses would you expect to find in high schools today?
2. How would youngsters in the schools react to their curriculum?
3. Would the nation have experienced so dramatic an economic development given a system of public schools similar to the Latin Grammar School? Why, or why not?
4. What kind of occupations would likely be held in highest public esteem given a public school system emphasizing subjects of the Latin Grammar School? How would these "high status" occupations compare with the "high status" occupations we have today?
5. What differences in entertainment (perhaps in television and radio programs and films) would you expect in a society educated in a school system reflecting the values of the Latin Grammar School?
6. How would you personally feel about a public school system built along the lines of the Latin Grammar School? Why?
7. Have we gone too far in this country in emphasizing practical and vocational education? Why, or why not?
8. If you were to look 50 years into the future, would you expect schools to be more like or less like the Latin Grammar School than they are today?

cern, the nation's first normal school to train teachers was established in 1839. In the beginning, these normal schools provided only one or two years of formal education for those wishing to become teachers. But the precedent was set for formalizing the education of future teachers. Many institutions of higher education that today offer undergraduate and graduate study in a variety of disciplines began life as normal schools.

Prompted by Mann's work, public schools were established in all areas of the country. By 1860, 50.6 percent of the nation's children were enrolled in public school programs (*Historical Statistics of the United States,* 1975, p. 370). A majority of states had formalized the development of free school systems, including elementary schools, secondary schools, and public universities. In 1867, a National Department of Education was established as part of the federal government. By the late 1860s, many of the basic patterns of American education were in place. The persistence of many of these patterns is a tribute to the vision, patience, and political skills of Horace Mann.

Education from the Civil War to 1900

The post-Civil War years were characterized by an unprecedented growth in American industry. Technological innovations of all kinds had the effect of reducing the demand for unskilled labor. The demand for workers who had some knowledge of value in the workplace intensified the need for educated employees. Of course, this need reinforced the trend to make school programs more oriented toward the practical world as well.

An additional development during this time was the great increase in the number of immigrants coming into the country. These people needed both skills useful in the workplace and an orientation to the values of their adopted homeland. These needs placed new demands on the schools, and there was a great increase in the number of schools during this period.

In the realm of school financing, the famous Kalamazoo case (*Stuart* v. *School District No. 1 of the Village of Kalamazoo,* 30 Mich. 69 [1874]) resulted in a ruling that the state legislature had the right to pass laws levying taxes for the support of *both* elementary and secondary schools. This established a legal precedent for public funding of secondary schools. As a result, there was a dramatic expansion in the total number of schools in the nation and in the total number of youngsters attending school as districts began to build large numbers of secondary schools. Because of a desire of many citizens to provide older youngsters with "useful" educational experiences, many secondary schools broadened programs to include more of the practical and applied arts.

Organizational activity on the part of teachers increased during this period. Before 1900, organizations that were forerunners of today's American Federation of Teachers and National Education Association were established (see Chapter 12 for a detailed treatment of the AFT and the NEA). Reports of such groups as the NEA's Committee of Ten and the Committee on College Entrance Requirements began to influence public school curricula. These groups, while suggesting schools should serve youngsters with varying future academic and career aspirations, nevertheless suggested that preparation for college and university study was the "primary" purpose of high schools. This orientation represented a temporary reversal of a century-long trend to view secondary education as a provider of more "practical" kinds of learning experiences.

Twentieth Century Education to World War II

During the first two decades of the twentieth century, the conflict between those seeing the high school as primarily serving the needs of the college-bound student and those seeing the high school as primarily serving more "practical" ends was resolved through a compromise. This compromise was revealed in a new conception of the high school as a "comprehensive" institution. The comprehensive high school came to be seen as an institution providing both academic and applied kinds of instructional programs. Debates

---

Box 2-3
Purposes of Secondary Schools

A great debate about secondary education has raged for years. On the one hand, there are people who say that secondary schools should have a rather narrow curriculum designed to prepare youngsters for the rigors of college or university life. It is more important that they learn how to think in high school than it is that they learn how to do something useful.

On the other hand, others argue that only a minority of youngsters ever graduates from a college or university. But all will be occupied in the workplace. Therefore, it makes sense for secondary schools to provide practical training that youngsters can use in making a living.

LET'S PONDER

Read the paragraphs above and respond to the following questions:

1. Some say the process of thinking is what schools should teach. This process stays constant over time. Specific knowledge, particularly vocational skills, changes so rapidly that what is taught in schools today may be irrelevant tomorrow. Therefore, schools should forget about teaching "practical" things. How do you feel about this argument? Why?
2. Has an emphasis on "practical" or "vocational" subjects tended to "water down" secondary school curricula? Are youngsters being cheated because their intellectual capacities are not challenged?
3. How well do secondary school courses that allegedly are designed to "prepare youngsters for college" in fact accomplish this task?
4. Do secondary schools have an obligation to train youngsters for leadership? Does this imply a program designed to prepare them for college or university positions? Defend your position.
5. Were you to look at public education 25 years from now, would you expect more attention or less attention in secondary schools to "practical" or "vocational" aspects of the program? Why?

about how much weight ought to be given to each of these major emphases continue even today.

Numbers of public schools and of public school learners increased tremendously during the first four decades of the twentieth century. Schooling became almost universal during this period. In 1900, only 50.5 percent of youngsters in the five- to twenty-year-old age group were in school. By 1940, 74.8 percent of this age group were enrolled (United States Department of Commerce. *Historical Statistics of the United States,* 1975, pp. 369–370). Given the tremendous growth in the total United States population between 1900 and 1940, these figures indicate that millions more youngsters were served by schools in 1940 than in 1900.

An individual who had a tremendous influence on education during this period was John Dewey. Dewey was born in 1859 and lived until 1952. His work continues to influence educational thought and practice.

Dewey viewed education as a process through which young people are brought into full participation in society. He saw the primary goal of education as individual growth and development. Thus schools should not set out to serve the goals of the society (for example, the production of electrical engineers if the society is short of electrical engineers) at the cost of overlooking the unique needs of the individual learner. Schools, Dewey felt, should produce a secure human being committed to his or her own continuing self-education.

Dewey believed that every learner actively attempts to explore and understand his or her environment. If this is so, then it would be helpful for youngsters to have a set of tools they might use to make sound judgments about those things they encounter. They need a process that can be applied to any unfamiliar situation. It is more important for a youngster to be familiar with this process than to know any specific item of information. The process is useful in a variety of situations. A specific item of information may have little utility beyond the situation in which it is learned. But the process may be useful in a variety of situations. The process that Dewey felt youngsters should learn was the scientific problem-solving method. Mastery of this method, Dewey felt, would give the child confidence in developing rational responses to the dilemmas that he or she would confront throughout life. Clearly Dewey's emphases on the individual and on teaching processes continue to have great influence on the schools.

Schools today also continue to be influenced heavily by an early-twentieth-century movement that developed first in France. Education in France became compulsory in 1904, and a special commission was established to determine which youngsters could be expected to benefit from regular instruction in public schools and which would be better off in special classes. In 1905, to help answer this large question, Albert Binet and his associates developed a test designed to predict learners' success in French schools. Soon educators from the United States and from throughout the world were seeking information about ways to measure intelligence. It is interesting that a test designed to predict school success was viewed as a test of intelligence.

The presumption was that the school program had been so designed that the most intelligent would do the best. (Today this idea is much debated. Some argue, for example, that the "most intelligent" resist school rules and procedures and do not do well.)

The testing movement expanded during World War I. The military needed a system by which they could quickly identify men who would be suited to a variety of necessary tasks. Intelligence tests were developed that were seen as capable of classifying individuals and assigning them to different levels of intelligence. A number of well-known group intelligence tests were developed during the war.

As an aside, it is interesting to note that some of these early intelligence tests were given to European immigrants. It was noted that immigrants from Western Europe did better than immigrants from Eastern Europe. (Hardly a surprising development, in that most tests were developed by Western Europeans or Americans trained by Western Europeans.) There is some evidence that the congressional passage of laws restricting the immigration of individuals from Eastern Europe came about as a result of the dissemination of these score differences. This development might be one of the first examples of the cultural bias that can be embedded in tests of this sort.

The testing movement, particularly intelligence testing and the IQ score, become heavily involved in education. With the advent of the testing movement, youngsters came to be classified and counseled on the basis of their IQ scores. Evidence abounds that many teachers' patterns of interactions with individual youngsters were related to those teachers' understanding of the learners' capabilities as revealed in their IQ scores.

In recent years, uses of intelligence tests, particularly group intelligence tests, have been challenged. The issue of cultural bias has been raised by blacks, Hispanics, and other minority groups. Others have argued that a factor so broad and diffuse as "intelligence" cannot possibly be measured by a single test. Situations have been brought to light where perfectly normal youngsters have been assigned to custodial institutions for the mentally retarded on the basis of a faulty IQ score obtained from a group intelligence test. The debate rages on. Though we are far from consensus on this issue, it is fair to say that educators today increasingly hesitate to predict the educational futures of youngsters based on a single measure, the IQ score.

As special circumstances and needs stemming from the wartime situation expanded interest in the testing movement, the World War I years also prompted renewed interest in the systematic investigation of education's purposes. The last year of the war, 1918, was a landmark year for education. In that year, the National Education Association's Commission on the Reorganization of Secondary Education identified seven specific goals for the public schools. These seven goals came to be known as education's "Cardinal Principles." They were:

1. Health.
2. Command of fundamental processes.

3. Worthy home membership.
4. Vocational preparation.
5. Citizenship.
6. Worthy use of leisure time.
7. Ethical character.*

*Commission on the Reorganization of Secondary Education. *Cardinal Principles of Secondary Education*. Washington, D.C.: United States Government Printing Office, 1918.

Box 2-4
The Cardinal Principles and Secondary Education Today

The Seven Cardinal Principles of Education of 1918 suggested that secondary schools should attend to education in each of these seven areas:

1. Health
2. Command of Fundamental Processes
3. Worthy Home Membership
4. Vocational Preparation
5. Citizenship
6. Worthy Use of Leisure Time
7. Ethical Character

(Commission on Reorganization of Secondaary Education. *Cardinal Principles of Secondary Education*. Washington, D.C. United States Government Printing Office, 1918)

LET'S PONDER

Read the information above and respond to the following questions-

1. Consider your own high school. Which of these cardinal principles received *most* attention in the curriculum? Why?
2. Consider your own high school. Which of these cardinal principles received *least* attention in the curriculum? Why?
3. What groups in our society would be most supportive of the principles of (a) vocational preparation, (b) health, and (c) citizenship? What groups in our society would be least supportive of these principles?
4. Suppose a high school attempted to establish a curriculum that gave equal weight to each one of these seven principles. What courses would be included? How would people in the community react? Especially, how would people having great political influence react?
5. Are some of these cardinal principles more important to you than others? If so, which ones? Why do you prize these principles more than the others? How do you think your ranking of the importance of these principles would compare with how our society in general would rank the importance of these principles?

These principles laid the groundwork for the comprehensive high school. They suggested that secondary schools should have broader purposes than simply preparing youngsters for colleges and universities. Publication of the Cardinal Principles stimulated an expansion of course offerings in high schools to meet the needs of students who were not going to be attending institutions of higher learning. It should not be supposed, however, that all high schools gave equal emphasis to each of the many subjects that came to be offered. In many, a good deal of attention (critics would say too much attention) continued to be given to college and university preparatory courses. At a minimum, however, discussions stemming from the publication of the Cardinal Principles did result in an expansion in the range of courses offered in most high schools.

Changes in the schools brought about by the Cardinal Principles and as a result of actions taken by other groups looking for a more practical orientation in the curriculum suggested that people increasingly saw education as a necessity for young people. Many concluded that if learning experiences were important and were being paid for by taxpayers, then young people should take advantage of the educational opportunities that were available. This attitude resulted in a tremendous expansion of compulsory attendance laws during the first twenty years of the twentieth century. By 1918, thirty states had such laws. Most required youngsters to stay in school until about age sixteen.

In the 1920s and 1930s, the influence of those who wanted the schools to respond humanely to the needs and interests of individual youngsters was strong. The term *progressive education movement* has been applied to the efforts of individuals who worked for these general goals. Supporters of the progressive education movement drew much inspiration from the work of John Dewey. The installation of counseling programs in the schools, which developed at a rapid rate particularly during the 1930s, represented a logical extension of Dewey's concern for individual development.

American Education After World War II

After World War II, the progressive education movement evolved into a loosely knit group of individuals supporting school practices that came to be known as *life-adjustment education*. In some of its more extreme forms, life-adjustment programs seemed bent on allowing youngsters to do whatever they pleased in schools. Systematic attention to intellectual rigor or subject-matter content was avoided. Critics suggested that youngsters were being shortchanged by schools that failed to provide them with needed understanding and skills. These critics attracted many followers. As a consequence, by the middle 1950s, support for life-adjustment education had diminished greatly.

Rarely can change in education (or, indeed, in other social institutions) be attributed to a single event. But in the fall of 1957, the launching of the first earth satellite, *Sputnik,* by the Soviet Union so changed the public's perception of education's role that many subsequent alterations in school curricula can be traced back to this single seminal event. *Sputnik* shocked the nation by challenging the presumed American technological supremacy. Those looking for an explanation placed a good deal of the blame on public education. Large audiences listened sympathetically to critics who told them that American schools had gone soft and that instruction in subject-matter content compared unfavorably with that provided youngsters in other countries. Instruction in the sciences was pointed to as a particularly weak area of the curriculum.

Reacting to pressures to "do something" about the schools, the federal government in 1958 passed the National Defense Education Act. This legislation resulted in a massive infusion of federal funds meant to improve the quality of education. Large-scale curriculum reform projects were launched, first in mathematics and the sciences and later in the social sciences. Special workshops were held on campuses across the nation during summer terms to upgrade the skills of teachers. There was a massive effort to revise and upgrade the quality of textbooks and the other instructional materials used in the schools. There were high hopes that a revolution in the schools could be carried to a successful conclusion.

Though the curriculum reform movement of the 1960s did result in some important changes, these modifications fell well short of the expectations of many who had supported the passage of the National Defense Education Act. Teachers who attended summer programs became proficient in the use of new techniques and materials, but only a small minority of all teachers participated in such programs. Many teachers who did not participate found themselves ill at ease with many of the new programs, and a majority continued doing things much as they had always done them.

Another problem involved the new instructional materials themselves. Many were developed by subject-matter specialists who had little if any experience in working with public school youngsters. Consequently many materials were written at a level of reading difficulty that was simply beyond large numbers of youngsters. Further, the issue of learner motivation was not attended to very well. Many young people simply did not find some of the new instructional materials very interesting.

Probably the changing youth culture of the 1960s did more than anything else to subvert the changes in the schools that were being pushed by those who wanted more "intellectual rigor" in the program. With the discontent of young people everywhere over official policies toward Vietnam and with the particular frustrations of economically concerned blacks in the cities, the ground was not fertile for a curriculum that appeared to be yet another effort to push the values of the "establishment" on the young. Increasingly, young people questioned the relevance of school curricula that seemed to favor esoteric intellectual subjects rather than topics of more immediate personal concern.

The last several decades have witnessed turmoil and unrest in public education. Schools have found themselves awash in a sea of hostile opinion. Some intellectuals have charged that schools have failed to teach critical intellectual content. Some youngsters have contended that school programs have not been responsive to their own needs. Civil rights groups have criticized the schools for being insensitive to the rights of various elements within the population, including racial minorities, women, and handicapped youngsters. Some religious groups have attacked schools out of a conviction that schools were promoting unacceptable values. Taxpayers have worried that public education had lost any commitment it ever had to cost containment. Other groups, too, have voiced concerns.

In the early 1980s, there were signs that schools were increasingly becoming a topic for major national debate. At the federal level, President Reagan deplored what he and his education specialists felt to be too much federal involvement in education. At the state level, action was taken in many states to change high school graduation requirements (generally with a view to making them "more rigorous") and to upgrade requirements for certification of teachers. There was great activity in the public education arena at the local level as well. The breadth of national interest in public education was reflected in the presidential election of 1984, when, for the first time in many years, the quality of public education emerged as a major campaign issue.

Some have viewed the great national debate over education negatively, while others have viewed it positively. The pessimists have suggested that the debate has been accompanied by a general public retreat from the idea that public education merits support. They foresee a decline in the overall quality of education as middle-class and upper-class Americans shift more of their education resources from public schools to private schools.

Optimists, on the other hand, have pointed out that public education has weathered crises in the past. What is involved now, according to this view, is an attempt to redefine the proper "role" of the school. Out of this assessment it may be possible that a more realistic view of the school will emerge that will hold educators responsible for something less than the unattainable objective of solving all social problems. As some optimists have expressed it, a school with more limited responsibilities might better serve the needs of the nation's young people because available resources would be brought to bear on a much reduced range of educational objectives.

The outcome of the introspective analyses of schools that the nation is experiencing today is not clear. When decisions are made regarding changes, it is highly probable that they will reflect the orientations of those individuals and groups who have worked hardest and organized best to promote their perspectives. Given this reality, educators who wish to have a voice in the future direction of their profession must become active participants in efforts to define the role of education. A decision to stand aside may leave the field to others who would shape the schools in ways that educational professionals may find objectionable. Active participation by educators will not ensure that all decisions will go their way, but the decisions will be made in full knowledge of the educators' professional views.

Box 2-5
Future of American Education

Some argue that the schools demand too little of youngsters. Young people can do much more than they are asked to do in school. Only a fraction of their intellectual power is tapped by schools. Today's "soft" programs produce lazy young people who learn little but "how to use time unproductively."

Others argue that schools do not pay sufficient attention to youngsters' individual differences. Schools, they say, are regimenting agencies. In a culture that prizes individualism, schools prize youngsters who conform. School practices kill creativity in many youngsters. Our society suffers because potential talents find their spirits crushed in the oppressive atmosphere of many schools.

LET'S PONDER

Read the paragraphs above. Then, respond to the following questions:

1. Do you think schools do demand too little of youngsters? Why, or why not? How would you go about determining a level of expectations that was "just about right?"
2. Suppose schools decided that their only objective was to teach rigorous school subjects to children. How would today's practices be changed? How would youngsters react? How would parents react? Would such a change be more popular in some communities than in others?
3. Are the schools "oppressive" places? Why, or why not? Can you think of any examples from your personal experience when a young person in school who is very bright has simply become so turned off by the system that he or she has performed only at a minimal level?
4. Can schools be both intellectually challenging *and* sensitive to individual differences? If such a thing were possible, what changes would have to occur in schools?
5. Were you to revisit a sample of schools twenty-five years from now, would you expect to find a greater or smaller emphasis on "developing youngsters' intellectual power" than you find in the schools today?

Recapitulation of Major Ideas

1. An understanding of educational history provides a context for viewing present educational practice and for reacting to proposed changes. From the New England Puritans, we get a legacy of concern for local control of schools and governmental concern for universal literacy.
2. Early secondary schools were private rather than public. The Boston Latin Grammar School emphasized study of the classics. The academies introduced more practical subjects into the curriculum. The first public high school did not appear until 1821, when one was established in Boston.

3. A key figure in the early and middle nineteenth century was Horace Mann. Horace Mann popularized the idea of the "common school." He pointed out that tax-supported schools could result in benefits not only for learners but for those paying the taxes as well.

4. After the Civil War, there was a great increase in the demand for educated workers to work in the burgeoning American industries. Additionally, thousands of immigrants were entering the country who needed a systematic introduction to the values of their new homeland. The demand for educational services, taken together with court actions establishing the legality of levying taxes to pay for schools, led to a great growth in public education between the late 1860s and 1900.

5. A giant figure in twentieth-century American education was John Dewey. Dewey emphasized educating children as individuals and teaching them the processes of thinking rather than specific pieces of isolated information. Dewey's followers and their progressive education movement pushed hard for changes in the schools in the direction of making the schools more humane. The great expansion of counseling services ranks as one of their successes.

6. Intelligence testing, originally developed in France, spread rapidly in American schools after World War I. In recent years, suspicions about the validity of measuring something as broad and diverse as "intelligence" on a single group test have made educators much less inclined to make judgments about youngsters based on IQ scores. Evidence also mounts that such tests may be culturally biased.

7. Education has been greatly influenced by external affairs. For example, the launching of *Sputnik* in the late 1950s prompted a tremendous curriculum reform effort in the United States. This effort was dedicated to the development of programs thought to have more "intellectual rigor." The impact of these efforts was reduced when protests over Vietnam, suspicions of blacks in the cities, and other developments led many young people to reject the new programs as irrelevant to their own needs and concerns.

8. Today a massive national reexamination of education is underway. Taxpayers are concerned that education is too expensive. Others believe that programs continue to be too "soft" and that children are not getting what they should be getting from school. Some youngsters believe that the schools are already much too concerned with intellectual learning and not concerned enough with individual differences. All of these perspectives suggest a debate that has a long time to run before any broad consensus can be expected.

Posttest

DIRECTIONS: Using your own paper, answer each of the following true/false questions. For each correct statement, write the word *true* on your paper. For each incorrect statement, write the word *false* on your paper.

1. Involvement of lay citizens in educational policy-making is a characteristic of the American public school system.
2. Many present school practices that were originally developed in response to real needs are maintained by tradition today.
3. There is general agreement about what goes on in a school where teachers are thought to be doing a "good job."
4. "Local control of schooling" is an idea that sprang from biblical interpretations made by the New England Puritans.
5. In general, the curriculum of the Boston Latin Grammar School was more "practical" and "vocationally oriented" than the curriculum of the academy.
6. Thomas Jefferson strongly opposed the idea that schools should lead children to place high value on democratic principles.
7. Horace Mann was strongly committed to the "common school," a school for the average person.
8. The decision in the "Kalamazoo case" supported the right of a state legislature to pass laws allowing local communities to collect taxes for secondary schools as well as for elementary schools.
9. Intelligence testing first developed in the United States and is regarded widely as one of the most important American contributions to education.
10. The Cardinal Principles constitute a set of goals for American schools that suggest that schools have responsibilities going beyond the transmission of academic content.

Summary

Today's public schools and the entire system of public education reflect ideals and values that have been evolving since the time of the Puritans. Many school practices today make little sense if examined in the absence of an understanding of their historic roots. Consequently it is important for teachers and prospective teachers to be aware of some of the key episodes that have shaped present practices.

There is evidence that American schools today are in a transitional phase. Pressures are coming from a variety of groups to change the way things are being done in America's classrooms. These pressures come from taxpayers' groups, from concerned parents, from youngsters, from intellectuals, and from a host of others. While the outcome of the confrontations among the members of these disparate groups cannot be predicted, change appears to be a certainty. As practitioners who will be working within the public school environment, whatever that might turn out to be, teachers have a personal stake in decisions that may affect the schools' future. Their influence may well be tied to their ability to relate proposals to what has been tried in the past, to evaluate the relative success of those past efforts, and to pass this information on to others lacking this information. Given this possibility, those teachers wishing to have an influence on the condition of their own profession will seek a grounded understanding of the historical roots of American education.

References

BUTTS, R. FREEMAN. "The Search for Purpose in American Education." *The College Board Review* (Winter 1974–1975): 3–19.

COMMISSION ON REORGANIZATION OF SECONDARY EDUCATION. *Cardinal Principles of Secondary Education.* Washington, D.C.: United States Government Printing Office, 1918.

CORDASCO, FRANCESCO. *A Brief History of Education.* Towowa, N.J.: Littlefield, Adams, 1967.

CREMIN, LAWRENCE A. *The Transformation of the School: Progressivism in American Education, 1876–1957.* New York: Alfred A. Knopf, 1961.

CREMIN, LAWRENCE A. *The Genius of American Education.* New York: Vintage Books, 1966.

CREMIN, LAWRENCE A. "The Revolution in American Education." *The Educational Forum* (Winter 1983): 249–250.

DAVIS, O. L., JR. (ED). *Perspectives on Curriculum Development, 1776–1976.* Washington, D.C.: Association for Supervision and Curriculum Development, 1976.

ORNSTEIN, ALLAN C. *Foundations of Education.* Chicago: Rand McNally College Publishing Co., 1977.

PERKINSON, HENRY J., (ED). *Two Hundred Years of American Educational Thought.* New York: David McKay, 1976.

RICHEY, ROBERT W. *Planning for Teaching: An Introduction to Education,* 5th ed. New York: McGraw-Hill, 1973.

SMITH, FREDERICK R., AND COX, C. BENJAMIN. *Secondary Schools in a Changing Society.* New York: Holt, Rinehart and Winston, 1976.

Stuart v. *School District No. 1 of the Village of Kalamazoo,* 30 Mich. 69 (1874).

TYACK, DAVID G. (ED). *Turning Points in American Educational History.* Waltham, Mass.: Blaisdell, 1967.

U.S. DEPARTMENT OF COMMERCE. *Historical Statistics of the United States Colonial Times to 1970: Part I.* Washington D.C.: Bureau of the Census, 1975.

3
Who Controls?

Objectives

This chapter provides information to help the reader to

1. Recognize the existence of a trend favoring more centralized control of public education.
2. Suggest arguments supporting and opposing local control as opposed to state and federal control of education.
3. Point out factors associated with the expansion of the federal government's role in education in recent years.
4. Note that the degree of control of education at the state level varies greatly from state to state.
5. Point out why federal programs have not always responded to the needs of individual school districts.
6. Cite the contributions of federal programs to the total educational program in the country over the past several years.
7. Indicate possible changes in educational goals that may be coming about as a result of an increasing centralization of authority over educational decisions by state and federal officials.

Pretest

DIRECTIONS: Using your own paper, answer each of the following true/false questions. For each correct statement, write the word *true* on your paper. For each incorrect statement, write the word *false* on your paper.

1. In the United States, most local school boards are composed of officials appointed by the governor and are charged with carrying out the governor's policies.
2. Federal programs in education have generally responded to needs identified by state and local school districts rather than to the needs of organized pressure groups.
3. In recent years, many educational decisions have been made in response to pressures brought by organized interest groups rather than by individuals.
4. The certification of teachers, administrators, and supervisors is a responsibility of state authorities rather than of local or federal authorities.
5. The sponsorship of vocational education programs in the schools has been assumed primarily by educational leaders at the federal level rather than by those at the state or local level.
6. There is an increasing trend for state governments to establish

minimum competencies that must be demonstrated by a student before he or she is permitted to graduate from high school.

7. There are more school systems in the country today than there were in 1940.
8. Pressure for bilingual education in the school has come primarily from federal rather than state or local education authorities.
9. School programs result from a blend of local, state, and federal influences.
10. The legal precedents currently being followed give state school authorities the right to make decisions that have priority over decisions made by local school authorities.

Introduction

American school practices reflect compromises among local, state, and national forces. Some of these forces involve actions of local, state, and federal governmental bodies. Others are nongovernmental influences that impinge on schools and school programs at the local, state, and national levels. The relative influence of the authorities at each of these three levels of governance has not remained constant over time.

In the governmental arena, American schools have been controlled traditionally by state governments. Though federal and local authorities have had roles to play, the primary responsibilities have resided at the state level. This arrangement is rooted in the most fundamental of American political documents, the United States Constitution. The Constitution makes no express mention of schools or of education. But the Tenth Amendment to the Constitution does provide some general guidance in its notation that "the powers not delegated to the United States by the Constitution nor prohibited by it to the States, are reserved to the States respectively, or to the people." These words imply that since the Constitution makes no mention of specific federal responsibility for education, that responsibility falls to the state and local authorities.

Based on this constitutional situation, states have adopted bodies of law relating to the operation of the schools. These laws have established centralized procedures for financing and managing systems of schools. Typically, systems are organized under the direction of a central state department of education. State legislation generally provides for local school authorities to implement general school law and policy decisions made at the state level.

Typically, state legislation has created systems of locally elected school boards to manage educational programs in individual school districts. These officials establish general policies for the districts in which they serve. They are charged further with raising local revenues as needed to supplement state support for instructional programs and for the construction of facilities.

They oversee the hiring of key administrative and teaching personnel. Consistent with state guidelines, these officials also have some discretion over some components of the program of instruction in local schools.

Since school board members are usually elected officials, they tend to reflect major community interests. The school board provides a forum for the expression of local concern. Furthermore, the board is a political vehicle capable of implementing a limited range of policies that reflect unique perspectives of the local community.

In recent years, this tidy assignment of different responsibilities within education to officials at different levels of government has begun to undergo some changes. For example, the federal government, operating under its constitutional authority to look after the "general welfare" of the population, has begun to play a much more direct role in education than was true in earlier times. Furthermore, because of the need to expend scarce tax dollars wisely, state legislatures in recent years have been asserting additional state control over local school operations. In general, the actions of the federal and state authorities have reflected a trend that has resulted in a reduction in the range of school decisions left exclusively to local school officials. In the sections that follow, the reasons for this trend toward greater centralization are explored. Furthermore, arguments that have been put forward in support of and in opposition to this trend are introduced.

"As you all know, funding responsibilities are shifting back to local governments."

Local Influences on the Schools

Sentiment for the local control of schools represents a value that runs deep. A random survey of speeches about school governance chosen from nearly any historical period is certain to include a good number of addresses featuring ringing affirmations of the importance of local control. Wirt (1977) pointed out that textbooks for administrators often praise the value of local control and, with minimal concern about the inconsistency, go on to tell would-be principals how to impose state educational policy on local districts.

Box 3-1
Number of Local Public School Systems: United States,
          1939–1940 To 1980–1981

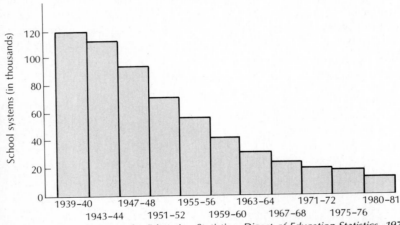

(Sources, National Center for Education Statistics. *Digest of Education Statistics, 1976 Edition.* Washington, D.C.: United States Government Printing Office, 1977, and National Center for Education Statistics. *Digest of Education Statistics, 1982 Edition.* Washington, D.C.: United States Government Printing Office, 1982)

LET'S PONDER

1. How do *you* account for the decline in the number of school districts?
2. What do you think might have been the reactions of people living in districts that became consolidated into larger districts?
3. What impact might consolidation have had on high school students? On junior high school students? On elementary school students?
4. What advantages and disadvantages for teachers do you see in consolidation? For administrators?
5. Do you think there will be more or fewer consolidations of districts in the future? Why?

Even some who administer federal programs do so out of a stated conviction that their actions are taken in support of the principle of local control.

The tradition of local control has long historical roots. Education frequently was a topic of debate in early New England town meetings. Indeed, regardless of geographic location, when communities were small and somewhat isolated from one another, few challenged the right of local leaders to exercise considerable control over what went on in the schools. This system reassured local people that appropriate values were being transmitted to the young. Furthermore, the system built a sense of community that cut across class and age lines. The system worked reasonably well so long as the communities and the problems remained small and manageable. When communities became larger, local decision-making involving the personal participation by the entire community became impractical. The growth of the communities resulted in districts' growing larger, in the consolidation of districts, and in a general increase in distance between the individuals making decisions about the schools and the individuals affected by these decisions.

Despite the changes in physical conditions in many American communities, the idea of local control remains very strong. In the subsections that follow, some arguments supporting and opposing the value of local control are introduced.

The Case *for* Local Influences on the Schools

Local communities know their own needs best. Though Americans in different parts of the country share many common values, still differences do exist. The special characteristics of people in individual communities are best understood by those people themselves. Certainly subtle differences peculiar to individual places cannot be fully appreciated by officials living in state capitals or in far-off Washington, D.C. It makes sense, then, for local communities to control the educational programs for their own young people. They know their needs and are capable of developing sound programs.

Local schools serve a unifying function for local communities. This function goes well beyond the school as a place for presenting formal information to the young. The schools provide athletic programs, school plays, evening classes for adults, voting sites for political precincts, and other services that are of great importance to the adult population of a community. Particularly, the achievements of the school athletic teams draw community members together. It is not uncommon for the remembrance of a shared moment of athletic excellence to be a positive unifying force years after the event. For example, in the 1980s in Schulenburg, Texas, a huge sign, somewhat weather-beaten, continued to proclaim: "SCHULENBUERG SHORTHORNS—STATE FOOTBALL CHAMPIONS 1972"; this years after the fact.

Throughout the land, merchants in small towns proudly display posters proclaiming their loyalty to the Butte Public Bulldogs, the Smithville Coal

Tenders, the Bryan Vikings, or some other team that provides a focus for community interest and discussion. When schools and their athletic teams are close to the community, a sense of belonging develops that is dear to the hearts of small-town America. Fear of losing this sense of togetherness along with the local school athletic teams has been an important motivator of those who have opposed school district consolidations.

Though there has been a trend in recent years for an increasing proportion of school funds to be provided from state as opposed to local sources, substantial revenues still are raised at the local level. Local control of education has meant that school board officials, in response to the wishes of the local community, have been able to set tax rates and generate revenue to provide the level of educational services desired. It should be pointed out that almost always, state authorities have decreed that certain minimum standards be met. But districts have typically had the option of providing more than these minimums. Given this situation, many districts have prided themselves on developing school systems far superior to those that have gone little beyond the levels required by the state. These districts have argued strongly for local control, noting that this control permits districts with parents and constituents interested in providing truly superior programs to do so. Without local control, it is alleged, no districts would lead the way in developing high-quality programs, and in time, all school systems would provide a level of services no higher than the existing minimum standards established by the state.

The right to hire teachers is a privilege that local educational leaders have defended strongly against state and national encroachment. There has been a feeling that teachers represent adult role models for young people. Therefore individuals compatible with the basic values of the local community must serve as teachers. To ensure that this indeed occurs, local leaders have insisted that teachers be hired by local rather than by state and federal officials. It is felt, too, that this procedure helps students learn because the teachers represent the kinds of adults the youngsters are used to encountering in their community. Consequently the credibility of these teachers does not come into question as frequently as would be the case were teachers very different from the community norm.

In addition to some of these specific arguments in support of the local control of schools, local control is defended on the general ground of its consistency with American political tradition. A core American value is the prizing of individualism. Individualism is thought to be less threatened by small local governmental authorities than by the larger, more distant state and federal authorities. Widespread adherence to this value supports local control of schools in that efforts by state and federal authorities to intervene are frequently seen as attacks on individual competence in local settings. People in local communities have a good deal of confidence in their personal abilities. This confidence, taken together with a strong belief in the value of the individual, makes a case for centering more control of schools at the local rather than at the state or national level.

The Case *Against* Local Influences on the Schools

Local schools may *think* they know their own needs best, but do they really? The local community is really part of a larger state community and a still larger national community. While there may be characteristics of the population in a given community that are special, it makes little sense to give local school people the authority to shape school programs geared heavily to these special characteristics. American society is increasingly mobile. Students must emerge from their school years capable of fitting in comfortably in communities anywhere in the state or the nation. Therefore it makes little sense to allow too much local control of schools. A very heavy dose of "localism" in school management can result in academic programs that do not equip students for life in the larger world beyond the local community.

The unifying function of school in the local community has been exaggerated. True, small towns continue to be highly dependent for much of their organized social life on programs associated with the schools. But in urban and suburban America, school programs represent only a tiny fraction of the opportunities available for citizens to come together. The relative importance of the small town that exists in isolation from a major urban center is declining. Resistance to the consolidation of school districts for the purpose of maintaining an individual identity for the small local community has little basis in logic. Consolidation is proposed in the first place because the numbers of students in existing districts are too low to be provided educational services efficiently. When consolidation is proposed, the community has already demonstrated that it either is already in decline or is failing to attract new residents at a rate commensurate with national averages. The call for consolidation does not cause the decline of the local community; it simply recognizes a decline that has already begun.

Permitting local school districts on their own initiative to raise taxes to provide services over and above state minimums discriminates against students in local districts unable or unwilling to levy taxes to provide services at these levels. This inequality fosters a tendency of affluent citizens to cluster together in individual communities where high housing costs keep out middle-income and low-income people. When citizens in these "silk-stocking" communities levy high school taxes, they create "ghettos of excellence" from which youngsters of middle- and low-income parents are excluded. It would be more equitable for taxes from these high-income areas to be collected at the state level. The state could then redistribute the money and raise the minimum standards in *every* district.

Absolute local control over teacher selection can result in teachers who mirror all the prejudices of the local community. If, for example, a community has few black residents, all teachers hired may be white. If there is a strong prejudice against Roman Catholics, subtle means may be used to ensure that the vast majority of teachers are Protestants. Such practices do not take into account that students should be prepared for the world, not for the local community. Given this reality, state and federal actions taken to ensure that local hiring practices have not been reflective of unacceptable biases are a reasonable and appropriate response to a potentially dangerous problem.

In response to the argument that local control is a reflection of the traditional value of individualism, it should be noted that in America, individualism has always gone forward within a social context. That is, the value has not been that "anything goes" in response to individual whims. Rather, individualism has been defined and limited by our society. There has been a strong tradition of collective help in support of individual development. The frontier farmer called in his neighbors when he roofed his barn. Lewis and Clark did not go alone to the Northwest frontier. This concern for the group and for the larger society suggests that in an age of great mobility, the local level of government may not represent the most appropriate level of control for American education. Rapid communication, the tendency of people to move frequently from community to community, and widespread concerns about similar educational problems suggest that, increasingly, control over education should be vested in state and federal authorities as opposed to local authorities.

Local Influences: Status Report

In this century, there has been a tendency for local school authorities over time to lose some of their control over education to state and federal authorities. This general pattern, however, should by no means be taken to suggest that local authorities today do not still exercise a profound influence over school programs in individual districts. They continue to make many decisions that give special flavors to individual school districts. But the range of their discretionary authority has tended to erode over time.

Efforts to professionalize education have typically sought the active involvement of state authorities. Clearly a policy decision has a wider immediate impact when it is backed by state authority. For this reason, decisions relating to many school personnel and program standards have been vested in state rather than local authorities. Particularly since World War II, there has been a great increase in the number of such standards adopted at the state level. Moves to implement and enforce these standards have tended to truncate the discretionary authority of local school officials to some degree.

At the federal level, organized interest groups have been able to secure the passage of legislation that has an impact on local districts. Specifically, programs relating to bilingual education, the treatment of minorities, vocational education, and the education of handicapped youngsters have been sponsored by federal authorities. Requirements placed on school districts by federal officials relating to the implementation of these programs have taken some program decision-making power away from local education officials. Today even very small districts are likely to have individuals charged with coordinating federal programs in the school system.

Box 3-2
Issues Relating to Local Control of Schools

LET'S PONDER

1. What kind of a community did you grow up in? How well do you think you were prepared for life beyond this community? Were there any features of your school program that responded to specific local political pressures?
2. Do you think the kinds of people elected to school boards are representative of the local community? Why, or why not?
3. Do decisions of school boards, in your experience, seem to be generally consistent with feelings of the local community? Can you cite any examples to support your conclusions?
4. What would have been the effects on your community had the school athletic programs been dropped? Was consolidation ever an issue in your community? If so, how did people feel about the question?
5. Do you think that increasing the authority of local school boards would tend to increase or decrease sexist or racist hiring practices in education? Why do you think so?
6. How different do you think communities are in the United States today? How different do school systems need to be?
7. If you were to predict the situation twenty-five years from now, would you expect local school authorities to have more or less authority than they have now?

Though there has been a clear tendency to remove some decision-making power from local educational leaders, the belief in local control of education remains strong. Indeed, in the first part of the 1980s, a federal administration philosophically opposed to increases in the power of the federal government increasingly took action to support the authority of local and state educational decision-makers.

State Influences on the Schools

Traditionally the greatest concentration of governmental power over public schools has been centered at the state level. Though state guidelines have influenced the school curriculum tremendously, they sometimes seem somewhat distant to the average citizen. Sometimes the heavy local press coverage of specific issues being weighed by local districts has given the erroneous impression that state influences on education are of relatively minor importance. Though local disputes may have a higher "visibility" among citizens in the local community, much more significant authority over education programs is found at the state than at the local level.

State control is exercised in a number of ways. State authorities typically control the certification of teachers, administrators, and curriculum supervisors, who are trained by colleges and universities. Preparation programs in these institutions are controlled by the state. Through the control of preparation programs and of certification requirements, state authorities establish minimal levels of quality for the educational professionals who will be permitted to teach in the schools.

State legislatures require that certain subjects and topics be provided in school curricula in all state districts. Requirements in the state of Illinois exemplify a pattern that is quite common in most states (though there is some variety in terms of the specific courses required). In Illinois, all schools must provide instruction in health, physical education, and United States history. Furthermore, schools are directed to include emphases on American patriotism, representative government, and the effects of alcoholic beverages (Hazard, 1978). To assure adherence to the prescribed state curricula, state authorities retain inspection rights over local district instructional programs.

In some states, state authorities adopt textbook titles for use in the schools. There is a good deal of variance in how this is handled from state to state. Some states—Texas, for example, identify a limited number of titles that are purchased and distributed to local schools. The districts may select other titles, but they must purchase them with local tax monies. Given a choice between using books purchased with state funds or levying local taxes to buy books instead, not surprisingly very few districts use textbooks that are not on the state adoption list. In other states, the titles identified by state education authorities are little more than suggestions that may or may not be adopted by local districts. Some states do not get into the textbook identification business at all.

The situation with regard to textbooks points up an important point about the state control of education. That is, while it is generally true that state authorities exercise a tremendous control over local programs, the actual degree of centralization of authority at the state level varies a good deal from state to state. In an exhaustive survey of administrative practices in the fifty states, Frederick Wirt and his students found differences among levels of state authority to vary according to traditional geographic regions. Relatively weak state controls were observed in the Northeast and in the Rocky Mountain states. States in the Midwest and the West generally had somewhat stronger state controls. The strongest general pattern of state control over education was found in six states in the Southeast. In terms of individual state extremes, Wyoming was observed to have the weakest state control over education and Hawaii the strongest—in Hawaii, there are no local school districts at all (Wirt, 1977).

The legal basis for state control is a nineteenth-century judicial decision that yielded what has come to be known as Dillon's rule. In essence, Dillon's rule holds that "the state can create and destroy all local units and it can grant or withhold authority for them to act" (Wirt, 1977, p. 164). The judicial precedent has provided the general authority for state educational authorities to hold local school districts accountable. This is an authority that state agencies have not been reluctant to use. As is noted in the subsections that follow, there is much debate regarding whether lodging control of education at the state level is a good idea.

The Case *for* State Influences on the Schools

Expertise in curriculum development and program management tends to be vested in relatively small numbers of individuals who have undergone special training. It is unrealistic to suppose that sufficient numbers of people will ever have the professional depth in these areas that is associated with first-class curriculum development and program management. Consequently it makes a good deal of sense to concentrate the relatively small pool of expert talent that is available at the state level. These talents can be directed toward developing curricula and program-planning guidelines that can be disseminated to local schools for implementation. This procedure relieves the local schools from difficult developmental tasks that may go beyond their talents and resources. It leaves the implementation responsibilities to officials at that level. These responsibilities accord more appropriately with the general level of expertise in local districts. Furthermore, when local officials are freed from curriculum and program development tasks, their time resources can be spent productively in the important area of fitting state guidelines to the unique characteristics of the local school districts.

State control of education promotes accountability. State legislatures mandate certain program minimums. Thus it is only logical that the responsibility for overseeing the implementation of these basic guidelines be undertaken by state rather than by local officials. Furthermore, purely from the perspective of efficient management, it makes sense to implement proven innovations in education at a state level rather than district-by-district. For example, should a fine new reading program be developed, action at the state level can install this program relatively quickly in every local district in the state. Were such a decision left to the local districts, squabbling could delay statewide implementation for years.

State control ensures that competent personnel will be hired to work in the schools. While certainly most local districts are managed by highly competent individuals, the possibility still exists for abuse, given the local district's power to hire teaching and administrative personnel. Clearly, some individuals are hired because of personal ties to influential people in the community. But through control of certification requirements, the state ensures all citizens of the state that all individuals will meet certain minimum criteria before they can be hired to work in the schools. Without this control, the professionalism of educators in the schools would not be as high as it generally is today.

In all areas, state control tends to professionalize education. State agencies act as a conduit for communicating information of all sorts to individual

Box 3-3
Comparative Levels of State Control Over Education in Different Regions

There is variability in the quantity of state control over public education in different regions of the United States. Note the following general patterns:

High Degree of State Control: — States of the Old South (particularly those where major battles of the Civil War had been fought)

Moderate Degree of State Control: — States of the Midwest and the West

Low Degree of State Control: — States of the Northeast and the Rocky Mountains

LET'S PONDER

1. How do you explain the relatively high degree of state control of education found in states of the Old South? Are there historical reasons? Would you expect to see changes in this pattern in the future? Why, or why not?
2. What accounts for the relatively low degree of state control in the Northeast? Are there historical reasons? Would you expect to see changes in this pattern in the future? Why, or why not?
3. How do you account for the low degree of state control over education that generally characterizes states of the Rocky Mountain Region? Are there historical reasons? Would you expect to see changes in this pattern in the future? Why, or why not?
4. What do you expect to see in the future in states in the Midwest and the West? Do you look for an increase in state control over education in these states or a decrease? Why?

school districts. New research results, opportunities to participate in state-wide assessment efforts, and a host of other possibilities for becoming linked to state and national professional efforts in education become available to even the most remote school districts in the state because of the existence of strong, central state-education agencies. A diminished influence for state-level education authorities would have a negative effect on the quality of programs in nearly every school district.

The Case *Against* State Influences on the Schools

At one time, individuals with high-level training in curriculum development and program management were few in number. While there might have been a historical case for concentrating the limited numbers of talented individuals in state education offices, this argument is no longer compelling. There has been a vast increase in the number of individuals managing local districts who have extensive preparation in sophisticated curriculum and program-planning skills. For example, even small districts today may have a superintendent with a doctoral degree. Many have individuals with doctoral degrees or at least extensive graduate training heading key curriculum and administrative departments. Any fair assessment would result in a conclusion that the diffusion of talent in education has reached down to even quite small districts today. These talented individuals are capable of doing more than simply implementing procedures sent down to them by officials in state offices.

State control of education tends to overlook diversity among America's local school districts. This diversity suggests the need to tailor school programs to the population of young people to be served. Further, there are issues of community values involved. Some communities wish an emphasis on area *A*, others on area *B*, and still others on areas *C* through *Z*. State-level officials do not take these important local differences into account. Consequently some programs promoted by state officials are simply not appropriate for certain communities. It would make better sense to increase the power of local officials to make substantial modifications in the school curriculum to fit unique local needs. State control interferes with their freedom to act as they know they responsibly should act.

No one argues with the need to be accountable. But assessment of school programs should be undertaken at the local level, not at the state level. State evaluators, because they must deal with information from all districts in a state, tend to assess programs based on state averages. These averages might not be appropriate for a given community. For example, a school district in a small community consisting of college professors who have always encouraged their children to read and have supported their efforts to learn in every way might have scores on a statewide test that look absolutely brilliant in terms of state averages. These scores might result more from the particular home backgrounds of these youngsters than from the excellence of their school programs. In such situations, it would make much more sense for local school officials to make year-by-year comparisons of the progress of students *within* the district. This information would reveal a good deal more about how well the program is "working" than assessment data based on state averages.

State control does not professionalize education. Rather, state control bureaucratizes education. Attempts to establish quality control result in a paperwork nightmare for local administrators. Furthermore, the effort to ensure that all individuals in schools have proper credentials is credible only if there is a pool of properly trained individuals available for hire. Often this is not the case. Nearly every state has "emergency certificates" of some kind that can be issued at the request of a local district to an individual with some deficiency in his or her formal training. Given the legal availability of these "exceptions," state pretenses as guarantors of "quality personnel" are something of a sham.

State Influences: Status Report

Evidence suggests that state control over education is increasing. In the early to middle 1980s, a trend emerged for the federal government to allow states to exert more control over how federal money for education was allocated and spent. State control seems to be increasing at the expense of local control as well. This latter trend is explained by the growing unwillingness of taxpayers to support education through a system of locally collected taxes on real property. The effect of this reluctance has been to shift a greater portion of school costs onto state as opposed to local revenue sources. As states more and more have become the major bill payers, they more and more have wished to look after their expenditures. Hence, state control seems very much on the upswing.

Beyond the trend toward states' picking up higher percentages of financial responsibility for the schools, a number of court challenges have been mounted in recent years that have implications for the issue of state versus local control. Litigants are contending that children should be guaranteed a "quality education" regardless of their district of residence. Decisions in these cases might require state authorities to equalize the funds expended for education in all state districts. This requirement will result in a diminished influence of local school authorities, who will be barred from using local revenues to provide programs in their districts that are greatly superior to or different from state-mandated "quality standards."

State legislatures throughout the nation have been consumed by two great enthusiasms regarding education in the past several years. First of all, they have become increasingly vocal on the point that schools must become "accountable." Second, they have been ever more attracted to the idea that certain "minimum levels of competence" be required of all students before they are permitted to graduate from high school. The "accountability" movement and the "minimum-competency" movement both promise an even greater concentration of power in state education agencies. Both will require the development of extensive statewide testing. It is clear that this testing will be developed and administered by the state education agencies. Local districts will be required to pass extensive data on to the state agencies for approval. Clearly the result will be another restriction of local control and an expansion of state control over education.

Finally, in recent years, the federal government has acted to strengthen state control over local education. Many federal programs are funneled through state agencies en route to local schools. State officials are charged with overseeing a good many of these programs. Their contacts with the officers for federal programs in local districts represent yet another example of the expansion of state control that has been witnessed over the past few years.

Educational trends are difficult to project, but little on the horizon suggests any imminent reduction in state control over education. Indeed, the trend toward an increasing concentration of administrative power at the state level seems quite likely to maintain itself for some time to come.

Federal Influences on the Schools

Though the federal government has been active in certain aspects of education for some time, this activity has increased dramatically in recent years. In modern times, acceleration of federal interest in the schools can be traced to the late 1950s. When the first Russian space orbiter, *Sputnik I,* was launched, an almost immediate public concern developed over the technical training being provided in the schools. A legislative response to this concern was the National Defense Education Act of 1958. This legislation provided monies to send teachers to special training programs to upgrade their skills. The impetus of this effort also resulted in a number of national curriculum projects, underwritten—in part, at least—by the federal government, that brought top talents together to develop new curricula for the public schools. Originally centering on the sciences, later these efforts expanded to include programs for developing new social science curricula as well. As a result of these efforts, influences of work supported by federal dollars began to shape a number of curriculum areas through the 1960s and on into the 1970s.

The impact of these federal curriculum-development efforts on school programs is difficult to assess. True, large numbers of new curricula were developed. True, many of these curricula represented promising new contributions to the field. But relatively small percentages of teachers were involved in special training programs where they were taught to use these materials. Some of these programs, additionally, suffered from being too heavily oriented toward the needs of the college-bound student. Some were simply not well suited to youngsters for whom graduation from high school would represent the end of formal schooling. For these and other reasons, these federally sponsored curriculum-development projects did not have as pervasive an influence on the schools as some might have hoped.

In the 1970s, federal involvement in education was directed less toward the establishment of specific curriculum programs. Rather, federal authorities moved as advocates of the rights of special groups of individuals whose interests may not have been well served by school programs developed by state and local authorities. The concern, then, of more contemporary federal involvement was about how certain groups of individuals were being treated by the schools rather than concern about the school curriculum, independent of its impact on these individuals.

Goldhammer (1978) identified a number of contributions to education that have resulted directly because of federal intervention. He noted such things as the following:

1. Vocational education has been established and has been built into programs at most levels.
2. Special programs have been developed for the handicapped and the disabled.
3. Bilingual programs have been stimulated.

4. New curricula in the sciences have been implemented.
5. Programs for out-of-school youth have become part of the responsibility of local school districts.
6. Adult and continuing education has become generally available.
7. Schools have had to respond more vigorously to the special needs of minority students.*

Federal involvement in education expanded in many areas during the decade of the 1970s. During this period, new programs were established in many of the categories identified by Goldhammer (1978). Older ones continued or were modified. Federal requirements helped reshape school practices throughout the nation.

In the early and middle 1980s, the federal government adopted a somewhat less activist role in terms of mandating programs to be installed in all of the nation's schools. Rather, there emerged a trend whereby the federal government allocated money to the states and provided general guidelines to govern how it was to be spent. Certainly many mandated federal programs

*Adapted from Keith Goldhammer. "The Proper Federal Role in Education Today." *Educational Leadership* (Feb., 1978): 350–353, pp. 350–351.

"We understand you ignored a Federal Guideline."

remained intact during this period. But when new programs were proposed and modifications to old ones were suggested, there was a tendency to allow state education authorities to assume a larger role in deciding exactly how state and local programs would respond to federal mandates.

Few dispute that the federal government has had an impact on school programs. But debate is heated over the issue of whether this involvement has been "good." Some of the positions taken in these discussions are highlighted in the subsections that follow.

The Case *for* Federal Influences on the Schools

The federal government speaks for the entire society. Because leaders in Washington receive signals from the entire population, they are positioned to take actions that represent the real national interest. For example, when national data reveal a deficiency in science and technical programs in the schools that might have long-term negative influences on our national defense capability, federal authorities can take action. While states and local authorities would probably be willing to take similar actions themselves, they simply do not have the information resources to detect emerging areas of need quickly. For this reason, the federal government must be empowered to make important decisions regarding school programs.

The interests of certain groups have not been well served by programs devised and implemented by state and local authorities. For example, in some places, educational resources diverted to programs serving minority groups have been meager compared with those diverted to programs serving students from majority groups. In many instances, children with learning handicaps have been very poorly provided for in the schools. In many areas, programs for adults wishing to upgrade their educational level have traditionally not been viewed as part of the schools' responsibilities. Since education properly serves the special needs of every segment of the population, there is a need for an authority to see that these needs are, in fact, met. Because federal decisions have an impact in all states and in all districts, the federal actions taken to help groups whose needs have traditionally not been well served have been highly appropriate. These actions have ensured that individuals can find programs to fit their special requirements regardless of where they live. The net result of these efforts is to upgrade the level of educational competence of the entire society.

Increasingly, we are becoming a nation of Americans, not a loose association of Texans, New Yorkers, Montanans, and citizens of other states. People move freely from place to place. The "NBC Nightly News" is seen in Bar Harbor, Maine; Tampa, Florida; Missoula, Montana; San Angelo, Texas; Independence, Iowa; Salem, Oregon; and nearly every other area of the country. Name-brand merchandise is on the shelves of commercial outlets

Box 3-4
Federal Control of Education

Mobility of our population is increasing. A student born in Florida may go to elementary school in Montana, high school in Texas, and attend a college or university in Pennsylvania. If he goes to graduate school, he may spend school time in several additional states.

As adults, Americans feel quite comfortable in moving from one part of the country to another. Indeed, this kind of movement taken together with our superlative transportation system and our capability of communicating instantly with any part of the country have made similarities of American towns and cities more striking than their differences.

Given this situation, it would make a good deal of sense for us to give up the illusion that local communities and states are somehow so different from one another that different sorts of school programs are needed. We are truly one nation. And, truly, what we need is one national school curriculum. There is a need for the federal government to manage education as a nation-wide enterprise. Such a system would assure maintenance of high levels of quality for youngsters everywhere. Furthermore, it would recognize in a programmatic sense that we are indeed one people.

LET'S PONDER

Read the selection above and consider the following questions:

1. What disadvantages, if any, do you see for a system of education that is controlled almost exclusively at the federal level? Could anything be done to overcome these disadvantages?
2. What advantages, if any, do you see for a system of federal control of education? What sorts of occurrences would result in a diminution of these advantages?
3. What is your reaction to the point that similarities of American towns and cities, regardless of their geographic location, are more striking than their differences? Do you have any specific evidence to support your view?
4. What do you think would happen to salaries of teachers were education to be controlled exclusively by the federal government? Why do you think so?
5. How likely do you think a federal takeover of all responsibility for education is? What would change the odds?

across the nation. Because our similarities today are more profound than our differences, our education system should be standardized to ensure that the individual who moves to a distant state will take along a set of competencies that will make adjustment relatively easy. Heavier federal involvement in education seems the most appropriate remedy to ensure that school programs everywhere will do a good job of providing youngsters for an adult role anywhere in the United States.

The Case *Against* Federal Influences on the Schools

It is a failure of logic to argue that the federal government speaks for the entire society. At best, the government represents only a majority view. At worst, the government represents a view that those in power believe "ought" to represent majority, whether it in fact does or not. Recall, for example, that during the Vietnam war, particularly during its final years, public opinion poll after public opinion poll revealed a majority of the population to be opposed to governmental policy. Yet for a long time government officials maintained a policy clearly running in opposition to this opinion. Given the uncertain record of the federal government as a responder to the will of the people, the prospect of increasing federal control over education is frightening.

Anyone who has worked with federal programs will report frustration centered on the heavy paperwork load involved. It is not surprising that the federal government wishes to defend the appropriateness of its expenditures by requiring adequate documentation from those receiving federal monies. But there is a real problem that results from the distance of federal authorities from the local schools. This distance requires that documents flow through a host of intermediate agencies. When the process begins, at the local school district level, the paperwork involved can be absolutely overwhelming. Today, with the growth of federal programs in the past several years, even the smallest school districts find it necessary to appoint someone to manage the paperwork associated with federal programs. Usually this is a full-time position. Should there be a vast expansion of federal involvement in education, the paperwork in local districts would be insupportably heavy.

The lack of differences from place to place in this country has been exaggerated. It is true that technological changes have brought us closer together, but strong local differences remain. Individual and regional differences are a core American value that would be seriously threatened were local and state control of education replaced by federal control. Furthermore, the ability to move from place to place remains, for many, a choice not taken. Significant numbers of people continue to be born, to live, and to die very close to their place of birth. The sense of place is a strong characteristic of Americans, and it is rightly supported by an educational system that reflects regional differences by developing programs at the state and local levels.

Federal programs have been disruptive to the operation of the school curricula. Many such programs have simply been imposed from above. The federal government has mandated that X be done, but the "how" has been left to the states and the local schools. Unsystematic introduction of new programs in the schools because of federal action has played havoc with systematic curriculum development. Curricula have become fragmented, and the principle of developing a logical progression of learning experiences has been violated. The net result may be less real learning for youngsters in the schools.

Federal Involvement: Status Report

As noted, there has been a tendency in recent years for the federal government to assign more decision-making about how federal money is to be spent to state and, to some extent, to local authorities. Whether this trend continues will depend on the philosophical orientation of individuals in places of responsibility in the federal government. It does seem certain, however, that some kind of federal involvement in education is likely to continue.

Some past complaints about federal involvement that have been voiced by state and local officials have come about because of a tendency of some federal actions to be taken in response from interest groups outside of organized education. For example, national organizations of Spanish-speaking Americans have been behind the federal effort to support bilingual education. Parents of handicapped children have pushed for more adequate school programs for their children. One result of this trend has been a perceived failure of the federal government to develop programs directed at needs that those within local and state educational needs have seen as pressing. This may well suggest a future where state and local education officials will have a much more active role in lobbying the federal government for action in areas they deem to be important.

Local, State, and Federal Influences: Some Final Thoughts

It seems clear that local districts are continuing to yield additional control to state education authorities. Both local and state authorities are having increasing numbers of restraints placed on them because of federal actions in education. Several implications for future teachers are suggested by these trends.

First of all, because many decisions affecting educational practices in local districts are going to be made at the state and national levels, teachers are going to need to develop professional perspectives going beyond their local community. If they are to have some influence on these decisions, they are going to have to affiliate with and play an active role in groups having a voice in the state capital and in Washington, D.C.

Second, teachers can expect more demands for evidence that their youngsters are learning. Because many of these demands are going to come from state and not local authorities, the kinds of anecdotal remarks about individual youngsters that would suffice for parents or principals will not suffice. Given the number of teachers and learners involved, it seems clear that the states will increasingly demand evidence of achievement as provided by objective tests of some sort. Indeed, the political demand for information at the state level may be outrunning the "state of the art" in test development. That is, adequate testing technology may not be available to deliver, responsibly, the kind of information that is wanted. But given political pressures, states may be forced to give some available tests, whether adequate or not.

Teachers, if they are to have some voice in the matter of assessing their students, must be prepared to argue their case at the state, not the local level. To protect themselves from inadequate and inapproriate testing programs, teachers will have to develop a more sophisticated understanding of the whole area of learner assessment than many have had in the past.

Teachers may be called on to deal with youngsters in their classrooms who are quite different than those they were trained to teach. Federal laws, such as Public Law 94-142,* are going to result increasingly in the placement in regular classrooms of students who formerly spent their entire day in special classrooms. This law and others on the horizon suggest that teachers will need to engage in professional upgrading of their skills through much of their careers. As a consequence, in-service education for teachers is certain to take on important new dimensions.

Finally, to put matters in perspective, we need to reemphasize that in the final analysis it is the individual teacher who will "make a difference." While policy questions related to issues of federal, state, and local authority do influence the range of individual teachers' actions, still the primary influence on youngsters is the teacher. So though we may be heartened or disheartened by trends related to the political control of education, we must not lose sight of the individual who is going to "make" or "break" any program: the all-important classroom teacher.

Recapitulation of Major Ideas

1. Traditionally most control over education has rested at the local level of government. There is evidence that today state authority is increasing at the expense of local authority.
2. In general, state educational authorities provide general guidelines related to the content of the school curriculum, the establishment and management of local school districts, and the certification of the professionals who work in the schools.
3. Local school-district authorities are charged with implementing state guidelines. They oversee the day-to-day management of the schools. They control most aspects of hiring personnel to fill professional and nonprofessional vacancies in the schools.

*See Chapter 16 for an extensive treatment of this legislation.

4. There has been a great reduction in the number of school districts in the country over the past forty years. Consolidation has made it possible to build larger schools and to provide more adequate services. Consolidation has been opposed on some occasions because of the feeling that there will be a negative impact on the local community as a result of the loss of a school or a school district bearing the community's name.

5. Supporters of local control of education base most of their arguments on the idea that local people know local needs best. Opponents of this view suggest that, given an increasingly mobile population, schools must prepare students for life in the larger society. Excessive local control, these critics contend, can result in the development of school curricula having little utility to students outside of the local area.

6. In recent years, state legislatures have been increasingly interested in passing "accountability" legislation and "minimum-competency" legislation. Laws reflecting these trends have placed increased responsibilities on state departments of education. They support the general increase in the power of state educational authorities over local educational authorities.

7. State control over the certification of teachers establishes a minimum level of quality control. Furthermore, the state, through its relationships with colleges and universities, works to maintain high standards.

8. Federal influences in education have been exercised largely because of pressures brought to bear by organized interest groups. Most of these interest groups have represented individuals not working within public education. Federal action has been taken to ensure that certain groups whose interests were seen as being ill served by existing programs would receive instructional programs consistent with their unique needs.

9. In general, there seems to be a trend toward increased state and federal involvement in education. Thus teachers are going to have to keep abreast of the developments occurring in state capitals and in Washington, D.C.

Posttest

DIRECTIONS: Using your own paper, answer each of the following true/false questions. For each correct statement, write the word *true* on your paper. For each incorrect statement, write the word *false* on your paper.

1. In the United States, most local school boards are composed of officials appointed by the governor and are charged with carrying out the governor's policies.

2. Federal programs in education have generally responded to needs

identified by local school districts rather than to the needs of organized pressure groups.

3. In recent years, many educational decisions have been made in response to pressures brought by organized interest groups rather than by individuals.

4. The certification of teachers, administrators, and supervisors is a responsibility of state authorities rather than of local or federal authorities.

5. The sponsorship of vocational education programs in the schools has been assumed primarily by educational leaders at the federal level rather than those at the state or local level.

6. There is an increasing trend for state governments to establish minimum competencies that must be demonstrated by a student before he or she is permitted to graduate from high school.

7. There are more school systems in the country today than there were in 1940.

8. Pressure for bilingual education in the schools has come primarily from federal rather than state or local education authorities.

9. School programs result from a blend of local, state, and federal influences.

10. The legal precedents currently being followed give state school authorities the right to make decisions that have priority over decisions made by local school authorities.

Summary

Traditionally state educational authorities have exercised the greatest degree of control over public education. Today the control of state departments of education is increasing at the expense of local control. States are picking up a higher percentage of school funding than was true in former times. State legislatures are directing state school authorities to hold local districts accountable for educational expenditures and for the levels of competence demonstrated by secondary-school graduates.

In recent years, there has been a dramatic growth in the involvement of federal authorities in education. In general, federal programs have developed because of efforts mounted by special-interest groups who have felt that their needs were not being well served by school programs. Emphases on bilingual education, vocational education, education for adult learners, and the education of handicapped students have been reflected in federal programs. Increased involvement by federal authorities has been viewed as a mixed blessing by local officials.

In general, it is fair to say that education in the United States is becoming increasingly governed by state and federal actions as compared with local actions. An implication of this trend is that teachers in the future are going to have to keep abreast of developments occurring in state capitals and in Washington, D.C. If teachers' influence on educational policy is to be felt, that influence probably will have to be expressed through representatives of professional organizations who speak with state and national legislators.

Finally, it must be remembered that regardless of where basic educational policy decisions are made, ultimately the classroom teacher is the person who must implement them. Though teachers may be happy or unhappy about the increasing influences of state and federal authorities, they should take solace in an understanding that the teacher remains the pivotal figure in determining whether programs and youngsters fail and succeed in the schools.

References

BARRY, JOSEPH E. "Politics, Bilingual Education, and the Curriculum." *Educational Leadership* (May, 1983): 56–60.

FRAZIER, CALVIN M. "State/Federal Role in Curriculum Development." *Educational Leadership* (Feb., 1978): 339–341.

GOLDHAMMER, KEITH. "The Proper Federal Role in Education Today." *Educational Leadership* (Feb., 1978): 350–353.

HAZARD, WILLIAM R. *Education and the Law,* 2nd ed. New York: Free Press, 1978.

KOERNER, J. D. *Who Controls American Education?* Boston: Beacon Press, 1968.

NATIONAL CENTER FOR EDUCATION STATISTICS. *Digest of Education Statistics, 1976 Edition.* Washington, D.C.: United States Government Printing Office, 1977.

NATIONAL CENTER FOR EDUCATION STATISTICS. *Digest of Education Statistics, 1982 Edition.* Washington, D.C.: United States Government Printing Office, 1982.

SCHUSTER, JACK H. "Out of the Frying Pan: The Politics of Education in a New Era." *Phi Delta Kappan* (May, 1982): 583–591.

SHANNON, THOMAS A. "The Emerging Role of the Federal Government in Public Education." *Phi Delta Kappan* (May, 1982): 595–597.

WIRT, FREDERICK M. "School Policy, Culture, and State De-Centralization." In Jay D. Scribner (ed). *The Politics of Education.* The 76th Yearbook of the National Society for the Study of Education, Part II. Chicago: National Society for the Study of Education, 1977, pp. 164–187.

4
How Curricula Are Organized

Objectives

This chapter provides information to help the reader to

1. Name the general bases used for organizing curricula.
2. Explain why curriculum organization is important for learning.
3. Describe the advantages and disadvantages of subject-centered curricula.
4. Point out the features of curricula organized according to a broad-fields approach.
5. Suggest the possible relationships between the curriculum organization and the nature of the subject matter.
6. Point out how the needs of society influence curriculum organization.
7. Describe the factors to be considered in implementing curricula that respond to individual needs.

Pretest

DIRECTIONS: Using your own paper, answer each of the following true/false questions. For each correct statement, write the word *true* on your paper. For each incorrect statement, write the word *false* on your paper.

1. Because they have gone through a common preparation program, few teachers disagree about what should be emphasized in school programs.
2. In Puritan New England, schooling was seen as a mechanism that could keep children from falling into the hands of the Devil.
3. Throughout history, it has been a common practice to organize instruction in schools in such a way that knowledge is separated into different academic subjects.
4. According to those favoring a "structure-of-disciplines" approach to teaching, learners should be familiarized with the basic organizing ideas of academic subjects or disciplines.
5. Critics of subject-centered curricula point out that the "real" world is not divided into separate subjects, such as history, mathematics, and science.
6. An advantage of the broad-fields curriculum is that large numbers of teachers have the breadth of training necessary to deal successfully with the approach.
7. Proponents of "needs-of-society" curricula point out that learners are motivated by programs associated with this approach.
8. Critics of the "needs-of-society" orientation say programs associated with the approach needlessly force learners to delay their choice of a career.

9. Jean Piaget has identified a number of developmental stages through which all individuals are thought to pass.
10. In the view of supporters of "learner-centered" curricula, an important strength of programs associated with this approach is the placement of learners at the center of the planning process.

Introduction

As principal of a medium-sized middle school, Marge Henry finds that many of her problems with her thirty-eight faculty members concern disagreements about how the curriculum should be organized. Many of the fifth- and sixth-grade teachers favor a learner-centered approach that emphasizes experiences more than subject-matter content. They tend to believe that individual development is the primary mission of the school.

Another group of teachers believes that education should prepare youngsters to move smoothly into the adult world of work. They are convinced that the needs of society should be analyzed and that the school program should be directed toward meeting these needs. They are fearful that learner-centered approaches may result in programs that provide youngsters with no useful social skills.

Still another element in the faculty, represented by fairly large numbers of seventh- and eighth-grade teachers, are suspicious of both the learner-centered and the society-centered approaches. They dismiss learner-centered curricula as "frivolous" and point out that the needs of society change too frequently to provide a sound basis for course planning. The teachers in this faction believe that the traditional emphases on academic subjects represent the best foundations upon which to build the school program. They are particularly wary of innovations that they feel might "dilute" or "water down" the academic program.

These teachers and the views they represent are found in American schools everywhere. Partisans of these basic positions are very sincere in thinking their view the "best" or the "most responsible." These philosophical differences point up the great difficulty involved when policy decisions are needed that specify what is to be taught. Clearly such decisions tend to support some philosophical positions and to run counter to certain others. Professional educators need to be familiar with these orientations and to understand the curriculum decisions that logically flow from each. The elements of the operating school program did not just get there by chance. They were put in for a purpose. That purpose relates to the philosophical premises of those people who set up the program. For example, if a high school requires four years of mathematics for all graduates, this requirement suggests that there is a good deal more support for a subject-centered curriculum than for a learner-centered curriculum in this district or in this school. On the other hand, a high

List some of the subjects you took in elementary school, junior high school, and senior high school in the spaces provided at the left. In spaces at the right, suggest reasons or motives that you think might have been used to justify inclusion of these subjects in the school program when they were first introduced.

Subjects   Reasons

_____   _____
                          _____
_____   _____
                          _____
_____   _____
                          _____
_____   _____
                          _____
_____   _____
                          _____
_____   _____
                          _____

LET'S PONDER

1. Do you find that most of your school subjects seem to have been included because of reasons related to importance of (a) the characteristics of the individual learner, (b) the needs of society, or (c) the subject matter of the academic disciplines?
2. Were all subjects in schools you attended directed to serving just one of the stated purposes of the school (see "a," "b," and "c" in question 1 above), or were each of these purposes served by at least some courses?
3. In the future, would you expect most new courses to serve "a," "b," or "c" (refer to question 1, above). Why?

school with few, if any, required courses above and beyond those the state requires for graduation and very large numbers of elective courses probably belongs to a school or district with a heavy commitment to learner-centered curricula.

Look at the "Subjects in the Curriculum" box. See if you can explain why some of the subjects you studied during your elementary- or secondary-school years were included in the curriculum.

If you had some difficulty in identifying the purpose of some of the subjects you took in school, you need not feel bad. Many people find it very difficult to identify the specific purpose that a school subject is supposed to be serving. Indeed, many teachers of particular school subjects would have difficulty in responding were someone to press them hard about the basic justification for including their subject in the school curriculum. The difficulty comes, in part, from the length of time that has passed since the individual subjects were first introduced. Today many courses are maintained more because of tradition ("We've always taught American history to high school juniors") than because of a specific educational purpose. To understand how some of these courses got into the curriculum, it is necessary to look back in time for an example.

In early Puritan schools, education was viewed as a vehicle for keeping the young from falling into Satan's snares. The Puritan curriculum included a heavy dose of religion and morals. Bible study was considered critical. Even reading exercises were heavily laced with Puritan moralism. Clearly here, the major concern was perpetuating a norm of behavior considered "right" by the controlling group. Puritan education might be thought of as being heavily guided by the "needs-of-society" objective of schooling. Today courses such as "contemporary problems," "courtship and marriage," and "the free enterprise system" are in the tradition of Puritan moralism. They reflect pressures to transmit certain core values to the young. While certainly, today, the society permits a much greater latitude of behavior than was tolerated in Puritan days, still there is some legacy in the schools to serve the "needs of society." To do otherwise, in Puritan days, was to "serve Satan." Thus, for the Puritans, the rationale for moral education in the schools was a simple one: to prevent the child from falling into the Devil's clutches. Today the consequences of not serving the needs of society are not so crystal clear. For this reason, we find it more difficult to pinpoint the reasons that some of our present-day needs-of-society courses are in the curriculum.

The lesson of this review of Puritan moralism is that school subjects, when they were initially introduced into the curriculum, bore a clear relationship to certain expectations that people had about schooling. With the passage of time, however, these assumptions about the "way the world is" have altered. However, many elements of the school program have remained in place despite dramatic changes in how the members of society view their world. Thus it is sometimes difficult to describe today the exact function of courses, the role of which was understood with perfect clarity at the time those courses were first introduced. This point needs to be kept in mind as you read the following sections, which expand on curricula organized according to the nature of the subject matter, the needs of society, and the characteristics of the learners.

Nature of the Subject Matter

Throughout history, one of the most common ways of organizing the curriculum has been a division along the lines of disciplines or academic subjects. Even in Roman times, educational programs were separated into subjects based on the assumption that there were disciplines (or bodies of knowledge) that were related in some natural way. Learning was thought to be easier when young people were introduced to knowledge that had been preorganized into academic subjects, such as "mathematics" or "music."

Even today, people who organize school curricula around academic subjects accept the general view that scholars in individual disciplines have developed reliable, responsible, and precise ways of knowing about the world. They believe that there is merit in having learners master certain kinds of information. They believe that learning this content enables youngsters to gain control of their own destinies. Indeed, some bodies of knowledge are perceived to be so important that they are absolutely essential for everyone. Subjects that have been described frequently as "essential for all learners in American schools include English, history, science, and mathematics. Usually courses dealing with these major subject areas are mandated by state law. These laws have resulted from a feeling that an individual cannot be thought of as properly "educated" until he or she has a firm foundation in several of the academic subjects.

Exactly *which* subjects are "musts" for learners has been the subject of considerable debate. Perhaps not surprisingly, scholars in each subject have found "compelling" reasons for placing very heavy emphasis on their own specializations. Conflicts among partisans of different academic subjects have become familiar events in state capitals throughout the nation as legislators have called on expert witnesses to help them define the essential elements of a "basic education."

FUNKY WINKERBEAN   Tom Batiuk

(Funky Winkerbean by Tom Batiuk. © 1981, Field Enterprises, Inc. Courtesy of Field Newspaper Syndicate.)

Some have argued that the debate ought not to center so much on the titles of appropriate courses as on what organizational features characterize each academic specialization. A good deal of attention to the "structure of the disciplines" (the organization of the individual academic subjects and how professionals in these disciplines ask and answer questions) developed after the fall of 1957, when the Soviets launched a small satellite named *Sputnik*.

Concerns spawned by the launching of *Sputnik* prompted a meeting of thirty-five prestigious scientists and educators at the small town of Woods Hole, Massachusetts. This group came together to discuss ways of improving education. They concluded that school courses ought to be reorganized around something called the *structure of the discipline*.

Each academic subject, or discipline, was seen as being characterized by a few key organizing ideas or principles. These principles are used by scholars in these disciplines to frame important questions and to analyze and evaluate their data. Scholars and educators at the Woods Hole conference determined that much of the difficulty of American education resulted from courses that were little more than random collections of isolated information. What was needed, they felt, was a reorganization of courses to teach not these isolated "facts" but the organizing ideas or principles that represented the structure of each discipline taught in school. Curricula that encouraged youngsters to master the structure of the disciplines were thought to be better able to stimulate sophisticated thinking and to involve youngsters in problem-solving activities similar to those that occupied leading professional scholars.

Because professional scholars were familiar with the structure of their own disciplines, recasting school curricula along these lines, it was thought, would provide an avenue that would attract the active involvement of these scholars in developing school programs. An underlying theme was that students who during their public school years became thoroughly familiar with the structure of the disciplines would be ready to do more advanced work in college. Indeed, in one sense, the structure-of-disciplines approach might be thought of as a scheme to prepare youngsters more efficiently for rigorous university programs terminating in Ph.D. degrees.

Interest in the structure-of-disciplines approach was reflected in a proliferation of federal activities in education beginning in the late 1950s. During the 1960s, there were a tremendous number of new curriculum projects that were attuned philosophically with the structure-of-disciplines approach. There was heavy involvement of leading scholars in the academic disciplines. Among these projects were the following: The Biological Science Curriculum Study (BSCS); The Physical Science Study Committee (PSSC); The Earth Science Curriculum Project (ESCP); and The Intermediate Science Curriculum Study (ISCS).

During this time, some of the traditional subjects in the curriculum were challenged by proponents of some of the newer disciplines. For example, some individuals questioned the place of history in the curriculum. Concerns about the "legitimacy" of history were raised by those who were bothered by historians' inability to identify a definitive "structure" supported by a general set of common principles. The relevance of history was questioned, therefore, and some sentiment arose for the newer behavioral sciences, such as psychology and sociology—disciplines with a more discernible "structure." History has maintained itself, but definitely such courses as sociology and psychology have cut into the numbers of youngsters in history programs, particularly those history courses taken as electives.

Advantages of the Subject-Centered Approach

One often-cited advantage of subject-centered curricula is that the individual subjects tend to organize content that contains many common elements. For example, mathematics courses of all kinds tend to have much more common content than would be found in a mixture of mathematics, English, and French courses. This commonality of content is thought to facilitate learners' understanding. Learning is thought to come more easily when youngsters encounter material that is limited in scope and logically related.

Subject-centered curricula are widely accepted by the general public. As the most traditional form of organizing school programs, this pattern has been imbued with a certain "respectability" because of its long familiarity to parents and other patrons of the school. Thus subject-centered curricula provide a certain sense of stability that many find attractive. Teachers, for example, may appreciate the security of knowing that they will be teaching familiar subjects. Administrators may feel more confident in explaining this kind of organizational pattern to parents.

Another frequently cited strength of subject-centered curricula is that the content organization is much the same as that encountered by teachers in their own educational programs. It is natural that teachers who have experienced sixteen or more years of subject-centered curricula in public schools and in colleges and universities will be disposed favorably toward this organizational pattern.

Subject-centered curricula tend to make large use of textbooks. These texts nearly always assume a subject-centered approach. For example, there are separate mathematics, English, and French textbooks. Though they exist, textbooks that represent a fusion of content from these three subjects are rare indeed. Because of the subject-centeredness of textbooks, there is some incentive for teachers to support a subject-centered curricular approach. For many the sequence of textbook chapters provides a "natural" organization that is attractive. Even those teachers who "skip about" from chapter to chapter make use of the organization within individual chapters.

Though too much reliance on textbooks has been criticized, the use of texts does have certain advantages, considering the alternatives. If information that is gathered conveniently within the covers of a given textbook were to be duplicated in the form of journals, newspapers, documents, and other information sources, literally dozens of expensive items would have to be purchased. Storage difficulties could be enormous. Also teacher planning might become a task of enormous complexity as dozens of information sources were reviewed in the search for items of relevance for daily lessons. So, while few deny that textbooks should be supplemented by additional materials, many teachers stoutly defend their advantages as efficient vehicles for storing a great deal of important basic information.

Disadvantages of the Subject-Centered Approach

Subject-centered curricula do have their disadvantages. While individual courses in a subject-centered curriculum have a certain internal consistency, it is by no means clear that the world is organized into "history," "mathematics," "English," "French," and the other separate subjects usually found in such organizational schemes. Learners do not encounter reality as, for example, mathematics content or English content. Rather, the world is encountered "all of a piece," or as a "whole." Since the world is not divided into individual subject areas, critics of subject-centered curricula suggest that the schools should not place so much emphasis on separate subjects. What is needed, many believe, is a curriculum that is more interdisciplinary in nature. That is, the school curriculum ought to focus more on the "real problems" of living and draw on a number of sources to help learners deal with these problems.

Critics of the subject-centered curriculum suggest that dividing knowledge into individual subjects creates artificial barriers. Such a practice assumes that the learners will be able to integrate the information from the various subject areas as they need it to deal with problems. But many learners do not do this easily. For example, some learners write almost error-free prose for their English teacher but turn in papers in other classes that contain many mistakes. ("This is history. We aren't *supposed* to write perfect papers here. That's for English. Here we learn names and dates.")

Many learners have complained that the subject-centered pattern of organization does not provide them with "relevant" learning experiences. For example, a student studying algebra may well ask, "Why should I study this stuff? What good is it?" Those who would like something different from a subject-centered approach suggest that algebra could be more meaningful if the focus were on "real problems" rather than on "algebra." In such a setting, there would be more incentive for youngsters to learn algebra as they perceived its connection to the real world.

Other critics of the subject-centered approach have suggested that too many courses in such programs have not kept up with the "knowledge explosion." Today new knowledge is being generated at a very rapid rate. This development poses great problems for the subject-centered curriculum in that most traditional courses have assumed a relatively stable, if not static, body of knowledge. Too many such courses are simply behind the times. They have not proved capable of quick adjustment. Consequently the contents of many such courses are obsolete.

Broad-Fields Curriculum

One interesting approach meant to resolve some of the criticisms that have been directed against the subject-centered curriculum is the "broad-fields curriculum." In the broad-fields curriculum, two or more traditional subjects are combined into "broad areas." These broad areas sometimes center on large themes or strands, such as "industrialism" or "evolution." Using these basic themes, instructional planners prepare lessons that draw on knowledge from a number of different subject areas. This approach has been promoted

---

Box 4-2
Relative Attractiveness of Different Teaching Assignments

Assume you are a certified teacher who has just graduated from a college or university teacher preparation program. Suppose you have been offered teaching positions in two different districts. Salaries and general working conditions are about the same in each place. You will be expected to teach five classes a day at the high school level. Your assignments for each district would be as follows:

School District One	*School District Two*
Period 1 American History	Period 1 Technology and Society
Period 2 American History	Period 2 Technology and Society
Period 3 World History	Period 3 Planning Period
Period 4 Planning Period	Period 4 Militarism
Period 5 World History	Period 5 Militarism
Period 6 World Geography	Period 6 Dynamics of Leadership

LET'S PONDER

How would you feel about accepting a position in either one of these districts given these teaching assignments? Respond to the following questions.

1. In general, would you prefer District One or District Two? Why?
2. In which case would you have had better college or university preparation for your task? Why do you think so?
3. In which case do you think you would have the more difficult time in locating appropriate instructional materials? Why?
4. How do you think learners would react to courses in the two districts? Why do you think so?

---

as a device for breaking down the barriers that separate knowledge into different subject areas. Learners, it is assumed, will be better able to apply knowledge if they are given exposure to the broad-fields approach.

The approach is not without its problems. One major difficulty is that few teachers possess the breadth of knowledge in different academic specialties that would enable them to draw freely and easily on a number of different areas. With very few exceptions, teachers' college and university courses have not been organized according to a broad-fields approach. Consequently many do not feel well enough prepared to teach in this way.

Needs of Society

The "needs of society" represent another major point of departure for curriculum organization. Curricula developed from this perspective may have one of several basic emphases. Among these are curricula organized according to "problems approaches" and curricula organized to promote "citizenship development."

The problems approach has been favored by educators who believe that the school program should provide learning experiences that will enable learners to develop skills and insights related to pressing social problems. Supporters argue that ensuring social survival is the key misssion of the schools. To accomplish this objective, they believe that youngsters must be introduced to difficult contemporary problems during their school years and must be given opportunities to think through potentially useful solutions to these problems.

The problems approach bears a close resemblance to the broad-fields approach. Information from a variety of disciplines is drawn on as youngsters and their teachers attempt to develop reasoned responses to pressing issues. In the problems approach, the emphasis is always on pressing social problems. The broad-fields curriculum may or may not use social problems as a central focus. Thus the problems approach might be thought of as a subset, centering on pressing issues, of the wider and more general broad-fields curriculum.

Another orientiation stemming from the basic needs-of-society orientation is the citizen-development approach to curriculum organization. Proponents of this approach point out that citizens in a society need to have certain basic skills in order to make a contribution to the society. There is a heavy emphasis on identifying and teaching those things that will be "useful" to learners in their role as adult citizens. Vocational training of all kinds is assigned a high priority. Though by no means universal, there is some tendency for partisans of this position to be very wary of courses in the school that do not have a clear relationship to what students will be doing as working adults.

The citizenship-development approach has had broad appeal for large numbers of pragmatically oriented Americans. Frequently, attacks on "frills" in school are manifestations of concerns being voiced by those who want the program to be more clearly tied to the future career and vocational needs of youngsters. Recent educational history has demonstrated a reluctance of voters to provide funds for school programs not having a demonstrable connection to the world of work. Some educators have noted that this attitude has been transmitted to a good many youngsters, who not infrequently ask teachers such questions as: "Why do I need to know this? What good is it going to do me?" These questions clearly flow from the idea that there should be some practical utility to education—a position that is central to the citizenship-education approach.

Strengths of the Needs-of-Society Orientation

Like the broad-fields approach, the organization of curricula around the needs of society draws together information from a variety of separate academic subjects. This process helps break down the idea that knowledge is compartmentalized artificially in "boxes" we label *history, English, mathematics, physics,* or something else. In other words, needs-of-society curricula help youngsters integrate knowledge from a variety of sources as they use it to take a look at the world as it "really is."

Proponents of needs-of-society curricula point to the motivational advantages of organizing programs around "reality." For example, if a class is oriented toward a career a youngster is interested in, the desire to learn the material may be greatly increased; a learner might find it a much more pleasant task to learn mathematics in the context of studying to be a pilot rather than going page by page through a traditional mathematics textbook.

There is also an important motivational appeal that accompanies a focus on important social problems. Youngsters more easily see the relevance of a topic such as "consumer rights" than of "decision making in ancient Sparta." Social problems are likely to have been a topic of concern at home. Many traditional topics may seem to youngsters to be of interest to absolutely no one except the classroom teacher. Little wonder, then, that they prefer to deal with issues that seem to hold the interest of the wider community.

Weaknesses of the Needs-of-Society Orientation

A major problem of the needs-of-society orientation is the difficulty of identifying just what "needs" should be addressed in the school program. There is a danger that these needs will be identified hastily and that they will be very narrow in scope. For example, courses that seek to prepare youngsters to deal with current social problems or for a specific job ignore the inevitability of change. Given problems pass away; new problems emerge. Technical changes alter job requirements tremendously over time. When needs are thought of too narrowly, there is a danger that the curriculum will consist of courses that provide youngsters with information that will be obsolete by the

Box 4-3
How "Practical" Should the Curriculum Be?

Robert Peterson's father owns a used car lot. Robert, a sixth grader, helps out after school. He strips cars of mirrors, chrome, hub caps, and other exterior ornaments and trim. With his father's help, he organizes these items in some large bins in the main office area where customers are invited to look for something they might need. For his help, Robert's father pays Robert 10 percent of what he takes in from sales of these items. Robert has several hundred dollars in his own bank account that have come to him from these sales.

Robert's father has told him that, as he gets older, he will take on more responsibilities in the business. He also will have an opportunity to make more money. Some day Robert hopes to be a full partner working side by side with his father. His father has the same wish.

In school, Robert takes "History of Latin America," "Arithmetic," "English Composition," "Spelling," and "Science." He does not care too much for school, but he does well enough to keep out of trouble. His father and mother don't say anything to Robert, but they suspect that some of the things he is studying are not really very important.

LET'S PONDER

Read the paragraphs above and respond to the following questions:

1. Which of the school subjects do you suspect Robert likes least? Why?
2. What could be done with this "least favorite" subject to make it more acceptable to Robert? Would this be a responsible change?
3. Which courses would you expect Robert to like best? Why?
4. Should Robert's school offer some entirely different courses to better suit his needs? If so, what would those courses be?
5. Would it be a good idea for schools to offer courses that parents and youngsters considered to be "relevant" to their youngsters' present and future needs? Would this approach cause any problems?
6. Are there some courses that are "musts" for everyone regardless of the roles they will play as adults? Why do you think so?

time they leave school. Such programs will not provide learners with the kind of general learning they need to adapt easily to changing conditions.

Critics of the needs-of-society orientation have taken the approach to task because of the tendency of such programs to encourage youngsters to make career choices too early during their school years. The approach, they allege, encourages this behavior because if youngsters are to be "properly motivated," teachers need to know what the youngsters intend to do as adults so that their instruction can respond to these interests. Carried to a logical extreme, youngsters would be forced into career or vocational tracks very early. In fact, this practice has been followed in many other countries. But in the U.S. there has generally been a recognition that youngsters' interests change over time. Consequently there has been a reluctance to lock youngsters into a premature career choice.

Those needs-of-society curricula focusing on social problems have not always been popular with parents and other adults. There is some fear that the school will impose a set of values or a set of responses to these problems that are inconsistent with those held by the parents. Some are distrustful of teachers and their ability to engage learners in a consideration of problems in a way that will not be inherently critical of cherished American institutions. It is arguable that these concerns are legitimate. But the concerns certainly are real enough to have made school authorities in many locations extremely cautious about reorganizing the school program around a social problems approach.

Characteristics of Learners

A third orientation for school curricula centers on the "characteristics of learners." There have been several programmatic responses to this orientation. Among these are programs centered on the "psychological development" of youngsters and programs centered on "learners' interests." In the sections that follow, there is some elaboration of the central threads of each of these approaches.

Psychological Development of Learners

It is possible to organize the school program around the psychological principles associated with growth, development, and the nature of learning. A number of years ago, a leading figure in educational psychology, Robert Havighurst (1953), developed a list of what he called "developmental tasks." He hypothesized that as individuals grow up, they are faced with different types of tasks that must be mastered in a given order. One approach to curriculum development would involve the creation of courses that would provide youngsters with proper developmental-task experiences in an appropriate sequence.

In recent years, the work of the eminent Swiss psychologist Jean Piaget has received a good deal of attention. Piaget has identified a number of developmental stages that he believes all individuals go through. These developmental stages and some of their basic characteristics are noted below:

1. *Sensorimotor stage (birth to age 2):* During this period, the child moves from simple reflex actions to some more clearly goal-oriented behavior.
2. *Preoperational thought stage (ages 2 to 7):* Intellectual thought develops gradually. The child tends to be self-centered. He or she is not able to

accept the perspective of others. Toward the end of this period, more concern for others and interaction with others' views develops. The child tends to "center" on the most obvious characteristics of a situation and has very little understanding of more subtle contributing factors. Responses tend to be to immediate stimuli. There is little systematic evaluation of previous experiences that might help explain immediate stimuli. The child is not able to see cause–effect relationships.

3. *Concrete operations stage (ages 7 to 11):* In the early phases of this stage, the child is able to solve tangible sorts of problems. Later he or she can deal with more abstract issues. Information directly perceived from the "real" world can be assigned to appropriate categories.

4. *Formal operations stage (ages 11 to 14):* During this period, youngsters begin to think as adults. Abstract ideas can be handled even in the absence of concrete or tangible examples. Thinking is possible about things that are remote in terms of their geographical placement or time.*

One variant of the learner-centered curriculum would involve developing courses in such a way that expectations were consistent with Piaget's stages. For example, given such a program, seven-year-olds would not be expected to deal with highly abstract thinking. The entire program would be geared to ensuring some congruence between the youngsters' level of development (their "stage") and the nature of the intellectual tasks they would be expected to perform in school.

Learners' Interests

There has been some sentiment for organizing the school program around the interests of the learners. An early proponent of focusing heavily on the unique features of individual youngsters in planning educational experiences was the eighteenth-century French philosopher Jean Jacques Rousseau (1712–1778).

Rousseau, as he studied the world, concluded that civilization as conceived of by human beings making decisions in groups was corrupt. If this were true, clearly no case could be made for educating youngsters according to a needs-of-society approach. This would result only in the corrupt social values' being visited on the next generation.

In Rousseau's view, children were born innately "good." Whatever evil might come to characterize them later in life was imposed by the negative influences of their society. To remedy this lamentable situation, Rousseau suggested that the school should protect the child from society. Furthermore,

*Adapted from Flavell, 1963.

the school should let the child's naturally good instincts unfold with a minimum of disruption.

Rousseau believed that people pass through four distinct growth phases on the way to maturity. From birth to age five, he saw feeling, perceptual skills, and muscle coordination as developing. At this stage, the child's education should protect him or her from societal restraints and permit him or her to experience directly the consequence of any actions.

During the next stage, from ages eight through twelve, Rousseau suggested that there ought to be no formal education. The child should simply be allowed to do what comes naturally and to learn from experience. Rousseau perceived experience alone as an adequate teacher.

The next stage, from ages twelve through fifteen, he saw as a time when education could become more formal, but this formal education was not to be heavy-handed or prescriptive in nature. Rather, it was to consist primarily of making learning opportunities available to youngsters. Educators' roles were primarily motivational. They were seen as stimulating youngsters' curiosity and prompting them to *want* to pursue such subjects as astronomy, geography, and agriculture.

Rousseau saw the final stage of development occurring between the ages of fifteen and twenty. During this time, he thought that individuals developed refined human-relations skills, an appreciation of beauty, and a complete sense of personal and religious values. Young people in this age category were to be encouraged (but certainly not forced) to study such things as religion and ethics.

Though not carrying the ideas to the same extreme as Rousseau, many critics of more traditional education have suggested that more attention ought to be paid to individual differences. Some have described schools as agencies of oppression that tend to stifle individual youngsters who will not be "molded." Many curricular innovations directed toward "humanizing" school programs are clear linear descendants of the thought of Jean Jacques Rousseau.

A famous American educational philosopher, John Dewey, has long been associated with learner-centered instruction. Dewey believed that the curriculum should be constructed out of the actual experience and curiosity of the child. It should be noted, however, that Dewey did not reject the idea that traditional subject matter could be included in the curriculum. He believed, however, that this subject matter should be related to youngsters' experiences and should not simply be imposed as information that was purported to be "good" and "useful" in and of itself.

Strengths of Curricula Based on Learners' Characteristics

Probably the most important "strength" of learner-centered patterns of organization is that they place concern for individual youngsters at the center

Box 4-4

Comparing Your School Program and the Ideas of Rousseau

Rousseau believed that children were born naturally "good." Society tended to corrupt young people as they grew toward maturity. Thus, if we were ever to have a society of "good" people, we would need to protect them from the present corrupt society as they grew to maturity. To accomplish this, he proposed that the school protect youngsters from society's evil influence and encourage youngsters to follow many of their own inclinations.

LET'S PONDER

Think of your own education and respond to the following questions.

1. To what extent was your schooling based on the assumption that young people are basically "good?"
2. How much freedom did you have to select what you studied?
3. Were there attempts to meet individual differences when you were in school? If so, what were they?
4. How would citizens in your community react if you tried to persuade them that the schools should be re-organized to follow practices suggested by Rousseau?
5. How do your personally feel about Rousseau's position? Do you think young people would profit from schooling of this type? Why, or why not?

of the planning process. They remind educators that their primary mission is to serve young people and to provide experiences that will enable them to live enriched and meaningful lives.

Learner-centered plans for organizing the curriculum have the potential to break down artificial barriers among subject areas. When youngsters' interests are the basis for planning and organizing courses, then specific information can be drawn from a variety of academic specializations, as appropriate. Not only does this approach free up knowledge from its artificial "compartmentalization" within such traditional subject areas as history and English, but it also tends to provide a more motivating learning environment.

Weaknesses of Curricula Based on Learners' Characteristics

Some critics of learner-centered curricula ask, "Is it necessary for each generation to reinvent the wheel?" What they are questioning is the efficiency (or inefficiency) of this approach to organizing the school program. They note that learner-centered programs frequently ignore the cumulative nature of knowledge throughout history and attempt to teach even the most basic ideas through the "discovery" method rather than simply providing them to youngsters and insisting that they be learned. In some of its manifestations, the approach seems to assume that nothing is learned unless the youngster re-creates it for himself or herself.

Others challenge the assumption that youngsters are the best judges of what is important and relevant for them. These critics suggest that catering to the whims of unsophisticated learners leads to knowledge that is both shallow and fragmented. They fear that, given free choice, large numbers of young people either will not study at all or will study frivolous topics. In today's complex world, these critics charge that it is irresponsible to allow youngsters to pursue this type of educational experience.

Curricula Today: State of Present Practices

A review of curricular patterns in America's schools today would reveal quite a variety, but it is highly unlikely that any examples would be found of "pure" subject-centered curricula, society-centered curricula, or learner-centered curricula. In practice, programs reflect a blend of the three general orientations. But there are clear and important differences in the relative emphasis given the different orientations that go into these many curricular blends.

Some districts continue to place a heavy emphasis on traditional subjects. Others have a strong commitment to career education and vocational education, reflecting a heavy emphasis on a needs-of-society orientation. A few school districts present youngsters with a great freedom of choice in deciding how to spend their time in school (limited, of course, by state requirements). These districts' curricula suggest a heavy commitment to the learner-centered orientation.

Differences among these emphases in districts result from differences in what individual communities want from their schools. Schools tend to reflect community desires. It is no accident, then, that some districts emphasize one kind of instruction and other districts quite a different kind of instruction. The diversity in the schools is a testament to the high values Americans have placed on citizen control of education. Thus, in the final analysis, no parts of the school program are there simply by random chance or by accident. They are there because they respond to a need or a value that is felt deeply enough so that leaders in education have felt compelled to respond with a course, a topic, or a special subject area in the school.

Recapitulation of Major Ideas

1. Teachers within a given school or a given district may have severe differences in terms of their perceptions how the school program should be organized. These philosophical differences can be a source of faculty discord.

2. Many traditional components of the school program are there for reasons that, today, are obscure. However, they tended to respond to a very real need at the time they were first included.

3. Historically one of the most common ways of organizing the curriculum has been to divide the program into separate academic subject areas. This approach is attractive in that most teachers have received their college and university training under systems where programs were organized in this fashion. Parents also are generally familiar with this approach and many feel very comfortable with it.

4. The launch of *Sputnik* by the Soviets in 1957 precipitated a crisis in American education. One result was a great participation by college and university professional scholars in curriculum development. Many programs developed in the early 1960s seemed to be directed toward helping young people think as scholars think.

5. Subject-centered curricula have been praised because of their ability to draw together related topics into coherent "packages" for learners. They have been criticized because they tend to give learners the impression that knowledge is fragmented and that information learned in one class has little relevance in other settings.

6. Broad-fields curricula represent attempts to draw on information from a number of subjects and to apply it to a central theme or problem. While the approach does break down barriers separating school subjects, few teachers have been trained in any depth in the large number of subjects from which information might have to be drawn. Thus some teachers do not find it easy to adjust to a broad-fields orientation.

7. Needs-of-society curricula presume that youngsters need certain skills and competencies to function as productive adults. Such programs tend to emphasize broad problem-solving skills and career and vocational training. Some critics allege that they fail to take into account that conditions change rapidly and that youngsters may emerge from such learning experiences with outmoded information.

8. Learner-centered curricula focus either on theories of psychological development or on freedom of learner choice. Programs reflecting this latter emphasis tend to assume that schools can be a force that represses individualism and that youngsters should be given a great deal of freedom in deciding what to learn in school. Others say that unsophisticated youngsters are unable to make reponsible choices and that too much electivity in school programs is a bad thing.

9. No schools have curricula that are *pure* examples of "subject-centered" curricula, "society-centered" curricula, or "learner-centered" curricula. All are blends of the three basic types. But there are considerable differences in the relative emphasis given each type in individual schools.

Posttest

DIRECTIONS: Using your own paper, answer each of the following true/false questions. For each correct statement, write the word *true* on your paper. For each incorrect statement, write the word *false* on your paper.

1. Because they have gone through a common preparation program, few teachers disagree about what should be emphasized in school programs.
2. In Puritan New England, schooling was seen as a mechanism that could keep children from falling into the hands of the Devil.
3. Throughout history, it has been a common practice to organize instruction in schools in such a way that knowledge is separated into different academic subjects.
4. According to those favoring a "structure-of-disciplines" approach to teaching, learners should be familiarized with the basic organizing ideas of academic subjects or disciplines.
5. Critics of subject-centered curricula point out that the "real" world is not divided into separate subjects, such as history, mathematics, and science.
6. An advantage of the broad-fields curriculum is that large numbers of teachers have the breadth of training necessary to deal successfully with the approach.
7. Proponents of "needs-of-society" curricula point out that learners are motivated by programs associated with this approach.
8. Critics of the "needs-of-society" orientation say programs associated with the approach needlessly force learners to delay their choice of a career.
9. Jean Piaget has identified a number of developmental stages through which all individuals are thought to pass.
10. In the view of supporters of "learner-centered" curricula, an important strength of programs associated with this approach is the placement of learners at the center of the planning process.

Summary

In general, there are three basic types of curriculum organization schemes. These are (1) subject-centered curricula, (2) society-centered curricula, and (3) learner-centered curricula. Today no district has a *pure* subject-centered curriculum, society-centered curriculum, or learner-centered curriculum. Practices tend to reflect a blending of the three types. But philosophical differences among districts are reflected in the relative emphasis given each of the basic organizational types.

Subject-centered curricula have the longest history as bases for organizing the school program. Many teachers have been trained under such programs at colleges and universities. Many parents are familiar with this organizational pattern. Some critics suggest that subject-centered curricula artificially divide knowledge into the various subject areas. Supporters argue that this organization makes it easier for youngsters to learn because similar information is clustered together in a logical fashion.

Curricula organized according to a needs-of-society approach tend to emphasize vocational and career training. There is an attempt to make instruction in the school compatible with the "real" needs of individuals when they enter the adult world of work. Some critics allege that these programs tend to be too narrow in their conception and teach skills that soon become outdated. Supporters point to the motivational advantages of teaching youngsters things they will be able to use.

Learner-centered curricula represent a third general type. Building heavily on the thought of Rousseau, who perceived youngsters as being born in a state of innocent "goodness" and in need of protection from a "corrupt" society, programs heavily oriented in this direction give youngsters a great number of choices in deciding what to study in school. Critics have charged that such programs foster weak and frivolous learning because youngsters lack the sophistication to make sound choices. Proponents say that these programs tend to place the learner where he or she belongs, at the center of the instructional planning process.

The particular emphasis placed on each of the three basic orientations reflects the values of the individual school community. Differences among school programs testify to the great diversity characterizing American cities, towns, and rural communities.

References

BROUDY, HARRY S. "What Knowledge Is of Most Worth?" *Educational Leadership* (May, 1982): 574–578.

BRUNER, JEROME. *The Process of Education.* Cambridge, Mass.: Harvard University Press, 1960.

DOLL, RONALD C. *Curriculum Improvement, Decision-Making, and Process,* 4th ed. Boston: Allyn and Bacon, 1978.

FLAVELL, JOHN H. *The Developmental Psychology of Jean Piaget.* Princeton, N.J.: Van Nostrand, 1963.

FRIEDENBERG, EDGAR Z. "A Perspective on the Core Curriculum." *McGill Journal of Education* (Spring 1982): 99–108.

GOODLAD, JOHN I. *The Dynamics of Educational Change.* New York: McGraw-Hill, 1975.

HAVIGHURST, ROBERT J. *Human Development and Education.* New York: Longmans, 1953.

HAWLEY, WILLIS D. "Some Problems with the Paideia Proposal." *Education Week* (Nov. 24, 1982): 20.

HUNKINS, FRANCIS P. *Curriculum Development: Program Improvement.* Columbus, Ohio: Charles E. Merrill, 1980.

MCNEIL, J. D. *Curriculum: A Comprehensive Introduction.* Boston: Little, Brown, 1977.

UNRUH, GLENYS G. *Responsive Curriculum Development.* Berkeley, Calif.: McCutchan, 1975.

5
Computers and Schools

Objectives

This chapter provides information to help the reader to

1. Recognize the dramatic increase in the use of computers in school settings.
2. Identify selected applications of computers in education.
3. Point out problems associated with implementation of computer-oriented school programs.
4. Describe a number of assumptions that support efforts to increase educators' involvement with computers.
5. Realize that setting variables have much to do with the success or failure of computer applications in education.

Pretest

DIRECTIONS: Using your own paper, answer each of the following true/false questions. For each correct statement, write the word *true* on your paper. For each incorrect statement, write the word *false* on your paper.

1. There are more computers in use in public schools today than there were 10 years ago.
2. One argument supporting computer use in schools is that they are becoming a pervasive feature of modern life.
3. All school computer programs are based on the best information we have about how youngsters in the school learn.
4. It takes only about two hours for a good programmer to write a computer program requiring about one hour of classroom instructional time.
5. There is evidence that twenty years from now computers will have completely eliminated the need for classroom teachers.
6. Software used in today's school settings in many cases has been developed in nonschool settings.
7. Some schools have rushed to buy computers without first deciding exactly how these new tools would contribute to the effectiveness of the school program.
8. It is probable that in the future all teachers will be trained to exactly the same level of proficiency in the area of computer use.
9. In addition to their potential value in the area of instruction, computers in the schools can also be an important program management tool.
10. There is some evidence that young people are attracted to working with computers.

Introduction

In the 1880s, the push to end our dependence on the horse was on. By 1885, George Daimler had invented a high-speed internal combustion engine and fitted it to a carriage. It worked. In 1891, two Frenchmen, René Panhard and Émile Lavassor, produced the first automobile that looked like it was designed to be powered by an engine and not pulled by a horse. A year later, the American Charles E. Duryea made an enormously important technological breakthrough with his invention of the spray carburetor.

By the mid-1890s, there was much talk about automobiles and the mechanically minded wealthy were driving them. For most people, however, the new invention remained an interesting and expensive novelty. That the automobile had "arrived" did not become clear until Henry Ford broke important new ground in production technology with the development of assembly line manufacture. The enormous productive capacity of Ford's techniques resulted in the manufacture of over fifteen million Model T's in the years between 1908 and 1927.

The genius of the early automobile pioneers ultimately brought relatively inexpensive transportation into the hands of Americans of virtually every social class. The arrival of the automoblie had profound economic and social effects on the nation. In the economic realm, for example, the automobile industry grew from nothing to a position of dominance in American industry. In the social area, traditional patterns of chaperoned and otherwise closely supervised dating broke down as the automobile provided a means to speed young couples away from the concerned eyes of their elders. Residential patterns changed as the automobile gave people the freedom to live at some distance from their work. In short, it is not too much to say that the automobile was an invention that transformed American life. Once it became widely available, things were never again as they had been before.

Today we are in the middle of another technological revolution that promises to change the world at least as profoundly as the automobile changed that of our grandparents and great grandpaents. This revolution centers on that marvel of technology, the computer. Computers are not new, but, as happened with the automobile, technological advances are making computers more widely available and are dramatically increasing the kinds of things they can do. Computers are becoming a pervasive feature of modern life. Today thousands of Americans own their own microcomputers.* Projections are that in the future the computer will be as much a part of the typical home as the telephone or the television set.

Given the explosion in computer technology and the dramatic expansion

---

*A "microcomputer" is a small, generally portable computer of a type sometimes called a "personal computer." Somewhat larger computers are called "minicomputers." The largest computers, both in physical size and capacity, are the "mainframe computers" that tend to support major research operations and other very complex data management functions.

of practical application of computers in virtually every sector of life, it is not surprising that computers are playing ever larger roles in educational programs. Thousands of computers already are in the nation's schools. Thousands, if indeed not millions, more may be added in the years ahead. Computers, the logic goes, have done wonders for businesses, governmental agencies, and for individuals. Therefore, any school that does not wish to fall behind must provide youngsters with some exposure to them.

Typically, school programs that feature exposure to computers are described as promoting the general goal of *computer literacy*. Computer literacy is a much-used term that often the users do not take time to define. Though some proponents of computer literacy might take issue with this definition, many would accept the following conception of the term:

Computer literacy: A state characterizing individuals who (1) have acquired a certain minimum level of competence in loading and using software on a given computer or computer system, (2) have acquired general knowledge about these processes so that these skills may be transferred relatively easily to other software and computer systems, and (3) have lost any initial fear they might have had of working with computer software and hardware.

For individuals not familiar with some of the more commonly used computer terminology, "software" refers to the programs that run in computers and "hardware" refers to the equipment that runs them.

In the sections that follow, issues relating to alleged advantages and disadvantages of using computers in schools will be raised. Additionally, some specific applications of computer technology in school settings will be introduced. Finally, there will be a discussion of some issues related to what teachers should know about computers and how they should approach learning about computers.

Computer Use in the Schools: Some Alleged Advantages

Probably the most compelling argument for introducing students to computers in the school is that such knowledge, increasingly, seems necessary for economic survival in our society. Checkout clerks at the grocery store pass items over an electric eye that keys transactions directly into a computer-managed accounting system. Lawyers use computers to trace common law precedents. Law enforcement officials use them to get almost instantaneous reports back on the "record" of any traffic violator who has been pulled over. Virtually every life activity relies more and more on computers, and it is evident that youngsters in the schools today are going to be working with them

Box 5-1
Computers in the School: A Real Need or "Keeping Up With the Jones?"

The following statements were made by two speakers at a recent school board meeting.

Speaker A: We need computers in our schools and *now!* As usual, our schools are lagging behind. My 13-year old kid knows more about computers and programming than any teacher on the staff. That's a disgrace. Computers are the wave of the future. We should have a significant amount of *required* computer instruction for every student. We need to train teachers in this area, and we need to spend a significant sum to purchase a large quantity of computers for our kids to use in school.

Speaker B: This computer thing has a strange and familiar ring to it. Remember when teaching machines were going to do all of these wonderful things? Where are they now? I'll tell you where, they're sitting on storeroom shelves gathering dust. Now let's be honest. Do we *really* know what we'll teach kids about computers or are we mainly interested in being able to boast a bit to our neighbors that "Johnny's taking this high tech computer work in school . . . don't know much about it myself, but it's cracked up to be first-rate stuff."? Are we just jumping on another expensive bandwagon? Is *everybody* really going to have to know about computers, or is that just what salespeople tell us so we'll buy more school computers? I say we need to go slow on this one. We've been "taken" before. Let's not let it happen again.

LET'S PONDER   Read the comments of the two speakers. Then, answer these questions:

1. How do you react to speaker A? Why?
2. How do you react to Speaker B? Why?
3. If you were to make a speech of your own to the board on the advisability of expanding school programs involving use of computers what would you say? How would you defend your position to critics?

throughout their adult lives. Computer training of some kind in the schools is viewed as a valuable kind of vocational training that will be of great help to youngsters when they enter the employment market.

Many proponents of expanded school programs involving computer use point out that computers have value in teaching many present school subjects more efficiently. The computer, for example, has infinite patience. Even the most dedicated of teachers can lose keen-edged enthusiasm after going over similar material a number of times with youngsters who are slow to grasp it. Computers, though, do not suffer this kind of emotional fatigue. They can be programmed to feed chipper responses back to youngsters on the fiftieth or one-hundredth time they make a given kind of mistake. Computers do not get irritable.

Computers can increase the frequency of interaction a youngster has with the source of instruction. In a large classroom, even under the best of circumstances, a teacher can engage in direct conversation with only a few students at a time. The opportunities for an individual youngster to interact with a teacher are very restricted. On the other hand, a child who works with a computer program can interact many more times during a given instructional period with a computer than he or she could interact with a teacher responsible for an entire class of learners. Frequency of interaction of this sort is thought to help youngsters learn new material.

Computers have the technical capacity to provide instruction geared to a wide range of ability levels. Educators have long desired to provide instructional programs that are truly individualized, that are truly designed to fit the very special needs of individual learners. The computer is a tool that has the potential to allow this kind of instruction to take place. Computer programs can be prepared that vary enormously in complexity and that provide appropriate challenges to youngsters with very different kinds of interests and needs. Their flexibility in this regard, some feel, goes well beyond what might be expected in programs developed and delivered by the classroom teacher.

Improving the problem-solving skills of learners has long been a hoped-for outcome of many school programs. Computers, with their ability to store enormous quantities of information and to process it quickly, potentially can help youngsters work on much more challenging kinds of problems than they would be able to handle without the help of computers. Proponents of expanded computer use in public education point out that computers can greatly increase the range of problems students can confront in school settings. Learners exposed to well-designed curricula that take advantage of problem-solving potentials of computers may leave school with much more sophisticated kinds of problem-solving skills than typify youngsters who have not had such training.

In some areas, at least, there is evidence that instruction that is delivered by a carefully constructed computer program can speed up the rate at which learners acquire new knowledge. One researcher, for example, found that computer-assisted instruction reduced by 20 to 50 percent the time required for a learner to learn a subject to the same level of proficiency as would have been required in a more traditional approach (Senter, 1981).

Finally, computers are thought to be highly motivating for learners. Proponents point to the proliferation of arcades using computer-based video games as partial support for this contention. They point, too, to the high level

Box 5-2
Do Computers Provide *Proper* Motivation for Young People

The following remarks were made by a parent speaking to a school board meeting.

As a concerned citizen of this community, a parent, and a taxpayer, I'm as interested as can be in having schools that are up-to-date and cost efficient. But I have some real qualms about this computer business. The board proposes to pay almost $1,500 for each of some 50 computers to be placed in classrooms throughout the district. The point is made that youngsters are tremendously interested in working with computers and that there are some real learning benefits to be had from allowing them to work with them. That may be, but I have some concerns.

All you have to do to determine youngsters' ``real'' interest in computers is to walk into any computer store in the city. Are there clusters of youngsters gathered around demonstrations of software featuring geography, history, mathematics, or other important school subjects? No way. The mobs are around machines running cheap thrill game programs. In my judgment, without incredibly close supervision, we are going to turn classrooms into computer game parlors when we buy microcomputers for the schools. While youngsters who succeed in loading game programs and playing out twenty-first century space fantasies might be motivated, I suggest strongly that their motivation will not be directed toward productive ends. There is real potential here, I believe, for microcomputers in the schools to divert attention away from the important objectives of school learning.

LET'S PONDER

Read the above remarks. Then answer these questions.

1. How accurate a depiction of youngsters' attitudes toward computers is the statement? Why do you think so?
2. What evidence can you cite that might support the speaker? Oppose the speaker?
3. If you were to make a public statement reacting to this individual, what might you say?

of learner interest in computers that has been noted when computers have been introduced into public school classrooms. In short, youngsters not only do not share a frequently observed adult fear of computers but actually appear eager to work with them and to learn from them. In some schools, teachers have found that the promise of "more computer time" has been a very effective kind of a reward to offer to youngsters to urge good performance on other types of academic tasks.

Computer Use in the Schools: Some Concerns

Today, virtually no one argues that computers are simply a passing fad that may well go the way of the nineteen-cent hamburger, the hula hoop, or the franchised trampoline center. Evidence abounds that computers are here to stay and that they are altering ways of living and thinking in ways that can barely be imagined. The recognition of the arrival of the computer age does not suggest, however, an absence of controversy regarding the place of computers in school programs. Some critics point out that schools may be rushing to embrace the computer too quickly. As a result, the great potentials of the innovation may fail to be realized.

One problem facing educators interested in installing numbers of microcomputers in the schools and in providing students with experiences designed to promote computer literacy has to do with the issue of software quality. The software (or computer programs) for many (if, indeed, not most) microcomputers in the schools originally was designed for use in nonschool settings. Much has been quickly adapted from software initially designed for use in the business world. Furthermore, many computer programs sold to schools have been written by programmers who have little background in education. As a result, much of the software presently available is not of good quality. Even the better software, as Daneliuk and Wright have pointed out (1981), needs to be adapted to fit the special needs of individual schools and individual students. Such adaptation requires careful attention by individuals who are proficient both in programming and in the special needs of educators and learners. At the present time, very few people have both of these essential qualifications. Though the situation is improving, much of the software in use in the schools still is not first rate.

A particular problem with much of this software is that its writers have failed to attend to principles derived from sound learning theory. For example, some software in use in the schools is written in such a way that youngsters who make an incorrect response are given something more interesting to do on the computer than youngsters who respond correctly. This design flaw is inconsistent with long-established principles of learning that urge teachers to use rewards to encourage correct rather than incorrect responses.

In response to the issue of mediocre software, some concerned educators have suggested that an effort should be undertaken to train educators to become sophisticated computer programmers. This response has a certain appeal. Such training, however, is both costly and time consuming. School districts are hard pressed to find the dollars required to pay for this kind of training on a very large scale. Furthermore, even when trained individuals are available, software development is an extremely time-consuming activity. Commenting on this situation, Senter (1981, p. 60) estimated that "for every hour of computer-assisted instruction, between 20 and 200 hours of writing time are required." The result of all this is that it may be some time before large numbers of people trained both in education and in computer programming are available to produce large quantities of software specifically designed for use in schools.

Other critics have suggested that schools have moved too quickly to require learners to master "BASIC" and other widely available and popular computer languages. They point out that other languages, perhaps less widely known, really are more appropriate for school learners. They see the rush to commit to a currently popular language as just one symptom of a larger problem that some call *bandwagonism.*

Bandwagonism is a tendency for schools to go after a new program or technology not so much because its worth has been proved as because a failure to do so will make them appear "behind the times." Schutz (1981) has suggested that many computers have been purchased more out of a desire to appear technologically up-to-date than out of any real understanding about how computers should be used in school programs.

In closing this section, we want to reiterate the point that critics of computers in the schools are not objecting to the general idea of introducing youngsters to using software and hardware. What they are objecting to is *irre-*

"I can accept and process data, but I have trouble generating it on my own."

sponsible use of computers. They argue that educators should insist that school programs emphasizing computers feature software designed specifically for school use, consistent with sound learning theory, and clearly consistent with promoting the general learning objectives of the school. Computer education for youngsters that includes these program design features has a real potential to provide important benefits for youngsters in the schools. Without them, such programs may fall short of expectations. The range of these expectations, to some extent, is revealed in present applications of computer technology in public education. Some examples will be introduced in the sections that follow.

Academic Program Applications of Computers

In general, computer-oriented programs in the schools can be sorted into two broad categories. First of all, there are special courses focusing on the study of computers as the basic subject matter. These are much more typical of secondary schools than of elementary schools, but some courses of this type are found at virtually every level of public education. Typically, such courses emphasize the development of programming skills. Youngsters are taught one or more computer languages and are provided with learning experiences designed to allow them to apply their knowledge as they develop and to test programs they have written. The demand for such courses generally is high. In many parts of the country, school districts have been hard pressed to find sufficient numbers of teachers with qualifications to teach courses of this kind. Certainly, teachers with skills in teaching learners to write programs and to use computers, particularly microcomputers, seem certain to remain in high demand in many parts of the country for at least the next several years.

The second kind of setting in which a youngster is likely to encounter a computer in the school is in one of his or her regular required-for-graduation courses. Increasingly, computers are being introduced in such programs as mathematics, English, the social studies, and the sciences. Microcomputers in such classes often are used for two basic purposes. Primarily they are being used to present learners with an opportunity to master subject matter that is introduced by software that deals with course-related content. In working with such software, youngsters sit at the computer, load the programs, and follow instructions. As a result, youngsters are provided with opportunities to learn content, and they become familiar with basic elements of computer use.

In addition to teaching learners course-related content and basic computer literacy skills, some of these programs also provide limited opportunities for youngsters to develop rudimentary program-writing skills. Because of the necessity to cover other kinds of content, such courses ordinarily do not attempt to develop programming skills to levels as high as those that might be expected of youngsters in a full-time computer course. Some youngsters, however, do become surprisingly proficient. What appears to happen is that the interest levels of youngsters are so stimulated by the limited exposure to programming they get in class that they continue studying programming on their own outside of the formal classroom setting. Today it is not at all unusual for a junior high school or a high school teacher to admit that sizable numbers of youngsters in his or her class have developed programming skills that go well beyond those of the teacher. Fears of "falling behind the kids" have stimulated many teachers to put in extra time either on their own or in classes to learn more about programming.

As noted in a previous section, much of the software presently available for use in the classroom is deficient. For example, though computers can be pro-

---

Box 5-3
Computers In, Teachers Out?

The following statement was made by a teacher speaking to some colleagues in the teachers' lounge.

They used to say, "Programmed texts are going to put us out of a job." I laughed, and I was right. They used to say, "Teaching machines are going to put us out of work." I laughed then, too, and again I was right. Now they're saying, "Computers are going to put us out of work." Friends, I am *not* laughing. In fact, I'm scared to death.

I went to a meeting on Friday. Saw some things that blew my mind. Computers that take in assignments, give tests, award grades, and . . . and I am dead serious on this one . . . *really* individualize instruction. I mean the darn thing analyzes what a student knows and then gins up tailor-made programs. For those nonreaders, and we've all got some, right, the crazy machine even delivers material through an artificial voice simulator. I'm told a couple of technicians can keep 40 or 50 of these things going full time with almost no breakdown time. Needless to say some of our cost-conscious board members are stumbling over one another to endorse this "significant educational breakthrough."

These things might create some excitement of a positive kind over at the Taxpayers League. But me, I'm scared. Just plain scared.

LET'S PONDER

Read the statement above. Then, answer these questions.

1. How real is the possibility that computers will result in massive layoffs of teachers? Why do you think so?
2. Does the speaker have more reason to fear computers than teaching machines or programmed textbooks?
3. How would you respond to this individual if you had heard his remarks in the faculty lounge?

grammed in such a way that they are incredibly responsive to the individual differences of learners, most software has not been designed with this kind of individualized instruction in mind. But the capability *is* there. And given time for software development, classroom teachers who include computers in their instructional programs may be able to tailor instruction to the needs of individual youngsters in ways thought impossible in years gone by. Certainly at this point it appears very likely that the roles of computers in school academic programs will continue to expand in the years ahead.

New Computer Applications for School Program Management

Computers have played important support roles to school managers and administrators for many years. Management of budgets and payrolls are examples of areas that have had a fairly long history of computer support in school settings. While such traditional computer applications continue to be important, use of computers to perform management tasks of various kinds is expanding. Today, many classroom teachers are using microcomputers to assist them in managing instructional accounts, maintaining grades, and keeping track of other kinds of learner data. One area that has witnessed an extraordinary expansion involves the use of computers to provide information about the relationship of classroom instruction to the adopted guidelines from the school district and state.

Increasingly, states and school districts are responding to the concerns of citizens that acceptable quality levels of programs be maintained. In many parts of the country, specific directives have been given to teachers regarding the kinds of learning youngsters should take away from exposure to their courses. The trend for state governments to insist that certain essential elements be treated in each course in the curriculum of grades K to 12 is accelerating. The need for teachers and administrators to provide evidence that classroom instructional programs are in compliance with such requirements has resulted in a great growth in the use of computers for program management.

Suppose, for example, that a given state decided that all Introduction to Chemistry courses had to produce learning related to a number of "critical outcomes." Each critical outcome could be assigned a numerical indicator that could be used to identify it in a computer program management system. For example, there might be ten "critical outcomes" and they might be notated as follows:

notation	critical outcome
.01	manipulative laboratory skills
.02	use of skills in acquiring data

.03	use of skills in ordering/sequencing data
.04	experience in oral and written communication of data in appropriate form
.05	experience in concepts and skills of measurement using relationships to standards
.06	use of skills in drawing logical inferences, predicting outcomes, and forming generalized statements
.07	experience in skills in relating objects and events to other objects and events
.08	experience in applying defined terms based on observations
.09	experience in identifying and manipulating the conditions of investigations
.10	applications of science in daily life

In a given school, a teacher might develop a number of units for his or her chemistry course and provide numerical identifiers as follows:

notation	*unit title*
.01	The Elements
.02	Basic Compounds
.03	Identifying Unknowns
.	.
.etc.	. etc.

For this course, the teacher might also develop a number of expected learning outcomes or objectives. These, too, could be assigned numerical identifiers. Such a scheme, in part, might look like this:

notation	*objective*
.01	Learners will recognize and describe properties of elements listed on the periodic chart.
.02	Learners will become familiar with techniques chemists use to identify unknown compounds.

These notation systems would allow all of this information to be stored by a computer system. Listings of these kinds sometimes are referred to as a computer "menu." They tell us what the numerical notation we have used to store information in the computer represents.

Once information such as that illustrated above has been placed into a computer, it becomes possible to make a relatively quick and easy determination of how an instructional program is tied into each critical outcome. Suppose a state education official had an interest in investigating how the chemistry teacher's program was responding to the critical outcome involving "use of skills in drawing logical inferences, predicting outcomes, and forming generalized statements." The teacher who had placed information about critical outcomes, units, and objectives into a computer using the notation system described could use the computer to demonstrate a display that would show every unit and objective that was tied to the critical outcome in which the state official was interested.

To illustrate how part of this information might appear, look at the following display:

critical outcome	*unit title*	*objective*
.06	.03	.02

This might even be condensed to appear:

.06.03.02

To interpret this information, we need to go back to our menu. From the menu, we learn that .06 refers to the critical outcome of interest "use of skills in drawing logical inferences. . . ." The .03 refers to the unit on "identifying unknowns." The .02 refers to the objective that states "Learners will become familiar with techniques chemists use to identify unknown compounds."

Box 5-4
Are Computers Making Teaching More Difficult?

The following letter to the editor was written by a disgruntled teacher.

They told us computers were going to make life easier. They said we would have more time to teach our youngsters. They pointed out that "at last" individualized instruction would become a reality, not a dream. They were wrong.

Since we have had microcomputers in our rooms there has been an enormous increase in demands for us to store information that we never had to keep track of before. They think that since we have this "wonderful new tool" that we should be assuming dozens of new record-keeping responsibilities. The bottom line of all this is that I have less time to teach today than I did fifteen years ago. The only winners are the people who sell computers to the school. My youngsters certainly are no better off.

LET'S PONDER

1. How accurate do you believe the comments of the teacher to be?
2. If you were a principal in this building, how might you respond to this teacher's concerns?
3. Is there a possibility that microcomputers can seriously undermine teachers' effectiveness? Why do you take this position?

Thus, in plain language, .06.03.02 lets the official know that critical outcome number .06 (the critical outcome of interest) is being addressed by unit 3 (identifying unknowns) and that students are expected to perform at the end as indicated in objective 2 (Learners will become familiar with techniques. . . .). An audit of a teacher's program can be made in just a few minutes when this kind of information has been stored in a computer. Otherwise, it might take days and even weeks to gather and assess such information.

Concerns about school programs delivering sound and responsible instruction to learners are reflected in a trend for state departments of education to assert more and more control over program contents. Given this trend, it seems very likely that uses of computers to oversee components of teachers' instructional programs will be even greater in the future than it is today. Experts predict computers in the years ahead will be used increasingly in the schools to perform managerial tasks of a diversity that can barely be imagined today.

Learning about Computers: Suggestions for Prospective Teachers

Few doubt that teachers in the years ahead will be increasingly involved with computers as part of their expected classroom and professional routine. Individuals preparing to teach find themselves faced with the necessity of informing themselves about a subject that, until recently, received scant attention in college-of-education programs.

The swift infusion of computers into the schools has caught even experienced teachers by surprise. Many are struggling to learn as much as they can about this unfamiliar, sometimes intimidating, and thoroughly fascinating new tool. Large numbers of prospective teachers, too, are surprised to learn that, in addition to developing sound understandings of a number of school subjects and general instructional planning and teaching procedures, they now must understand a good deal about computers. For individuals with prior experience in working with computers, this new obligation represents no real concern. For some others, however, the prospect may produce understandable anxieties.

In our opinion, people planning careers as teachers ought not to worry excessively about how they will fare with computers in the classroom. The kinds of training they will need may well prove to be a good deal less sophisticated and demanding than they might imagine. In the subsections that follow, a number of principles are introduced that should allay some of the fears that even individuals who initially admit to little enthusiasm for learning about and working with computers might have.

Principle One: Prospective Teachers Need Not Fear the Computer.

Most teachers will not be called upon to teach learners how to become programmers. That responsibility falls to specially trained individuals. For the majority of teachers, the use of computers will involve tasks such as loading and running programs developed by others. The amount of knowledge required to oversee this kind of activity does not require a commitment of an enormous amount of time. Certainly no special training in mathematics or science is required.

Part of the fear many prospective teachers have when they think about learning about computers relates to the specialized vocabulary that those who are familiar with computers seem to use so easily. Casual references to terms such as "moving cursor," "ROM," "floppies," and others can cause real panic on the part of someone who does not know the jargon. The terminology used does not refer to ideas that are so profound that only a brilliant few can master them. Actually, in most cases they refer to objects and processes that are not especially complex. A beginner who takes a few minutes to look at a glossary of terms related to computers will quickly appreciate the accuracy of this statement. Indeed, a little study of such a glossary can provide a beginner with enough specialized terms to begin the game of intimidating others who are not "in the know." For those who might be interested in some frequently used terminology, a short computer-terminology glossary has been provided at the conclusion of this chapter.

Principle Two: Knowledge About Computers Learned Using One Machine Transfers Relatively Easily to Other Types and Brands.

A visitor to a large computer show may see hundreds of booths displaying individual units of hardware and software that are claimed to be substantially different from those being peddled by competitors. Indeed, there are important ways in which these items vary. But the fundamental characteristics associated with the basic operation of most computers, particularly of microcomputers—the kind being placed in most school classrooms—differ very little. Controls may vary in sophistication. Positioning of various switches and so forth may not be the same. Generally, however, the same general kinds of behaviors are required of an operator of brand *X* and brand *Y*. This commonality suggests that when teachers master procedures for using one type or brand of school computer they generally can adapt rather quickly to using another type or brand.

This statement has importance for prospective teachers. There are many types and brands of computers available today. It is quite possible that the type and brand used by the college or university to introduce undergraduate students to computers may be different from the type and brand an individual student might find in use in the school where he or she initially starts to teach. Ordinarily, people find that the transition from working with the computer they originally encountered in a training situation to working with computers of a different type or brand is not a difficult one.

Principle Three: The Computer Will Extend What Teachers Can Do, Not Reduce the Range of Their Responsibilities.

When one reads articles about the incredible capabilities of computers we already have and the even more exciting capabilities that will be available soon, there may be a temptation to conclude that soon computers will be doing "everything." Among this "everything" might be all the responsibilities that now are taken care of by classroom teachers. In other words, in the future computers might replace most if not all teachers. In our view, this is a groundless fear.

The argument that "technology will replace the teacher" has been heard before. In the 1960s, for example, some people worried that their jobs would be jeopardized in the rush to wire schools for educational television. In the early 1970s, many mathematics teachers wondered whether the proliferation of hand-held calculators signaled a potential end to the need to teach basic mathematics courses in the elementary school. In each of these cases, the new

---

Box 5-5
Let's Wait Until the Good Ones Come Out

The following statement was made by a speaker at a school board meeting:

They tell us knowledge in general is doubling every eight years. And I understand that computer knowledge is developing even faster than that. Take my own son. He used to have one of these small computers that used a cassette tape. When it came out, he thought it was wonderful. Today, he thinks it's a piece of junk. As far as he's concerned it's a Model T in a supersonic transport world. He's after me to buy some extra-high-speed multiple disc-drive stuff, the cost of which you would not believe.

Well, the point of all this is should we be buying computers for the schools *at this time?* I mean, we definitely should have them, but are we going to get stuck with a lot of outdated equipment and then not have the money to buy the really good new stuff? It might be a good idea for us to jump off the bandwagon and wait five years. We might get a much better computer set-up for our money then than we can get now.

LET'S PONDER

1. What arguments can you think of that might support the position of this speaker?
2. What arguments can you think of that might oppose the position of this speaker?
3. What are your personal feelings on this issue? Why do you feel as you do?
4. What do you think the response of the school board was? Why do you think so?

technology proved to be much less of a threat to teachers' jobs than some initially had feared. The same in all likelihood will be true of the computer.

Human beings are incredibly diverse and complicated organisms. Though certainly there are some commonalities that join together members of the human race, individuals still have personal characteristics that are so different and complex in nature that no machine, no matter how sophisticated in design, seems capable of adequately responding to them. To achieve some kind of a functioning communication link between a learner and a transmitter of information, there needs to be another complicated intelligence involved—another human being, the teacher. Teachers can "read" the subtle variations in temperament and mood, which is an aptitude that is necessary in planning instruction for a given youngster. Certainly the availability of the computer to assist in the delivery of instruction adds tremendously to the teacher's repertoire of responses, but, the computer alone seems unlikely to be an effective instructional tool unless it becomes part of a larger program managed by the teacher. For this reason, computers pose little real threat to teachers' employment.

Principle Four: Proficiency in Using Computers Demands "Hands-On" Experience.

Prospective teachers who are interested in learning about computer use in education need to do more than read some good articles and books. Computers are going to be available to them in their classrooms. They are going to be charged with supervising youngsters as they spend some time working with computer programs. These responsibilities suggest that the teacher's knowledge about computers must be something more than an ability to speak knowledgeably about the subject. The teacher must be able to "do something" with computers, and, even more importantly, must be able to lead youngsters as they "do something" with the computer.

Expertise of this kind demands direct "hands-on" kinds of experience. There is nothing like loading and running a program to help a beginning teacher appreciate the kinds of frustrations that a youngster might encounter in doing the same thing. The hands-on approach also has the potential to make much clearer and understandable some information that when described in the rather dry and dusty language characterizing instruction manuals appears much more difficult than it really is. If you doubt this point, consider that millions of youngsters have learned to play the game *Monopoly* by being invited to play the game by someone who knows how. They have picked up the rules as they have played the game. The game, if one knew nothing about it except as it is described in the printed rules, might appear hopelessly complex to a beginner. The same kind of hopeless feeling sometimes comes over a computer novice when he or she begins reading an instruction booklet. If this introduction is accompanied by some practice time on the computer itself, however, anxieties generally fade away and are by a confident "I-can-do-this" feeling. This surge of confidence is essential for teachers who are just beginning to understand how computers work and how they may be used in the school classroom.

These principles certainly are not meant to deal with every issue a prospective teacher interested in learning to work with computers will confront. They do, however, suggest some general areas of concern that have been voiced by a good number of beginners. We wish to close this section by reiterating the point we made at the beginning. Individuals preparing to teach any subject at any grade level are capable of learning enough about computers so that they may reasonably supervise learners' work with computers in the schools. The subject is not nearly so complex, confounding, and impossibly "deep" as many beginners think it is. Learning to work with computers should be viewed as no more or no less of a challenge than learning to work with the many other kinds of instructional tools that are available to today's teacher.

Recapitulation of Major Ideas

1. Computer technology is expanding at an astonishing rate. This new technology is creating dramatic changes in our entire society. It may have as deep and lasting an impact on how we "see the world" as did the invention of the automobile in the generation of our grandparents and great grandparents.
2. There has been a dramatic expansion in the number of computers being used in the schools. They may number in the millions or at least in the very high hundreds of thousands in the years ahead. Increasingly, schools are being charged with producing students characterized by "computer literacy." In general, the term implies that students should have some basic familiarity with working with computers and should have no fear of this kind of equipment.
3. A number of advantages have been cited for introducing computers to school children. One point that frequently is made is that computers are becoming a pervasive feature of our society and that youngsters who do not know how to work with them will be at a disadvantage. Some people feel computers can help teachers to teach certain subjects more efficiently. Others point out that computers may be able to give certain students more personal attention than they can get from a teacher. Others note that computers may be able to help learners work with more complex kinds of problems. Still others take note of the ability of computers to motivate youngsters.
4. A number of individuals have raised some concerns about present computer programs in the schools. They note, for example, that much of the available software is not as good as it should be. Few educators, who are solidly grounded in learning theory, know how to develop

computer programs. Hence, many programs are being developed by people who know relatively little about teaching and public school youngsters. Other critics suggest that school administrators have acted to jump on the "bandwagon" before really good computer programs are available and that such administrators have more of an interest in appearing up-to-date than in having first-rate computer experiences available for learners.

5. Today, a number of academic applications of computers are being made. There are some courses that teach programming skills directly. These are free-standing courses carrying such titles as "computer programming," "introduction to programming," and so forth. In many other courses, there is a trend to deliver some of the content using computers. Today, large numbers of computers are being used to support instruction in such areas as mathematics, science, English/language arts, and the social studies.

6. The roles of computers in the area of school program management are expanding. Many states are requiring individual teachers to demonstrate that their instructional programs are following state guidelines calling for coverage of certain topic areas. Some teachers have already begun using computers to maintain records of what they are doing in their courses to satisfy any state program auditors who may ask for evidence that state guidelines are being followed.

7. Prospective teachers at all grade levels and in every subject area should work toward some basic working understanding of computers. All have a strong likelihood of being asked to supervise youngsters' work on computers as a normal part of their instructional responsibilities. The task of learning sufficient information about computers to manage school youngsters' work with computers is not as difficult as some might imagine. This kind of expertise certainly lies within the intellectual power of virtually all potential classroom teachers. Learning about computers should be viewed as no different than learning about other instructional support tools that are in the repertoire of professional classroom teachers.

Posttest

DIRECTIONS: Using your own paper, answer each of the following true/false questions. For each correct statement, write the word *true* on your paper. For each incorrect statement, write the word *false* on your paper.

1. There are more computers in use in public schools today than there were 10 years ago.
2. One argument supporting computer use in schools is that they are becoming a pervasive feature of modern life.

3. All school computer programs are based on the best information we have about how youngsters in the schools learn.
4. It takes only about two hours for a good programmer to write a computer program requiring about one hour of classroom instructional time.
5. There is evidence that twenty years from now computers will have completely eliminated the need for classroom teachers.
6. Software used in today's school settings in many cases has been developed in nonschool settings.
7. Some schools have rushed to buy computers without first deciding exactly how these new tools would contribute to the effectiveness of the school program.
8. It is probable that in the future all teachers will be trained to exactly the same level of proficiency in the area of computer use.
9. In addition to their potential value in the area of instruction, computers in the schools can also be an important program management tool.
10. There is some evidence that young people are attracted to working with computers.

Summary

The revolution in computer technology may well transform the nature of our society much as the automobile did in the first decades of the century. Knowledge in this fascinating new area is developing at an astonishing rate. Increasingly the new world that is evolving seems one that will demand at least some level of expertise with computers on the part of most, if not all, productive citizens. This recognition has resulted in enormous pressures on public schools to accelerate the rate at which they are installing programs designed to familiarize youngsters with computer use. Such programs seem certain to increase in number in the years ahead.

For prospective teachers, the computer revolution has introduced a need to learn about an instructional tool that was barely mentioned in textbooks for educators even five years ago. While some teachers certainly approach this need with some fear, it is not probable that most teachers will need to have an especially sophisticated grasp of computers. For most, sufficient expertise to allow them to develop "computer literacy" in youngsters will suffice. Though definitions vary, in general "computer literacy" will be thought of as characterizing individuals who are able to load and operate computer programs with some proficiency and who have lost any initial fear they might have had in working with computers.

Schools will be faced with a number of problems as they work to increase numbers of computer-related experiences for youngsters. A particularly difficult situation has to do with the quality of available computer programs or software. Much that is presently available has been developed by individuals who are not educators. There are few people available today who have both sound groundings in learning theory and in computer programming. It is hoped their numbers will increase in the future. In the meantime, though, school officials must be cautious in evaluating computer programs to ensure that they truly are appropriate to meet the needs of public school youngsters. This may well prove to be one of the most challenging administrative responsibilities of the next decade.

References

ANDERSON, RONALD, KLOSSEN, DAVID, AND JOHNSON, DAVID. "Why We Need to View Computer Literacy Comprehensively." *Education Digest* (March, 1982): 19–21.

BECKER, HENRY J. "Cost vs. Effectiveness—Roles for Microcomputers in the 1980's." *NASSP Bulletin* (Sept., 1982): 47–52.

BOWMAN, RICHARD F., JR. "A Pac-Man Theory of Motivation." *Educational Technology* (Sept., 1982): 14–16.

CORNELIUS, RICHARD. "Don't Buy a Computer—Buy Software." *NASSP Bulletin* (Sept., 1982): 22–25.

DANELIUK, CARL, AND WRIGHT, ANNETTE E. "Instructional Uses of Microcomputers: The Why, What, and How of the B.C. Approach." *Education Canada* (Fall 1981): 9.

DYRLI, ODVARD EGIL. "Computers and Other Electronic Aids: High Tech Teaching." *Learning* (November, 1982): 29.

GRETH, CARLOS VIDAL, BRANAN, KAREN, ROSEN, SHERI, and MACKEY, MAUREEN. "Computers in the Schools: What's Really Happening Around the Country?" *Learning* (Oct., 1982): 30–50.

LEVIN, DAN. "The Computer Takes Root." *The American School Board Journal* (March, 1983): 25–28.

ROBLYER, M. D. "The Case For and Against Teacher-Developed Microcomputer Courseware." *Educational Technology* (Jan., 1983): 14–17.

SCHUTZ, RICHARD E. "Programmatic R&D, Educational Technology, and Cooperative School Improvement." In Marcella R. Pitts, (Ed.). *A Bright Promise But a Dim Future: Researchers Examine Potential of Educational Technology.* Proceedings, Council for Educational Development and Research. Washington, D.C.: Council for Educational Development and Research, 1981: 39–57.

SENTER, JOY. "Computer Technology and Education." *Educational Forum* (Fall 1981): 55–64.

WILLIAMS, DENNIS A., AND MCDONALD, DIANNE H. "The Great Computer Frenzy." *Newsweek* (Dec. 27, 1982): 68.

Appendix: Glossary of Computer Terminology

BASIC. Beginner's All-purpose Symbolic Instruction Code. A versatile and popular computer language used extensively by educators, especially with learners being introduced to computers for the first time.

Binary digits. One and zero. Used to code information and store it electronically in a computer.

CAI. Computer-Assisted Instruction. The application of computers to help individuals learn.

Chip. A tiny piece of silicon containing an integrated circuit.

COBOL. COmmon Business Oriented Language. A higher level programming language developed for use in business.

Computer. An electronic machine that performs rapid, complex calculation and/or has the ability to compile and correlate data.

Cursor. An indicator on a computer terminal display screen that tells the operator the precise point on the display that will be altered by the next entry.

Database. A file containing specialized information in a format that makes it readily accessible by a computer.

Debugging. The process of locating and removing errors from a computer program.

Diskette. See Floppy Disc.

Downtime. A period of time when a computer is not functioning properly or not working at all.

EPROM. Erasable Programmable Read Only Memory.

Execute. To perform the operations specified by a computer instruction or program.

Floppy Disc. A flexible disc widely used to store data in microcomputers.

FORTRAN. FORmula TRANslation. A high level programming language designed for scientific studies.

GIGO. Garbage In—Garbage Out. A reference to the idea that bad or faulty input leads to bad or faulty results.

Hardware. The machines or equipment of a computer system.

High-Level Language. A language that is more English-like than machine language-like. See Machine Language.

Integrated Circuit. A solid-state electronic circuit on a single layer of silicon.

Interface. An electronic go-between used to connect the computer to another device such as a disc drive.

Interpreter. A computer program that translates and executes expressions one at a time.

Keyboard. A typewriter-like instrument for putting information into a computer.

Line Printer. A device that prints computer output as letters, numbers, or other symbols.

Load. To enter data into a program or to enter a stored program into memory.

Loop. A sequence of program instructions that are repeated until an exit command is given or until a predetermined completion point is reached.

Low-Level Language. A computer programming language that is closely related to "machine language." See Machine Language.

Machine Language. A language consisting of instructions that a computer can recognize and execute without translation into more simple forms. Usually expressed in terms of ones and zeros.

Microprocessor. The memory unit of a computer, often called a *chip*.

Microsecond. One millionth of a second.

PASCAL. A relatively new, higher level language that is being used extensively with personal computers.

PROM. Programmable Read Only Memory. This is ROM that is programmed by the user, not the manufacturer. See ROM.

RAM. Random Access Memory. Also called *read-write memory*. A high speed memory that can be accessed in about one millionth of a second.

ROM. Read Only Memory. Memory produced by the manufacturer that the user cannot employ to store additional information or for other purposes.

Software. Computer programs. In school settings, sometimes referred to as *courseware*.

Solid state. Refers to electronic components such as diodes, resistors, and transistors that are made of solid materials as opposed to glass tube-type materials.

Time-Sharing. The distribution of computer processing time among many users simultaneously.

6
Current Issues in Education

Objectives

This chapter provides information to help the reader to

1. Recognize that schools operate within a very politicized environment.
2. Cite approaches made to use schools to eliminate *de facto* segregation.
3. Point out recent developments in bilingual and multicultural education.
4. Indicate examples of how legislation designed to prevent discrimination based on sex affects schools.
5. Note some probable causes of declines in public confidence in education.
6. Describe some recommendations made recently by several groups interested in upgrading the quality of the nation's schools.

Pretest

DIRECTIONS: Using your own paper, answer each of the following true/false questions. For each correct statement, write the word *true* on your paper. For each incorrect statement, write the word *false* on your paper.

1. Educational policy is not much influenced by larger societal issues.
2. In many instances, the patterns of residence of different racial groups in American cities indicate the existence of *de facto* segregation.
3. Multicultural education has been promoted as a means of developing understanding among members of different cultural groups.
4. Bilingual education is designed to force all school learners to master two languages.
5. Few school districts have difficulty in meeting bilingual education requirements.
6. In "mainstreaming," there is an attempt to educate the handicapped learner in the "least restrictive environment."
7. All educators agree that the schools are institutions that can solve all major problems facing our society.
8. Though sometimes they are critical of certain school practices, American taxpayers have never wavered in their willingness to accept higher taxes to support public education.
9. Today, many groups are concerned about the quality of education being provided by the public schools.
10. A majority of the states have legislation requiring some measure of competency of high school graduates.

Introduction

Any discussion of contemporary issues in education must begin with one fundamental understanding: The schools are a reflection of the society within which they operate. Educational issues, then, must be viewed within the context of larger societal issues.

Large and important social issues have had a profound influence on the schools because public education operates through a system of public consent. Issues such as depressions, unemployment, and civil rights that arouse the population at large inevitably influence public education as well. These social influences are exerted through a number of channels.

In most school systems, local opinion is exercised through freely elected school boards. Local citizens, too, exercise some additional control through their ability to vote on school-funding issues of various kinds. The extent of this sort of control varies from place to place, but almost everywhere, there is at least some "ballot box" power exercised by the public over the operation of the local school system.

At the state level, legislatures exercise tremendous controls over what schools may and may not do. Laws relating to curricula and even to teachers' salaries regularly come down to local school districts from the state capital. A few states even centralize the selection and purchase of textbooks for use throughout the state. Such regulations, administered through central state education departments, give state governments great authority over the operation of the schools.

During the 1970s, there was a broad expansion of federal control over education. During this period, laws were passed requiring local schools to take specific actions with regard to such issues as programming for girls, for ethnic and racial minority, and for handicapped youngsters. Since 1980, there has been a general slowdown in efforts to expand federal authority over education. Indeed, during this period, there has been a moderate reversal of the trends of the 1970s, and, in general, there has been an increasing inclination of federal authorities to leave more decisions about schools to state and local authorities.

Though at various periods of time, federal, state, or local authorities may exercise varying degrees of control over public education, governments at some level have always been willing to impose the perspectives of society on public schools. Some critics of public education have ignored this reality and have put the blame for programs they do not like exclusively on the backs of school administrators. The truth is that school officials themselves exercise relatively little control over the basic programs of the school. These tend to be "givens" that are demanded by the larger society as reflected through local, state, and federal governments.

Schools, then, are very sensitive to public sentiment as it is reflected through the actions of governments. Governments make decisions slowly. Changes are preceded by debates among proponents of contending posi-

"We're grateful Mr. Alford could take time out of his busy superintendent's schedule to give us his views on the state of our school system."

tions. In a democratic decision-making process where votes are not counted until all have had their say, it is idle to hope for speedy changes. This system preserves the democratic process, but it also ensures that some individuals in the society will find the rate of change disappointingly slow.

Today, many issues being debated in our society have worked through the governmental decision-making systems to the point that policies have been established that are beginning to influence school programs. A number of these issues are introduced in the sections that follow.

Civil Rights

Schools have long been a focus of civil rights' concerns. For years, minority groups have looked on public education as a mechanism for moving their young people into the mainstream of American life. Political philosophers from the very earliest days of our country have hoped that the schools would be places where youngsters from different social and economic strata could meet and mix freely.

To some extent, this has occurred, but the ideals of breaking down all barriers among classes and preventing elitism have never been completely realized. The difficulty of attaining these ideals is evident, given the cultural diversity of all the groups in the American population. The view persists, however, that more can and ought to be done to ensure at least a mutual respect and acceptance of all groups. In recent years, the general concern about civil rights has been translated into a number of political decisions that have had important consequences for the schools.

The Segregation Issue

Racial segregation continues to be a difficult issue facing the American schools. The landmark *Plessy* v. *Ferguson* decision of 1896 (163 U.S. 537, 16 S. Ct. 1138, [1896]) upheld a state's right to segregate learners according to race. In 1954, in the famous *Brown* v. *Board of Education* decision (347 U.S. 483 [1954]), the Supreme Court overturned the "separate-but-equal doctrine" laid down in *Plessy* v. *Ferguson* that had provided the legal basis for segregated public-school systems.

In the *Brown* case, the court observed that segregating youngsters on the basis of race denied them equal educational opportunities. In particular, the court noted that segregation had a detrimental impact on black children. Therefore segregated education was declared "inherently unequal." There was a directive that segregated schools be eliminated with all deliberate speed. This action made *de jure* segregation, or segregation supported by governmental action or inaction, illegal.

The *Brown* decision, however, did not eliminate *de facto* segregation. De facto segregation is segregation that exists but is not supported by statute. For example, in many cities there are neighborhoods that are nearly 100 percent black and neighborhoods that are nearly 100 percent white. This racial separation is not permitted by government laws (indeed, it cannot be so required). Nevertheless it does exist. Such segregation is *de facto* but not *de jure* segregation.

Considering the language of the *Brown* v. *Board of Education* decision, it was evident to many people that some advantages would accrue to both black and white youngsters were they to attend school together. But the *Brown* decision, though it eliminated (in time) legally segregated school systems, did not ensure that there would necessarily be much racial mixing in many schools because of *de facto* segregation and because of a long-standing tradition of neighborhood schools. If all youngsters in the neighborhood were black, then all youngsters in the school would be black. If all were white, then all youngsters in the school would be white.

Many people who believed that some benefits would come from schools attended by both blacks and whites were unhappy when they observed that residential patterns kept many schools as segregated as they had been before the *Brown* decision. Pressures to change this situation led to proposals to bus youngsters to schools outside of their home neighborhoods for the purpose of achieving a racial balance in all schools. These proposals set off a fire storm of controversy that rages yet.

Proponents have suggested that busing represents the only realistic way to ensure that all youngsters have the benefit of some association with youngsters of other racial groups. They argue that it is idle to hope that neighborhood residential patterns will become integrated quickly enough for the same sort of racial mixing to occur "naturally" in traditional neighborhood schools. Unless the difficult decision to bus youngsters is taken, too many black youngsters and too many white youngsters will remain in all-black or all-white schools, perpetuating the "inherently unequal" situation that the Supreme Court found unconstitutional in *Brown* v. *Board of Education*.

Critics have pointed out that forcing youngsters into long and tiring bus rides may be destructive to the educational process. Others have been concerned about the quality of the schools the youngsters would attend once the bus ride was over. Still others point to the costs of massive busing programs. In Los Angeles, for example, the cost of busing youngsters during the 1978–1979 school year was $12 million (Summers, 1979). Some have suggested that this money spent on busing could be put to more important educational uses.

Busing has not been the only response to the *de facto* segregation issue. In some districts, voluntary integration plans have been tried. Though the specifics vary, attempts are made to encourage parents of black youngsters to agree voluntarily to send their children to schools in predominantly white neighborhoods and parents of white youngsters to agree voluntarily to send their children to schools in predominantly black neighborhoods. One interesting variant among voluntary integration plans has been the *magnet school* concept.

Magnet schools have been established, among other places, in Houston and Los Angeles. The idea is to establish a number of schools with very high-quality programs, perhaps each specializing in a certain area, in different parts of the city. Parents throughout the city are given the opportunity to examine the programs at these schools and to apply to send their youngsters to the one that most impresses them. The high quality of the programs at magnet schools has proved reasonably attractive to many parents of white youngsters, who have been willing to enroll their children even in magnet schools situated in traditionally black neighborhoods.

Another device that has been used to break down *de facto* segregation is changing the number of grades in any one school. Instead of the tradition of elementary schools each having grades kindergarten through six, some districts have realigned the grade levels. Some schools, for example, might have only grades one and two (in such a building, there might be as many as ten or twelve separate first-grade and second-grade classrooms), others with only grades three and four, and still others with only grades five and six. Because within any given neighborhood attendance boundary there are not sufficient first- and second-graders to fill an entire building, the youngsters must be brought in from a much wider attendance area. In some cases, they are brought in from the entire district. Usually this means some kind of busing, but it eliminates the argument that some youngsters will be bused away from well-equipped schools because all youngsters in the same grade level attend the same building.

The painful reality is that a good deal of racial segregation continues to exist in American schools. No easy solution is in sight. Perhaps the difficulties experienced in dealing with this issue do have one important lesson for educators and those interested in education; that is, the schools reflect the larger society of which they are a part. If a given condition continues to exist in the

Box 6-1
The Question of Busing

Some have said that busing, a policy designed to combat *de facto* segregation in schools, has resulted in increased residential segregation. More specifically, some have suggested that fears of city-dwelling whites that their children would be bused to distant schools has led to a "white flight" from the cities. This has resulted in many city neighborhoods losing their white population. Consequently, rather than promoting integration in schools, some contend that busing is tending to produce schools that have fewer racially integrated classrooms than before busing was introduced.

LET'S PONDER

Read the paragraph above. Then, respond to the following questions:

1. How do you react to the argument in the paragraph above? Do you have any evidence to support your position?
2. Assuming that there has been "white flight" of some degree in response to busing policies, how permanent a phenomenon do you think this is? Will people adjust to busing in time? Why, or why not?
3. Some have argued that those who attack busing on the grounds that it is tiring for youngsters basically are racists. They note that for years youngsters living in rural areas were bused to school. Complaints about busing, they say, came about only when there was a question of busing black youngsters to white neighborhoods and vice versa. How do you react to this argument?
4. On the first day busing started in Los Angeles, 17,000 youngsters failed to appear in school. A number of them ended up in private schools. Some critics of busing suggest that its long-term consequences will be schools populated only by sons and daughters of the poor and near poor. All others will send their children to private schools. How do you react to this contention?
5. If you had a crystal ball and were able to foresee school policies as they will exist twenty-five years from now, would you see more school busing than we have now or less?
6. Assuming that it is desirable for children to attend integrated school classrooms, are there alternatives other than busing that have a reasonable chance for successfully achieving this objective? If so, what are those alternatives? Why haven't they been widely discussed or implemented?

larger society, then it is unlikely that that condition can be rooted out of the schools with ease. Neighborhood residential patterns and other features of our society suggest that *de facto* segregation continues to be very much a part of American life. It may well be that no attempt to eradicate *de facto* segregation in the schools will be capable of success so long as *de facto* divisions of racial groups endure in other areas of social life, despite our best efforts to eliminate their *de jure* status.

Multicultural and Bilingual Education

Recent emphases on multicultural and bilingual education represent another manifestation in the schools of the public interest in civil rights. These emphases constitute something of a break with traditional practices. Traditionally the schools were seen as being charged with "Americanizing" minorities. They were thought to be the finest expression of the "melting-pot" ideal, where peoples of different backgrounds would be heated in the crucible of education and cast as new ingots characterized by a set of values unique to Americans. Given this view of minorities, it is not surprising that schools for years tended to downplay the differences and the contributions of different ethnic groups.

While perhaps well intentioned, school practices based on the melting-pot notion had what some critics believe to be negative consequences for youngsters who came to school from nonwhite and non-European ethnic backgrounds. Some evidence exists that such youngsters developed negative self-images because the school program tended to make them ashamed of their cultural heritage. The dropout rates of such youngsters have always been high, perhaps, certain critics suggest, because of their feelings of alienation from a school system that, by implication, has frequently suggested they are less worthy than majority-group youngsters.

Today many schools have installed or are installing multicultural programs. Sometimes these programs involve separate courses. Sometimes they involve infusing multicultural content within existing courses. One of the objectives of such programs is to help minority youngsters develop a more positive sense of their self-worth. Typically this involves learning about their own cultural heritage so that they can develop the same sense of roots that many youngsters of white European descent have picked up from their study of traditional American history.

Multicultural programs, however, are not directed only at minority youngsters. Part of the difficulty that such youngsters have experienced is that majority-group youngsters have little appreciated the cultural perspectives and history of minority groups. Consequently multicultural programs are directed as much toward the majority group as toward the minorities. There is a feeling that prejudice will be diminished when the majority of youngsters have some appreciation of the values and contributions of the minorities.

In addition to developing special multicultural programs that focus on disseminating information about the minorities, another thrust of the interest in multicultural education has been improvement in the quality of all educational experiences made available to minority-group learners. Stemming from President Lyndon Johnson's "Great Society" concern for education of economically deprived and minority-group youngsters, a great deal of attention has been focused on improvement of the instruction directed toward

Box 6-2
Multicultural Education

In recent years, there has been a trend to introduce multicultural perspectives into the curriculum. The reason this has been done is that youngsters coming from cultural minorities, in the past, have sometimes taken away from school an impression that something is "wrong" with them and their cultural group. Furthermore, because they have known nothing about most minority cultures, youngsters from the cultural majority frequently have developed unfortunate stereotypes about members of cultural minorities. Some have felt these mistaken perceptions can be remedied by exposing them to responsible information about cultural minorities in the school.

LET'S PONDER

Read the information in the paragraph above. Then, respond to the following questions:

1. How valid do you consider the argument that, traditionally, members of minority groups may have received the impression that their cultural perspectives were "less worthy" than those of the majority? Why do you say so?
2. Will the introduction of multicultural studies into the schools promote harmony among learners? Why, or why not?
3. Is there or is there not a danger that emphases on multicultural studies can sow suspicions and lead to hostilities among members of different cultural groups? What evidence supports your position?
4. Many proponents of multicultural studies reject the idea that the schools should serve as a "melting pot" for all cultural groups. How do you react to their position? Why?
5. Should multicultural programs be targeted only for members of cultural minorities or should they be required of all learners? Why do you say so?
6. Is it necessary to "water down" the curriculum to make room for multicultural studies? Why, or why not?

these youngsters. For example, surveys have revealed that most teachers have not been drawn from minority groups. Clearly, increasing the efforts to recruit teachers from the minorities has been one response. Another has been the requirement by state teacher-certification agencies of some university-level training in culture and perspectives of minority groups. It is too early to determine the impact of these changes on minority-group youngsters, but the interest in doing something to strengthen the instruction for these learners suggests that a good deal of attention will continue to be directed toward this area in the years ahead.

Bilingual education represents an important dimension of the total multicultural emphasis. People learn cultural values and perspectives largely through language. This fact has had important implications for youngsters in the United States, who, with very few exceptions, have been exposed to English at school. Clearly, the mastery of subjects at school has required the mastery of English. This has placed a burden on youngsters who do not speak English as a first language at home. They have been expected to learn a new language and at the same time compete with native speakers to achieve success in school. Many have done so successfully, but others have experienced problems.

The issue of language discrimination came to court in 1974. In *Lau* v. *Nichols* (414 U.S. 563 [1974]), the Supreme Court ruled that requiring learners who did not understand English to use the same materials and the same facilities as English-speaking learners constituted unequal treatment. Subsequent court decisions and actions by the U.S. Office of Civil Rights have resulted in mandated bilingual programs.

The major characteristic of bilingual education programs is to provide non-English-speaking youngsters instruction in their native language until they can compete effectively in English. Thus the districts must identify youngsters coming to school from homes where English is not spoken as the primary language. Next, school officials must ascertain the language "dominance" of these youngsters. If their knowledge of English falls below certain levels, then it is up to the school district to provide instruction in their home language. The idea is to help youngsters achieve success at school during the time they are adjusting to using English as a primary vehicle for learning.

Not everyone is happy about bilingual education requirements. In 1983, for example, a task force of the Twentieth Century Fund, a private research organization, recommended that federal funds for bilingual education be used instead to fund programs specifically designed to improve English language proficiency. The position of the Twentieth Century Fund task force is consistent with that of some other critics who feel that existing bilingual programs may be prolonging a dependency on a language other than English. These critics feel that English is critical for individuals who seek to take full advantage of the benefits of American society. Hence, they are concerned about programs such as bilingual education that, in their view, might in any way stand in the way of a youngster's mastery of the English language.

Federal laws mandating bilingual education have presented school districts with some real challenges. Something that has surprised school officials is the wide array of languages spoken by youngsters at home. A recent survey in the Houston Independent School District revealed that 98 different languages were spoken at home by youngsters attending schools in that city. Subsequent analysis revealed several of these to be dialects of the same language, and the original total was reduced from 98 to 89. These languages included Romany, Tagalog, Yiddish, Arabic, Armenian, and Punjabi.

The diversity of first languages has produced great staffing and materials problems for school districts. For example, how many teachers are there who are both certified and fluent in Punjabi or Armenian? Meeting the requirements for mandated bilingual education has been very difficult for districts where there are groups of people speaking languages that few teachers know. This problem appears certain to remain a difficult one for school districts in the years ahead.

In conclusion, bilingual education and the whole concern about multiculturalism must be thought of as a manifestation of a more general trend in education. This trend seeks to go beyond the long-standing rhetoric about "meeting individual differences" and, in fact, to take specific actions that will lead to appropriate educational experiences for all learners.

Sex Discrimination

In recent years, a good deal of civil rights activity has focused on sex discrimination, particularly against females. One of the cornerstones of the movement is Title IX of Public Law 92-318, Education Amendments of 1972. This legislation prohibits discrimination based on gender. The opening sentence reads, "No person in the United States shall, on the basis of sex, be excluded from participation in, be denied benefits of, or be subjected to discrimination under any education program or activity receiving Federal financial assistance."*

Though most people think of Title IX as it relates to athletic programs, the law clearly is directed at sex discrimination in any educational program or activity. It has prompted great debate in the education community. In order to clarify the intent of the legislation, numerous court actions have been filed. Opinions have shown no clear and certain direction, and both opponents and proponents of federal action to prevent sex discrimination have been elated at some times and frustrated at other times.

Analysts have pointed out that in one sense this legislation seems to run counter to a number of court decisions made in earlier civil rights cases. While the "separate-but-equal" doctrine has been declared unconstitutional by the courts in cases involving racial segregation, Title IX seems to suggest that "separate-but-equal" may be an acceptable doctrine when applied to sex discrimination cases.

In summary, the final history of Title IX has yet to be written. Court cases continue to refine the meaning of the legislation. It is clear, however, that the law has had an impact on sex discrimination in school programs and activities. Doubtless, future court decisions will result in more changes in this general area.

Education for Handicapped Students

Another focus of the civil rights movements has been education for handicapped learners. In 1971, the Pennslyvania Association for Retarded Children brought a suit against the state for an alleged failure to provide retarded

*United States Statutes at Large, 1972, vol. 86 (Washington, D.C.: United States Government Printing Office, 1973), p. 373.

Box 6-3
Sexism in the Schools

Title IX has placed an intolerable burden on public education. It is another example of the federal government caving into pressure groups with little regard for the implications of legislation for public schools. We are being told now that athletic money *must* be allocated for girls' programs on the same basis as it is allocated for boys' programs. *But,* girls' programs draw very few spectators. They simply do not pay their own way. If girls' athletics made money on the same basis as boys' programs, then a case could be made for equalizing athletic expenditures for both sexes. But that not being the case, a requirement that as much be spent on girls' athletics as on boys' athletics is going to have devastating consequences for school budgets. In the end, both boys' and girls' programs may be hurt.

LET'S PONDER

Read the paragraph above. Then respond to the following questions.

1. Is it logical to assume that increases in expenditures for girls' programs will come at the expense of boys' programs? Why, or why not?
2. Some argue that better girls' programs will attract, in time, more spectators to girls' athletic contests. How do you react to this contention.
3. Does Title IX, in your view, represent an irresponsible intrusion of federal authority into the affairs of the public schools? Why, or why not?
4. Some have argued that even without Title IX girls' athletic programs would have come in for more monetary support as time went on. Do you agree? Why, or why not?
5. Do you foresee more or less emphases on women's athletics in public schools in the years ahead? What evidence supports your position?

children with an appropriate public education (*Pennslyvania Association for Retarded Children* v. *Commonwealth of Pennsylvania,* 343 F. Supp. 229 [1972]). A year later, a suit was brought in the District of Columbia on behalf of all out-of-school handicapped children. In this case, it was charged that children having a variety of handicapping conditions were denied access to public education. In both the Pennsylvania and the District of Columbia cases, the courts ruled that all children, regardless of any handicapping condition, enjoy a right to a publicly supported education.

Court decisions were buttressed by the Education Amendments of 1974 (U.S. Congress, Public Law 93-380, Education Amendments of 1974). Title VI-B of this legislation required state education agencies to submit to the U.S. Commissioner of Education long-range state plans for providing educational services to all handicapped children.

Another relevant piece of legislation was the Education for All Handicapped Children Act (P. L. 94-142). This act required that "a free appropriate'' public education be provided for all handicapped children between the ages of three and eighteen in each state, to begin not later than September 1, 1978. This act not only specified a deadline for compliance but also stipulated that handicapped youngsters were to be educated in the "least restrictive environment." This requirement led to what has come to be termed *mainstreaming*.

Mainstreaming refers to the effort to educate handicapped learners in regular classrooms to as great an extent as possible. They may spend part of the day in special instruction to meet unique needs, but whenever possible, they are to work alongside regular youngsters in regular classrooms.

Public Law 94-142 also called for the required involvement of the parents of handicapped youngsters in decisions about the kinds of educational settings their youngsters would experience. The act requires an individualized educational plan (IEP) to be worked out for each handicapped learner in a cooperative planning effort involving the parents and trained school people. Furthermore, there is a proviso for periodic assessment of the progress of each handicapped learner.

Some assumptions underpinning Public Law 94-142 are similar to those supporting efforts to use the schools as a vehicle for promoting racial integration. First of all, it is presumed that an education characterized by classrooms that enroll a great diversity of individuals will lead to greater tolerance and understanding of differences among individuals in the society at large. Second, there was a suspicion that special programs for the handicapped may have been as deficient as special schools for blacks in days when segregated schools were common in certain areas of the country. There was some evidence, too, that a disproportionate number of minority youngsters were in special classes. This imbalance led some to conclude that some placement decisions had been made on the grounds of racism rather than the existence of legitimate handicapping conditions.

The passage of Public Law 94-142 has put new pressures on teacher preparation programs. Additionally, special efforts have had to be mounted to reach in-service teachers. Today very few teachers have had special training in teaching youngsters with handicapping conditions. To respond to this situation, many school districts have had to provide in-service programs to provide teachers with some expertise in dealing with youngsters who are now part of their regular classes because of the requirements laid down in Public Law 94-142. Colleges and universities have adjusted teacher preparation curricula to provide prospective teachers with some basic information about mainstreaming handicapped youngsters.

At this point, the profession is still somewhat confused about how best to respond to Public Law 94-142. Many teachers are very concerned about their lack of formal preparation to work with handicapped learners. In some places, these concerns have resulted in serious teacher morale problems. The rapid developments in the area of serving handicapped youngsters have created a number of problems for educators at all levels. It is clear that these problems will be a focus of professional concern for some time to come.

Disenchantment with Public Institutions

Over the last twenty years, a series of events have acted collectively to shatter public confidence in numerous institutions. One critical event was the unpopular Vietnam war. To many, the government during this period appeared unwilling to respond to citizens' concerns. The handling of dissent during this period acted to diminish public confidence not only in the national political leadership but in the military establishment, the FBI, the CIA, and state and local police agencies as well.

Not long after the war ended, the Watergate scandal erupted. For months, the public was greeted by almost daily revelations of corruption at the highest levels of government. When it was all over, confidence in many government institutions was at a low ebb. Concerns about job security, about price stability, and about other areas intensified doubts about the quality of public institutions of all kinds. Education was not immune from this escalating public skepticism. In some respects, education may have been more vulnerable to public expressions of displeasure than some other social institutions. Unhappiness with the education establishment could be easily expressed by voting "no" on school tax levies of various kinds.

Although criticism of education may have become more common in recent years, there is nothing new about it. Throughout our history, education has received its share (some would say more than a fair share) of blame for social ills. It may well be that criticism has resulted because public expectations of what the schools could do have been unreasonably high. Some have seen education as a solution for every social problem. Frequently—perhaps too frequently—educators have willingly appeared to accept the responsibility for solving social problems well beyond the capacity of the schools. When racism, poverty, crime, unemployment, and other social problems have persisted, perhaps it should not have been surprising that vocal members of the public have charged the schools with failing to discharge their responsibilities. After all, didn't a good many educators seem to suggest that education *could* take care of these problems? It may well have been better for education's reputation if educators had made no commitments about the schools' capacity for solving deep-seated social problems by themselves.

Education may have become an especially tempting target for public criticism in an era of general suspicion of traditional institutions because of the generally modest social esteem of educators. It is regrettably true that a good many people feel that a person does not need to know very much to be a teacher. Teaching has not been viewed as a rigorous professional discipline demanding a high level of intellectual ability. Furthermore, there is a tendency for some people, at least, to feel that they are educational "experts" because they have spent time in public schools and "know" what good teaching is. Given that the vast majority of adult Americans have been educated in public schools, this view would appear to make everyone (or nearly everyone) an "expert." Perhaps this fact accounts for the willingness of large numbers of people to go public with critical comments about the schools.

Box 6-4
Public Disenchantment with the Schools

Schools fail to lead. Schools only react. They never initiate. They are simply creatures of established authority. They do not adapt quickly to changing conditions. They tend to promote the values of those in power. Political power tends to be vested in the middle-aged and in the conservative. Therefore, schools tend to reflect the values of these people. Little wonder then in an age when television can galvanize the public in a matter of days behind a given issue, that schools have been seen as "out of touch." They are stodgy. They are slow. They are nineteenth century institutions in a twentieth century world. How then can they merit respect?

LET'S PONDER

Read the paragraph above. Then, respond to the following questions.

1. Do schools lead, or do schools follow? Provide some evidence for your answer.
2. To what extent are schools a simple reflection of a middle-aged conservative "establishment?" What evidence supports your answer?"
3. Are schools out of touch? If so, how? If so, why?
4. Is it ever possible for schools to please the "public?" Why, or why not?
5. Are schools nineteenth century institutions in a twentieth century world? Why, or why not?
6. The writer of the paragraph seems to imply that schools are generally run by conservatives. Does this mean that conservatives are not among those criticizing the schools? Why, or why not?

For whatever reason, schools as important social institutions are being subjected to a public scrutiny that appears to have grown increasingly critical in recent years. Today there is no unshakable consensus that schools are doing "good things" or that all teachers are commendable role models for young people. People contemplating a career in education must have the intellectual toughness to enter a profession that seems to be less universally admired than formerly. They must be prepared to demonstrate the merit of what they are doing to a skeptical public whose faith in education is no longer a "given."

Quality of Education

For much of the 1980s, there has been a continuing national discussion on the subject of the "quality" of American public schools. In response to this general concern, U.S. Secretary of Education Terrel H. Bell appointed an eighteen-member National Commission on Excellence in Education in 1981.

The Commission delivered its report in mid-1983. The report, entitled "A Nation at Risk: the Imperative for Educational Reform" noted that students in the United States performed poorly in critically important academic areas compared with those in other industrialized countries. Despite years of a strong public commitment to education, large numbers of both adults and students are still severely deficient in reading skills. The Commission reported, for example, that 13 percent of American seventeen-year-olds were functionally illiterate (National Commission on Excellence in Education, 1983).

The Commission suggested that the rate of technological development of the nation is in jeopardy because of school programs that are not producing sufficient numbers of young people with solid grounding in science, mathematics, and other basic skills areas. The Commission made recommendations calling for extended school years, more rigorous courses in important basic skills areas, and a system of teacher salaries that would reward merit rather than longevity (see the box on "Improving Educational Quality" for a discussion of some of these issues).

This report prompted a great deal of public discussion. Proposals of various kinds were developed to provide for merit pay for teachers and for more rigorous graduation requirements. One implication of the proposal was that more resources would have to be devoted to public education, but the Commission did not identify specifically the sources of funds required to pay for suggested improvements.

About the same time the National Commission on Excellence in Education made its findings public, a second study group, sponsored by a private research organization, the Twentieth Century Fund, announced its conclusions regarding public education in the United States. This report expressed great concerns about the level of training provided in mathematics and the sciences, particularly in advanced courses. Part of the problem was viewed to be inadequately prepared teachers. The report suggested, among other things, that the federal government reward teachers financially for professional improvement. The report also spoke to the need to improve the proficiencies of youngsters in use of the English language. Such proficiency was viewed as an absolute necessity for individuals seeking to maximize their opportunities in this society.

Still another effort to improve educational quality during the early and middle 1980s was launched by a task force of the National Governors' Association. On the assumption that economic growth requires an educated population, the Governors' Association task force developed a list of specific competencies needed for employment in the areas of reading, writing, mathematics, speaking, science, reasoning, and computer science (Peirce, 1983). The task force succeeded in getting the National Governors' Association to adopt as policy a commitment to have individual governors work for educational reform in their own states. High on the list of intended reforms are efforts to institute systems to pay teachers based on merit not seniority and to improve learners' performances in basic skills areas.

Box 6-5
Improving Educational Quality

In 1983, the National Commission on Excellence in Education made the following recommendations for improvement of programs in the nation's schools:

1. There should be rigorous courses in English, mathematics, the sciences, the social studies, and computer sciences. More emphasis should be placed on foreign language study.
2. There should be an effort to increase the school year from the present average of about 180 days to 200 to 220 days.
3. Teachers' raises, promotion, and tenure should be based on merit, not seniority.
4. Colleges and universities should raise entrance requirements to encourage public schools to place greater emphases on basic courses noted in item one.

LET'S PONDER

Read the material above. Then, respond to these questions.

1. What changes would you expect to see in the schools if item 1 above were implemented?
2. Of the items listed above, which would you expect to be accomplished first? Last? Why do you think so?
3. What special difficulties do you see for implementing each of the four items noted above?
4. How probable is it, in your opinion, that each of the above recommendations will be implemented?

An important part of the general debate over the quality of education is the concern for the caliber of American teachers. Many people feel that not enough has been done to attract superior people to teaching. Some of the difficulty is thought to relate to teachers' salary levels. A 1983 report of the Carnegie Foundation (*Houston Chronicle*, Aug. 24, 1983) noted that the percentage of school budgets going to teachers had declined in the ten years from school year 1972–1973 to school year 1982–1983. Teachers salaries were said to be less competitive with those of other professions at the end of this ten-year period than at the beginnning. This change, the Carnegie report implied, has much to do with the 50-percent drop in the number of college-bound high school students who expressed an interest in becoming teachers.

Issues associated with school quality are extremely complex. Because fears about the nation's continued capacity to increase the overall standard of living have become pervasive and because problems in this area seem closely associated to the quality of knowledge being imparted to young people by the schools, debates overall the relative excellence of the nation's schools seem certain to remain a centerpiece of public policy decisions.

The Revolt of the Taxpayers

There is a tie between the "quality of education" issue and the taxpayer's revolt. Some have argued that many who profess an interest in "educational quality" are really seeking a reduction in the breadth of school programs to focus on a limited number of "basic" subjects such as mathematics, science, history, and English with a view to reducing school costs and, hence, school taxes.

Schools are particularly easy targets for citizens concerned about tax levels. School budgets and building issues require affirmative votes by the electorate. Taxpayers' frustrations stemming from those actions of government that cannot be attacked directly often have been expressed in school elections where citizens do have the right to vote "yea" or "nay" on money issues. In recent years, many school measures have failed to pass. Some districts have had to close schools for part of the school year because of a lack of funds. In 1983, the San Jose, California public schools actually went bankrupt.

The taxpayer revolt has been one of several factors leading to frustration and anger among public-school teachers. Feeling powerless in their efforts to achieve some semblance of economic security, many teachers have become increasingly militant members of their professional organizations and unions. Teachers' strikes have become almost an annual event in many parts of the country.

Accompanying the growth in teachers' militancy has been a growing polarization of teachers and administrators. Many teachers have come to see administrators as little more than front men for school board members—who, in the eyes of many teachers, do not have teachers' interests at heart. In many districts, mutual distrust between administrators and teachers has made teaching a less desirable profession than it once was. Certainly, extreme hostility between administrators and teachers does not exist everywhere, but in some areas, the situation has led large numbers of teachers and administrators to leave the profession.

Teachers' strikes and public arguments between administrators and teachers have been seen by some taxpayers as additional evidence that "something is wrong" with education. Increasingly they have come to the conclusion that they have not received a fair return on the tax dollars expended on public education. In particular, they have been upset about the use of the property tax as an income source for schools.

Certain taxpayers' groups have been very concerned about differences in property evaluations from one school district to another. Because of different evaluations and different tax rates, the very same house in two different districts could be assessed annual school taxes that vary by hundreds of dollars. In general, taxes in more affluent areas are higher than in less affluent areas. One consequence of this has been that relatively poor districts have had less money to spend on schools than relatively rich districts. As a result, a number of court suits have been filed challenging property taxes as a source of school revenues.

An important case in this area was the *Serrano* case of 1971. In *Serrano* v. *Priest* (5 Cal. 3d 584 [1971]), the court accepted the view that education is a fundamental right and that making the quality of an individual's education dependent on the wealth of a school district was unconstitutional. The effect of this decision was to reemphasize the responsibility of the state for providing education to youngsters and to suggest that a form of financing be devised that would not discriminate against youngsters living in less affluent areas. Following the *Serrano* decision, a number of court actions were filed in other states. Efforts to dislodge property taxes as the primary source of school funds have met with mixed results. But the issue is still very much alive, and attempts to find alternative ways to pay for schools are being debated in a number of states. In general, efforts have been directed toward getting state governments to collect money and distribute a like amount per learner to every school district in the state. Such a change may have both positive and negative implications for education.

On the positive side, there may be a more equitable distribution of income to school districts. Differences among buildings and programs in districts should be reduced. With revenues coming from the state rather than as a result of local tax elections, school leaders may find that they have more time to develop curriculum and instruction, since they will not have to worry so much about preparing school-tax election campaigns.

On the other hand, there is a possibility that funding coming directly from the state government rather than from a combination of state and local sources may result in more state control and regulation of local schools. Some foresee the establishment of a common salary schedule for all teachers in a state, more state control over curricula, and state involvement in other areas that traditionally have been left to local authorities.

A more general impact of the taxpayers' revolt and leveled (or even diminished) rates of school funding may well be in the area of teachers' selection and recruitment. Though critics, including taxpayers, have voiced a constant concern about "quality" education and "better" teachers, few have suggested that there might be a relationship between quality teaching and financial remuneration. But that relationship seems to be a very real and persistent one. Consistently the college undergraduates with the highest scores on scholastic aptitude tests select major fields where the beginning salary levels for college graduates are higher than those of beginning teachers. Although people certainly go into education for reasons other than salaries, if salary differentials are too wide, it may prove difficult to attract quality people to teacher preparation programs.

In the final analysis, however, it is well to return to the argument introduced at the beginning of this section. Is the taxpayers' revolt really in support of "quality" education, or is "quality education" simply being used as a code phrase to cover a desire for the reduction of taxes? Although no one denies that many Americans have experienced financial problems in recent years, whether the best remedy lies in a reduction of support for school programs is by no means clear. However, in a time when many people feel that they are being helplessly buffeted by economic forces they do not understand, it may not be surprising that schools and any other vulnerable consumer of public revenues will be called to render a closely scrutinized account. That the taxpayers' revolt may not yet have reached high tide is a fact that educators may have to live with.

Competency Testing

Over the past twenty-five years, it has become a relatively common practice to pass youngsters from one grade to the next on the basis of age rather than on the basis of educational attainment. Certainly there have been exceptions to this generalization, but by and large this pattern has attracted a wide following. This system has been termed *social promotion.*

Social promotion became common for several basic reasons. First, some research studies indicated that retaining a youngster at a given grade level because of low achievement was not a productive strategy. All too frequently when this was done, there was no discernible improvement in youngster's performance during the second year in the same grade. Further, some evidence was found that some unhealthy side effects were likely to result when a learner was required to repeat a grade. Many learners in this situation were found to come out of the experience with a sense of personal failure and diminished self-esteem.

Furthermore, many teachers found it difficult to work with classes where youngsters' ages varied widely. For example, assuming some youngsters had been held back once or twice since starting school, a sixth-grade teacher might have a class with learners varying from eleven to fourteen years of age. Because of the physical and social differences of youngsters of different ages, supporters of social promotion felt it best to move youngsters through school systematically in age-based groups. Though youngsters would vary greatly in terms of their understanding, it was presumed that teachers would be skilled enough to individualize their instruction to accommodate these differences.

Critics of social promotion questioned the ability of teachers to vary instructional practices to meet the specialized needs of groups of youngsters varying greatly in their level of academic achievement. Concerns about social promotion accelerated during the 1970s. During this time, more and more people became concerned that because of social promotion, youngsters could graduate from high school and receive a diploma without mastering basic content and skills. Rising out of this concern was the "minimum-competency testing movement."

The basic assumption of minimum competency is that basic content and skills can be specified. Furthermore, it is assumed that they can be measured by a carefully developed test. Advocates of minimum-competency testing propose that such tests be used to determine whether or not an individual who has completed high school should be awarded a diploma. A number of states and districts have adopted minimum-competency testing. The tests are given some time prior to graduation. Those who fail are placed in a remedial program to remedy deficiencies. The tests must be passed before a diploma will be awarded.

By the mid-1980s, over thirty-five states had passed minimum-competency requirements of some kinds. Other states were considering similar legislation. Not surprisingly, legal challenges to this legislation were beginning to appear. In a key case in Florida, a federal judge ruled in 1983 that the state could legally deny diplomas to high school seniors who had failed the state's functional literacy test. Encouraging news from the courts and broad-spread support for the view that a high school diploma ought to imply something in terms of mastery content and skill suggest that legislators' enthusiasm for competency testing probably will continue.

A number of justifications have been offered for competency testing. Some have seen it as a means of restoring "credibility" to the high school diploma. They argue that today diplomas represent nothing more than attendance. Properly, they contend, the diploma should assure employers of some minimum level of competence.

Others suggest that the establishment of minimum-competency require-

Box 6-6
Competency Testing

Today, the competency testing enthusiasm is sweeping the land. Well over half of the states have some sort of competency testing legislation on the books. It is instructive to note that it has been necessary to go to legislatures to get the job done. School officials have failed to heed the groundswell of support for competency testing. By dragging their feet they have prompted people to go to legislatures where their voices cannot be ignored. Regardless of how it has been done, today at last America's schools seem on the road once again to some semblance of academic respectability.

LET'S PONDER

Read the paragraph above. Then, respond to the following questions.

1. Will competency testing ensure "academic respectability?" Why, or why not?
2. Will competency testing cause teachers to work harder on planning lessons? Why, or why not?
3. Will competency testing attract a more talented individual to the teaching profession? Why, or why not?
4. What impact on youngsters do you expect competency testing to have in the long run? Why?
5. What is your personal reaction to the competency testing movement?
6. Twenty years from now would you expect more or less emphasis on competency testing? Why do you say so?

ments will increase public confidence in the schools because (1) their institution will suggest that schools are responsive to the desires of the public, and (2) there will be available evidence that something tangible is being obtained in exchange for scarce school tax dollars. Other proponents suggest that learners will work harder in school as a result of a fear of not graduating if they do not pass the competency tests. Still others see competency testing as encouraging teachers to be more effective. They contend that competency tests will force teachers to do a better job of fitting their instructional practices to the special needs of individual youngsters.

Competency testing, however, is not without its critics. A very basic difficulty involves identification of the content and skills that are essential. Once this has been accomplished, there remains the formidable task of designing valid and reliable tests to ascertain the performance levels of youngsters in these areas. The general issue of "fairness" has been raised by a number of individuals who have reservations about competency tests. They note that some evidence points to very high failure rates on the part of children from certain minority groups. "Aren't such tests culturally biased?" they ask. There have been charges that the tests are tools of racists and majority-culture elitists.

Other critics question the use of competency tests as motivational tools. They wonder whether the tests really motivate youngsters or whether they lead only to learner frustration, cheating, and other efforts to subvert the system. Another group of opponents questions the limited range of competency tests. Even assuming that good and valid tests are devised, they sample only a small portion of what youngsters experience in school. There is some doubt in the minds of these critics about the wisdom of making judgments about the worth of a given school's programs based only on the scores of youngsters on competency tests.

Recapitulation of Major Ideas

1. The social and political issues of the larger society have a direct impact on education. Educational issues and problems cannot be discussed without consideration of the issues confronting the larger society.
2. Racial segregation in schools continues to be a perplexing social issue. Throughout history, the schools have been viewed as institutions capable of resolving important social issues. This may be an untenable expectation. It is likely that schools, as part of the larger society, cannot solve these problems until they are resolved in the society as a whole.
3. Multicultural education is an important civil rights issue that has received great emphasis within public education. Multicultural education seeks to overcome ethnic stereotyping in the curriculum, to provide ethnic-minority children with a sense of self-worth, and to encourage the majority culture to appreciate perspectives of minority cultures.
4. Bilingual education developed largely because of court rulings indicating

that learners who did not speak English as a native language were being denied equal treatment.

5. Title IX of Public Law 92-318 prohibits discrimination based on sex. As a result, classes formerly open to members of one sex have been opened to members of both sexes. Considerable confusion continues regarding specific implications of Title IX in the areas of athletics and extracurricular activities.

6. Federal legislation requires that handicapped learners be educated in the "least restrictive environment." This means that where possible handicapped youngsters are to be educated in regular classrooms.

7. In recent years the public has become increasingly suspicious of many traditional institutions, including the schools. This disenchantment has been expressed in many ways. In general, there has been a feeling that money spent for education has not produced the best possible results.

8. Questions about levels of "educational quality" have concerned Americans in recent years. Proposals have been made to increase the academic rigor of school programs and to upgrade the overall quality of the instructional staff.

Posttest

DIRECTIONS: Using your own paper, answer each of the following true/false questions. For each correct statement, write the word *true* on your paper. For each incorrect statement, write the word *false* on your paper.

1. Educational policy is not much influenced by larger societal issues.
2. In many instances, the patterns of residence of different racial groups in American cities indicate the existence of *de facto* segregation.
3. Multicultural education has been promoted as a means of developing understanding among members of different cultural groups.
4. Bilingual education is designed to force all school learners to master two languages.
5. Few school districts have difficulty in meeting bilingual education requirements.
6. In "mainstreaming," there is an attempt to educate the handicapped learner in the "least restrictive environment."
7. All educators agree that the schools are institutions that can solve all major problems facing our society.
8. Though sometimes they are critical of certain school practices, American taxpayers have never wavered in their willingness to accept higher taxes to support public education.
9. Today, many groups are concerned about the quality of education being provided by the public schools.
10. A majority of the states have legislation requiring some measure of competency of high school graduates.

Summary

The past several decades have proved challenging for educators. New civil rights legislation has required schools to take new action in such areas as racial integration, multicultural education, sexism, and education of the handicapped. These changes have had to be accommodated in an atmosphere of mounting public skepticism regarding the overall quality of education being provided in the schools. Tight budgets and reluctance of citizens to raise school taxes have proved frustrating at times.

On the other hand, in the 1980s public education has moved into the national spotlight and has become a major focus of public debate and concern. Today many issues relating to the schools are being more widely discussed than they have been for years. Optimists within education feel that this kind of a national focus on education, in the long run, has a potential to make public education better than it has ever been.

References

CHRONICLE NEWS SERVICES. "Teachers are Receiving Smaller Share of Educational Spending, Report Says." *Houston Chronicle* (Aug. 24, 1983): section 2, p. 7, cols. 1–6.

HUSÉN, TORSTEN. "Are Standards in U.S. Schools Really Lagging Behind Those in Other Countries." *Phi Delta Kappan* (March, 1983): 455–461.

KRIST, MICHAEL. "The New Politics of State Education Finance." *Phi Delta Kappan* (Feb., 1979): 327–432.

"A National at Risk." Final Report of the National Commission on Excellence in Education. Washington, D.C.: United States Department of Education, April, 1983.

PEIRCE, NEAL R. "States Tackling Risk of Improving Education." *Houston Chronicle* (Aug. 15, 1983): section 3, p. 1, cols. 4–6.

RUBIN, LOUIS. *Curriculum Handbook: The Disciplines, Current Movements, Instructional Methodology, Administration, and Theory.* Boston: Allyn and Bacon, 1977.

SAPON-SHEVIN, MARA. "Another Look at Mainstreaming: Exceptionality, Normality, and the Nature of Difference." *Phi Delta Kappan* (Oct., 1978): 119–121.

SMITH, VERNON, BARR, ROBERT, AND BURKE, DANIEL. *Alternatives in Education: Freedom to Choose.* Bloomington, Indiana: Phi Delta Kappa, 1976.

U.S Statutes at Large, 1972, Vol. 86. Washington, D.C.: United States Government Printing Office, 1973.

VALVERDE, LEONARD A. (Ed). *Bilingual Education for Latinos.* Washington, D.C.: Association for Supervision and Curriculum Development, 1978.

PART

II Teachers

7
Reasons for Teaching

Objectives

This chapter provides information to help the reader to

1. Identify several reasons that motivate people to go into education and to remain in the profession.
2. Recognize the diversity of teaching situations and realize that this variety provides opportunities for teachers with a variety of personal interests to find positions compatible with their own priorities.
3. Identify both the positive and the negative characteristics of teachers' roles.
4. Begin to take stock of his or her own motivations for considering a career in teaching.
5. Note that an individual who might be a happy and competent teacher in one setting might be an unhappy and only marginally effective teacher in another setting.

Pretest

DIRECTIONS: Using your own paper, answer each of the following true/false questions. For each correct statement, write the word *true* on your paper. For each incorrect statement, write the word *false* on your paper.

1. Few teachers can identify a single factor as *the* feature of teaching that got them into the profession or that maintains their interest in the profession.
2. It is very uncommon for secondary-school teachers to enter teaching because of a love of the subject they will be teaching.
3. For many teachers, contact with a group of colleagues who are educated and congenial is an important reason for remaining in the profession.
4. Many teachers are attracted to the profession because of the extended summer-vacation period.
5. Some teachers say that they stay in teaching because the profession provides a great deal of variety from day to day.
6. There is universal agreement that the profession of teaching attracts the top talent in our country.
7. Teachers almost never mention their satisfaction with the "importance" of their work as a reason for staying in the profession.
8. Because teaching conditions vary so dramatically from place to place, many new teachers find themselves working in an environment far different from what they had initially expected.

9. Many teachers find themselves stimulated when youngsters master something that the teachers have worked hard to introduce.
10. The changing of classes, the rounds of meetings, the discussions with parents, and the constant potential of "activity" provide a high level of interest for many teachers.

Introduction

Why teach? Why, indeed? The question is a good one. Certainly it merits serious consideration by anyone considering a career as a teacher. But like so many simple questions, the "why teach?" question has no simple answers. Teachers are complex human beings (as are we all). The conditions under which they work reflect a diversity that defies generalization. Given the differences among teachers and among their workplaces, the great variety of reasons that teachers give when asked to explain their career choice is not surprising.

For some teachers, love of the subject matter is the primary motivator. Many high school teachers, in particular, enter the field because they have been "turned on" by mathematics, history, biology, or some other subject. They hope to light some intellectual fires under new generations of young people. Others are interested in the personal development of young people as they grow to maturity. They feel that they can help these youngsters bridge the gap from childhood to adulthood with less pain than they themselves perhaps experienced.

Still others find the variety that characterizes the teacher's day to be stimulating. They enjoy going to work knowing that each day will be different. Some teachers find the nine- or ten-month school year attractive. While many must work during the summer, others find time for taking courses, traveling, and pursuing hobbies.

Some teachers feel a social obligation as transmitters of the culture to upcoming generations. They derive deep satisfaction from their identification with the long line of professional educators who have assumed the responsibility for providing to the young their insights related to productive citizenship.

Some teachers enjoy working and socializing with other teachers. Colleagues tend to be fairly well read, interested in people, and congenial. They tend to be warm and supportive. Many teachers' best friends are drawn from among their co-workers.

Probably no single reason motivates any given person to select teaching as a career or to remain in the profession. For most people the decision results from a consideration of a number of factors. Clearly, however, some factors are weighted more heavily in the decision than others. In the sections that follow, we will be considering a number of the reasons that teachers frequently cite for their commitment to their profession. These reasons should be regarded as representative but not as exhaustive. Given the diversity of personalities in teaching, it would be impossible to deal with all the reasons that prompt people to remain in the classroom.

As a beginning, it might be beneficial to take a look at how three individual teachers have made satisfying lives for themselves by fitting their own personalities into teaching situations that meet their own clusters of needs. Barbara Castanella teaches in a high school in an exclusive coastal community between Los Angeles and San Diego. Fenton Dragstedt teaches in a junior high school in a small town in the northern Midwest. Willard Stiles teaches primary-grades youngsters in a school situated in the old central-city area of a large city on the Eastern Seaboard.

BARBARA CASTANELLA

Barbara's alarm rings at 6:30. She rises quickly, looks out over the swimming pool at the center of her apartment complex, and pops a light breakfast into the microwave oven. After a hasty second cup of coffee, she gathers her school papers, locks the door to her apartment, and walks briskly down the steps and over to the breezeway where her car is parked.

Slipping easily into her antique classic Morgan with the three-inch leather hood strap, she varooms her way out of the driveway and onto the palm-lined boulevard. Ten minutes later, she turns into the faculty parking area at Chester A. Arthur High School. From the lot, she walks through the elaborately landscaped grounds to the main entrance. She heads for the main office.

As is her usual practice, she greets the secretaries, makes some small talk with other arriving teachers, and sorts through the materials in her box. Precisely at 7:30 she is on her way to her room to prepare for the day.

Barbara's biology classroom is tidy and attractive. Looking around, Barbara notes with satisfaction the gleaming microscopes in their brightly polished glass cases. The potted plants in the windows and the ferns draping gracefully below the macrame hangers are doing well. The starfish, shrimp, and echinoderms in the salt-water aquarium seemed to have had a good night. This quick review completed, Barbara quickly lays out the lab equipment her students will be needing. Scalpels, glass slides, and other paraphernalia are handled with the deft touch and the clear appreciation of the professional.

Barbara Castanella considers herself both a biologist and a teacher. She has a master's degree in marine biology and has begun doctoral-level study in the area. She finds biology exciting, and her mission in life is to ignite a similar enthusiasm in her students. Her greatest satisfaction in teaching comes when she converts a student's mild interest in biology to an abiding passion. Among her most prized treasures are letters from former students who have gone on to do fine work in biology in colleges and universities. She is particularly proud of two former students who have Ph.D.'s in marine biology and teach the subject at major universities.

For Barbara, love of biology and love of teaching are inseparable. She has some difficulty in keeping calm when some colleagues argue that "schools should teach students, not subjects." She argues that subjects and students simply cannot be separated. For Barbara Castanella, good teaching means teaching both subjects and students.

FENTON DRAGSTEDT

Fenton Dragstedt's alarm rings at 6 A.M. He gets up without disturbing his wife. Dressing quickly, he heads for the kitchen. He plugs in the coffee pot, listens for some reassuring percolating sounds, and opens the front door, where the morning paper lies waiting.

From 6:00 to 6:30 is Fenton's private time. Sometimes he works on school papers. Sometimes he reads the newspaper. Sometimes he just drinks a little coffee and thinks. He relishes this time of morning as a needed "fortification for the day."

At 6:30, Fenton wakes his wife. She, in turn, rouses the twins. Erik and Jon are sleepy-headed thirteen-year-olds who grump their way out of bed only when they sense their mother's voice has taken on its "I mean business" tone. By 6:45 or 6:50, the family is seated around the breakfast table. Promptly at 7:10, Fenton gathers his schoolwork in his brief case and leaves the house for the six-block walk to school.

Fenton Dragstedt's family has lived in this community for four generations. He knows personally nearly all of the parents of his students. In a good many cases, he knows or has known their grandparents and even their great-grandparents. On his way to school, he waves a familiar "hello" to the folks who've just come in from working "graveyard" at the canning plant and are gathered for breakfast in Ernie Johannesen's place. Mike Fuller is out on the walk this morning sweeping down the area in front of his Western Auto store. Fenton and Mike exchange a few words about the Vikings and about the soaring cost of home heating oil. Crossing the street, Fenton strolls through the square by the band shell and across the street on the other side. One more block and he turns into the walkway leading to the main entrance of Lincoln Junior High School.

As he enters the main office, Fenton notices the large Elgin on the wall. 7:30. Precisely. Fenton notes with satisfaction that he is right on time . . . just as he is every day. After a quick check in his box, he goes down to the cafeteria. At 7:40, they let in the early-arriving youngsters. Fenton has charge of the early-morning activity program. He has arranged for a couple of television sets to be brought in. He found a Ping-Pong table at a rummage sale for five dollars and borrowed Mike Fuller's truck to bring that in. A number of checker and chess sets have been found. Fenton is working on Coach MacMillan to let the youngsters shoot baskets in the gym in the morning. The coach is worried about his newly finished floor, but Fenton thinks he is "weakening" on the issue. Fenton remains in the cafeteria supervising students until 8:15, when they report to their first classes.

During the day, Fenton Dragstedt teaches three sections of eighth-grade American history and three sections of seventh-grade English. At noon, he leaves the door of his room open and invites any youngster who passes by to drop in and chat. Fenton brings his lunch in a paper bag. Typically he eats a sandwich while he is talking to a student about football, mag wheels, bicycle frames, or any one of a hundred other topics. After school, Fenton works with the student council. Sometimes he gives a hand to the coaching staff.

Fenton Dragstedt is committed to his community. He senses great value in the stability that continuity over several generations has given to him and others in his family. He believes his role is to help youngsters toward self-understanding. When asked, he's likely to say that teachers should help youngsters get interested in something: "I don't care what it is, but something. If I can get them interested in history or English, that's great! But if it turns out to be sports, or working on cars, or entering the county fair, well, that's all right too. What we're about is training up young folks to be happy and contributing adults. My job is to give them the confidence and enthusiasm that comes from the pursuit of an important interest. I think I'm helping to shape the kind of community that future generations of my family will want to live in. And, to me, that's very important."

WILLARD STILES

It's 6 A.M., sharp. Hard rock pounds briefly out of the clock radio in the quick instant before Willard Stiles punches the stop button. Getting up, shaking his head, and stretching, Willard tries to get the circulation going. He enjoys his day but wonders to himself, "Why does it have to start so early?" Quickly dressing, he settles into the kitchen with a cup of instant coffee and some toast. On the table before him are a few papers he needs to go over before he can return the set to his class. He'd meant to finish last night, but he just didn't have the energy. Working quickly, he makes comments on the few remaining pieces of work and stuffs them into his briefcase. At 6:30, he leaves his apartment and heads for the bus stop.

The 6F bus pulls in at 6:38, right on time for a change. Willard gets on, requests a transfer, and settles down for the bumpy ride to Fort Point. At Fort Point, he catches the 10L bus for the dreary ride through the old central-city area. Passing by neighborhoods of decrepit apartments and boarded-up businesses, he arrives at his Thirty-first Street stop at 7:25. He leaves the bus and looks up at Banner Elementary School. It is a three-story brick building, vintage 1890, set back slightly from the street on a "lawn" of pot-holed asphalt. A few youngsters are running around the building, though they won't be admitted until 8 A.M.

Willard uses his main-door key, swings open the creaking oaken door, and strolls down the hall toward the office. Nothing much in his box today. Joe the principal and a couple of other teachers exchange some light comments. Then Willard heads to his second-floor room. On the outside of the door there is a formica sign that reads: "4th Grade—Mr. Stiles." Willard enters his classroom, straightens up the bulletin board, and begins thinking through the structure of his day: reading, then social studies, then PE, then lunch, then science, then math, then art, and . . . finally . . . dismissal time. A tall order considering his youngsters.

Willard has described his class as a "real United Nations." He has blacks, Chicanos, Chinese, Vietnamese, and other racial and cultural minorities. Most come from very poor families. Most are very deficient in basic skills. Many, though certainly not all, do not receive a great deal of support at home to do well at school. It is probably true to say that a majority of Willard's youngsters prize the "knowledge of the street" more than the "knowledge of the classroom." Willard often muses about what would happen if standardized tests assessed street knowledge rather than classroom knowledge. He says his youngsters would "blow the top off" the norms in any such test.

But Willard really doesn't want such a test. In fact, his life is dedicated to convincing youngsters that street knowledge is limiting; it has value only in an immediate, localized area. But classroom knowledge, at least "good" classroom knowledge, has utility in a much broader arena. Willard sees his task as one of opening the eyes of his youngsters to the world beyond their inner-city neighborhood. He says, "These kids are not dumb. Many of them are very, very bright. But they just don't see any need to 'get good at' school tasks. I see my job as providing a bridge between a world where success on school tasks means something and their world, where success is not always highly prized. I have lots of failures. Kids I worked with three, four, and five years ago are on the streets. Some already have a lengthy arrest record. But there are a few, too, who are developing into pretty decent people. I like to think I've had a hand in that. I like the heavy odds I work against here. It's a challenge. You have to develop a high tolerance for losing because there are lots of failures in a situation like this. But for me, the successes perhaps are even more appreciated because I know that they have come about against odds that most bookmakers would call a 'long shot.'"

Barbara Castanella, Fenton Dragstedt, and Willard Stiles all have different motives for continuing their careers in education. For Barbara, teaching has provided an outlet for her abiding interest in biology. For Fenton, working with young people has been a means of ensuring continuity of values that he sees as basic to the kind of pleasant community that he wishes to maintain for future generations. For Willard, the pleasure comes from facing a challenge and "getting through" to some youngsters whom others might write off as "failures." Certainly these capsulized statements of these teachers' motives are somewhat simplistic. Clearly their satisfaction with their careers results from a cluster of factors. But it is probably fair to say that the motives mentioned are the primary forces maintaining their commitment to the profession.

The motivations of Barbara, Fenton, and Willard represent only a small sample of those that prompt people to commit themselves to a career in teaching. In the sections that follow, a number of motives are introduced.

FUNKY WINKERBEAN

By Tom Batiuk

(Funky Winkerbean by Tom Batiuk. © 1972, Field Enterprises, Inc. Courtesy of Field Newspaper Syndicate.)

Nice Working Conditions

When asked about their reasons for going into teaching and remaining in teaching, many teachers comment on their favorable impression of their conditions of work, both the physical environments within which they work and the kinds of people with whom they work. Some who have worked outside of education tend to be particularly vocal in their support of the idea that educators enjoy especially good working conditions.

Arguments Supporting the "Nice-Working-Conditions" Motive

Many teachers do indeed have very nice physical facilities in which to work. Many newer schools are located on large plots of well-maintained land. The interiors are light and cheery. Furthermore, since the buildings tend to be scattered throughout a community, ordinarily teachers can drive to work without having to get caught up in downtown-area traffic jams. Even many older buildings are well maintained. In many districts, the summer months witness a fever of activity as rooms are painted, floors are refinished, and all aspects of the physical plant are made ready for the fall. Schools, after all, are public property. Many districts, therefore, take care to see that their buildings and grounds are something in which the community can take pride.

There is an autonomy in teaching that many people find appealing. Though there are occasional visits from principals and coordinators, by and large

---

Box 7-1
Comparing Motives for Teaching

LET'S PONDER

Read the short descriptions relating to Barbara Castanella, Fenton Dragstedt, and Willard Stiles. Pay particular attention to their motives for teaching. Then, respond to the following questions:

1. How would you distinguish among the motives given by Barbara, Fenton, and Willard for teaching?
2. Do you tend to agree with the motives of any one of these individuals more than the others? If so, which one? Why?
3. Which one of these individuals has motives for teaching that are least appealing to you? Why?
4. If one of these individuals was going to work with you as a member of a teaching team, which one would you prefer? Why?
5. Do you think all of these people are responsible teachers? Why, or why not?

teachers spend their days unsupervised by others. When they close the door to their teaching area, they function as autonomous professionals. Many teachers find this a very satisfying situation. In general, teachers have a good deal of freedom to develop their instructional programs according to their own preferences.

Many teachers report tremendous satisfaction in working with "high-caliber" people. In general, teachers are well educated, people-oriented individuals. Few are profane. Few remain long in the profession who have grating, unpleasant personalities. Many dress, if not stylishly, at least with some concern for personal appearance. In summary, a good many teachers live the ideals of the middle class. Many teachers find themselves very comfortable in working with people sharing these values.

Though certainly there are exceptions, many teachers continue to have altruistic rather than materialistic motives. Many are truly dedicated to a life of helping others. Though salaries are not high, "rewards" tend to come in terms of self-satisfaction from helping youngsters develop. There is a community of common purpose that binds many teachers together. Many teachers derive a tremendous amount of psychological support from their relationships with colleagues who share their concerns for others.

Because of tenure laws and because of tradition, few teachers get fired. Teachers who do a reasonably good job enjoy fairly high job security, which reduces the anxiety level of teachers (at least with respect to employment security) below that of people following other occupations. Teachers tend to begin work under the assumption that they will be allowed to continue. This security provides teachers with a feeling that administrators are there more to help than to find fault. For many, this kind of atmosphere contributes to effectiveness in the classroom and builds a commitment to the profession.

Arguments Refuting the "Nice-Working-Conditions" Motive

Television and films have given many people a distorted image of school buildings and grounds. Though exceptions exist, there is still a tendency to depict schools in very affluent suburban areas. These educational palaces with their multiacre campuses and half-million-dollar landscaping scarcely typify most American schools. In fact, in an era of tightening budgets, the physical condition of many buildings and grounds is declining. In some areas, this has happened by design. Certain administrators, sensitive to a taxpaying public that is ever-vigilant for evidence of spending for "frills," have taken to cutting budgets for maintenance to provide a public impression that the money is being spent for instruction, not for building maintenance. In many places, a well-landscaped school ground has become a public relations liability rather than a public relations asset.

Though many beginning teachers assume that they will have a great deal of autonomy in teaching their classes, frequently this turns out not to be the case. Because of the public demand for accountability, districts increasingly are standardizing their curriculum. This standardization means not only that districts are insisting that professional course curriculum guides be developed for use throughout the district, but that teachers, in fact, follow the guides. Demands for the competency testing of youngsters seem destined to ensure even more standardization of the instructional program in the future. If all youngsters in a district are to be assessed by a common test, then it is only natural that the district administrators will be interested in the instructional programs being used in the school classrooms. This interest may well mean an increasing incidence of classroom visits by district administrators bent on monitoring the instructional practices of classroom teachers.

Television frequently depicts principals and teachers enjoying an easy, comfortable relationship. Often they engage in warm banter and convey the impression that a principal and a teacher are coequal professionals dedicated to doing a good job with youngsters. In reality, this kind of warm and open relationship does not always exist. In some schools, the principals deliberately keep themselves at a personal and social distance from the teachers. They justify this behavior by pointing out that they are responsible for making the "difficult" decisions, and that when these decisions have to be made, it is best that they be made on the basis of evidence rather than on the basis of any personal friendship that may have developed between principal and teacher.

Though teachers do enjoy considerable job security, administrators do have ways of dealing with teachers whom they view as "not pulling their weight." For example, a high school teacher might be assigned classes requiring five separate preparations. An elementary teacher might be given groups of difficult, unruly children year after year. The simple legal protections of employment that many teachers enjoy certainly do not ensure that the conditions of work will be pleasant.

Though some teachers clearly are motivated by altruistic motives and are sincerely committed to helping others, many others do not have such motives. In every school, there are teachers who are "simply putting in their time." A good number of these people may have outside activities or business interests that command the lion's share of their enthusiasm. For many of these individuals, teaching simply provides a way of ensuring a regular check at the end of the month. In a school with large numbers of such marginally committed teachers, new teachers cannot expect lively discussions in the faculty room centered on helping youngsters by improving school programs. In almost every building, teachers find certain of their colleagues less than congenial and less than committed to their profession.

Lack of Routine

Lack of routine is cited by many teachers as a characteristic of teaching that they find particularly appealing. This characteristic appears with great frequency in the comments of teachers who worked as secretaries or in some highly routinized job such as a production assembly. Many teachers find the variety of experiences provided in teaching to be highly stimulating and highly rewarding.

This variety takes several forms. Clearly the diversity of youngsters in itself ensures that no day will be a carbon copy of any other day. Teachers also generally enjoy some discretion over what they do within each class period. Finally, there is a "season" to the school calendar of cocurricular and social events that changes with the months of the year. If a teacher begins to weary of youngsters' endless discussions of football, there is solace in the knowledge that soon basketball, and then track, baseball, and other spring sports will become the compelling enthusiasm. For elementary teachers, in particular, Columbus Day, Thanksgiving, Valentine's Day, and other holidays provide opportunities to "do something a little different."

Arguments Supporting the "Lack-of-Routine" Motive

Many classrooms are very exciting places. Youngsters represent a cross-section of the school community served. They bring a tremendous diversity of interests, enthusiasms, and competencies to the classroom. Where teachers establish an atmosphere in which youngsters feel free to get involved actively in the program, the teacher's day will not be boring. Many teachers appreciate this diversity.

In particular, many teachers receive continual stimulation from the comments of their youngsters. Recall that even seniors in high school have not had a great deal of experience in living. Youngsters in schools, regardless of their age, frequently make some truly "memorable" comments. Teachers with a sense of the humorous and incongruous find their days brightened by many of these remarks. For example, one of the authors, working with a group of seniors, noticed that the term *feudal* appeared on a number of pages in the reading. Thinking this might be a problem term for some youngsters, he asked if anybody could define it. A hand shot up: "That's a simple one. A 'feudal society' is one of those places where everybody in one person's family is fighting everybody in another person's family." A good guess . . . but no cigar. An elementary teacher friend of the authors reported her difficulty in suppressing a smile when a second-grader came up and said, "We learned a new song at church. A brand new one I bet you've never even heard of. It's called 'Amazing Grace.'" Examples of this sort abound. The refreshingly innocent comments of young people are a constant delight to many teachers.

Teachers do enjoy a good deal of flexibility in planning individual lessons. This enables them to change the pace and modify materials to meet the special needs of their youngsters. There is a good deal of artistry involved in developing schemes that "get through" to some learners, and many teachers enjoy their freedom to design approaches that can get the job done. In accomplishing these objectives, teachers operate quite autonomously. They are treated as professionals, and a good deal of faith is placed in their expertise. Many teachers draw deep satisfaction from the confidence that administrators place in them to do what is "right" for their young people.

Box 7-2
How Your Own Teachers Viewed Their Professional Environments

LET'S PONDER   Think about your own elementary, junior high school, and senior high school. Now, try to imagine how those buildings were viewed by the teachers. Respond to the following questions:

1. Were the physical facilities in these buildings of a type that teachers probably found attractive? Was there a place for teachers to get away from their classrooms and sit down with other teachers?
2. How do you recall interpersonal relationships among members of the teaching staff? If you remember them as having been good, can you suggest what might have contributed to this situation? If you remember them as having been bad, can you suggest what might have contributed to this situation?
3. How were relationships between teachers and administrators? Were teachers generally comfortable around administrators? Do you recall any teachers being clearly intimidated by administrators?
4. What kind of people were most of your teachers? Were they really committed to teaching? Were they just putting in their time while their real interests were devoted to other things?
5. Were the grounds around these schools well kept? Were schools attractive kinds of places to which teachers could point with pride?
6. How would you feel about working with teachers in some of the schools you attended? What kind of a teaching staff would you most like to work with?

There is abundant change even within the school day itself. Assemblies, pep rallies, plays, band and orchestra recitals, and a number of other events take place during the school day at irregular intervals. After school, there may be building meetings, professional-organization meetings, and a number of recreational opportunities, including such activities as teachers' bowling leagues and teachers' volleyball teams. For teachers who seek them and need them, the profession offers a tremendous variety of experiences.

Arguments Refuting the "Lack-of-Routine" Motive

For all the talk about flexibility, teaching tends to be a highly routinized profession. Teachers' professional lives in many schools begin and end according to the dictates of the buzzer or the bell signaling class changes. If a lesson should take sixty minutes but periods are only fifty-five minutes in length . . . too bad. The lesson must give way to the rule of the clock. Cutting the day into periods of equal length makes program management easy. It may be that good learning has been sacrificed to administrative convenience. Certainly there is no indication that schools in large numbers are abandoning their heavy commitment to a schedule dictated by the clock. This commitment suggests that teaching cannot properly be thought of as a profession characterized by a lack of routine.

Beyond the issue of clock time for classes, many other elements of the teacher's day are highly routinized. Attendance must be taken and reported every day. In elementary schools, a lunch count must be taken and reported. The same sequence of classes must be faced day after day. If Johnny Smith comes in making sarcastic remarks today with the ten o'clock group, it is certain that three months from now he will be walking through the classroom door at the same time. In elementary schools, recess occurs daily at the same time. Lunchroom duties, playground responsibilities, hall patrol duties, and many other tasks appear with wearisome regularity at predictable intervals throughout the school year.

The curriculum itself is highly predictable in districts with well-developed curriculum plans. In many districts, teachers must treat topics within subject areas in a certain prescribed order. Little flexibility remains to them in this regard. In some elementary schools, a definite order is established by administrative decree for teaching subjects during the school day. Typically, reading is taught first thing in the morning. In many districts, teachers have no freedom to alter the prescribed subject-by-subject sequence in the elementary program.

Many teachers find that learners vary little from year to year. After a number of years of teaching, some secondary-school teachers, in particular, begin their classes by announcing to students that they have already heard "every excuse" for not getting assignments completed. In fact, some say that students' excuses are so predictable that teachers enjoy sharing with one another any "new ones" students come up with. One high school teacher, a friend of the authors, reported his delight one morning in having a student tell him that he "really intended to bring the assignment in. It was done and was resting on the kitchen table. At the last minute, with a careless brush of the hand, the assignment was knocked to the floor. As luck would have it, the paper fell into the dog's milk. At that very moment, a younger brother opened the back door. The ravenous dog ran in, charged the milk bowl, and eagerly consumed the milk-soaked paper." Truly a heartrending story . . . worthy of an F+.

Youngsters' attitudes at various times of the year, according to many teachers, follow a highly predictable pattern. Generally they are easiest to work with in the fall. Then, as the winter holidays approach, they begin to get very excited about Christmas and the extended vacation. In elementary schools, in particular, youngsters become extremely excitable during the few days before their vacation begins. January and February are usually reported as "blah" times by teachers. Youngsters seem hard to motivate, and the pros-

Box 7-3
How Routinized is Teaching?

LET'S PONDER

Recall your own experiences in elementary school, junior high school, and senior high school. Then, respond to the following questions:

1. Can you describe a typical day from your elementary school years? Your junior high school years? Your senior high school years? How much routine was there?
2. To what extent do you think teachers had discretion to change routines while you were in school? What is your evidence that they did or did not have this discretion?
3. Thinking about classes you had when you were in school, how much discretion do you remember teachers having had in deciding how classes would be organized and what would be taught?
4. Did you have a system of buzzers or bells in schools you attended? If so, to what extent did these provide a sense of routine? Did times allotted for individual classes ever interfere with teachers' abilities to cover material adquately? If your schools had no buzzers or bells, were there other ways to signal length of classes?
5. Do you think your teachers felt each class of learners was different or that they expected each class to be "more of the same?"
6. What is your view of teaching? Do you think there is a lack of routine as compared to other occupations, or do you think teaching is characterized by a high degree of routine? Why do you think so?

pect of any vacation-time relief from school seems hopelessly remote. Things pick up a little around spring-vacation time. Late spring, any time after April 15, is sure to witness serious outbreaks of "senioritis" in many high schools. Large numbers of seniors simply go through the motions in premature anticipation of walking across the stage to receive their diplomas. All youngsters become extremely excited as the end of school approaches. Many schools require teachers to collect and turn in all books two or three days before school is dismissed in the spring. Those final two or three days, when youngsters are supposed to be productively occupied in school even in the absence of learning materials, try the ingenuity of even very experienced teachers.

While certainly there is some variety in teaching, in general the profession is highly routinized. Patterns of learner behavior are quite predictable. Procedures follow a fairly constant sequence each day. Even the curriculum itself may provide so much structure that little flexibility remains for the teacher. Given these conditions, it is perfectly understandable that some teachers describe themselves as following the same rut year after year.

Importance of Teaching

Many teachers report that their commitment to the profession results from their belief that they are doing something very important. They sense a deep obligation as transmitters of the culture to new generations. In a complex, technically oriented society such as our own, teachers bear a heavy responsibility. They must produce young people who have the talent and the inclination to become contributing citizens accomplished in a number of important skills. Without competent teachers, the social fabric would be threatened. Large numbers of teachers take a good deal of satisfaction from their key position as conduits through which important attitudes and understandings are passed on to the young.

Though teachers are not particularly well paid, many surveys reveal teachers to be highly respected members of the community. Many teachers believe that this respect attests to the importance people attach to their profession. Concerns of parents about the progress of their youngsters in school reinforce the idea that what goes on in classrooms is important. Such signals that they are "doing something worthwhile" gratify many who have elected teaching as their chosen profession.

Arguments Supporting the "Importance-of-Teaching" Motive

Is teaching important? Well, of course it is. There was a time when the necessary knowledge could be provided to the young by family members. But as societies became more complex and division of labor more common, it was impossible for individual family members to provide the range of information and skills young people needed to become contributing adult members of the community. As the need for specialists was recognized, the profession of teaching evolved. In our own country, teaching as a profession has assumed increasing importance over the past hundred years. Today, we have rigorous standards for teachers. We require youngsters to attend schools. Dropouts become a matter of abiding public concern. Every signal suggests that teaching is indeed an "important" occupation.

In recent years, there has been an increasing demand for teachers to be "accountable." This means that the public expects teachers to succeed in their attempts to teach important information to the young. Were teaching lightly regarded, there would never have been a ground swell of public support for the accountability movement.

Teachers' salaries today, while not lavish, certainly are much higher than they were in years past. These increases have come about because people have recognized that without adequate salaries, competent people will not be attracted to the profession. Today almost no one argues that "anybody will do" for a teacher. The public expects "quality people" to instruct the young, and progress is being made to provide salaries that will attract competent individuals.

Increasingly schools are being recognized as important vehicles for social change. Mention any social problem and someone is sure to say, "What is needed is better education." Lawmakers at the federal and state levels have been active as never before in requiring schools to provide instruction to populations of youngsters who, it is believed, have not always been well served. Action, too, has been taken to require schools to emphasize subjects and topics that may have been skirted or ignored in the past. This interest by legislative leaders is a recognition of the important role that teachers play.

Standards for teacher preparation are growing more rigorous. Furthermore, once hired, teachers find themselves faced with obligations to "keep current." Many states require teachers to complete work toward a master's degree in order to keep their certification current. Others have in-service requirements that must be met as a condition of continued employment. All of these things reflect a concern for teacher quality. This concern suggests that teaching is clearly a profession that nearly everyone considers "important."

Arguments Refuting the "Importance-of-Teaching" Motive

Is teaching important, really? Or is its alleged "importance" simply something that clever people have devised to make well-intentioned but not particularly capable individuals accept as an alternative to a decent salary? Are teachers, in a sense, "paid" for belonging to an "important" profession rather than for their instructional services? If their instructional services were truly prized, wouldn't salaries be high enough to attract none but the best?

While teachers are accorded some respect, their social status does not begin to compare with that accorded other professionals. Physicians and lawyers, for example, tend to stand much higher in the social "pecking order." Indeed, many people do not consider teachers professionals at all. How, they ask, can people with so little academic training—sometimes as little as four years of college—pretend to think of themselves as professionals? Many see teachers as civil servants who do good and respectable work, but who are really rather ordinary kinds of people.

The scores that people going into teaching make on standardized tests tend to be lower, on the average, than the scores of people majoring in many other areas. Some argue that these scores indicate that teaching attracts intellectual mediocrities. If teaching were really important, they say, would not teacher preparation programs attract the very brightest students?

Teachers above all tend to exemplify the values of the American middle class. They believe in the work ethic. They dress in conservative fashions. Politically they tend to occupy the middle of the road, with a slight shift to the conservative side. They tend to be transmitters of information rather than

Box 7-4
The Importance of Teaching

LET'S PONDER

Some argue that teaching is one of life's most important activities. Others argue this point. They point out that teaching does not attract the most talented individuals in our society. Reflect on these positions as you respond to the following questions:

1. From your own observations of conditions in schools you attended, what degree of importance would you say was attached to teaching in your community?
2. What social status did teachers enjoy in your community? Do you think your community was typical? Why, or why not?
3. Would we be better off if all teachers were drawn from people who scored in the top five percent of those taking the Scholastic Aptitude Test? Why, or why not?
4. Do teachers undermine their own credibility by talking too much in terms of slogans such as "open education," "meeting individual differences," and so forth? Why, or why not?
5. How important do you think teaching is? What evidence is there to support your position?

creators of information. Teachers rarely break new ground in any area. Some argue that they do not do the important work of discovering new insights and producing new information. They simply pass on the work done by others to their youngsters. While certainly this is a valuable function, it does not begin to compare in importance with the contributions of those who truly work on the frontiers of knowledge.

Finally, teachers as a group are enchanted with high-blown phrases. They talk endlessly about such things as "individualizing instruction," "reaching every child," "open-concept instruction," and "self-paced learning." Few are able to talk knowledgeably about what these things mean in terms of specific classroom practice. For many teachers, giving a familiar practice a fancy new name is enough. It gives them the illusion that they are doing something novel and important. The public is well aware of this charade. Consequently, when a new name is trotted out, most people nod a weary approval, well aware that nothing basic has really changed. Teachers are considered generally "nice" people. If they wish to pretend that their work is important or that "team teaching" or some other enthusiasm of the movement will save the world, well, that's all right. No harm done in letting them have their fling. But most thoughtful people do not really see teaching as a serious, rigorous, "important" profession.

Excitement of Learning

"When I teach a youngster something, there's something electric in the air." That comment comes from a teacher whose greatest satisfaction in teaching comes from watching youngsters begin to grasp and understand what they are being taught. Many teachers report pleasure in observing youngsters' self-confidence grow as they master material that they once thought to be very difficult.

Many teachers themselves were eager learners in school. Many recall their own excitement as they began to grow confident in their understanding of new material. The hope of prompting their own learners to enjoy similar experiences motivates many individuals to go into teaching, particularly people wishing to teach in high school who hope that the stimulation they derived from their college and university courses can be transmitted to high school students.

Arguments Supporting the "Excitement-of-Learning" Motive

To teachers who attach high value to the material they are teaching, few things in life are so satisfying as a group of youngsters who are beginning to understand what they are being taught. If the material is presented in an interesting way, they may get very excited. Hands may wave in the air. Shouts may punctuate the lesson. Eager discussion may follow. At the end of the day, in the eyes of the teacher, at least, the youngsters may all stand a little taller as they reflect on their new-found confidence.

There is an important interplay between learners' excitement and teachers' performance. When youngsters do well, teachers find it gratifying. They are prompted to devote more time to the preparation of lessons. Many teachers report that they enjoy preparing for a class of responsive youngsters. Positive reactions from learners provide a very important psychological "payoff" to large numbers of teachers.

When youngsters are content and doing well, administrators and parents tend to be happy. This happiness may well be reflected in comments to the teacher about the high quality of his or her work. Thus the excitement of learning—a motive in and of itself—tends to generate other conditions that lead to teachers' satisfaction. These conditions tend, in turn, to cause teachers to place an even higher personal priority on learners' enthusiasm for their program.

Many youngsters like their teachers as people. They look up to them and admire them. This tends to be particularly true of youngsters in the lower elementary-school grades. Most teachers sense the positive feelings that youngsters have toward them. Many, particularly beginners, are concerned that such feelings may be lost if "things don't go right." When youngsters do well in their work and are excited about it, many teachers feel reassured that a foundation has been set for continued warm working relationships with the youngsters. Thus the excitement of learning becomes very, very important. When it is there, teachers feel good about themselves and about their youngsters. For large numbers, the enthusiasm generated by an excited group of learners represents the most important reason for the continued commitment to education.

Arguments Refuting the "Excitement-of-Learning" Motive

If teachers choose to base their decision to remain in the profession on their ability to "excite learners," then they will be disappointed. Certainly they will get through to some youngsters, but despite their best efforts, some youngsters will remain unenthusiastic. A few may be openly hostile. Given the tremendous cross-section of humanity represented in many classes, it is unrealistic to presume that even the finest imaginable lesson will strike a responsive note with every learner. Teachers who set a standard of reaching 100 percent of the learners with every lesson are foreordained to fail.

Some things that youngsters must learn in school just are not terribly interesting, but our society has decreed that they must know them. Certainly, imaginative teachers can devise techniques for presenting such information in ways that prompt some enthusiasm, but the truism remains that some topics simply lend themselves better to prompting learners' interest than do others. A teacher who expects to have no more difficulty in motivating youngsters in one topic than in another is being unrealistic.

Certain critics argue that by its very nature, some important learning cannot be "exciting." They point out, for example, that youngsters can make little progress in mathematics unless they master the multiplication tables. Yet for most children, this mastery involves hard, slogging work. True, many youngsters perk up once they have mastered this material, but many are very discouraged and less than enthusiastic as they are going through the process of learning it. Teachers must expect that youngsters will not be "up" all the time. No matter how well presented, some will find certain topics a dreary experience at best. Teachers must prepare to accept occasional negative comments from their learners and to keep these comments in a proper perspective. A complaint today from a youngster does not mean he or she has "turned off" on the teacher or the course. Given a changed set of circumstances, the same person can become very much interested in what is going on in class.

Producing learning experiences that excite youngsters is very hard work. The competition is stiff. Learners are conditioned to the polished performances of television actors who are backed by platoons of writers and technical directors. It is unrealistic to expect teachers who must work with learners every day to compete effectively with those once-a-week performers who transfix youngsters seated in front of a television screen. Given this competition, no teacher should base a commitment to the profession on his or her ability to excite and entertain youngsters. At least, teachers should not expect to accomplish this feat every day. To do so is to be committed to a "no-win" situation.

Finally, it must be remembered that youngsters' attitudes are conditioned by many factors outside the control of the teacher. Some may have terrible home situations. Others may work long hours after school. Others may be in trouble with the law. Any one of a hundred variables can influence a learner's reaction to a lesson. Given this reality, it is not logical to hope to work continually in an environment where learners are excited about what the teacher is doing.

Why Teach? Some Final Thoughts

The motives discussed in the preceding sections represent a small sample of those given by teachers for staying in the profession. Any one of a number of other reasons might have been cited, but those included are reasonably representative. It should be remembered that almost no one becomes committed to teaching on the basis of a single factor. Likewise almost no one remains in the profession unless he or she finds a number of satisfactions in teaching. Some of these are prized more than others, but all contribute to the decision to remain or to get out.

The important consideration for someone considering a career in education is the accuracy of his or her perception of the attractive features of the profession. If someone is going to teach, for example, because of "pleasant working conditions," what evidence does he or she have that the working conditions are indeed pleasant? If there is an intention to become a teacher because teachers do important work, what evidence does he or she have that this statement is true? Individuals interested in becoming teachers need to consider not only their motivations but the accuracy of their perceptions. When perceptions are accurate, then the decision rests on reason. When inaccurate, it rests on fantasy. In the latter case, introduction to the real world of teaching may prove shocking and disappointing.

Recapitulation of Major Ideas

1. There is no simple answer to the question "Why teach?" It depends on the inclinations of the individual involved. It may also depend on demands unique to a particular school situation.
2. Many teachers go into teaching initially because of a love of their subject matter. This tends to be especially true of people seeking careers as high-school teachers. Others are interested in the personal development of children and see themselves as a "bridge" between childhood and adulthood.

3. Many teachers say that they enjoy their nice working conditions. These include both the nature of the building they work in and the kinds of people with whom they associate during the day.

4. Though some physical plants are very nice, others are not. Some districts view finely maintained buildings and grounds as a plus. Others view them as a political liability that may draw patron complaints that too much money is being spent on maintenance and not enough on instruction.

5. Relationships between administrators and teachers vary enormously from place to place. Some teachers enjoy very open and harmonious relationships with principals. Others are intimidated by their principals and have as little contact with them as possible.

6. Lack of routine has been cited by many teachers as a very important reason for their continuing to teach. This reason tends to be very high on the list of individuals who have worked as secretaries or in other jobs where they felt confined.

7. Teachers do enjoy a good deal of flexibility in planning what goes on during a given class period. However, the curriculum may prescribe the order in which topics are treated and the materials to be used. Again, the degree of autonomy varies considerably from place to place.

8. Many teachers find working with youngsters a stimulation in itself. Learners' refreshing candor and unexpected comments make teaching a profession unlike any other. Other teachers find that this novelty wears thin after a few years. They report that learners' behaviors tend to fall into predictable patterns.

9. Views vary considerably with regard to the "importance" of teaching. Those supporting its importance, among other things, suggest that teachers are responsible for transmitting much of the culture to the young. Those questioning teaching's importance point out that teachers command low salaries and that the profession may not always attract top talent.

10. Individuals considering a career in education need to consider their own motives. Once these motives are identified, they need to check the accuracy of their perceptions of what teaching is really like. If, for example, they think they are going to be working in a "nice environment," they need to see what the range of school environments is. Unless their perceptions are accurate, they may be bitterly disappointed when they begin their careers and confront the real world of the schools.

Posttest

DIRECTIONS: Using your own paper, answer each of the following true/false questions. For each correct statement, write the word *true* on your paper. For each incorrect statement, write the word *false* on your paper.

1. Few teachers can identify a single factor as *the* feature of teaching that got them into the profession or that maintains their interest in the profession.
2. It is very uncommon for secondary-school teachers to enter teaching because of a love of the subject they will be teaching.
3. For many teachers, contact with a group of colleagues who are educated and congenial is an important reason for remaining in the profession.
4. Many teachers are attracted to the profession because of the extended summer-vacation period.
5. Some teachers say that they stay in teaching because the profession provides a great deal of variety from day to day.
6. There is universal agreement that the profession of teaching attracts the top talents in our contry.
7. Teachers almost never mention their satisfaction with the "importance" of their work as a reason for staying in the profession.
8. Because teaching conditions vary so dramatically from place to place, many new teachers find themselves working in an environment far different from what they had initially expected.
9. Many teachers find themselves stimulated when youngsters master something that the teachers have worked hard to introduce.
10. The changing of classes, the rounds of meetings, the discussions with parents, and the constant potential for "activity" provide a high level of interest for many teachers.

Summary

Teachers provide a bewildering variety of responses to the question "Why teach?" The range of answers is understandable considering the incredible variety of schools in this country. Additionally, public schools enroll a cross section of the entire population. Whatever diversity there is in the country is represented as well in the schools.

Among the many characteristics of teaching that teachers mention as motives for staying with the profession are (1) nice working conditions, (2) lack of routine, (3) the importance of teaching, and (4) the excitement of learning. Examination of each of these four motives reveals that the profession is divided with regard to its accuracy in characterizing teaching. This division is not surprising, considering the diversity of our massive public education system.

The lack of consensus regarding what factors teachers see as "true about teaching" points up the necessity for prospective teachers to do some serious investigating on their own. It is not enough for undergraduates seeking a career in education simply to think through their motives in an intellectual sense. They must go beyond this to check the accuracy of the perceptions they have about teaching. Given an accurate understanding of the real world of teaching, they will be prepared for what they find when they teach. But an inaccurate understanding may well precipitate a hasty decision to change to another occupation.

References

BARTH, ROLAND S. "Educators Can Come Through the Crisis of Self-Confidence." *Education Week* (Oct. 20, 1982): 20.

BORTON, TERRY. *Reach, Touch, and Teach: Student Concerns and Process Education,* 2nd ed. Santa Monica, Calif.: Goodyear Publishing, 1978.

GEORGIADES, WILLIAM D. H. "Is Teaching Beneath Our Dignity?" *Houston Chronicle* (Dec. 3, 1982) Section 2 p. 11.

GOOD, THOMAS L., BIDDLE, BRUCE J., AND BROPHY, JERE E. *Teachers Make a Difference.* New York: Holt, Rinehart and Winston, 1975.

GREER, MARY, AND RUBINSTEIN, BONNIE. *Will the Real Teacher Please Stand Up?* Santa Monica, Calif.: Goodyear Publishing, 1978.

HENSON, KENNETH T., AND HIGGINS, JAMES E. *Personalizing Teaching in the Elementary School.* Columbus Ohio: Charles E. Merrill, 1978.

MARTORELLI, DEBRA. "Is Teaching a Female Ghetto?" *The Instructor* (Sept. 1982): 30–32, 34.

RUBIN, LOUIS. *Facts and Feelings in the Classroom.* New York: Viking, 1973.

SHARP, D. LOUISE. *Why Teach?* New York: Holt, Rinehart and Winston, 1957.

STUART, JESSE. *To Teach, To Love.* New York: Penguin Books, 1973.

TRAVERS, ROBERT M. W., AND DILLON, JACQUELINE. *The Making of a Teacher.* New York: Holt, Rinehart and Winston, 1975.

8
Who Are the Teachers?

Objectives

This chapter provides information to help the reader to

1. Identify the kinds of family backgrounds from which teachers tend to be drawn.
2. Point out the major job-related concerns of teachers.
3. Describe employment prospects for teachers.
4. Recognize teachers' attitudes toward various aspects of their professional roles.

Pretest

DIRECTIONS: Using your own paper, answer each of the following true/false questions. For each correct statement, write the word *true* on your paper. For each incorrect statement, write the word *false* on your paper.

1. The ratio of women to men in the teaching profession has stayed the same for the past 90 years.
2. Traditionally, large numbers of teachers have had parents who were blue collar workers.
3. Today a male teacher is more likely than a female teacher to have had a parent who was an upper-class or upper-middle-class professional person.
4. Both elementary- and secondary-school teachers identify discipline as one of the most important problems with which they must deal.
5. Today, the vast majority of elementry- and secondary-school teachers hold at least a bachelor's degree.
6. There tends to be more demand for teachers in some teaching fields than in others.
7. Evidence suggests that throughout much of the middle and late 1980s, the supply of new teachers will be less than the demand for new teachers.
8. In general, today's learners spend fewer days in school each year than learners did in 1900.
9. The percentage of teachers who are black is about the same as the percentage of the total population that is black.
10. Teachers rarely are asked to participate in curriculum development activities.

Introduction

Teachers are part of what may be the largest occupational group in the country. Including students, well over sixty million Americans are involved in education as their primary occupation. This figure includes between two and three million classroom teachers. The importance of their work is revealed in the somewhat surprising statistic that nearly three in ten Americans are actively involved in the educational process.

The large number of teachers and their great dispersion throughout the country point to one clear conclusion: tremendous differences are represented within the total group of classroom teachers. Blacks, whites, Mexican-Americans, native Americans, and a host of other ethnic groups are found in the ranks of the teaching profession. Likewise, teachers from urban, suburban, small-town, and rural areas are represented. Indeed, we might cite almost any characteristic used to categorize people and feel comfortable in saying that some people having this characteristic are teachers.

For all this diversity, certain characteristics tend to be found more frequently among teachers than among others. Though there are great differences, a number of studies have found certain kinds of persistent patterns among people who have chosen to teach. In this chapter, we examine some of these patterns in an attempt to provide some general answers to the question, "Who are the teachers?"

In looking at characteristics of teachers, we will introduce information focusing on the personal and family backgrounds of teachers, the employment situations of teachers, and the issue of demand for teachers' services.

Personal and Family Backgrounds of Teachers

Teachers' Families

One of the first systematic studies of teachers' characteristics was conducted in 1911. This study revealed that most teachers were sons and daughters of native-born Americans. The fathers tended to be farmers or tradesmen (Rodgers, 1976). Few teachers came from families headed by upper-class or middle-class professionals.

The association of teachers with middle-class and lower-middle-class family backgrounds has been quite consistent over time. There is evidence, however, that somewhat smaller numbers of teachers have been drawn from these backgrounds over the past fifteen to twenty years. By the decade of the 1970s, still nearly half of the nation's teachers continued to come from a working-class or farm background, but there was a clear trend for a larger number of teachers to be drawn from families of higher occupational status than had been the case during the earlier years of the century. Perhaps this change results from a broadened appreciation of education's importance. One study in the early 1980s reported that if more federal money were avail-

Box 8-1
Selected Teacher Characteristics in the Years 1961 and 1981

	1961	1981
Percentage of Female Teachers	68.7	66.9
Percentage of Male Teachers	31.3	33.1
Percentage of Married Teachers	68.0	73.0
Percentage of Single Teachers	22.3	18.5
Percentage of Widowed, Divorced, or Separated Teachers	9.7	8.5
Highest Degree Held		
Less than Bachelor's	14.6	0.4
Bachelor's	61.9	50.1
Master's or 6 Years	23.1	49.3
Doctor's	0.4	0.3

*Data are from National Center for Education Statistics. *Digest of Education Statistics 1982*. Washington, D.C.: United States Government Printing Office, 1982. p. 55.

LET'S PONDER

1. How do you account for differences in percentages of males teaching in 1961 and 1981? Would you expect this trend to continue? Why?
2. How do you account for the higher percentage of married teachers in 1981 than in 1961? What would you expect the figure to be in 1991? Why do you think so?
3. How do you compare the overall educational levels of 1961 and 1981 teachers? What would you expect the figures to look like in 1991? Why do you think so?

able, more Americans would wish to spend it on education than on health care, welfare, or defense (Hodgkinson, 1982).

Male and Female Teachers

Historically teaching has attracted varying percentages of men and women at different periods of time. Relatively large numbers of men were in the profession in the latter decades of the nineteenth century. The figures for some specific decades are as follows:

1869–1870	38.7% of teachers were males
1879–1880	42.8% of teachers were males
1889–1890	34.5% of teachers were males
1899–1900	29.9% of teachers were males

Data from National Center for Education Statistics. *Digest of Education Statistics, 1976 Edition.* Washington, D.C.: United States Government Printing Office, 1977. p. 36.

Box 8-2

Changing Percentages of Male and Female Teachers Employed in Elementary and Secondary Schools

	1929–1930		1939–1940		1949–1950	
	Elem.	Sec.	Elem.	Sec.	Elem.	Sec
Males	9.8%	35.2%	11.0%	41.8%	8.8%	43.2%
Females	90.2%	64.8%	89.0%	58.2%	91.2%	56.8%

	1959–1960		1969–1970		1980–1981	
	Elem.	Sec.	Elem.	Sec.	Elem.	Sec.
Males	11.6%	51.3%	15.0%	53.2%	16.9%	51.1%
Females	88.4%	48.7%	85.0%	46.8%	83.1%	48.9%

Data adapted from National Center for Education Statistics. *Digest of Education Statistics, 1976 Edition.* Washington, D.C. United States Government Printing Office, 1977, and from National Center for Education Statistics. *Digest of Education Statistics, 1982 Edition.* Washington D.C.: United States Government Printing Office, 1982.

LET'S PONDER

1. What general trends do you observe in terms of male and female employment in elementary and secondary schools at these different time periods?
2. How do you account for the decline in the percentage of male elementary teachers in 1949–1950 as compared to 1939–1940?
3. What factors do you think might have been associated with the decline in the percentage of female secondary school teachers between 1929–1930 and 1959–1960?
4. What factors might have played a role in the increase in the percentage of male elementary schools that occured between 1959–1960 and 1969–1970?
5. There was an increase in the percentage of male elementary teachers both between 1959–1960 and 1969–1970 and between 1969–1970 and 1980–1981. Why do you suppose that the percentage of males increased more in the first ten-year period than in the second?
6. If you were to project what these figures would look like for school year 1990–1991, what would the male and female percentages be? What led you to this conclusion? What could happen that would make you wish to adjust your predictions sometime in the future (perhaps two or three years from now)?

After the turn of the century, the percentages of men in education began a long decline. In school year 1919–1920, for example, the percentage of male teachers fell to only 14.1 percent of the public school teaching force (National Center for Education Statistics, *Digest of Education Statistics, 1976*, p. 36). Salary conditions, alternative employment opportunities, and the lower status attached to teaching contributed to the decline in the percentages of men in the teaching profession. These conditions were particularly influential in shaping the decisions of married men with families to look toward other career options.

Since about 1920 there has been a general increase in the percentage of male teachers in the schools. By the 1980s, male teachers accounted for between 30 and 40 percent of all public school teachers.

Historically there have been significant differences in how male teachers and female teachers have been distributed in elementary schools and secondary schools. Look at Figure 8-2. What differences do you observe in the percentages of men and women in elementary and secondary schools at different times?

Selected Other Personal Characteristics

Training of teachers.   Tremendous progress has been made in the professional preparation of teachers in this century. As late as 1918, fully one half of the nation's teachers lacked any formal training for their positions. At this time, one sixth of all teachers lacked even a tenth-grade education (Rodgers, 1976).

Certification standards for teachers have been adopted nationwide only during the past fifty to sixty years. As late as 1926, for example, fifteen states still had no definite scholarly requirements for teachers (Rodgers, 1976). As recently as 1961, nearly fifteen percent of teachers in public schools did not have a bachelor's degree; today more than 99 percent of public school teachers have a bachelor's degree or some more advanced degree (National Center for Education Statistics. *Digest of Education Statistics, 1982 Edition*, p. 55).

Racial Characteristics.   Overwhelmingly, teachers in the United States are white. A survey conducted by the National Education Association in the 1970s (NEA, 1972) revealed that about 8 percent of teachers are blacks. This figure is somewhat smaller than the 11.5 percent of the general population that is black. A more recent survey found that blacks constituted only 5 percent of all beginning bachelor's-degree teachers in 1981 (National Center for Education Statistics. *The Condition of Education, 1983 Edition*, p. 204). This may suggest a trend for fewer blacks to enter the teaching profession than has been the case in the past. Among other racial groups, Hispanics accounted for 2.4 percent, Asian and Pacific Islanders for 0.7 percent, and American Indians or Alaska Natives for 0.3 percent of beginning 1981 bachelor's-degree teachers (National Center for Education Statistics. *The Condition of Education, 1983 Edition*, p. 204).

Age and Teaching Experience. On an average, the teaching population has become older and more experienced since the first survey of teachers' characteristics in 1911. In 1911, the average age of teachers was twenty-four. The typical teacher had five years of experience.

A 1981 survey revealed the typical teacher to be thirty-seven years old and to have taught twelve years. Until quite recently, there was a surplus of teachers in the country. As a result, fewer teachers were hired each year than in past times. One consequence was a "graying" of the population of teachers. Projections now are for modest teacher shortages for the middle and late 1980s. If these shortages develop, more new teachers may be hired, and average ages and years of experience may decline.

Employment Situations of Teachers

Much of the discussion in this section refers to either *elementary* or *secondary* education. These terms tend to obscure the reality that large numbers of teachers work in intermediate schools, generally referred to as either *middle schools* or *junior high schools*. Although intermediate schools have some characteristics of schools housing the lower elementary grades and some of the senior high school, they actually represent a third distinct tier of American education. Regrettably, statistics about education in this country almost invariably refer to only elementary education and to secondary education. Therefore no mention is made of middle schools or junior high schools in this section.

One of the most striking features of American schools is the commonality of certain patterns that persist across vast expanses of geographic territory. The relative ease of obtaining a teaching certificate in State *X* after having initially worked in State *Y* supports the idea that the similarities among American school districts are more significant than the differences.

FUNKY WINKERBEAN   Tom Batiuk

(Funky Winkerbean by Tom Batiuk. © 1979, Field Enterprises, Inc. Courtesy of Field Newspaper Syndicate.)

Classes and Work Schedules

Not surprisingly, given the typical organizational patterns of elementary and secondary schools, elementary- and secondary-school teachers have somewhat different schedules of work. There are some differences in numbers of learners in average elementary- and secondary-school classes. In 1981, for example, elementary school teachers in nondepartmentalized buildings had an average of 25 pupils in each class. In the same year, secondary school teachers had an average of 23 pupils in each class (National Center for Education Statistics. *Digest of Education Statistics, 1982 Edition.* p. 55.)

The figures for the elementary school represent a dramatic reduction from class sizes of fifteen and twenty years ago. In 1955, for example, elementary teachers averaged over 30 learners in their classrooms. There has also been something of a decrease in the size of secondary school classes, but at this level, average class sizes have been below 30 for some time. Figure 8-3 illustrates some changes in average class size over time.

Most secondary-school teachers work in departmentalized buildings. One survey revealed that on an average, they teach about five periods a day, have one unassigned period a day, supervise homerooms and study halls, and perform other duties as assigned. In addition, secondary-school teachers get a short break for lunch in the middle of the school day, typically averaging thirty to forty minutes in length. With few exceptions, secondary-school teachers are not expected to eat lunch with their students.

Many elementary-school teachers work with the same group of youngsters

---

Box 8-3
Some Changes in Elementary-School and Secondary-School Class Size From 1961 to 1981

AVERAGE NUMBERS OF LEARNERS PER CLASS:

	1961	1966	1971	1976	1981
Non-Departmentalized Elementary Schools	29	28	27	25	25
Secondary Schools	28	26	27	25	23

Data are from National Center for Education Statistics. *Digest of Education Statistics, 1982, Edition.* Washington, D.C.: United States Government Printing Office, 1982. p. 55.

LET'S PONDER

1. What general trend do you observe in average class sizes at the elementary level? At the secondary level?
2. What would you expect these figures to be in 1991? Why do you think so?
3. What advantages do you see for reduced class sizes? What disadvantages do you see?
4. Do you think class size has any bearing on youngsters' learning? Why do you think so? Can you find evidence to support your case?

throughout the entire school day. In recent years, however, a trend has developed to "departmentalize" elementary schools. That is, certain teachers are responsible for teaching specific subjects not just to their own group of pupils but to all pupils at a given grade level. For example, if there are three fourth grades in a school, one teacher might teach all of the arithmetic, another all of the science, and another all of the social studies. In such departmentalized elementary-school programs, the movement of pupils from room to room is less common than in secondary schools. More typically, the teachers rotate from room to room.

Though the situation is improving, large numbers of elementary-school teachers still have no unassigned periods during the school day. Indeed, significant numbers have no break at all in their contact with pupils from the minute they arrive in the morning until they go home in the afternoon, particularly in those schools where the teachers must eat lunch with their youngsters. It is common for teachers to eat in their own classrooms in schools having no central cafeteria facilities. (Food is usually wheeled into individual classrooms on special carts from a central district food-preparation center).

Box 8-4
Changes in Average Number of Days in the School Term

1870	1890	1910	1930	1950	1970	1980
132.2	134.7	157.5	172.7	177.9	178.9	178.8

*Data are from National Center for Education Statistics. *Digest of Education Statistics, 1982.* Washington, D.C.: United States Government Printing Office, 1982. p. 35.

LET'S PONDER

1. What factors do you associate with the rather short school terms in the nineteenth century?
2. What forces might have been at work to increase the length of the school term between 1910 and 1930?
3. How do you account for the greater changes in the length of the school term between 1898 and 1930 than between 1930 and 1970?
4. What forces today would tend to support a longer school term? What reasons are given by people favoring a longer school year? How do you evaluate their logic?
5. What forces today would tend to support a shorter school term? What reasons are given by people favoring a shorter school year? How do you evaluate their logic?
6. As a teacher, would you prefer a longer school year or a shorter school year? Why?

In some schools, all elementary teachers are expected to go out and supervise youngsters on the school playground after lunch until the afternoon classes start.

Not surprisingly, there has been a good deal of attention given to the intensity of the pupil–teacher contact in many elementary schools. Many have recognized that a teaching schedule that provides no breather for the teacher during the day drains energy reserves and saps enthusiasm. Pressures are mounting to provide all elementary teachers some unscheduled time during the school day, but despite these efforts it is likely to be some time before the unassigned period is as common at the elementary-school level as at the secondary-school level.

In most districts, teachers teach about 180 days each year. In addition, it is typical for districts to require a few additional days, in the range of 3–6 days, for workshops and other professional in-service activities. Today's teachers teach for more days during the year than did their counterparts in earlier times. Note the school-year information provided in Figure 8-4.

Teachers and Their Learners

The learners themselves constitute a very important variable in the teacher's work environment. There is evidence that there have been some important changes in the kinds of youngsters in schools today compared with earlier times, particularly in secondary schools.

In the nineteenth century, high schools were designed for a very small percentage of the population. With few exceptions, high schools served students who were preparing to go on to colleges and universities. High schools enrolled a very small percentage of the population. For example, in school year 1869–1870, only 1.2 percent of the entire school population was enrolled in a high school program. By school year 1979–1980, this figure had jumped to 32.9 percent (National Center for Education Statistics. *Digest of Education Statistics, 1982 Edition.* p. 35) The nature of the population of high school students served by teachers in the 1980s is very different from that served by secondary-school teachers in the 1870s.

A number of factors are associated with changes in the school population, particularly at the high school level. Among these has been a feeling that high schools should serve everyone, not just those going on to a college or university after graduation. Additionally, employment legislation has made it difficult for young people under the age of sixteen or eighteen to find work. Many have stayed in school who, in earlier times, would have been employed. Also, the decline in the farm population has resulted in a diminished demand for teenagers' services on a full-time basis to work the land. Finally, mandatory attendance laws and other related legislation have resulted in more students staying in school longer.

All of these things have changed the nature of the student population with which today's secondary teachers must work. At both the elementary and sec-

Box 8-5
Changes in the Percentage of Five- to Seventeen-Year-Olds Enrolled in School

1870	1880	1890	1900	1910	1920	1930	1940	1950	1960	1970	1980
57.0	65.5	68.6	71.9	74.2	78.3	81.7	84.4	83.2	82.2	86.9	87.7

*Data are from National Center for Education Statistics. *Digest of Education Statistics, 1982 Edition.* Washington, D.C.: United States Government Printing Office, 1982. p. 35.

LET'S PONDER

1. Why were the percentages of youngsters in school relatively small before 1900?
2. What social changes are associated with increases in these percentages?
3. Would you expect most of the increase to have been among younger or older children?
4. Though the 87.7 percent figure for 1972 is impressive, still it is considerably less than 100 percent. Who are the remaining 12.3 percent? Why were they not in school in 1980?
5. Would you expect these enrollment percentages to stay about the same, increase, or decrease in the years ahead? Why?
6. Do you think increasing percentages of the total population of five- to seventeen-year-olds in school has made teachers' jobs easier or more difficult? Why?

ondary levels, it is fair to say that educational programs enroll the vast majority of young people in the five- to seventeen-year-old age group. In school year 1979–1980, 87.7 percent of these youngsters were enrolled (National Center for Education Statistics. *Digest of Education Statisticss, 1982 Edition.* p. 35).

Today's young people have better school attendance than their counterparts in years gone by. In school year 1869–1870, and average of 59.3 percent attended daily. By school year 1919–1920, this figure had jumped to 74.8 percent. More recently, in school year 1979–1980, 90.2 percent of the enrolled learner population attended every day (National Center for Education Statistics. *Digest of Education Statistics, 1982 Edition.* p. 35).

Changes in the nature of the population of learners have created new challenges for teachers. One implication of these changes is that teachers must work with a cross section of learners that mirrors much of the diversity of the entire society. Many youngsters may not share attitudes and values of their teachers. They may find inconsequential many things that teachers prize, and they may prize things that their teachers see as having little value. These differences in how the world is viewed can cause difficulties in teacher–learner relationships. They can be a basis for classroom management problems.

Concerns about classroom management or discipline rank high among issues bothering teachers. Numbers of surveys have revealed that worries about discipline and learners' attitudes characterize large numbers of teachers. The issue is a particular problem for secondary school teachers. But even among teachers who work with lower elementary school youngsters, classroom management and control problems rank high on lists of professional problem areas.

Educational leaders have not been unresponsive to challenges faced by teachers in dealing with the incredibly diverse learner population in the schools. Great strides have been made to ensure that teachers will work in areas for which they have been properly trained. Teachers' confidence is bolstered when they are assigned to teach material that they are prepared to teach. But for all the progress that has been made, work remains to be done in this area.

For example, a recent survey of beginning teachers revealed that substantial numbers were teaching in areas outside of their major areas of preparation. About 16 percent of elementary school and high school teachers in this group were assigned to teach courses outside of their primary areas of specialization. The situation proved to be somewhat worse at the middle school/ junior high school level, where nearly 19 percent of these teachers were so assigned (National Center for Education Statistics. *The Condition of Education, 1983 Edition*. p. 210).

Assignments of this kind result in part from the necessity to "find somebody" to cover the courses that must be taught. (For example, if there is only one certified physics teacher and six classes of physics to be taught, someone else will have to teach one class. This assumes each teacher teaches five classes each day. The teacher of the extra physics class may or may not be well grounded in the subject.) While administrative necessity explains many cases of assignments out of major areas of expertise, still many teachers feel that too many of these assignments are made. Efforts to reduce numbers of teachers assigned to teach in areas in which they are ill-prepared seem certain to continue.

In addition to the issue of the appropriate assignment of teachers, educational leaders in recent years have recognized the desirability of employing people to assist teachers in meeting the diverse needs of their learners. These nonsuperivsory personnel have been labeled variously as *paraprofessionals* or as *teachers' aides*. A recent survey revealed that over 116,000 such individuals were employed in the nation's schools (National Center for Education Statistics. *Digest of Education Statistics, 1982. Edition*. p. 53). The availability of this additional adult help has enabled many teachers to provide better learning experiences for their pupils and students.

At the same time, teachers have had to learn new management skills as they have sought to take advantage of the services of these nonsupervisory people. Extra planning time has been required. But most teachers have adjusted well to this situation. They appreciate the flexibility they enjoy in planning and operating their instructional program that becomes possible with the availability of additonal help. Clearly, the preponderance of evidence suggests that numbers of nonsupervisory instructional support people in the schools will increase if money becomes available to fund these positions.

Teachers' Nonteaching Duties: Selected Aspects

Extracurricular Work. Teachers continue to be heavily involved in extracurricular work with students. (Sometimes the term *cocurricular* is used these days to suggest that such activities really support the entire school program and are not something "extra" added on.) Extracurricular work can involve teachers in supervising clubs, working bleachers to ensure order at assemblies and athletic contests, overseeing the loading of school buses, and taking tickets at school functions of various kinds.

In recent years, there has been a trend toward rewarding teachers monetarily for their work in many of these areas. Particularly, work associated with athletic contests and supervising youngsters when school buses are loaded have tended to become "paid activities" in many districts. There is a trend, too, toward paying teachers for work with large student organizations. Many teachers, for example, receive an extra stipend for serving as the advisor to the student council.

In general, extra remuneration for work in the extracurricular area tends to be more prevalent at the secondary-school level than at the elementary-school level. Organizations for students are more numerous at that level, and teachers' organizations first began pressing for additional financial rewards for this kind of work at the secondary-school level. Even where extra remuneration is available, the amounts tend to be insignificant in terms of the time that teachers spend working with pupils and students in extracurricular activities. Few take on such responsibilities out of any hope of financial reward. Rather, they look on their involvement as a way of understanding their youngsters better as individuals. Many who have worked with student clubs and organizations for years with no thought even of asking for remuneration feel that the insights they have gained into their young people have provided a more-than-adequate reward.

Curriculum Work. It comes as a surprise to some new teachers that they will be spending a good deal of their time planning curricula in addition to teaching. After a spate of interest in the 1960s in the idea that curricula are best designed by a few "experts" at national curriculum centers, in recent years there has been a renewed interest in curriculum development at the local level. This trend has been supported by two arguments. On the one hand, it is alleged that local people have better knowledge of the characteristics of local youngsters than do individuals, no matter how talented in the finer points of curriculum design, who live elsewhere. Second, it is alleged that teachers do a more effective job of teaching curriculum materials that they have participated in developing.

Nearly every district has one or more curriculum committees at work revising old curricula or developing new curricula in several subject areas. These teachers typically work closely with central district office personnel who may have special training in curriculum development. Frequently, too, consultants from other districts and from college and university curriculum centers are brought in to help in the development process. Work on curriculum committees gives teachers an opportunity to interact with other trained professionals. In addition to providing an opportunity to sharpen curriculum development skills, the experience can provide an important psychological link to the entire profession of education. It takes the teacher out of the classroom and helps him or her develop a richer sense of community with the millions of other professionals working for a more effective educational program in the schools.

Faculty Meetings. Faculty meetings are a feature of teachers' lives in nearly all schools. The quality of these meetings varies tremendously, but from an unscientific count of teachers' comments taken in teachers' lounges in schools across the country, the authors have concluded that many teachers occasionally have negative feelings about faculty meetings.

One problem is that the meetings frequently are held after school. At this time of day, teachers have already "fought the good fight." They are tired from hours of interactions with youngsters and anxious either to get home or to get busy on some paper correcting or planning tasks. The typical faculty mood at four o'clock in the afternoon would challenge even the most talented motivation expert. Yet the meetings do serve important purposes. They build a sense of community among the faculty, and they provide an opportunity for faculty members to provide input that can have implications for the school curriculum. They also afford an opportunity for an exchange of views among teachers, counselors, administrators, and others with responsibility for the overall school program.

There is little evidence that there will be any significant changes in this regard in the immediate future. And though teachers sometimes grumble about attending meetings when they are tired after a long day in the classroom, probably most, if pressed, would oppose a move to eliminate faculty meetings entirely. They do perform an important function.

Teacher Supply and Demand

Two factors influence the demand for teachers' services. One of these is the size of the learner population to be served. If the supply of teachers goes down or stays the same and the size of the learner population goes up, the demand for teachers increases. Conversely, if the supply of teachers stays the same or goes down only slightly and there is a large decrease in the size of the learner population, the demand for teachers' services decreases.

As suggested by the discussion in the previous paragraph, demand for teachers' services does not depend only on the size of the learner population. It depends also on the number of teachers available. Assuming that the population of learners stays about the same, when the supply of teachers decreases, there is an increased demand for their services. Similarly, when the supply of teachers increases, the demand for their services decreases.

The difficulty in analyzing what has happened to the demand for teachers' services in recent years is that, unlike the situations described in our hypothetical examples above, neither the size of the learner population nor the supply of teachers stays constant. Both tend to change simultaneously. Therefore, in looking at the outlook for teacher employment, we need to consider trends related to the size of the learner population and trends related to the total numbers of teachers available for hire. In the sections that follow, we will look at each of these issues separately. We will then examine prospects for teacher employment over the next several years.

Size of the Learner Population

Wide use of the birth control pill, beginning in the late 1950s, has had tremendous consequences for the schools. The pill provided families with an easy, virtually certain mechanism for limiting numbers of children. Many families did elect to limit the number of children, and the number of youngsters entering the schools began to drop. The reduction was felt at the elementary-school level. There was a delayed effect at the secondary-school level because large elementary classes had to progress year by year through the elementary program and into the secondary schools before any of the smaller elementary-school groups arrived in the junior and senior high schools. By this time, enrollments have begun to drop throughout the secondary-school level as well as in the elementary schools. These figures reveal a trend of a gradual decrease in overall enrollment levels in American schools:

	1970	1978	1981
Total Enrollment	45,909,088	42,611,000	40,168,373
Elementary* Enrollment	32,577,326	28,455,000	27,289,119
Secondary* Enrollment	13,331,762	14,156,000	12,879,254

*Elementary includes learners in grades K–8, and secondary includes learners in grades 9–12.

Data are adapted from National Center for Education Statistics. *The Condition of Education, 1980 Edition.* Washington, D.C.: United States Government Printing Office, 1980, p. 58, and from National Center for Education Statistics. *The Condition of Education, 1983 Edition.* Washington, D.C.: United States Government Printing Office, 1983, p. 14.

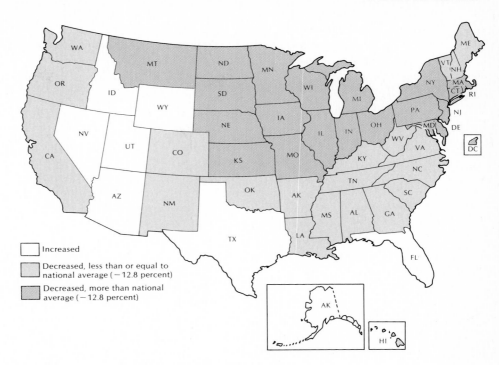

FIGURE 8-1.

Percent change in public elementary/secondary school enrollment between 1971 and 1981, by state. Public elementary/secondary school enrollment dropped from 46.1 million to about 40.2 million by fall of 1981, a decrease of nearly 13 percent. The Mid-Atlantic and North Central States experienced the sharpest declines.

From the National Center for Education Statistics, *The Condition of Education,* 1983 Edition. Washington, D.C.: United States Government Printing Office, 1983, p. 15.

One result of the decline in numbers of learners has been the elimination of overcrowded schools in many areas of the country. Indeed, in some places, schools have closed because of dramatic declines in enrollment levels. There are dramatic place-to-place differences in school enrollments. Some of these can be observed in Figure 8–1. For example, though there is an overall pattern of enrollment decline, certain fast-growing sunbelt areas are experiencing dramatic increases in school enrollments.

For people thinking about careers in education, there may be an initial tendency to find information about declining overall school enrollments depressing. But enrollment decline by itself does not necessarily suggest that demands for teachers will not be good in the years ahead. Demand for teachers, though connected in part to the number of learners in the schools, also relates to the numbers of individuals seeking to become teachers. We will look at some information related to this issue in the next section.

Trends in Teacher Supply

There is evidence that undergraduates in colleges and universities follow quite closely the available information about changes in public school enrollments. There is evidence, too, that they tend to assume that when enrollments go down, demands for teacher services will decrease. For example, until 1973 enrollments in teacher preparation programs tended to increase each year, in keeping with growing public school enrollments. Since 1973 there has been a dramatic decline in the number of individuals in such programs. This decline has been of such a magnitude that it seems clear that teacher shortage, not teacher surplus will be an important issue throughout much of the middle to late 1980s. Some authorities believe that prospects for teacher employment may be brighter during this period than they have been for years. Box 8-6 illustrates the emerging picture of teacher shortage.

Box 8-6
Some Trends in Numbers of New Teacher Graduates and Demands for Services of New Teacher Graduates

Fall of Year	Estimated Supply	Estimated Demand	Supply as Percent of Demand
1982	139,000	108,000	128.7
1983	138,000	146,000	94.5
1984	138,000	142,000	97.2
1985	135,000	175,000	77.1
1986	156,000	187,000	83.4
1987	177,000	192,000	92.2

*Projections are from National Center for Education Statistics. *The Condition of Education 1983 Edition.* Washington, D.C.: United States Government Printing Office, 1983. p. 182.

LET'S PONDER

1. In which of the above years was there an indication of the greatest oversupply of teachers?
2. In which of the above years was there an indication of the greatest undersupply of teachers?
3. Based on the trend you see here, would you estimate that there will be a higher or lower demand for teachers in the late 1980s and early 1990s than is projected to be the case in 1987? Why do you think so?
4. What general conditions tend to produce an oversupply of teachers? An undersupply?

Employment Patterns and Teaching Specialty

Some kinds of teachers are more in demand than others. The "high demand areas" tend to vary somewhat depending on a number of conditions. For example, at the secondary-school level, industrial arts teachers are in especially high demand when the national economy is booming and many other employers are seeking their services. They tend to be more available to work in schools in times of national economic recession.

Relative demand for some specializations tends to remain fairly constant. For example, generally the demand is good for mathematics and physical sciences (chemistry and physics) teachers at the secondary level whereas the demand for social studies instructors is not so high. Elementary teachers with strong preparation in mathematics and reading tend to be generally harder to find than those with certain other areas of emphasis. Table 8-1 indicates some recent information about the percentages of new teachers in various fields who were hired to teach either full time or part time.

Table 8-1. Percentages of May, 1981 Teacher Education Graduates in Selected Fields Who Applied to Teach and Who Were Either (1) Hired Full Time, (2) Hired Part Time, or (3) Not Hired	Field	Percentage Hired To Teach Full Time	Percentage Hired to Teach Part Time	Percentage Not Hired to Teach
	General Elementary	67	12	21
	Special Education	80	5	15
	Secondary Social Studies	65	11	24
	Secondary Mathematics	74	7	19

Derived from information from National Center for Education Statistics. *The Condition of Education, 1983 Edition.* Washington, D.C.: United States Government Printing Office, 1983, p. 190.

Given projections for increasing teacher shortages in the middle and late 1980s, it may be that higher percentages of applicants will be offered positions in the years ahead. (For information about the shortages, refer back to Box 8-6.)

Recapitulation of Major Ideas

1. Historically teachers have come from rural or working-class families. Today large numbers still come from these kinds of families, but increasing numbers come from families of higher economic status.
2. There have been interesting variations in the percentages of males and

females employed in education at different times in our history. Until quite recently, only small numbers of males worked in elementary schools. Today, there is a trend for elementary schools to hire more male teachers and for secondary schools to hire more female teachers.

3. Early in this century, certification requirements and educational requirements for teachers were ill defined. Many lacked any formal training. Today, virtually all teachers hold at least a bachelor's degree.

4. An overwhelming percentage of teachers are white. Black teachers represent a smaller fraction of the population of teachers than blacks represent of the population as a whole.

5. Teachers today tend to be older and to have had more classroom teaching experience than their counterparts from the earlier part of this century.

6. There has been a trend for class sizes to go down over time. Secondary school classes are slightly smaller than elementary school classes, but size differences between classes at the two levels are not nearly so dramatic as they once were.

7. In most districts, teachers work with students for about 180 days each year. Many also work a few additional days on such activities as workshops, curriculum development, and other school-related tasks when learners are not present.

8. Enrollments have been dropping over the past few years. At first, this drop was felt at the elementary level. By this time, it has been felt throughout the entire K–12 system.

9. Enrollments in teacher preparation programs have tended to go down faster than enrollments in schools have fallen. This situation suggests that the middle to late 1980s may be a time of national teacher shortage.

Posttest

DIRECTIONS: Using your own paper, answer each of the following true/false questions. For each correct statement, write the word *true* on your paper. For each incorrect statement, write the word *false* on your paper.

1. The ratio of women to men in the teaching profession has stayed the same for the past 90 years.

2. Traditionally, large numbers of teachers have had parents who were blue collar workers.

3. Today a male teacher is more likely than a female teacher to have had a parent who was an upper-class or upper-middle-class professional person.

4. Both elementary- and secondary-school teachers identify discipline as one of the most important problems with which they must deal.

5. Today, the vast majority of elementary- and secondary-school teachers hold at least a bachelor's degree.
6. There tends to be more demand for teachers in some teaching fields than in others.
7. Evidence suggest that throughout much of the middle and late 1980s, the supply of new teachers will be less than the demand for new teachers.
8. In general, today's learners spend fewer days in school each year than learners did in 1900.
9. The percentage of teachers who are black is about the same as the percentage of the total population that is black.
10. Teachers rarely are asked to participate in curriculum development activities.

Summary

Historically teachers have tended to be drawn from families of blue collar workers and farmers. In recent years, however, there has been an increasing trend for teachers to be drawn from families representing a broader economic spectrum.

The extent of teachers' formal preparation for their responsibilities has improved dramatically in this century. Before 1920, large numbers of teachers had almost no formal training. Today, nearly every teacher has at least a bachelor's degree and has received extensive preservice professional training in education.

Schools enroll a higher percentage of the total population of five- to seventeen-year-olds than in earlier times. Furthermore, there is evidence that the percentage of enrolled learners attending daily is higher than in earlier times. Finally, the school year has grown progressively longer throughout this century, presently averaging about 180 days per year. All of these things suggest that teachers today have contact with learners for longer periods each year than they did in the past.

Evidence suggests that numbers of individuals entering teacher preparation programs have declined even more rapidly than public school enrollments have declined. As a result, it is anticipated that teachers will be in relatively short supply throughout much of the middle to late 1980s.

References

GOOD, THOMAS L., BIDDLE, BRUCE J., AND BROPHY, JERE E. *Teachers Make A Difference.* New York: Holt, Rinehart and Winston, 1975.
HODGKINSON, HAROLD L. "What's Still Right With Education?" *Phi Delta Kappan* (Dec., 1982): 231–235.

NATIONAL CENTER FOR EDUCATION STATISTICS. *The Condition of Education, 1980 Edition.* Washington, D.C.: United States Government Printing Office, 1980.

NATIONAL CENTER FOR EDUCATION STATISTICS. *The Condition of Education, 1983 Edition.* Washington, D.C.: United States Government Printing Office, 1983.

NATIONAL CENTER FOR EDUCATION STATISTICS. *The Conditon of Education, 1983 Edition.* Washington, D.C.: United States Government Printing Office, 1977.

NATIONAL CENTER FOR EDUCATION STATISTICS. *Digest of Education Statistics, 1982 Edition.* Washington, D.C.: United States Government Printing Office, 1982.

NATIONAL CENTER FOR EDUCATION STATISTICS. *Projections of Education Statistics to 1986–1987.* Washington, D.C.: United States Government Printing Office, 1978.

RODGERS, FREDERICH A. "Past and Future of Teaching: You've Come A Long Way." *Educational Leadership* (Jan., 1976): 282–286.

9
The Teacher's Philosophy

Objectives

This chapter will help the reader to

1. Identify the basic elements of any philosophy of education.
2. Clarify his or her personal philosophy of education.
3. Identify the main differences between several philosophical systems.
4. Identify specific educational practices that are based on different philosophical positions.

Pretest

DIRECTIONS: Using your own paper, answer each of the following true/false questions. For each correct statement write the word *true* on your paper. For each incorrect statement write the word *false* on your paper.

1. Philosophy is a nice intellectual exercise but has little to do with the "real world."
2. There is one philosophy of education upon which nearly all educators agree.
3. Metaphysics is the study of the nature of reality.
4. Epistemology is the study of the nature of knowledge.
5. Axiology is the study of the nature of values.
6. The perennialist believes that there is a core of knowledge that should be learned by all.
7. Perennialism takes the position that knowledge is constantly changing.
8. Progressivism views human nature as basically good.
9. The main focus in progressivism is on subject matter.
10. Essentialism is basically inconsistent with American culture.
11. Essentialism sees the arts and the humanities as the most important subjects in the curriculum.
12. Reconstructionists believe that time-honored truths from the past need to be reconstructed and taught to learners.
13. Reconstructionism takes a scientific view of nature and values.
14. Existentialists believe that every learner should take exactly the same program in school.

Introduction

The school board meeting had begun quietly enough. Reports on building maintenance had been received. A few contracts for minor repairs had been approved. The superintendent had been authorized to begin a search for a new personnel director. But then something happened that transformed a placid . . . some might say a boring . . . meeting into an emotional firestorm.

It all started when the associate superintendent for curriculum made a report on the scores of youngsters in the district on a battery of recently administered standardized tests. The scores were not as high as in previous years. This revelation prompted some heated discussion among various board members, but the debate really became highly charged only when the board decided to invite comment from members of the public who were in attendance.

The first speaker identified himself as a member of the taxpayers' league. He noted that the decline in scores represented "yet another instance" of public monies being used for unproductive purposes. The teachers, he pointed out, simply were "not getting the job done." "My people," he went on to say, "want to be darn sure somebody is watching the store. Who is it that is responsible for seeing that teachers teach what they're supposed to teach? Is that person really holding these teachers to account? Certainly these dismal test results suggest otherwise."

These remarks were accompanied by a good many approving nods of the head of certain others in the audience. One of these individuals jumped quickly to his feet when the first speaker had concluded. Picking up on the same general theme, he pointed out that when he was in school, youngsters had certain facts they had to memorize "or else." "It is obvious," he noted, "that young people are naturally lazy and won't work unless they are expected to do so. We need to quit coddling these kids. If we have to, we should get out that paddle, get these kids into some good textbooks, and not let up on them until they *know* this important material." He concluded by pointing out that the curriculum had become "softened" by the introduction of too many electives and that youngsters were being denied that "important discipline" of exposure to subjects that they initially might not find either interesting or easy. Many in the audience applauded these remarks . . . but not everybody.

Shaking her head in disagreement, a woman in the front row stood and was recognized. She began by identifying herself with the idea that "something is not right with the schools" that had prompted the comments of the earlier speakers. But her identification of what was "wrong" and her prescription for change were much different. "The real problem is not with *how* things are taught but with *what* things are taught," she pointed out. "There are too many courses of a vocational nature. We are too much concerned with train-ing students for jobs. What we need is more emphasis on the classics. What-ever happened to the humanities? We want people who can *think*, not people who only know how to change an oil filter. Ten years from now cars might not even have oil filters, but ten years from now these youngsters will have to think. Let's go back to the classics. Let's help our young people learn to rea-son regardless of what future occupation they follow." These remarks drew some scattered applause and an isolated "Amen!" or two, but a larger num-ber of comments such as "impractical," "ivory tower stuff" and "irrelevant" were heard.

Next a man on the right-hand side of the room stood up and shocked the crowd into an attentive silence with the observation that "Test scores are meaningless and people should stop worrying about such trivial matters." "Tests," he pointed out, "do nothing but ask kids to regurgitate isolated facts. Who in this room can name the capitals of every state? Does anyone here feel seriously handicapped if he or she can't do it? Then why should we get upset about scores on tests that involve questions about matters that are equally unimportant." The speaker went on to suggest that because of rapid change, most textbook knowledge was obsolete. "What the schools need to do," he asserted, "is to help youngsters accommodate to change. They need to learn that what we have today is not what we will have tomorrow. They need to learn how to shape our tomorrows. And the way to do that is *not* to have schools cram in outdated facts and subject the children to critical evaluations based on how they do on questions about those facts."

These comments elicited cheers from some in the audience. Others stood up and started shouting counterarguments. Individual board members looked very uncomfortable. Finally, the chairman seized his heavy gavel and began beating a furious tattoo on the lectern. The superintendent looked tired and defeated. How, he wondered to himself, could anyone administer a school district when there were so many different opinions regarding what should be done?

How relevant is this scene from the board meeting for the prospective teacher? *Very* relevant. Teachers must make decisions about the content to be taught. Deciding what is to be taught requires teachers to respond to an important philosophical question: What knowledge is worth knowing?

Second, teachers, by definition, work with learners. How individual teachers interact with learners depends on their general philosophical position regarding the nature of human beings. Are they basically "good" or basically "evil"? Clearly those teachers who see people as basically good tend to work with their learners in ways dramatically different from those who see people as basically bad.

A third variable that teachers must deal with is their individual understanding of what is "moral" or "right" conduct. Teachers differ in terms of how to determine moral behavior. Some make the determination through intuition. Others rely on situational variables. Still others use some objective measures.

Still another variable distinguishing individual teachers is their view of what constitutes "correct thinking" on philosophical questions regarding rules of inference and consistency. For example, how are conclusions to be defended? Is intuition enough? Or must there be some reliance on evidence? If so, what kinds of evidence are appropriate, and how must they be organized?

Clearly, teachers must be aware that different individuals (themselves included) perceive the nature of the world and of knowledge in many ways. An understanding of different perspectives helps teachers to maintain open lines of communication with others. Frequently, when teachers and other educators have not taken into account that others may be seeing the world

Box 9-1
Purposes of Schooling and Teachers' Attitudes

Speaker A: "Schools should emulate a factory or a business model. Specific information must be identified that learners must acquire. Teachers must be held responsible for teaching that content. Schools and teachers should be rated in terms of the degree to which this content is mastered by students and the cost-effectiveness of the procedures used to transmit it to learners."

Speaker B: "Schools should prepare learners to move immediately into the world of work. They should be able to make change, to keep accurate records, and to perform basic skills associated with the occupations of their choice. Businesses should not have to do the schools' work for them. These youngsters should be prepared and ready to go to work beginning with their first day on the job."

Speaker C: "Schools should teach youngsters mathematics, sciences, literature, history, and foreign languages. Most other subjects should be eliminated. Furthermore, most electives should be eliminated. Because our society changes so rapidly, it is essential that the essential 'truths' of these traditional disciplines be mastered. Armed with the kinds of thinking abilities that come from mastery of this content, youngsters will have something to 'hang on to' as they adapt to change."

Speaker D: "Our society is full of injustices. Schools should be dedicated to teaching youngsters to transform society to make it more sensitive to individual needs. Courses should prepare youngsters to be political activists who are eager and willing to challenge existing political, economic, and social practices."

LET'S PONDER

Read the statements by each of the speakers. Then, respond to these questions.

1. What basic differences do you note among positions of these speakers?
2. If you were a school board member, how would you respond to concerns of each speaker in an open meeting? How would you accommodate differences without hopelessly offending one or more of them?
3. Which one of these speakers has a position closest to your own? Most distant from your own?
4. What is your own view about the "proper" function of the schools?

differently from themselves, they have run into unexpected opposition when changes in the school program have been proposed. An appreciation of these differences and a sensitivity to them can make life much more comfortable for teachers when communicating with others. Certainly a basic understanding of various philosophical positions does not guarantee a solution to problems, but it does lead to an understanding of the sources of difference that can facilitate cooperation and compromise.

Everything teachers do in schools goes forward supported by a given set of assumptions. Often these assumptions have been little noticed. But today, given increasing public interest in the substance of what is being taught in the schools, certain groups of people are challenging some traditional school practices. These challenges also represent an attack on the assumptions upon which these practices were based. Teachers need as never before to recognize not only the assumptions underpinning their own practices, but also those supporting the positions advocated by school patrons demanding change.

In short, teachers need to be prepared to defend what they are doing. They need a philosophical base from which to operate, and they need some grasp of the philosophical foundations on which their critics are building their arguments. As a beginning, prospective teachers might review some of the categories of questions that must be answered as they begin working out their own philosophies of education. These categories are introduced in the sections that follow.

Metaphysics (or Ontology)

Metaphysics is concerned with the nature of reality. Questions in this category cannot be answered by application of the scientific method. These questions tend to be speculative and focus on such issues as the nature of cause-and-effect relationships. For example, do cause and effect exist in reality, or are they simply a creation of our mind? Is there a purpose to the universe, or is life basically meaningless? Are humans essentially spiritual beings, or are they creatures that exist in a particular time and space with no meaning beyond self? Is there a set of constant and unchanging principles that guides the operation of things and that therefore can be discovered? Is reality a constantly changing thing that is always relative, therefore making a search for truth fruitless?

All of these questions are metaphysical. Obviously we cannot conduct experiments to test our answers against scientific evidence. To some people, these questions may seem very abstract and hopelessly remote from the everyday world of the schoolteacher. But such is not the case. Consider, for example, that in recent years some people have argued that the primary purpose of education is to help youngsters achieve "happiness." This implies that "happiness" has been identified as an answer to a metaphysical question about what the central purpose of life ought to be. Given this orientation, some critics of more traditional school practices have suggested that there is no subject matter worth knowing that is not of clear and pressing interest to the individual youngster. Therefore, some have suggested that the schools should permit youngsters to determine what they will study and that above all, the schools should provide for learners' freedom and individual choice.

Those advocating such practices have made a number of philosophical assumptions about reality. They reject the idea that there is a limited number of known principles that explain reality and that should be mastered by all youngsters. Furthermore, they perceive human beings to be essentially good and trustworthy. Basic to this position is an assumption that if only individuals are given freedom, then they will intuitively do what is "good."

Another group of parents and citizens whom teachers frequently encounter is convinced that there are certain unchanging principles that should be taught to learners. These people tend to believe that individual experience is an unreliable guide to "proper" action. They generally reject the idea that people intuitively choose what is "best." In their view, teachers must exert control to ensure that youngsters will do the "right" thing. This position, too, derives from a metaphysical stance about the nature of human beings.

Indeed, many divisive issues in education *are* devisive because people have arrived at different answers to basic metaphysical questions. Teachers who are familiar with the nature of metaphysical questions—and more particularly with the reality that answers to such questions cannot be tested for their "truth" against scientific evidence—are better prepared to understand the assumptions that undergird views about school practices and procedures that may differ from their own. Teachers with these insights know when an argument is based on metaphysics (and cannot, therefore, be proved with evidence) and when an argument is not based on metaphysics (and can be challenged with evidence). Some knowledge about the nature of metaphysical questions, then, prepares teachers to discern arguable issues from positions that rest on personal, perceptually based conclusions about the nature of "reality" that cannot be challenged by appeals to logic.

Epistemology

A second major category of philosophical questions is epistemological questions. Epistemology is concerned with the nature of knowledge. Since educators are concerned about the discovery and transmission of knowledge, teachers have an especial interest in this category. One of the basic epistemological issues is the question of whether certain knowledge about "reality" is possible. Some maintain that there is no possibility of obtaining knowledge about ultimate reality. Others counter that it is possible to identify a set of principles that represent "true knowledge." Still others argue that there are no principles that are "true" in all sets of conditions, but that there is knowledge that is "true" in certain situations. Stated in another way, what these people contend is that knowledge functions in a particular situation, and all that we can know is what is "functional."

Another basic epistemological question centers on what might be described as ways of knowing and the reliability of methods of knowing. Basically the issue is one of whether knowledge comes from revelation, from authority, from intuition, from the senses, or from reason or experimentation. Today many people have a bias supporting the position that knowledge comes from scientific experimentation. Indeed, among many people this idea is so generally accepted that few individuals challenge it at all. But in some instances, many of us who generally accept that knowledge comes from scientific experimentation take actions actions based on intuition. We just "feel" that a certain action is "right."

Those who have religious convictions frequently include revelation as a source of knowledge. They act on the basis of knowledge that has been "revealed" to certain individuals by a supreme being. In this country, the tradition of separation of church and state—in part, at least—seems to have been supported by a rejection of the idea that revelation represents a generally acceptable and reliable source of knowledge, though even today there are some who reject this view. Consider, for example, the pressures that some religious groups have brought on the schools to introduce the view of creation as revealed in the Book of Genesis as an alternative to Darwinian natural selection.

Many other cultures in the world place a much lower premium on knowing through scientific experimentation than does our own. Because of differences in perception regarding how knowledge is best acquired, we frequently have difficulty in understanding the perspectives of people living in these unfamiliar cultural settings. In working with learners, it is particularly important for teachers to understand how other cultures presume that knowledge is best acquired. Without such understanding, the practices of other peoples may seem strange or even funny to youngsters who learn about them for the first time. Teachers have an obligation to open learners' eyes to the reality that we bring some "cultural blinders" of our own along when we look at other people. Though we are committed to the view that knowledge comes best from scientific evidence, there is nothing necessarily "correct" about this position in any absolute sense. It is simply a reflection of how we see the world at this time.

Teachers' approaches to teaching content to learners says a good deal about their own answers to basic epistemological questions. For example, a teacher who insists that learners master specific facts and principles that others have discovered operates on the assumption that there is such a thing as true knowledge. Other teachers, who are more interested in teaching the processes of problem solving, imply that there is no ultimate "truth" and that it makes better sense for youngsters to learn some skills that will be useful to them in arriving at answers that are situation-specific.

Some subjects in the curriculum tend to include instructional practices that derive from alternative conclusions regarding the source of knowledge. For example, instruction in the humanities is frequently premised on the assumption that knowledge results at least as much from intuition, feeling, and reason as from scientific experimentation. Critics who do not understand the appropriateness of an approach to truth through any process but scientific experimentation have sometimes labeled the humanities "soft" subjects. That is, they are "soft" compared with the "hard" sciences, with their heavier reliance on scientific experimentation.

The labels *hard* and *soft* have nothing to do with the difficulty of the subjects. Rather, they relate to the sources of knowledge deemed appropriate within each discipline. Debates over the worthiness of "soft" subjects and "hard" subjects have important curricular implications. For example, if a decision is made that only knowledge that is scientifically verifiable is important, then there will be a much heavier emphasis on the sciences than on the humanities. On the other hand, if other sources of knowledge are considered important,, humanities-oriented courses, will very likely receive a good deal of emphasis.

(© 1983 Joel W. Pett in the Phi Delta Kappan. World Rights Reserved.)

Axiology

Should teachers stress the acquisition of knowledge or the moral and character development of their learners? Is there a standard of moral behavior that teachers should emphasize? These questions relating to the nature of values and ethics are axiological questions.

One important emphasis within axiology is the issue of whether life is worth living. What is the nature of existence? Does life have any meaning? Answers to these questions, particularly as they are formulated by learners, are of great interest to teachers. For example, the rising rate of suicide among young people in our society leads to a conclusion that many people have concluded that life has no meaning (or at least not one worth living for).

Drug problems in schools can be related to the issue of the value and worth of life. Many who use drugs are convinced that the highest good amounts to seeking immediate pleasure and living for the moment. In traditional philosophy, such attitudes are collectively referred to as *hedonism*. Though many youngsters in schools would be unable to define *hedonism*, they are acting in ways to convey to us that hedonism represents their basic philosophy of life. If, indeed, the intense pleasure of the moment is perceived as the highest good, then a temporary narcotics high makes sound logical sense. Such logic actuates the behavior of large numbers of youngsters in our schools.

Of course, hedonism is not the only perspective flowing from a consideration of axiological questions. Some, for example, take the optimistic view that life is absolutely worth living over the long run and that the highest good is something other than short-run pleasure. Some people with this orientation see the highest good as self-realization or self-perfection. Many star athletes in our schools have this orientation. Social reformers of all kinds who believe in the perfectability of the human condition also tend to reflect this general position.

Others find life's purpose through religion. They accept the view that there is a divine purpose to life and that every human being has a divine reason for being. They see the highest good being served in the effort to understand God's will and to strive to meet God's expectations.

An important axiological question of a slightly different kind centers on the nature of "right conduct." How should a person behave? What is moral behavior? How does a person know when he or she is doing the "right" thing? In answering these questions, some argue that there are certain universal principles or laws that provide guidelines for behavior. For example, some point to the Ten Commandments as an example of such universal guides to appropriate behavior. Others reject the idea that there are guidelines that fit every set of circumstances. They contend that morality of behavior is situation-specific. For example, some argue that American combat against Hitler was moral but that American combat in Vietnam was not.

Teachers find themselves continuously faced with helping youngsters make value choices. Furthermore, they must make many value judgments themselves as they are asked to determine the appropriateness of learners' behavior, to evaluate programs, and to engage in dozens of other tasks requiring a moral commitment. Given the extent of these kinds of responsibilities, it makes good sense for teachers to have some familiarity with axiology.

Logic

One of the most frequently cited goals of education is to teach youngsters to think logically. The science of exact thought is a subfield of philosophy known as *logic*. Logic deals with the relationships between ideas and with the procedures used in differentiating between valid thinking and fallacious thinking.

There are several reasons that a knowledge of logic is important for teachers. First, logic helps teachers communicate more effectively by helping them arrange thoughts clearly. Second, logic helps teachers to evaluate the consistency of learners' reasoning. Third, logic helps teachers assess the factual adequacy and reliability of the new knowledge they encounter.

There are two general types of logic. The one most familiar to most people is deductive logic. Deductive logic begins with a general conclusion and then elucidates that conclusion with reference to particulars. Inductive logic, on the other hand, begins with particulars. Reasoning, then, is designed to help people arrive at a general explanatory principle.

The choice of a deductive approach or an inductive approach has implications for how teachers organize and present materials. When a deductive approach is selected, great care must be taken to ensure that learners will acquire a solid grasp of the major principle or idea before the teacher moves on to illuminate this idea or principle through the introduction of examples. Inductive approaches, on the other hand, demand that a tremendous number of examples be found. Furthermore, the teacher must make sure that these examples accurately represent the larger principle that, it is hoped, the learners will grasp. Typically it takes longer for a given body of content to be taught inductively than deductively (because the learners must work hard to grasp the essentials of the principle that explains the examples with which they have worked.) Consequently, time decisions must be made about whether inductive or deductive logic is to be followed.

In recent years, there has been a good deal of discussion about which is more effective, inductive teaching or deductive teaching. Research on this issue suggests that neither approach is demonstrably superior to the other. A much more important issue is how teachers take learners through the lesson, regardless of whether it is organized inductively or deductively. Clever teachers who help youngsters to grasp relationships among ideas and to sort out valid and logical arguments from invalid and illogical arguments find that their learners do well regardless of whether an inductive or a deductive sequence is followed.

Philosophies of Education

A personal philosophy emerges out of responses to questions rooted in metaphysics, epistemology, exiology, and even logic. The final "mix" of responses of any teacher has a great deal to do with how he or she reacts to his or her responsibilities in the classroom. As important as these categories of concern, which have occupied philosophers for centuries, are the number of philosophies of education that have emerged. These philosophies represent clusters of ideas. Each tends to attract individuals who have answered many of the basic metaphysical, epistemologic, axiological, and logical questions in similar ways. Individual teachers' philosophies tend generally to identify with one of these broad general philosophy-of-education categories. A number of these are introduced in the subsections that follow.

Perennialism

Perennialism views truth as unchanging or "perennial." In the view of the perennialists, education should focus on the search for and the dissemination of these unchanging principles. Though they grant that changing times bring some surface-level alterations in the problems people face, they feel that the real substance remains basically unchanged over generations. Furthermore, the experience of human beings through the centuries has revealed those truths that are worth knowing.

Box 9-2
Reactions to Basic Philosophical Issues

LET'S PONDER

A number of categories that long have concerned philosophers have been introduced in this chapter. As you begin working toward a personal philosophy of education, you will need to respond to some very basic questions. How do you feel about each of the issues raised in the following questions;

1. Do you believe there are constants in life, or is life always changing? What do you see as the essential nature of human beings? What do you see as the basic meaning of life?
2. How do you think knowledge is acquired? Do you believe everything should be verified by evidence? What is your subject specialization? Does that in any way influence your view of the nature of knowledge?
3. Do you believe that there are universal moral values? What do you see as the worth of living? What criteria should be used in judging right from wrong?
4. How do your answers in the three areas above relate to one another? Are your answers consistent? If not, why not?

The schools, suggest the perennialists, should bring learners to know these truths. Whether the learners see as "relevant" the academic content necessary to reveal these truths is an unimportant consideration. The schools should not pander to what youngsters believe to be important. The schools are charged with preparing young people for life. When they have mastered the truths discovered through the centuries, they will come as adults to appreciate the content that, as learners in the school, they might not see as relevant at all.

School curricula should be the same for all youngsters. Critically important are those subjects that most clearly reveal long-standing truths about the human condition. Perennialists are particularly attracted to courses in the humanities and in literature, which are thought to be especially useful in illuminating critically important insights.

Learners are expected to ingest the content presented to them by teachers and ask few questions. Teachers are perceived to be bearers of the wisdom of the centuries. Consequently they cannot be reduced to a position of engaging in debates with youngsters who have yet to master the basic truths. Because there is much to be learned, youngsters must work very hard in the perennialist's view. Assignments should be rigorous. When necessary, the teacher should not shrink from disciplining youngsters as they are pushed to develop their intellectual powers.

Progressivism

Stemming from the work of figures such as John Dewey, progressivism approaches the work of the school from a perspective at some distance from that of perennialism. Progressivism views change as the essence of reality. Unlike perennialists, progressives do not believe that there is a knowable body of unchanged truth that has been developed through the centuries and that each learner must master. The schools, then, should not teach youngsters any set of unchanging principles but should prepare them to accommodate to changing conditions.

Progressivism views knowledge as a tentative explanation that may fit present reality well but that has no claim to being "true" forever. Life presents ever-changing conditions. It is the task of the educated person to develop solutions that fit situations as they arise. Knowledge, then, represents a tentative explanation of a present problem, and it must have some practical significance.

Progressives view human beings as basically "good." Therefore, if people are allowed freedom, generally they will choose the best course of action. This idea suggests that some considerable choice be given to youngsters in the schools. It is assumed that options will be selected that will turn out well for them.

Progressives view teachers as advisers or guides who help youngsters make sense of problems they face in a changing environment. There is a heavy emphasis on developing youngsters' problem-solving skills. Many progressives feel that inductive approaches are particularly well suited to meeting this objective because inductive teaching does not provide learners with a general explanation but requires them to develop an explanation of their own that will explain some phenomena to which they are exposed.

It is basic to progressivism that an individual in all likelihood will learn what relates to his or her interest better than something in which he or she has no interest. Furthermore, it is assumed that youngsters will be more motivated to learn information that holds a promise of helping them solve porblems that they regard as personally important. Consequently, many progressives place a high premiun on attempting to identify content that youngsters regard as relevant.

With regard to this latter issue, we need to pause to point out that some adherents of the progressive philosophy have carried the issue of "relevance" far beyond what John Dewey and other early progressives advocated. Dewey, for example, believed that a learner should not be allowed to study simply the content that he or she found personally interesting. He saw a need for the teacher to control the learning environment so that meaningful growth would take place. Dewey believed that subject matter can be organized in ways that take advantage of youngsters' interests. When teachers take the time to do this, Dewey believed, then the learners' problem-solving abilities are much improved. In summary, Dewey did not object to having youngsters learn unfamiliar content, but he did suggest that the content be organized to take advantage of youngsters' interests.

Some later progressives went far beyond Dewey's ideas to suggest that the entire school program should center on the interests (critics would say the "whims") of the learners. In classrooms characterized by extreme "learner-centeredness," the youngsters pursued activities of dubious significance. For example, a class might study Indians by building a paper teepee in the room and eating the food the Indians were supposed to have eaten. In many such programs, there was an assumption that "the experience is the thing." In too many classrooms, youngsters rarely applied the information they learned to developing serious problem-solving skills. Such practices tended to give critics ammunition to suggest that the entire progressive movement was anti-intellectual. Though Dewey and other leading American progressives most certainly had not supported the extreme "learner-centeredness" position, the entire progressive movement was tarred by critics' concerns about what was going on in some classrooms organized by proponents of "the experience is the thing." Consequently, there has been something of a tendency for educators in recent years not to identify themselves publicly as "progressives."

Essentialism

Essentialism began as an organized philosophical movement within education in the 1930s. A basically conservative movement, essentialism began as a reaction to some of the more extreme variants of progressivism. In some respects, it can be viewed as a swing back toward the position of the perennialists, but there are some important differences. Though essentialism as a formally organized philosophical positon is relatively recent, it follows a tradition of long-standing importance, even dominance, within American education.

Essentialism holds that there is a core of knowledge and skills that should be taught to all learners. This view begins to sound suspiciously like perennialism, but there is this important difference. Recall that the perennialists feel that there is a body of known general "truths" that youngsters should learn through exposure to the humanities and literature. Essentialists, on the other hand, hold that what all youngsters should be taught are those "essential" things that a mature adult needs to know to be a productive member of the society. These "essential" things may change from time to time. There is no emphasis on "truths" that are believed to be constant from generation to generation. Essentialism is practical and pragmatic.

Essentialism dwells on the practical aspects of life and feels that the school should "waste" little time on engaging youngsters in reflective speculation. Schools should teach youngsters factual information, which they are to learn and retain. Serious knowledge is perceived as residing primarily in the sciences and the technical fields. The arts and the humanities are considered fine for personal pleasure, but they are not among the essentials needed to help youngsters to become productive members of society. Many essentialists tend to view such subjects as "frills" in the school. When budgets are tight, they tend to suggest that these frill subjects be cut first.

The essentialist feels that priorities in the schools should be placed on essential subjects. The authority of the teacher, hard work, and discipline in the classroom are important values. Essentialists tend to approach the world from the position that human beings are not basically good. Therefore the untrained child must be shaped by education to become a productive member of society. Essentialists expect teachers to discipline youngsters to ensure that they will put forth the effort that, it is assumed, they will not put forth in the absence of such pressure.

A curriculum that an essentialist might view as "ideal" would consist of scientific, technical, vocational, and other subjects seen as having some potential "usefulness." There are only a limited number of such subjects. All youngsters should follow this same program. Teachers are expected to transmit this essential core of information.

Perhaps more than any other educational philosophy, essentialism seems to reflect central American priorities. It reflects the values of hard work and the practical "can-do"spirit of Americans. These perspectives can be traced back to the earliest days of our country. Recall that even Benjamin Franklin was interested in making programs in school "more practical" in nature. Some suggest that essentialist ideas are so ingrained in the thinking of many people about what schools ought to be that they are seldom even challenged. Certainly programs in most American schools suggest that this philosophy continues to be a highly potent force.

Reconstructionism

Reconstructionists believe that society has been strained nearly to the breaking point. This strain has come about because of unprecedented developments such as the advent of atomic power, the worldwide struggle between totalitarian and nontotalitarian states, and the widespread direct involvement of civilian populations in war. These developments have so stretched the existing social arrangements that societies are no longer able to make systematic adjustments to changing conditions. What is needed is an entirely new social order. This social "reconstruction" is necessary to humankind's survival.

Reconstructionism seeks to build society afresh. In this new world, there will be a heavy emphasis on economic abundance, human welfare, and democratic decision-making. Reconstructionists point to the need to act positively on the shared long-term goals of the human race. Specifically, they favor the formulation and implementation of plans of action that are clearly directed toward the achievement of these goals.

Reconstructionists believe that the schools should lead the way in building a new and better society. Rather than teaching outdated information, the schools should prepare youngsters for change and, beyond that, for "reconstructing" their society to meet changing conditions. Reconstructionists place a heavy faith in insights from the behavioral sciences. They believe such knowledge can be used as the basis for creating a society where individuals can attain their fullest personal potentials. The schools, say the reconstructionists, should help youngsters critically evaluate the social institutions of their society to determine what changes might be necessary to provide the conditions that will promote the maximum development of individual human beings.

Reconstructionists believe that teachers have a direct and important role to play. Their role is not to communicate knowledge but to raise issues of social significance. Teachers are to exercise their persuasive talents to suggest to learners that some form of democratic society probably best ensures an environment in which people are encouraged toward the maximum development of their individual talents. There is an emphasis on active learning and on problem solving. Learning activities seek to help youngsters identify the nature of the ideal society and to suggest to them practical approaches to moving the "real" society in this direction.

Existentialism

There is some difficulty in characterizing existentialism because many individuals identified with the existentialist position reject the idea that existentialism is an all-embracing philosophical postion with tenets that are universally agreed upon. Still, there are some elements of the position that tend to characterize a good many individuals who identify with existentialism. We will discuss some of these (and their educational implications) here.

Existentialism begins with a focus on the very fact of one's individual existence. It begins with the premise that individual human beings fit into no grand design of God or of nature. Rather, individuals are born into an indifferent, alien, and purposeless world. To each person falls the task of constructing his or her own meaning and purpose for existence.

Existentialists are not at all concerned with speculation about ultimate reality or truth. In fact, they reject the notion of absolute truth. All truth, all meaning is individual. Existentialism asks each person to question his or her own reasons for living. Out of this sort of self-examination, individual human beings may identify personal purposes for living and recognize that their individual lives do have value. Yet though individual people have this recognition, in the totality of the universe each life is only a meaningless speck.

Existentialism urges people to ask questions about the nature of their own personal existence. Reason alone is not thought capable of providing answers. Therefore a great deal of emphasis is placed on the subjective elements of existence. Understanding of individual purposes for living comes not through logical thought processes alone but through feelings that go beyond logical analyses.

For existentialists, the individual is responsible for everything that comes to him or her. Blame for failure cannot be assigned to the environment, to the family, or to another external influence. Given this reality, self-fulfillment becomes a very important objective. An existentialist orders his or her own priorities and creates his or her own freedom and success. Each individual must personally confront the question "How shall I live my life?" Thus no individual should be forced to conform to standards that are established by others. The only acceptable values are those an individual chooses freely for himself or herself. The basis of morality is personal freedom.

The educational implications of existentialism include a heavy emphasis on individual choice, individual freedom, and individual responsibility. Essentially, the individual must educate himself or herself and ought to make the important decisions regarding personal behavior, the courses of study followed, and the methods of learning utilized. Education should not be directed only toward sharpening the intellect. Rather, education should also include attention to attitudes, feelings, values, and other subjective components.

For existentialists, it is impossible to describe one school subject as "more important" than any other. Such a statement would imply that the subject was more important for everyone. It is not possible to identify anything that is good for everyone. The worth of any subject must be assessed by each individual in the light of whether he or she sees it as contributing to a personal understanding of the meaning of existence. Thus existentialists generally do not support curricula asking learners to master the conclusions or generalizations of others. Rather, they seek after a curriculum that encourages a personal construction of reality on the part of each individual. What is important is not the conclusions that result from study but individual commitment to pursue personally relevant answers. It is in this seeking after a personal meaning that gives meaning to an individual's life. And, say the existentialists, the schools should provide youngsters with opportunities to extend their sensitivities, as they attempt to work out meaningful personal solutions to the all-important question, "What is my purpose?"

The role of the teacher, according to those who subscribe to existentialism, is to serve neither as a transmitter of knowledge nor as a consultant to the learner. Rather, the teacher should be a person who can assist each individual in the class to succeed in the search for self-realization. To accomplish this, teachers must be personally involved with their learners. Above all, the teacher must act as a person who is committed to freedom. He or she must have courage and be willing to take risks. In sum, the teacher is expected to model the independence and the courage of the existentialist through his or her own actions.

Teachers' Philosophies and Educational Issues

Clearly teachers' philosophies have a great impact on how teachers see educational issues. Much conflict about schools results when teachers and others in charge of school programs bring different philosophical perspectives to bear on important problems. When there are wide divergences of opinion between school people and the public they serve, there is likely to be trouble. Not many years ago, there was a very bitter confrontation between school leaders and many parents in West Virginia over the issue of including the version of Creation as outlined in the Book of Genesis in the biology curriculum. Examples of hostilities that can result when the philosophical orientations of educators and community members are at odds are legion. Few districts of any size have avoided major controversies that, at bottom, amounted to disputes among people with different philosophical positions.

Given this situation, it might prove worthwhile to take a moment to consider a number of present-day educational issues and to speculate on how people from different philosophical orientations would react to them. For example, consider the back-to-the-basics movement. With which educational philosophy would this movement be most compatible? How would perennialists, essentialists, progressives, reconstructionists, and existentialists differ in their definition of what is basic? Another issue to be considered might be career education. How would people with differing educational philosophies respond to this issue? As teachers consider answers to these questions and to similar ones related to other contemporary problems in education, they become more adept at anticipating potential reactions to possible solutions to these problems. They become more effective spokespersons for their own positions when they know, in a philosophical sense, where their adversaries are "coming from."

Recapitulation of Major Ideas

1. Behind every teaching method and every plan for organizing a school is a set of assumptions. When these assumptions are understood, teachers are in a better position to defend the logic of what they are doing and to understand why some people may be critical of certain school practices.
2. Metaphysics deals with the nature of reality. Metaphysics relates to teaching in terms of thought about educational goals, the selection of appropriate content, and attitudes toward the general nature of learners. Metaphysics asks such questions as the following: Is there a body of universal knowledge to be learned? Who should decide what is to be learned? Are learners basically good and trustworthy?
3. Epistemology deals with the nature of knowledge and influences teaching at the point of determining what type of knowledge should be

---

Box 9-3
How School Practices Reflect Philosophical Orientations

School practices do not "just happen." They are instituted in response to one or another philosophical position regarding what is "true," "right," "correct," or "good."

LET'S PONDER

Read the statement above and respond to the following questions.

1. Think of examples in the schools that represent practices that might be consistent with views stemming from each of the following kinds of educational philosophy. Describe each example as specifically as possible. Tell why you believe it to be consistent with this philosophy.
   perennialiism
   progressivism
   essentialism
   social reconstruction
   existentialism
2. Compare your answer to the questions posed in the previous box, "Reactions to Basic Philosophical Issues," with each of these educational philosophies. Does any one of these philosophies seem closer to your own personal philosophy? Which one (or ones), and why?
3. Now that you know something about each of these philosophies, would you wish to change your responses to any of the questions posed in the preceding box? If so, what would those changes be, and why would you make them?

taught and of determining the reliability of different ways of knowing. Basic questions epistemology asks include the following: Is knowledge really possible? Should knowledge that is taught be functional or abstract? Do we acquire knowledge best through experimentation, intuition, or revelation or by some other means?

4. Axiology deals with the nature of values and relates to the teaching of moral values and character development. It considers such issues as the purpose of life and what constitutes "right conduct." It asks such questions as the following: What is right behavior? How does a good person act?

5. Logic centers on clarity of thought and the relationships among ideas. It provides people with a methodology for making clear distinctions between valid and fallacious thinking. For this reason, educators are very much concerned that learners develop a sound logical framework.

6. The educational philosophy of perennialism holds that universal truths and values do exist. Properly, then, education should consist of the search for and the dissemination of these truths and values.

7. Progressivism developed in reaction to some of the views of the perennialists. Progressivism holds that knowledge is ever-changing and that the best approach to knowledge is through scientific experimentation. Individuals are believed to have a basically "good" nature. Consequently, progressives suggest that they should play an active role in their own learning and be charged with making some personal decisions about the nature of that learning.

8. The educational philosophy of essentialism might be thought of as a reaction against some of the more extreme manifestations of progressivism. As a philosophy, it seems to represent a very widely held American view of what education ought to be. The focus of essentialism is on the teaching of knowledge that is essential or useful for individuals who will play productive roles as adult citizens. Teachers are expected to provide this kind of knowledge to learners and to take a leadership role in guiding them toward its mastery.

9. Reconstructionism suggests that the role of the school is to teach learners how to remake society in such a fashion that the general human condition will be improved. There is a heavy emphasis on teaching youngsters to analyze social conditions with a critical view to their improvement. There is an assumption that change is a constant and that it can be used to produce better conditions for all humankind.

10. In general, existentialism holds that there is no universal purpose to life. Humans simply exist. Each person must accept that he or she is bound to die and that when that happens all will be over. Whatever is to happen is to happen within the span of an individual's own life. Since one's own life is all there is, each individual ought to be

responsible for shaping that life in his or her own way. Personal freedom is the dominant value of existentialism. For schools, this implies maximizing the individual choices and the independent decision-making of learners.

Posttest

DIRECTIONS: Using your own paper, answer each of the following true/false questions. For each correct statement, write the word *true* on your paper. For each incorrect statement, write the word *false* on your paper.

1. Philosophy is a nice intellectual exercise but has little to do with the "real world."
2. There is one philosophy of education on which nearly all educators agree.
3. Metaphysics is the study of the nature of reality.
4. Epistemology is the study of the nature of knowledge.
5. Axiology is the study of the nature of values.
6. The perennialist believes that there is a core of knowledge that should be learned by all.
7. Perennialism takes the position that knowledge is changing constantly.
8. Progressivism views human nature as basically good.
9. The main focus in progressivism is on subject matter.
10. Essentialism is basically inconsistent with American culture.
11. Essentialism sees the arts and the humanities as the most important subjects in the curriculum.
12. Reconstructionists believe that time-honored truths from the past need to be reconstructed and taught to learners.
13. Reconstructionism takes a scientific view of nature and values.
14. Existentialists believe that every learner should take exactly the same program in school.

Summary

The philosophies underpinning educational practices have great importance for classroom teachers. It is from these philosophies that the assumptions flow that support school practices of all kinds. Consequently the philosophical orientation of a given individual has great relevance to how he or she will be likely to view a given education program. In defending their own practices and in understanding the potential views of others regarding these practices, teachers ought to have some understanding of the major streams of philosophic thought in education.

Any individual who enters education must recognize than in the pluralistic American society, there will be many views regarding what constitutes good and sound educational practice. The criticisms made of certain educational programs need not necessarily be taken as evidence that something is basically "wrong." Rather, they should be weighed in the realization that these criticisms indicate that critics come from a different philosophical orientation than those who support the existing school programs. When objections to these programs result in program changes, this suggests that the philosophical orientation of a minority has captured the support of a great many people. The policy change suggests that the former minority position has been reborn as a majority position (at least, a majority of those committed enough to put pressure on decision makers). Because of the importance of these philosophical shifts for school programs and policies, professional educators need some understanding of the philosophical orientations that may undergird calls for change.

References

BUTLER, J. DONALD. *Four Philosophies and Their Practice in Education and Religion*, 3rd Ed. New York: Harper & Row, 1968.

KNELLER, GEORGE F. *Introduction to the Philosophy of Education.* New York: John Wiley & Sons, 1964.

LAPP, DIANE, BENDER, HILARY, ELLENWOOD, STEPHAN, AND MARTHA, JOHN. *Teaching and Learning: Philosophical, Psychological, Curricular Applications.* New York: Macmillan Publishing Co., 1975.

ORNSTEIN, ALLEN C. *An Introduction to the Foundations of Education.* Chicago: Rand McNally, 1977.

PANDY, SIDDHESHWAR NATH. *An Existential Analysis of the Free School Movement.* College Station, Texas, an unpublished doctoral dissertation, Texas A & M University, 1978.

WINGO, G. MAX. *Philisophies of Education: An Introduction.* Lexington, Mass.: D. C. Heath, 1974.

10
The Roles of the Teacher

Objectives

This chapter provides information to help the reader to

1. Identify the multiple responsibilities of teachers.
2. Point out the specific skills that teachers need to fulfill the various roles they must play.
3. Note potential conflicts between and among teachers' roles.
4. Suggest the personal problems some teachers experience as a result of the necessity to fulfill multiple role expectations.
5. Describe possible solutions to the dilemmas that teachers face in dealing with multiple roles.

Pretest

DIRECTIONS: Using your own paper, answer each of the following true/false questions. For each correct statement, write the word *true* on your paper. For each incorrect statement, write the word *false* on your paper.

1. Though teachers play many roles, they usually find that their college preparation programs have given them adequate background to feel comfortable in fulfilling all of them.
2. A frequent complaint of teachers is that they must deal with too much paperwork.
3. Today it is generally recognized that teachers do not adequately serve the instructional role of teaching when they restrict their activities to telling learners information and making assignments.
4. Because many schools have counselors, teachers do not have to be much concerned with counseling responsibilities.
5. The public relations functions of schools are best left to professional specialists, and teachers should not be involved in this area.
6. Many states require teachers to take course work to maintain a valid teaching certificate.
7. Because they are involved in a relatively low-pressure profession, teachers suffer psychological or emotional stress only rarely.
8. Most teachers report that their evaluation as a "good" or an "ineffective" teacher depends almost exclusively on their ability to transmit information effectively to the youngsters in their classrooms.
9. Today, teachers in large urban areas may find it more difficult to establish close relationships with parents than formerly.
10. The phenomenon of "teacher burnout" has become increasingly common in recent years.

Introduction

Teachers' roles are incredibly diverse. Many teachers find themselves responsible for tasks that they had scarcely imagined existed in their undergraduate days. Certainly many things that they do have had to be learned on the job rather than from any special training. Some of these tasks seem marginally related at best to a conception of the school as an institution dedicated to transmitting information to the young. Indeed, the variety of teachers' responsibilities and the occasional incompatibility of the many roles they must play frequently place a severe strain on members of the profession. Many beginning teachers, in particular, find themselves feeling overwhelmed by the wide range of responsibilities for which they will be held to account. Let us consider, for a moment, what a typical new teacher might experience.

In mid-August, though the anxieties were there, the overriding emotion of our new teacher was enthusiasm to "get started at last." Student teaching had been survived. Indeed, it had been enjoyed. Confident from this positive experience, our new teacher looked forward to working with learners without having a supervising teacher or a university coordinator to worry about.

Excitement had continued to build with the arrival of the invitation to report to school for orientation sessions a few days before the beginning of the school year. The day of the orientation meetings arrived, and our new teacher was among the first to walk into the building. The day got off to a wonderful start. There were rolls, doughnuts, coffee, and lots of informal conversations with more experienced teachers. The old-timers had been wonderful about welcoming the newcomers and offering to help them learn the ropes.

Later in the morning, at a large general session, the superintendent welcomed the staff to another school year. After some wistful wondering about "where the summer has gone," he charged the staff to work hard to "make this year our best ever." The superintendent certainly seemed to be a nice person. Our new teacher felt good about working in a district where the top administrator seemed so concerned about youngsters.

The rest of the morning was devoted to a tour of the school district that had been specially arranged for the new teachers. After a quick bus ride by a number of school buildings in various parts of the district, the new teachers were deposited at the complex of central administrative offices. After more coffee, an assistant superintendent came in and gave an orientation talk illustrated with overhead transparencies. He pointed out the administrative and managerial arrangement of the district with frequent references to flowcharts. For many of the new teachers, the complexity of the management scheme seemed a bit overwhelming. There were assistant superintendents, subject-matter coordinators, curriculum directors and curriculum assistants, a media director, a personnel director, a finance manager, a federal programs director, and many more. Most of the new teachers were glad that they did not have to take a test on all of this information. Many felt some anxiety about whom they would contact from among this bewildering array of people should they have problems. But the afternoon promised to be more satisfying. They were to report to their individual buildings.

Certainly our new teacher felt better when, after a nice lunch, the secretary in the main office provided a warm welcome, pointed out the newcomer's name on a faculty mailbox, and went in to tell the principal that the "new teacher" had arrived. A very personable individual, the principal came out and escorted the new teacher to his office. "At last," thought our new teacher, "I'm going to find out something specific about my teaching." The principal opened with some small talk about the new teacher's family, university, and general background. He was just beginning to say a few words about the nature of the youngsters in the school when the phone rang. It was the secretary reminding him of the principals' meeting at the downtown central administration complex. He put down the phone, made apologies for having to be "at least three places at once," and returned our newcomer to the charge of the main office secretary.

The secretary began to brief our new teacher on some of the management procedures followed in the building. She started by explaining how the attendance register was to be kept. She went into some detail about how each of the large number of symbols at the top of each register page were to be used. She went on to the question of the lunch count and how it was to be passed on to people working in the school cafeteria. There was also some discussion of selling lunch tickets and special provisions for those entitled to federally subsidized meals.

As our newcomer's eyes grew wider, the secretary went on to procedures for putting daily announcements into the teachers' boxes and how these were to be read at the beginning of each school day. Next, the procedures for working with school counselors (there were three different kinds of referral forms) and with the school nurse were explained. The secretary was especially emphatic regarding the procedures to be followed to release a youngster from a classroom to the custody of an unknown adult. The secretary explained that all parents and others with authority to pick up children from classes during the school day had first to check with the main office. The main office would provide them with a release authorization. No youngster was ever to be allowed to leave unless a requesting adult first presented the teacher with an approved release authorization. The secretary's orientation ended with a quick review of the forms relating to athletic injuries, payroll deductions for charities, bomb threats, and a bewildering variety of other things.

Having completed her orientation, the secretary turned over our new teacher to one of the assistant principals. The assistant principal, a very pleasant middle-aged woman, explained that faculty meetings would be held every other week on Tuesday afternoons. Attendance was mandatory. Additionally, she pointed out, all teachers were expected to serve as advisers for extracurricular activities. She had a list various clubs and organizations posted on her wall along with the names of the sponsoring faculty members. A few had no faculty sponsors listed. Our new teacher was advised to write these down and to let the assistant principal know which one might be of interest. The assistant principal would take a look at the wishes of all new teachers and try to assign them, so far as was possible, to serve as faculty sponsors of activities in which they had some interest. She cautioned, however, that everyone might not get his or her choice.

The assistant principal went on to explain that there would be a PTA meeting the third week of school and that parents would be invited to chat with the teachers in their classrooms. She concluded her remarks by pointing out that all teachers had one extra responsibility associated with keeping the school functioning. She noted that the job of "media coordinator" for the building had been vacated by a retiring teacher and that that responsibility had been assigned to our newcomer. This job would involve coordinating all orders for films, filmstrips, and other materials ordered from the central district media center. More specifically, the media coordinator would see to it that the films were ordered properly, received as ordered, and returned on time. The assistant principal said that the job was a good one for a new teacher in that it would provide an opportunity to get quickly acquainted with the entire faculty.

By the time the assistant principal's comments had concluded, it was time to go home. The day was over. Our new teacher, flushed with enthusiasm at the beginning of the day, was beginning to panic. During the entire day, almost nothing had been said about teaching youngsters. There seemed to be many expectations that had rarely been mentioned in the classes at the university. Anxiety was becoming more of a problem with each passing moment. Well, maybe tomorrow would be better. Or . . . shudder . . . maybe it wouldn't.

The kinds of concerns experienced by the hypothetical new teacher we have been describing are very common. Few beginning teachers have a good conception of the range of responsibilities they will face as professional educators. High levels of anxiety are chronic among first-year teachers as they worry about their ability to deal with all of the roles they must play. Most make the adjustment successfully. Perhaps this adjustment would have come more quickly had they had a better understanding of the many roles teachers are expected to fulfill before they arrived to assume their positions. In the sections that follow, some specific characteristics of these diverse responsibilities are described.

Teachers' Instructional Responsibilities

Despite the diversity of roles that teachers must play, teachers' instructional responsibilities are the most important. Without instruction, there would be no schools. It is this function that the institution of the school grew up to serve. Though the mix of other responsibilities that teachers have varies greatly from school to school, it is fair to say that all classroom teachers share a common responsibility for instruction.

In years gone by, *teaching* was thought to be generally synonymous with *telling*. The teacher was viewed as a dispenser of knowledge. Typically the teacher transmitted information by standing in front of the learners, who were arranged in neat rows of floor-bolted desks, and lecturing. Lectures were supplemented with related assignments. Tests were administered periodically to assess progress. To function in this kind of an arena, teachers needed a good grounding in their subject matter, a strong speaking voice, and an appropriate delivery style.

In recent years, this traditional style of teaching has been challenged. Critics of this old and familiar model of teaching have pointed out that today we live in the midst of a knowledge explosion. Because of accelerating rates in the development of new information, it is alleged that teachers cannot possibly be expected to keep up with all the current developments in their academic field. Teachers who followed the old style of acting as the single source of all information would be transmitting to youngsters a good deal of obsolete knowledge. These criticisms have led to a revision of professional educators' understanding of the instructional role of the teacher. Today teachers tend to be viewed not as exclusive sources of information but as "instructional managers." As instructional managers, they may use computer-assisted instruction, television, and a host of other information sources to transmit current knowledge to their youngsters.

The task of the teacher who functions as an instructional manager is much different from that of the teacher as a lecturer. The instructional manager tries to establish an environment in which learning can take place. Instead of doing all the talking, the teacher's primary function is to plan and direct learners' experiences. As noted previously, these experiences can involve youngsters with a wide variety of information sources. Though the kinds of learning experiences will vary according to the subjects being taught, the availability of resources, the characteristics of the learners, and other things, a common set of instructional planning tasks still faces all teachers who function as instructional managers. More specifically, all teachers need to (1) determine objectives, (2) diagnose learners, (3) plan instructional activities, (4) implement programs, and (5) evaluate learning outcomes.

Determining Objectives

In planning for instruction, the first task for teachers is to determine the learning objectives. Regardless of the subject being taught, there is a need to decide precisely what it is the youngsters should be able to do as a consequence of their exposure to the instruction. Statements about what they should be able to do, or "learning objectives," help teachers to plan learning activities that will result in youngsters' having the desired knowledge and skills at the end of the period of instruction.

Teachers who use learning objectives have a basis for deciding to include

Box 10-1
Thinking About Teachers' Roles

Too many prospective teachers emerge from their training in colleges and universities with the mistaken impression that they have only one role to play in the school. They may presume that their only responsibility is to transmit information to young people. Many find themselves in a state of shock when they are confronted by record-keeping responsibilities, playground management duties, extracurricular activities supervision, parental relations duties, and a host of other responsibilities. In fact, some are convinced that only a small fraction of their time is spent on instructional tasks.

LET'S PONDER

Read the paragraph above. Then, respond to the following questions.

1. As you think about the teaching position you hope to assume, what do you think you will spend most of your time doing? Why do you say so?
2. As you reflect back on your own teachers in school, what kinds of things do you remember them having to do that were not directly related to instruction?
3. As you look over some of the teacher responsibilities in the paragraph above, think about your own interests and abilities. Which of the responsibilities do you think you could do best? For which ones do you feel least well equipped?
4. Would it be possible for prospective teachers to learn all of the things they need to do as teachers in their college and university programs, or is it inevitable that most of these things be learned ``on the job?''
5. Do you think too much of teachers' time is taken up with noninstructional responsibilities? Why, or why not?

or not to include a given activity. If the activity bears some logical relationship to the learning objectives, then a case can be made for including it. If not, probably the activity should not be used. Learning objectives, then, help teachers avoid selecting activities that tend to be little more than "busywork" that bears little connection to what youngsters will be expected to have learned.

Learning objectives also serve a valuable function once a unit of instruction has been completed. If the youngsters have done well—that is, if the youngsters have mastered these objectives—then the teacher has a basis for concluding that the material was well taught. If certain objectives were not mastered, then the teacher can identify certain things that might be changed on another occasion when similar content is treated. In summary, then, learning objectives provide not only important checks on teachers as they plan for youngsters' learning but also an important source of information about the effectiveness of the instruction once units have been taught.

Diagnosing Learners

A second major task that teachers face in preparing for instruction is diagnosing learners' individual needs and interests. This function relates to the time-tested dictum that teachers should begin "where the learners are." That is, the instructional experience provided should be appropriate for the youngsters being taught. To cite an extreme example, it makes no sense whatsoever to try to teach a group of youngsters how to form the past tense of French verbs if they do not know the patterns of present-tense French verbs. Though this example is a bit extreme, if not downright farfetched, an astonishing number of beginning teachers still prepare lessons and units that have sparse chance for success because they are inappropriate for the youngsters being taught.

A particularly important aspect of diagnosis relates to the determination of youngsters' interests. It is far easier to motivate learners if they are working on a task in which they have some interest. Clearly not all topics that must be considered in school courses can be framed in a way that responds to the burning interests of the learners, but a surprising number can be adjusted to take advantage of youngsters' interests. These interests can be used as entry points for the teacher as he or she attempts to broaden the range of learner enthusiasm when a new topic is introduced.

Diagnosis also provides teachers with information related to the learning problems of specific individuals. Some youngsters might have hearing, vision, or other physical problems that influence their ability to profit from certain kinds of instruction. Others may have failed to acquire knowledge that the teacher mistakenly has assumed all class members to have. For some, previous learning experiences may have come too swiftly and may not have been accompanied by sufficient concrete experiences to make the content "stick." A variety of circumstances may have played a part in determining the readiness of a given youngster for new learning experiences. By judicious diagnosis, the teacher can make a determination regarding the appropriateness of proposed instructional experiences for individual youngsters in the classroom. Adjustments to the proposed instructional program can be made in light of this diagnostic information.

Planning Instructional Activities

Once learner objectives have been formulated and diagnostic data about individual youngsters have been considered, the teacher is ready to begin developing an appropriate instructional sequence. In planning an instructional sequence, the following elements must be considered:

1. Motivation of learners.
2. Inclusion of alternative methods of introducing the material.
3. Provision of opportunities for learners to apply new understanding.

4. Description of procedures to be used in giving feedback to learners and in enhancing their retention.

The specific instructional plan developed will vary in accordance with teacher variables, learner variables, and other situational variables. Certainly these broadly defined elements provide a good deal of room for exercising creativity.

Implementing Instruction

Perhaps the most difficult task for new teachers is implementing instruction, largely because of inexperience in working with youngsters and, sometimes, faulty expectations of what they can and cannot do. The pacing of instruction is an especially difficult problem for new teachers. Sometimes they find a class grasping a concept thoroughly after only ten minutes' time when fully forty minutes had been allotted in the lesson plan. On other occasions, something that appears simple to the teacher will require much more instructional time than had been anticipated.

In general, problems stem from the necessity to lead and interact with as many as thirty or thirty-five individuals at one time. Many situations develop, given this number of "human variables," that simply cannot be anticipated in the planning phase of instruction. With experience, teachers get a "feel" for the kinds of situations that develop. They develop a facility for changing and adapting quickly to meet needs that may emerge as the lesson unfolds.

For new teachers, development of competency in this area seems to require experience in working with youngsters. These skills are acquired more quickly when a prospective teacher works with youngsters and has his or her performance criticized by a knowledgeable supervising teacher or university student-teaching observer. Out of a recognition that expertise in this area requires actual "hands-on" experience in working with learners, many teacher preparation programs in colleges and universities are emphasizing extended periods of experience working in public school classrooms. In particular, there has been a trend to get prospective teachers into classrooms early during their undergraduate careers and to extend the length of the student-teaching experience.

Evaluating Learning Outcomes

A final instructional task of teachers is evaluating the learning of the youngsters in their classes. A central purpose of this assessment is to determine whether or not the learners have accomplished the established objectives. If they have not, they will have a very difficult time succeeding on subsequent material that assumes an understanding of material to which they have been exposed earlier.

Teachers frequently use examinations or tests to determine whether learning objectives have mastered. Formal examinations or tests are not the only options available to teachers as they attempt to assess the progress of individual youngsters. In some situations, a teacher might use a checklist to note whether youngsters are exhibiting behaviors that have been taught (for example, how many baskets can a fifth-grader make from the free-throw line in three minutes?). On other occasions, learners might be asked to prepare a demonstration or construct a project that can be evaluated by the teacher using certain criteria. Although the options available to teachers are many, all responsible assessment requires that some kind of specific evidence be in hand that provides a rational basis for teachers to decide whether individual youngsters have or have not mastered specific learning objectives.

In summary, the instructional responsibilities faced by teachers are demanding. Successful teaching demands a command of instructional skills that are critically important. It is not sufficient for a teacher simply to be well grounded in the subject matter he or she teaches. Given the diversity of the learner population with whom teachers must work, professional teaching requires an ability to adapt instruction to an incredible variety of situations.

"Miss Ritz is excellent in a one-to-one situation."

For the teacher, this suggests that mastery of the skills of preparing objectives, diagnosing learners, planning activities, implementing programs, and evaluating learners is a necessary adjunct to their mastery of the subject or subjects to be taught.

Teachers' Counseling Responsibilities

Teaching is one of the helping professions. It requires many personal contacts with young people in the classroom. Certain interpersonal-relationship skills are part of the repertoire of all successful teachers. Indeed, some have seen the interpersonal relations or counseling function of teaching as all but inseparable from the instructional function. Some understanding of the emotional condition of youngsters is essential before the instructional program can be designed in such a way that learning takes place.

Most secondary schools and some elementary schools have full-time or part-time counselors, but the existence of professional counselors in a building by no means relieves teachers from counseling responsibilities. In the first place, the ratio of learners to counselors is so high in most schools that counselors are forced to spend time working with the most difficult personal situations of youngsters. They simply cannot spend time counseling every learner in the building. Second, because youngsters tend to become very well acquainted with their teachers and to feel comfortable around them, teachers tend to be sought out by youngsters when they have a problem that they wish to talk about. Teachers need to be prepared for approaches from learners about personal difficulties. Furthermore, they need to know when a problem is beyond their capacity to help and when to refer a youngster to a counselor or some other specialist for assistance.

Good teacher counseling does not simply mean becoming a "friend" of the learner. Many beginning teachers confuse the roles of friendship and of counseling. A youngster asking for help about a problem is not asking for friendship, or, at least, he or she is not looking for a friend in the sense that a fellow learner is a friend. The objective of seeking help is to find help. Help is sought under the assumption that the teacher is a leadership figure capable of providing guidance that might help resolve a problem. The youngster looking for assistance from a teacher has different expectations than he or she would have in a relationship with most friends. When inexperienced teachers make the mistake of trying first to act as friends rather than leaders, the credibility of their advice is threatened. This can undermine the learner–teacher relationship in other areas, as learner and teacher roles become confused.

Many times, teachers do have a responsibility for counseling. The ways in which teachers talk to youngsters, the respect they show them in both verbal and nonverbal communication, and other things either support the building of the sort of rapport necessary for free and open communication or tend to

Box 10-2
The Elements of Instruction

What is wrong with American schools today is that teachers do not know their subjects well enough. What we really need are solid historians, scholars of English literature, accomplished mathematicians, and trained people in the sciences who have some *depth* in their subjects. If a person really knows his or her subject, he or she needs no further preparation for teaching. Given such knowledge, he or she knows all that an effective teacher needs to know.

LET'S PONDER

Read the paragraph above. Then, respond to the following questions.

1. Do you agree that mastery of subject matter is all a teacher has to have in order to be effective in the classroom? Why, or why not?
2. From your own experience as a student do you think most problems teachers had in schools you attended related to a poor grounding in subjects they were teaching? What evidence supports your position?
3. Think about the tasks of preparing objectives, diagnosing learners, planning activities, implementing programs, and evaluating learners. To what extent did your former teachers perform these tasks?
4. Considering again the tasks listed in question 3, would some instruction you received in schools have been better had your teachers paid more attention to one or more of these tasks? If so, which ones?
5. Assume you agree that teachers ought to know how to accomplish each of the tasks mentioned in question 3. How do you see yourself now in terms of your preparation to perform each of them? Which ones would you suppose would give greatest difficulty to beginning teachers? Why?

destroy it. Teachers need particularly to attend to the possible consequences of their actions for youngsters' self-images. Youngsters' self-perceptions have a great influence on their patterns of behavior. Self-images are learned through interactions with others. When the reactions of others are positive, self-images tend to be positive. When the reactions of others are negative, self-images tend to be negative. Teachers need to think about the impact their reactions to individual youngsters might be having on learners' perceptions of their own worth and dignity.

Good counseling seeks to help youngsters live and behave in more constructive and satisfying ways. Some youngsters in school never have learned how to achieve their own goals. Frequently they do not understand the consequences of their own actions. In working with youngsters, teachers seek to help them clarify their own goals. Then the youngsters are helped to focus on the kinds of behavior that seem most logically to have potential in facilitating movement toward those goals. When youngsters whose traditional patterns of behavior have been a problem begin to change, teachers knowledgeable in the counseling function of their professional role are quick to provide as much emotional support as possible.

A basic skill possessed by teachers who perform the counseling function well is attending. *Attending* means listening very carefully and seeing the world through the eyes of the youngster with whom they are working. A teacher who attends can help youngsters identify critical features of problems and help them sort out potential solutions.

In performing the counseling function, teachers must above all be personally secure people who themselves have positive self-concepts. An emotionally crippled teacher is scarcely in a position to help learners with serious problems. If the goal is to produce secure, confident, and self-assured youngsters, teachers must provide good adult role models.

Teachers' Administrative and Supervisory Responsibilities

Large numbers of teachers comment that the administrative and supervisory aspects of teaching are among the least enjoyable of their many roles. Many complain that so much time is spent on paperwork that more important work, such as preparing for lessons and working with individual youngsters, is neglected. Clearly the paperwork load of teachers has increased in recent years with the expansion of federal programs in the schools. Nearly all such programs require a good deal of careful record keeping.

Even without the special paperwork associated with programs underwritten by the federal government, teachers have a heavy administrative work load. Schedules must be developed. Learner records must be kept. Materials have to be ordered. Requests for films and other media have to be filed. Notes must be kept regarding committee work, school organizations, and teachers' professional groups. Though such tasks are sometimes not terribly rewarding for the teachers who must do them, they do seem to be necessary to ensure the smooth functioning of the school program. Many of these duties could be completed by clerks and other individuals, but generally speaking, monies have not been available for this purpose.

Among the most important of all teachers' administrative responsibilities is maintaining accurate attendance records. In most states, school districts receive money from the state based on the number of youngsters in attendance. The districts clearly have a heavy financial interest in seeing to it that they have dependable records to document the number of youngsters that have been claimed for purposes of securing state funds. The teacher's daily attendance record in many places is a vital link in this documentation chain. Serious errors could result in heavy financial losses for the district.

New teachers sometimes have difficulty in taking accurate attendance

Box 10-3
Teachers as Counselors

Statement by a high school mathematics teacher:

I view my job as teaching my students algebra. I want them to be able to identify critical elements of problems. I want them to become quick and confident at factoring. In short, I see myself as a builder of minds. I suppose some of my students have problems. I suppose some of them come from homes that are less than ideal. But I don't want to know about that. It might change how I teach. And after thirty years, I pride myself that everyone in my class gets equal treatment.

LET'S PONDER

Read the statement above. Then, respond to the questions that follow.

1. How do you react to the statement above? Does knowing something about individual youngsters and varying the program to meet individual needs constitute unfair treatment for some?
2. The individual making this statement seems to take rather a dim view of the counseling function of teaching. Do you agree with his or her position?
3. When you were in school, were there certain teachers students sought out when students had problems? Who were they? Why were youngsters attracted to them?
4. Some student teachers and first year teachers feel that learners they teach above all want a teacher who is a ''buddy'' or a ''friend.'' Do you agree that this is what learners really want? Why, or why not?
5. How does a teacher go about establishing a classroom climate where youngsters feel free to chat about personal concerns and yet continue to accept the teacher as a leader?
6. It has been argued that teachers who successfully fulfill the counseling role are perceived as leaders by youngsters seeking help. How can a teacher be perceived as a leader and, at the same time, be seen as someone who is not cold and aloof?

quickly. Indeed, one of the authors once observed a student teacher who regularly required twenty minutes to accomplish this task. This was too much time. It is essential that teachers develop ways to take attendance as rapidly and accurately as possible. Research has shown that the achievement of youngsters correlates with the amount of time they are actively engaged in learning tasks. This time is clearly reduced when the teacher takes too much time on a routine task such as taking attendance.

In addition to attendance, teachers keep records of youngsters' academic progress. There are a number of reasons for keeping this kind of information. First of all, this information can be used to review the effectiveness of the instructional program. For example, if grades or scores on a particular section of the course seem unusually low, some revision in procedures may be needed the next time this section is taught.

Court decisions in recent years provide another reason for careful documentation of learners' progress. Several of the cases have involved teachers who were taken to court by learners (or their representatives) who were dissatisfied with grades that had been awarded. In general, courts have been reluctant to overturn a grade based on a teacher's judgment *provided that* the teacher has supportive evidence and documentation to back up his or her grading decision.

A good many schools keep cumulative records on learners. A cumulative record is a file that follows a learner throughout his or her school career (at least it does so provided the youngster stays in the same school district). The cumulative file might contain such information as relevant health data, standardized test scores, grades, and assorted other information. Frequently, particularly in the case of elementary-school educators, it is part of the teacher's responsibility to keep information current in cumulative folders for the youngsters in their classes. Typically, entries are made only once a year. But if many data have to be entered, updating cumulative records can be a very time-consuming task.

In summary, administrative responsibilities tend to be professional tasks that teachers find challenging. Because they are individuals who work in a large governmental enterprise, however, it probably is idle to suppose that such duties may be greatly diminished any time soon. Realizing that in all likelihood paperwork is here to stay, most teachers try to develop effective procedures to deal with this important dimension of teaching.

Curriculum Development Responsibilities

It is very common for teachers to be called on to help central district administrators with curriculum revision and textbook adoption. In larger districts, a teacher might be asked to serve on a curriculum committee or a textbook committee consisting of a number of other teachers plus an administrator or two. These opportunities provide teachers with a chance to grow professionally by working closely with a large number of other educators. Benefits are particularly likely to accrue to those who have an opportunity to take part in a curriculum development project. Many teachers who have been so involved and who have been engaged in writing and trying out new materials report that their own instructional practices have improved as a direct result of this experience.

Curriculum work ordinarily does impose additional burdens on teachers' time. Frequently, committee meetings are held after school. Sometimes, they even occur on weekends. When meetings take place after school, the energy level of the participants, who have been teaching all day, may well be at a low ebb. Many who have participated under these conditions report that they find creative ideas extremely slow to come when they are so tired.

An additional frustration for many teachers when they first become involved in curriculum work is their feeling of being unprepared for the demands of their task. Although teachers generally get a reasonably sound grounding in basic instructional procedures in their undergraduate preparation programs, only rarely do they have much course background in formal curriculum-development procedures. Lacking a conceptual base for this kind of work, some teachers feel frustrated in their inability to articulate adequate responses to the ideas of one or two strong-willed individuals with whom they may be in basic disagreement. Because of their lack of expertise in the curriculum development process, many teachers emerge from an initial curriculum-development experience feeling that the final product is not as strong as it should be.

Many teachers do try to improve their understanding of curriculum development by taking in-service courses and by professional reading. In time, large numbers of them become quite proficient in this area. When they become comfortable with the curriculum development process, many teachers derive great pleasure from working in their own classrooms with programs that they have helped plan and organize.

Teachers' Responsibilities for Professional Growth

Preparation for teaching does not end with the award of a bachelor's degree. Because of the many roles that teachers must play and because of the unique demands of every teaching situation, teachers generally find a need to continue their professional preparation long after their graduation from a college or university. Even teachers who have been in the field for many years find themselves confronted from time to time with situations that go beyond their present level of expertise. In recent years, for example, federal legislation requiring the integration of handicapped youngsters into regular classrooms has prompted a massive in-service education effort designed to reach even teachers with years of successful experience.

In some states, teachers must take additional course work every few years in order to keep their teaching certificate in force. Other states require teachers who have a baccalaureate degree to take a certain number of additional courses in order to change their certificate from a temporary to a permanent status. For example, in the state of Washington, forty-five quarter hours of college-level work beyond the bachelor's degree must be completed before a teacher is given the standard certificate (the permanent certificate in that state). In addition to legal requirements, many school districts provide incentives for teachers to continue their professional growth. For example, they may offer salary increments for the completion of additional hours of course work.

Traditionally, teachers have sought professional growth through courses offered by colleges and universities. Courses are taken during the evening during those months when school is in session or during summer terms. In recent years, some challenges have been made to this approach to professional development. Critics have argued that college and university classes tend to enroll individuals from a number of school districts. The needs of individuals from these different settings may be so different that they simply cannot be well served in any one course.

Furthermore, it has been argued that university and college classrooms tend to be too isolated from the "real world" of teaching. Although few teachers say that educational theory has no importance, many critics of the professional growth courses offered by colleges and universities have contended that too frequently, practical applications deriving from theory have been absent from such programs. To meet such criticisms, a number of school districts, particularly the larger ones, have begun offering a number of professional growth programs of their own. These are usually offered in schools in the district. Some people argue that these courses provide a mechanism for responding well to the real needs of teachers. Others contend, however, that some of these programs have become so narrow that they fail to broaden the perspectives of the participating teachers.

There is little merit in attempting to determine which side is "right" in the debate between proponents of university and college courses as a source of professional teacher development and proponents of programs sponsored by local school districts as a source of professional development. Some logic does seem to support the idea, however, that when the objective is to solve specific local problems, district-sponsored programs may be best, and when the objective is to broaden the professional horizons of teachers by introducing them to new theories or innovative practices, college and university courses may be the best answer.

A third alternative selected by many teachers is wide professional reading. Though reading for professional development clearly does not have the benefit of accumulating credit hours, which, in many districts, may translate into higher salaries, it does provide an important resource for teachers simply interested in increasing the range of their professional competencies. Almost all subject-matter areas have large professional organizations that print periodicals dealing with issues of interest to members. These publications and many others are indexed in the *Education Index,* which is found in many public libraries as well as in nearly all college and university libraries. Many of these publications review recent books of interest to educators that focus on a broad array of themes.

Teachers' Public Relations Responsibilities

Teachers can have a great influence on how members of the public view the quality of education in a district. This is particularly true of parents. When youngsters in school have positive relationships with teachers, they tend to like school. When they like school and get favorable grade and deportment reports, parents are inclined to be satisfied with the quality of instruction their children are receiving. In many respects, then, public perceptions of education depend on the existence of positive and open communication between teachers and parents.

In recent years, a number of trends have acted to decrease the opportunities for easy parent–teacher contact, especially in larger districts. With increases in size, the physical distance between homes and schools has increased. This situation has been compounded by decisions to bus youngsters to schools far from their home neighborhoods to achieve a racial balance in schools throughout entire school districts. This physical separation between place of residence and the school has made it increasingly difficult for parents to get to the school and to know individual teachers well. A consequence has been that teachers in many instances have come to be viewed as an impersonal arm of distant school administrative authorities rather than as "real people" interested in working with the youngsters of parents with whom they are well acquainted.

Many teachers in large urban settings have worked hard to maintain strong links with parents. But when such efforts have not been undertaken, parents have become suspicious about educators' performance and, in a few instances, downright hostile. This can be extremely dangerous for educators' community standing. When parents begin to lose their faith in the excellence of the schools, the rest of the community is almost certain to follow suit.

Many prospective teachers and even experienced teachers who were raised in middle-class communities find it difficult to imagine groups of parents who are not active supporters of the school. This kind of support, however, is not necessarily typical of other groups in the society. The extent of this problem in some areas was revealed by a survey of parental attitudes toward the school taken in an attendance area in a central-city zone of a large West Coast city where one of the authors once taught. The survey revealed that parents and others in the community viewed the school as an institution second only to the police department as a potential threat to their style of life. Clearly this situation illustrates the need for teachers to work hard to establish open and credible communications with the parents of their learners.

A long-standing vehicle for promoting teacher–parent communication has been the parent–teacher organization. PTAs (Parent–Teacher Associations), PTOs (Parent–Teacher Organizations), and PTSAs (Parent–Teacher–Student Associations) are much more active in elementary schools than in secondary schools. In many districts, they provide opportunities for parents to work closely with teachers and for both parents and teachers to develop

Box 10-4
Professional Growth of Teachers

Statement of a middle school teacher:

I work with sixth graders. I teach English. Quite frankly, the English I learned even during my first two years of college goes far beyond what I need to know to work with these youngsters. Certainly, I have never had *any* occasion to draw on my own personal loves, *Beowulf* and Chaucer's *Canterbury Tales.* I teach grammar. I try to give these youngsters a feel for the basic elements of the English sentence. We do a few short stories. And, sometimes, we get into a little poetry.

Though I do not need additional background in my subject area, the state still requires me to take six hours of college course work every three years to maintain my certificate. I strongly object to this requirement. I do not need the additional English background. Courses in education are not helpful to me at this stage of my career. I get along well with my students. I have a large file of activities upon which I can draw. I have learned how to pace my instruction to accommodate varying situations. Though it may seem a little self-serving to say so, I don't think I really need additional professional preparation.

LET'S PONDER

Read the paragraphs above. Then, respond to the following questions.

1. Do *all* teachers need additional professional preparation after they begin teaching? Why, or why not?
2. The author of the statement above makes the point that the subject matter knowledge needed to work with sixth graders does not go much beyond what was learned during the first two years of college or university training. Do you agree with this statement? Should professional development requirements differ for teachers of different grade levels?
3. From your recollection of your own teachers, can you think of any areas of weakness that might have been improved by exposure to a professional development program? If so, what would have been the most effective kind of professional growth program to overcome these weaknesses?
4. Some argue that the best kinds of professional development programs are inservice programs sponsored by school districts. They contend that these programs can best respond to practical needs of teachers. Critics of this view suggest that most inservice programs are designed to solve problems of the district, not necessarily problems of the teachers. What are your feelings on this issue?

friendships. A limitation of the parent–teacher organization as a public relations forum is that many parents do not attend. Consequently it is not always clear that the group of generally supportive parents who do become involved are truly representative of the feelings of other parents and of the community as a whole.

In some districts, an effort to expand contacts with parents has been established around the idea of home visitations. Teachers make attempts to meet and chat with the parents of youngsters in their homes. A variant of this procedure is the small-meeting model, where a few parents are invited to meet informally with teachers and principals in a private home to chat about any issues that might concern them.

In general, there have been many attempts to arrange for positive teacher contacts with parents. Regrettably many parents never hear from a teacher unless their youngster is having some kind of a problem. Understandably, given this tradition, a note from school or a call from the teacher frequently produces initial anxiety. A parent answering the phone and learning that the teacher is the caller may well wonder, "What has Joan or John been up to this time?" To break the expectation that a contact from a teacher means bad news, many districts now encourage teachers to call parents when their youngsters have done some exceptionally good work in school. A call or a note from a teacher to convey a message that a youngster has done well can be a tremendously effective builder of parental support for the school program.

In addition to formal contacts with parents, teachers communicate almost continuously with parents in an informal sense. For example, comments written on a youngster's school papers may be read by parents. If the teacher's comments are insensitive or if there are grammatical errors, the teacher, though probably not by intent, has sent a very negative message about the school to the parents. Additionally, if youngsters take home written instructions relating to homework that are couched in vague language or contain grammatical errors, a similar negative impression will result. For large numbers of parents, these informal contacts are the only contacts they have with their children's teachers. Consequently, it is essential that any materials that may go home with a youngster be prepared carefully and reflect a high standard of educational practice.

In summary, the teacher's role in public relations is not one of aping Madison Avenue by developing a slick presentation to "sell" the school. Rather, the teacher's role is to keep communications channels with parents and other school patrons open so that free exchange of information about the school program can take place. Clearly, it is to the long-run advantage of teachers to take public relations responsibilities seriously. The best guarantee for the sort of quality educational programs that professional teachers want is a public that is enthusiastic in its endorsement of what teachers and the schools are doing.

Teachers' Roles: Some Reflections

As has been noted, teachers play many roles. Some of these roles have little to do with one another and may even be in conflict. Reflecting on the range of teachers' responsibilities, Mace commented, "Teachers are expected to be psychologists, sociologists, social workers, babysitters, coaches, club advisors and police. They are also expected to be patient and understanding while accepting verbal and physical abuse" (1979, p. 512).

Meeting these responsibilities places heavy physical and emotional demands on teachers. Even those who are in good physical condition and are used to hard work find teaching much more tiring than they had imagined it would be. (This reality frequently comes home with a vengeance to student teachers. Many find that they must go to bed at 7:30 or 8:00 P.M. to build up enough energy reserves to stand up to a full day of teaching. Most build up their stamina and find that they need less sleep as the experience goes forward.)

In recent years, evidence has begun to mount that the pressures of teaching take a severe emotional toll on some teachers. There have been frequent observations of a phenomenon known as *teacher burnout*. Usually after a number of years of service, individuals suffering from teacher burnout seem to lose their enthusiasm for teaching, undergo some minor personality changes, and lose interest in any sort of creativity in the classroom. Some burnout cases seem simply to have given up.

Though there are multiple explanations of burnout, certainly one contributing factor is the isolation of teachers from continuous contact with supportive adults. Teaching can be a lonely profession. Once the day begins, some teachers see no adults at all until their teaching duties are over. Probably a majority interact with other adults only over a hasty lunch. Because of the press of other duties, visits by administrators to classrooms are infrequent. Even less frequent are visits by other teachers. With no one looking in to see how things are going, some teachers begin to wonder whether anyone really appreciates their efforts. Some conclude that it makes little difference to anyone whether they are doing their best or just getting by.

Compounding teachers' isolation is the impression that many teachers get regarding "what counts" in terms of administrators' evaluation of their effectiveness. Because of infrequent visits of administrators to observe instruction, many conclude that their skills in helping youngsters learn are not considered as important as following school policies, turning in attendance reports and other paperwork on time, keeping adequate records, and accepting extracurricular responsibilities willingly. Whether this is an accurate picture of administrators' expectations is not at issue. The issue is that many teachers *believe* these to be the expectations that "count." Given this perspective, many do develop some serious doubts about the professional payoff of staying up until midnight to prepare exciting lessons for the youngsters in their classes.

Box 10-5
Teachers and Public Relations

LET'S PONDER

Respond to the following questions.

1. Do you think teachers ought to have to concern themselves with public relations? Why, or why not?
2. Suppose a large district decided that too many obligations were being shouldered by teachers. A decision was made to hire five public relations specialists to work in each elementary school and seven public relations specialists to work in each secondary school. Teachers were freed from any obligation to work actively in parent-teacher groups. In fact, all public relations responsibilities were assumed by these specialists.
   How do you react to this scheme? Would you expect community reactions to schools to become better or worse? How would teachers react to this idea?
3. From your experience in school, can you recall some things individual teachers did that tended to give parents and other citizens the impression that the school was doing a fine job? Did all teachers do these things? Why, or why not?
4. Do you recall any teachers whom you might describe as "public relations disasters?" What did they do? What were their motives?
5. Suppose you were asked by your principal to devise a plan to improve the image of your school among parents. What would your recommendations be?

We would not wish to conclude by leaving an impression that all teachers lose their enthusiasm for their profession. Clearly this is not the case. Many teachers look forward to each day at school with as much enthusiasm at the beginning of their twentieth year as at the beginning of their first year. Some experience very few, if any, anxieties arising from the multiple roles they must play. But it would be irresponsible to suggest that no teachers experience these kinds of problems. Many do. And their condition represents a real concern of thoughtful educators everywhere.

Recapitulation of Major Ideas

1. Teachers play many roles. They have instructional responsibilities, counseling responsibilities, professional growth responsibilities, curriculum development responsibilities, public relations responsibilities, and others as well.

2. In recent years, the instructional role of the teacher has changed from that of a dispenser of information to that of an instructional manager. As an instructional manager, the teacher is responsible for creating an environment where learning can take place. In this role, teachers determine learning objectives, diagnose learners, plan learning activities, implement programs, and evaluate learners' progress.

3. Teachers play an important counseling role. Many teachers prefer to seek out a teacher whom they know well rather than a counselor when they have a problem. Teachers need some basic counseling skills of their own. Furthermore, they need to know when to refer a youngster to a counselor for more specialized help.

4. Teachers who do an effective job of exercising the counseling function tend to be people who are secure and have positive self-images. They have the ability to use rational problem-solving skills. In general, they are models of the sorts of behaviors it is hoped youngsters will acquire.

5. Many teachers say they do not particularly enjoy the supervisory and administrative tasks they must perform. Protests against "all of the paperwork" are heard frequently in teachers' lounges. Many feel that administrative work takes time away from instructional tasks.

6. Teachers frequently have a hand in curriculum development efforts. Initially such work may be seen as difficult because few teachers during their undergraduate preparation programs receive much training in curriculum development. Teacher preparation programs typically place a much heavier emphasis on instructional skills than on curriculum development. Most who do have an opportunity to work on a curriculum development project report great professional benefits from the experience once it is completed.

7. Teachers have professional growth responsibilities. Many states require teachers to return for additional training at colleges and universities periodically as a condition of certificate renewal. In larger districts, extensive in-service programs may be sponsored locally. Whether university in-service courses or those developed in local districts are better continues to be a much debated issue.

8. Teachers play an important public relations function. Particularly, the kinds of relationships they establish with parents can influence how an entire community feels about the schools. Today, with an erosion of the neighborhood school concept, it is becoming increasingly difficult for parents and teachers to come together in nonthreatening situations where firm friendships can develop. Many districts are establishing programs that encourage teachers to contact parents when a youngster has done something good at school. Traditionally, parents have heard from teachers only when a youngster is in some sort of trouble.

9. Some teachers experience emotional problems arising out of the nature of their professional lives. Part of these difficulties may result from role conflicts. Part may stem from the isolated conditions under which many

teachers work. Part may come from feelings, whether accurate or inaccurate, that administrators are not really very interested in whether or not performance in the classroom is good or bad. Certainly many teachers do not experience problems, but the number who do are sufficiently high to represent a genuine concern of the profession.

Posttest

DIRECTIONS: Using your own paper, answer each of the following true/false questions. For each correct statement, write the word *true* on your paper. For each incorrect statement, write the word *false* on your paper.

1. Though teachers play many roles, they usually find that their college preparation programs have given them adequate background to feel comfortable in fulfilling all of them.
2. A frequent complaint of teachers is that they must deal with too much paperwork.
3. Today it is generally recognized that teachers do not adequately serve the instructional role of teaching when they restrict their activities to telling learners information and making assignments.
4. Because many schools have counselors, teachers do not have to be much concerned with counseling responsibilities.
5. The public relations functions of schools are best left to professional specialists, and teachers should not be involved in this area.
6. Many states require teachers to take course work to maintain a valid teaching certificate.
7. Because they are involved in a relatively low-pressure profession, teachers suffer psychological stress only rarely.
8. Most teachers report that their evaluation as a "good" or an "ineffective" teacher depends almost exclusively on their ability to transmit information effectively to the youngsters in their classrooms.
9. Today teachers in large urban areas may find it more difficult to establish close relationships with parents than formerly.
10. The phenomenon of "teacher burnout" has become increasingly common in recent years.

Summary

Teaching places a multiplicity of demands on teachers' talents. The various roles that teachers must play are not always compatible with one another. Consequently, many teachers feel a good deal of pressure as they attempt to deal with the day-to-day requirements of their profession. There is evidence that these pressures are increasing. Particularly alarming is the increasing incidence of teacher burnout, a condition some psychologists have paralleled with the battle fatigue that afflicts many combatants in time of war.

Among the roles that teachers must play are those involving instruction, counseling, administration, professional development, curriculum development, and public relations. The diversity of these roles comes as a surprise to many beginners. They falsely anticipate that they will spend their days almost exclusively on tasks associated with instruction. On the contrary, they will be pulled in many different directions by obligations and responsibilities that many may not even have considered during their undergraduate days. Today the successful teacher has to be able to shoulder many responsibilities, adapt to many situations, and exercise leadership under a multitude of circumstances. The profession requires individuals who are strong-willed yet adaptable to a wide variety of conditions.

References

AMIDON, EDMUND J., AND FLANDERS, NED A. *The Role of the Teacher in the Classroom.* Minneapolis: Paul S. Amidon, 1963.

ANDREW, MICHAEL D. *Teachers Should Be Human Too.* Washington, D.C.: Association of Teacher Educators, 1972.

EGAN, GERARD. *The Skilled Helper: A Model for Systematic Helping and Interpersonal Relating.* Monterey, Calif.: Brooks/Cole, 1975.

FELKER, D. *Building Positive Self-Concepts.* Minneapolis: Burgess, 1974.

GILSTRAP, R., AND MARTIN, W. *Current Strategies for Teachers.* Pacific Palisades, Calif.: Goodyear Publishing, 1975.

GROSS, BEATRICE. *Teaching Under Pressure.* Santa Monica, Calif.: Goodyear Publishing, 1979.

HAWLEY, RICHARD A. "Teaching as Failing." *Phi Delta Kappan* (Apr., 1979): 597–600.

JARVIS, F. WASHINGTON. "The Teacher as Servant." *Phi Delta Kappan* (March, 1979): 504–505.

MACE, JANE. "Teaching May Be Hazardous to Your Health." *Phi Delta Kappan* (March, 1979): 512–513.

STUART, JESSE. *To Teach, To Love.* New York: Penguin Books, 1973.

11

Classroom Management and Discipline

Objectives

This chapter provides information to help the reader to

1. Recognize that classroom management and discipline are a regular part of the responsibilities of all teachers.
2. Grasp selected operating principles associated both with classroom management and with discipline.
3. Note that the purpose of good management and discipline techniques is the development of learners' self-control mechanisms.
4. Recognize that teachers' responses to learner misbehavior must vary with the nature of the situation in which the misbehavior occurs.

Pretest

DIRECTIONS: Using your own paper, answer each of the following true/false questions. For each correct statement, write the word *true* on your paper. For each incorrect statement, write the word *false* on your paper.

1. Learner misbehavior occasionally occurs even in classes taught by very experienced teachers.
2. Classroom management and discipline are the responsibility of the school counseling staff, not classroom teachers.
3. Learners do not function well in classrooms where routines are well established; consequently, teachers in such classrooms tend to have many discipline problems.
4. A major purpose of discipline is helping learners develop a sense of self-control.
5. Creative teachers who avoid lesson planning probably experience fewer discipline problems than teachers who plan each lesson with care.
6. For any given learner misbehavior, there is a universally "correct" teacher response.
7. Because of the possibility of a court suit, a teacher ought to keep a written record containing information about a iearner's misbehavior.
8. A major principle to be followed with a view to minimizing discipline problems is to respect the personal dignity of learners in the classroom.
9. Sometimes teachers need to change the nature of the physical environment as they work to improve the discipline climate within a classroom.
10. It is a sound practice for teachers to discuss with learners a set of rules describing appropriate patterns of classroom behavior.

Introduction

Controlling youngsters in classrooms so meaningful instruction can occur challenges even teachers with years of experience. All teachers must deal with the issue. Few would rank managing and disciplining youngsters high on their what-I-like-best-about-teaching lists. Most, however, develop procedures for dealing with the necessity to provide an environment that will allow their youngsters to learn. In this chapter, we will introduce some systematic approaches to dealing with classroom management and discipline that experienced teachers have found to be effective.

It is not only teachers who are concerned about classroom management and discipline. These issues are also very much on the minds of parents and the public at large. For a number of years, the Gallup organization has been surveying the public regarding feelings about the problems of public schools. In annual surveys taken between 1969 and 1983, "discipline" was perceived to be the major problem facing the schools in every annual survey except that of 1971, when this issue was nudged out by concerns related to school finance and integration of the schools (Elam, 1983).

Though discipline regularly has been seen as a major problem facing the schools, there is evidence that the public does not place primary blame on schools or school people for originating the problem. In a 1983 survey, for example, the Gallup Poll found that most people surveyed regarded "lack of discipline in the home" and "lack of respect for law and order throughout society" as the major reasons schools were faced with discipline problems (Gallup, 1983; p. 37).

Regardless of where the "blame" for discipline problems resides, no one denies that they exist and that teachers must be prepared to deal with them if they are to establish themselves as successful educators. Individuals contemplating a career as teachers need to begin preparing themselves to manage and discipline youngsters in their classrooms. These are responsibilities they will face throughout their professional careers.

Before we begin our discussion of these important issues, we would like to suggest a caution. Much has been written in the popular press about discipline problems. Television dramas often feature unruly youngsters as stock characters. Some short stories and novels have depicted school classrooms as terrible places in which teachers and students engage in confrontations that routinely end in violence. Certainly such situations have existed, do exist, and regrettably, will continue to exist in certain schools. But these very negative instances, often illustrating the worst-case scenarios, should not be generalized to all of public education. To be blunt, average public classrooms are not places where violence and carnage are "typical." In general, teachers develop ways of working very productively with youngsters who, in the main, enjoy being in school. One has only to look at the millions of teachers who go pridefully and positively to work each day to recognize that while all teachers must deal with classroom management and discipline issues, these chal-

Box 11-1
Violence on Television Means Violence in the Schools

A caller on a recent talk show made these comments:

> There's so much violence on television now that it's no wonder the schools have lost control of the kids. These cable channels will put absolutely *anything* on the air, and it's mostly kids who watch. If kids see decapitations, casual knifings, and all sorts of unmentionable mayhem on television, they're bound to start seeing that sort of thing as ''normal.'' No wonder teachers are scared to death. No wonder violence is becoming a way of life in the schools. It's a tragedy, a real tragedy. And I just don't think there's a thing we can do about it.

LET'S PONDER

Read the comments above. Then, respond to these questions.

1. Do you think there is too much violence on television? On what do you base your opinion?
2. How much does violence on television affect youngsters' tendency to act in violent ways?
3. How probable is it that discipline problems in the schools result primarily because of violence on television?
4. Suppose you were asked to respond to the caller who made these remarks. What would you say?

lenges do not represent insurmountable barriers to success in the classroom. There is every reason to believe that new teachers in the future also will master techniques that allow them to manage and discipline youngsters so that all may profit from the instructional program.

Classroom management and discipline are closely related tasks, but each has its special characteristics. Each of these important issues will be discussed in major sections to follow.

Classroom Management

Classroom management refers to procedures teachers adopt and implement to ensure a smooth, routinized functioning of the classroom. Good classroom management ensures that limited class time is used to maximum advantage. Good classroom managers have developed techniques that allow them to discharge noninstructional responsibilities quickly and to move efficiently into the instructional heart of their classroom programs. Though individual teachers use a variety of techniques to facilitate good classroom management, a number of their practices tend to fall into rather generalized kinds of patterns. For example, there is a tendency for good teachers to establish clear rules and routines.

Establishing Rules and Routines

Smooth classroom instructional programs are characterized by a certain predictability. That is, youngsters understand what is expected of them, how they are to behave, and what the general "flow of events" is during a typical class session. Many teachers have found it worthwhile to be very explicit with learners regarding just what their classroom "rules" are and what normal classroom routines will be.

Discussion of classroom "rules" with youngsters is important because expectations of what kind of behavior is appropriate tend to vary from teacher to teacher. This means that a group of youngsters who, in the eyes of a new teacher with whom they are working for the first time in September, may appear hopelessly undisciplined may, in fact, be acting in ways quite consistent with expectations of the teacher who worked with them previously. Frustration both for teachers and youngsters can be avoided when teachers take time to formulate a set of rules specific to their own individual classroom. Depending on the nature of the learners and on the predispositions of the individual teacher, these rules may be developed, in part, jointly by the teacher and the learners. Rules may address a number of issues. Some of the following are typical of issues many experienced teachers wish made clear in their lists of classroom rules:

1. Expected behavior when learners come into the classroom.
2. Teacher signals the learners are to look for when the teacher is ready to begin the day's instruction and wants the undivided attention of the class.
3. Learner actions to be taken when he or she needs to leave the room.
4. Expectations about making up missed work.
5. Procedures to be followed to get recognition during a classroom discussion.
6. Procedures to be followed in preparing for dismissal.

Once a particular set of "rules" is established, this information must be communicated clearly to students. At a bare minimum, there should be a class discussion to clarify any points of confusion. With older youngsters, it is a good idea to make copies of the rules and distribute them to learners. Some teachers go so far as to make copies, discuss the rules, and give youngsters a short quiz over this material. Whatever procedure is adopted, the objective here is to ensure that learners understand precisely what the rules are and what the teacher regards as "correct" classroom behavior.

In addition to establishing sets of classroom rules, effective classroom managers think through carefully day-to-day routines they follow in working with their youngsters. These routines establish predictable patterns of occurrence for tasks or events that must be attended to each day. Organization of these tasks or events into routines serves several important functions. First of all, establishment of consistent patterns fosters efficient use of class time. Second, the patterns can easily be communicated to learners along with information about what their expected behaviors are to be while each task or event is occurring. Additionally, teachers must make a tremendous number of decisions each day. When they have well-established routines, teachers are able to devote their energies to dealing with unpredictable events that deserve their undivided attention.

Many kinds of tasks and events can be organized into routines. For example, decisions can be made about how such obligations as taking roll, handling special learner questions and concerns, making assignments, and returning learners' work are to be discharged. Over the years, experienced teachers have developed time-efficient mechanisms for handling these responsibilities. Beginning teachers often experience difficulty in accomplishing these tasks quickly. It is not unusual, for example, for an unwary novice teacher to spend as much as 20 to 25 percent of precious class time taking care of administrative responsibilities that, with some attention to organization, could be accomplished in a fraction of this time.

A failure to handle such duties in a routinized, organized, and systematic manner can result in a classroom environment conducive to the development of control problems. When tasks are not accomplished smoothly and efficiently, there tend to be long periods of time when youngsters are not productively engaged. This kind of nonfocused "slack" time may lead to loud talking (indeed, even to shouting matches) among youngsters, and the teacher may find it very difficult to calm the group and refocus attention on instructional activities. With sound, routinized management of recurring activities, this kind of slack will not develop, and the youngsters' attention will not be allowed long to wander off the planned instructional program. In the long run, this kind of organized, routinized environment will make life more enjoyable both for the teacher and for the learners.

Lesson Management

Successful lesson management can diminish possibilities that classroom control problems will occur. Several teacher skills are important here. One of the most critical has to do with the level of expectations the teacher has of his or her learners. A basic principle in lesson preparation is that of providing for youngsters' success. This principle places an obligation on teachers to ensure that the lesson demands learner behaviors that are realistically within their reach. Classroom control difficulties can result from poor lesson planning when youngsters sense that the teacher has placed them in a "no win" situation by expecting performance levels that are hopelessly beyond their capabilities. Every lesson ought to make provision for the differing capabilities of

Box 11-2
Contributors to Discipline Problems and What Teachers Might Do About Them

The following have been suggested as possible contributors to discipline problems in the school:

- Too much violence on television
- Home environments where youngsters learn little self-discipline
- Working mothers
- Declining influence of the church
- General permissiveness of the larger society
- Too many legal constraints on the schools standing in the way of their dealing firmly with problem youngsters
- Teachers who are ill-prepared to deal with discipline problems
- Too many youngsters from foreign cultures who do not respect traditional American values
- Laws that discourage drop-outs and that keep uninterested youngsters in the schools too long

LET'S PONDER

Read the list above. Then, respond to these questions.

1. How would you rank the above items in terms of your own view of the relative importance of each? On what do you base your opinion?
2. Of the above "contributors," which ones do you think teachers can influence the most? The least?
3. What would you do if asked to develop a specific set of responses a group of teachers in a school might take to deal with three indicators that you view as highly susceptible to teacher influence?
4. What would you do if asked to develop a specific set of responses a group of teachers in a school might take to deal with three indicators that you view as highly resistant (or, at least, partially resistant) to teacher influence?
5. Would you add any other "contributors" to the list above? If so, what would they be, and why would you add them?

learners and should provide some opportunities for those who apply themselves to succeed. Success in the classroom enhances the self-images of youngsters, makes them more positively disposed to the teacher and to school in general, and reduces the likelihood of classroom behavior problems.

Successful classroom lessons are characterized by an orderly flow from beginning to end. Beginning teachers frequently experience difficulty in making transitions from one part of a lesson to another as efficient and as smooth as they should be. Where transitions are ragged, "slack" time may well develop, and classroom control difficulties may surface as the youngsters' attention is diverted from the central thrust of the lesson. Many beginning teachers get into transitions-associated difficulty because they abandon the kind of step-by-step lesson planning that was required of them when they did their supervised student teaching.

Certainly it is true that many very experienced teachers manage to move a lesson along in a commendably smooth and sequential fashion without relying on formal lesson plans. This kind of ability, however, has resulted from years of practice. Over time, these individuals have developed a kind of intuitive, internal lesson plan that enables them to unfold step-by-step instruction almost on "automatic pilot." Few beginners are able to turn this trick. Written lesson plans can serve as invaluable organizational tools as preparation for instruction goes forward and can serve as important reminders of sequence when the lesson is being presented in the classroom.

Lesson plans should speak with great specificity about particular statements to be made or actions to be taken at transition points. For example, if youngsters are to be asked to read something after having been engaged in a classroom discussion, the lesson plan should make this point very explicit. Some beginners find it useful to go so far as to write down specifically what they will say to youngsters at this point in the lesson ("Take out your texts. Turn to page 46. Read from the top of page 46 to the bottom of page 52. Close your book when you have finished. If others are still reading, begin working the problems we discussed earlier. When everyone has finished reading, I'll call you to attention, and we'll discuss the material.") This kind of specificity can help a teacher think through his or her precise expectations and all of the steps required to get youngsters smoothly from one phase of a lesson to another.

Materials needed for a lesson must be prepared in advance. Furthermore, they must be organized in such a way that items the teacher needs are readily at hand and in the appropriate order and that items to be provided to the youngsters are arranged in such a way that they can be distributed quickly and with a minimum of disturbance. Some teachers find it useful to organize materials they will need sequentially in a manila folder..If large numbers of items are involved, placing numbers on individual items to indicate intended order of use may prove helpful, particularly in the event that materials are dropped or, for some other reason, get out of their proper order.

Many teachers find it useful to organize materials to be passed out to learners according to how youngsters are seated. If they are seated at tables, then enough items for youngsters at a given table can be sorted into a small pile before the class. Or, if the learners are seated in rows, then enough materials for each row can be counted out ahead of time. This kind of organization does consume some time before classes begin, but this time will pay handsome dividends during the instructional day. Distribution can be made quickly, and valuable instructional time can be saved. Furthermore, this kind of efficient operation reduces nonproductive "slack" time and minimizes opportunities for outbursts of disruptive behavior.

In summary, successful implementation of lessons demands careful plan-

ning. In the main, this planning is directed toward the end of promoting efficient use of time of a kind that maximizes important task-oriented activity
and reduces opportunities for youngsters' attention to be diverted into nonproductive channels.

Discipline

One point noted earlier deserves mention again. *All* teachers from time to
time experience discipline problems. Youngsters in public schools represent
an incredible diversity. This diversity taken together with their immaturity go
together to ensure that every teacher will occasionally be confronted with
youngsters who do not observe a behavior standard consistent with their
teacher's expectations.

In thinking about the issue of discipline, it is not uncommon for beginning
teachers to consider discipline as a problem that somehow interferes with
their instructional responsibilities. In a sense, this conception makes sense.
After all, discipline problems of a disruptive nature can play havoc on lessons
directed toward teaching reading, language arts, history, and other school
subjects. When looked at in another way, however, discipline can be viewed
not as something that interferes with instructional responsibilities but as an
instructional responsibility in its own right. That is, teachers have an obligation to "teach" discipline much as they have an obligation to teach other
subjects.

The goals of discipline-related instruction are to help youngsters develop
patterns of self-control and acceptance of responsibility. Few would argue
that self-control and an ability to accept responsibility are characteristics that
differentiate between children and adults. Hence, it makes sense to focus
school instruction toward development of these ends. Successful teachers
develop expertise in helping youngsters grow in terms of self-control and
management as they also develop expertise in promoting learner growth in
subject-matter content areas.

When discipline is viewed as a "normal" teacher responsibility, then
teacher actions in this area can be evaluated in terms of their relative success
in achieving the goals of discipline. That is, are responses effective in terms
of their ability to help youngsters grow in terms of self-control and willingness to accept responsibility? These criteria ought to be applied as we consider the effectiveness of individual teacher actions. In this connection, it
should be noted that youngsters do not all respond in the same ways to the
same kinds of teacher actions. That is, certain teacher behaviors might work
beautifully with youngster *A* in helping him or her become more self-controlled and responsible but have no positive influence on youngster *B* at all.
Hence, while there are certain patterns of teacher behavior that have been
found to be successful with large numbers of youngsters, it is a fallacy to
assume that mastery of a certain set of responses will assure a given teacher

Box 11-3
Teachers Shouldn't Have To Be Disciplinarians

The following letter from a teacher recently appeared in a local newspaper.

Editor:

I am one of the teacher dropouts . . . a "burned out" case, some might say. In college, I worked hard to master my subject, and, when I began teaching, I burned with a desire to help youngsters master and love the content that has come to mean so much to me. The stars went out of my eyes fast.

The conditions in my classroom simply prevented me from serving those youngsters who wanted to learn. My life was nothing but discipline, discipline, discipline. Ten years of worrying about keeping some kind of minimal control level have been just too much. These disruptive kids should be sorted out and placed in special classrooms. The counselors and administrators should deal with them. They shouldn't be allowed to ruin it for the good students (and for the good teachers, I might add). I had hoped to make a productive contribution to society as a teacher. But I rest my case as one of the defeated. In schools as they are today, there is simply no way for a committed teacher to operate in a professional manner.

LET'S PONDER

Read the letter above. Then, respond to these questions.

1. What is your general reaction to this letter to the editor?
2. In your own experience, did disruptive learners frequently interfere with the learning of other youngsters? How did teachers respond to such situations in your school?
3. Should counselors and administrators play a larger role in the area of discipline? Why, or why not?
4. Can committed teachers "operate in a professional manner" in the schools today? Why, or why not?

success in dealing with every discipline problem that might emerge in the classroom.

Preventing Serious Behavior Problems: Basic Principles

A number of basic principles have evolved over the years that underlie the actions of teachers who deal successfully with the issue of discipline. Responses to these principles may vary greatly from teacher to teacher and from situation to situation. The principles themselves, however, tend to remain relatively constant.

Respect Learners' Dignity. Even the very youngest learners in the school enjoy a certain self-esteem as human beings. They tend to react negatively when comments of teachers (and of others) appear to them as designed to undermine their personal dignity. Typically, this kind of thing occurs when a teacher loses self-control and makes comments generalizing beyond the specific misbehavior that may be under question. For example, an angry teacher may respond to a learner who has been interrupting another youngster's comments with a very cutting remark such as, "You're just never going to amount to anything. You can't get along with other people."

This kind of uncalled-for remark is a failure on two counts. First of all, it fails to speak specifically to the nature of the "problem" behavior and generalizes to a whole host of conditions that may bear little, if any, legitimate relationship to what the youngster has done. Certainly, it provides the learner no guidance whatever regarding either (1) what he or she has done wrong, or (2) how he or she might remedy the situation. Second, the statement comes through as a direct assault on the personal dignity of the learner. It is almost certain to diminish the teacher in the eyes of the youngster, and it may well lay a foundation for additional behavior problems in the future. If a youngster believes that a teacher has classified him or her as a "bad" person, then he or she has nothing to lose by acting in ways displeasing to the teacher.

On the other hand, when teachers' comments are couched in language that tend to support youngsters as persons and to focus more specifically on the nature of the unacceptable behavior and on specific ways it might be remedied, then learners tend to be more receptive. The teacher is rejecting the behavior, not the learner. This kind of communication is critical if teachers sincerely hope to help youngsters in terms of self-control and assumption of responsibility for their actions.

Provide Chances For Correct Behavior To Occur. It is not enough for teachers to point out the nature of a problem behavior and to suggest an alternative, more productive behavior. Youngsters must also be provided with legitimate opportunities to practice the productive behaviors. This means that teachers cannot pigeonhole youngsters as "troublemakers." To do so denies the possibility of achieving a permanent change of behavior, and a change of behavior in a more productive direction is what good discipline ought to be about.

To put this principle into practice, teachers need to demonstrate their faith in the essential "goodness" of learners by laying out clearly how they expect a youngster with problem behavior to act and by allowing him or her a chance to demonstrate this more productive pattern. Many problem behaviors will disappear when youngsters are provided with appropriate guidelines, are given an opportunity to demonstrate acceptable patterns, and are reinforced by the teacher for behaving in a manner more consistent with the teacher's expectations.

Discover the Nature of the "Real" Problem. Misbehavior in classrooms often results from circumstances having little, if anything, to do with the individual teacher or the individual class. The classroom may provide nothing more than a convenient forum for display for misbehavior that is deeply rooted in conditions completely external to the school. Something may happen in the classroom that simply may appear to a youngster with problems to be laying on one frustration too many. When this happens, he or she may respond with behaviors that the teacher finds unacceptable.

Youngsters come to school from backgrounds that are unbelievably varied. Frankly, some have home situations that are simply appalling. Homes where emotional tensions are the norm, battering of family members is a frequent occurrence, and financial disaster is a day-to-day reality provide little emotional support for children. Frustrations resulting from a combination of many factors can lead to misbehavior in the classroom. It behooves the

---

Box 11-4

Identifying Rules for Classroom Behavior and Responding to Misbehavior

Suppose you are a teacher new to a building. Your principal is very much interested in how you will handle classroom management and discipline problems. To see how well you have thought through these issues, the principal suggests that you do the following:

1. Prepare a list of about six rules that will govern learner behavior in your classroom.
2. Prepare a list of things you will do to reward or support or praise youngsters who behave consistently with these rules.
3. Prepare a list of penalties of three levels of severity for youngsters who fail to behave in accordance with these rules.
    a. Penalties requiring little major effort on the part of the learner.
    b. Penalties requiring a moderate effort on the part of the learner.
    c. Penalties requiring a good deal on the part of the learner.

LET'S PONDER

Read the above information. Then, respond to each of the above items. Then, answer these questions:

1. What age group of youngster did you have in mind when you made your responses? Would your responses have been different if you had another age group in mind?
2. Which did you find to be the most difficult of the three tasks above? Why?
3. How would you assess the potential effectiveness of each of the "penalties" you described in your response to item 3 above?

teacher to learn as much as possible about the personal lives of the individual youngsters he or she serves. Quite often, a misbehaving youngster is signalling a need for adult help and guidance and not expressing a malicious desire to be disruptive. While teachers seek to understand causes of misbehavior so learners can be helped to act in a more acceptable manner, issues such as lack of support at home should not interfere with the objective of rechanneling problem behavior along more acceptable lines. There are certain behavioral expectations that all individuals must meet if they are to be regarded as self-controlled and responsible people. This is true regardless of environmental difficulties they may face that are different from those faced by others.

Use a Variety of Techniques.   As noted previously, no single technique can be used as a "fail-safe" device that will remedy problem behavior of every misbehaving learner. Different learners respond to different techniques. Thus, teachers must be familiar with a variety of techniques they can use, as appropriate, to respond to disruptive situations. Several are introduced in the next section.

Responding to Inappropriate Behavior: Some Teacher Options

Teachers have a number of options available to them when learners misbehave. These options can be organized into a number of categories. Each category includes several responses that might be used to divert unacceptable behaviors into more productive channels. Options can be scaled along a "not severe" to "severe" continuum.

Supporting Self Control.   Youngsters must be provided opportunities to demonstrate appropriate behavior patterns. That is, teachers must give youngsters chances to behave "correctly." When minor misbehaviors occur, teachers might begin by "ignoring the problem." This response is based on an assumption that youngsters know the rules and will return to a more acceptable pattern if no large issue is made of a temporary aberration.

If this kind of planned ignoring fails to result in a change, then visual contact between the teacher and the offending youngster may be a productive alternative. Known in the trade as the "cold, hard stare," such a glance can communicate to a youngster that a particular behavior is not acceptable. The glance provides the student with a cue that says, in effect, "now is your opportunity to exercise self-control." When relatively minor behavior problems are involved, the teacher glance often works well. The technique can be accompanied by hand signals, nods of the head, and other nonverbal promptings that may reinforce the teacher's expectation of a behavior change.

Another option open to the teacher is that of "proximity control." This involves nothing more than the teacher taking action to move physically closer to the youngster who is misbehaving. Many teachers like to do this in situations where they spot unacceptable behavior during a time when they are in the middle of a presentation to the class and are hesitant to stop and break the flow of the lesson. They simply continue their presentation while moving closer to the youngster(s) with the problem behavior. Often this movement will result in a cessation of the nonproductive behavior pattern. Many learners find it difficult to misbehave when the teacher is nearby.

Nonverbal approaches may fail to remedy the problem behavior. As a first course of action, many teachers favor a "quiet word" with the offending learner. This action seeks to correct the inappropriate behavior through a quiet and firm spoken directive to the learner. With younger children, often it is sufficient simply to remind them of a classroom rule ("Remember, all of us must listen when someone else has been recognized.") The intent of the quiet word procedure is to let a learner know in unequivocal terms that his or her behavior is unacceptable, has been noticed, and should be changed.

Sometimes problem behavior is so disruptive that a more assertive verbal approach must be taken. It may be necessary to issue a verbal "command." The command should indicate specifically the nature of the misbehavior, suggest the nature of an appropriate alternative, and insist that the appropriate alternative be implemented forthwith. To be effective, a command must be delivered in a strong "I-mean-it" tone of voice.

Occasionally, it may be necessary to have individual conferences with learners who have not changed unacceptable behavior patterns even after having been provided with numerous verbal and nonverbal signals as well as with suggestions regarding more appropriate behaviors. Under such circumstances, it makes sense to schedule an "individual conference." The conference should be held when the teacher can speak with the learner on a one-on-one basis, free from the prying eyes and ears of other youngsters. During the conference, the learner should be encouraged to do a good deal of the talking. Questions such as the following often are posed during individual conferences:

What is the problem?
What are we going to do about it?
What will be the consequences for you if this kind of misbehavior continues?
How can I help you?

The purpose of the conference is to solve the problem, not to arrange for revenge on the offending youngster. Consequences that are discussed should be designed with a view to moving the learner to a pattern of self-controlled behavior.

All of these teacher responses have two general purposes. In the short run, they seek to change an unproductive pattern of behavior that may be interfering with the ability of youngsters in the class to learn. On the other hand, they seek to direct behaviors of offending youngsters into more productive channels. Often behavior change of this kind does not occur immediately. Professional teachers must be prepared to take the long view and to keep working with youngsters who, initially, may not change as rapidly as might be desired. With judicious use of some of the techniques suggested here, teachers can begin shaping learners' behaviors in directions that, in the long run, have potentials to serve them well.

Managing Classroom Environments to Diminish Potential Control Problems

Many experienced teachers find that making a change in the nature of the environment of their classroom facilitates good classroom control. Such changes may involve alterations in arrangements of physical objects, in seating patterns, or in other variables that go together to shape the overall context of a given classroom.

Seat Changes.   Recall that the objective of discipline is to help youngsters grow in terms of self-control or self-management. To provide conditions for this growth, sometimes it is desirable to make changes in assigned seating arrangements. For example, a misbehaving youngster may be seated in close proximity to other learners who tend to reinforce his or her undesirable behavior patterns. By removing a learner to a seat elsewhere in the classroom, the teacher sometimes can create a set of circumstances more probable to support a change in behavior in the desired direction.

In addition to changing seats to separate a given learner from others in the class who may be supporting unacceptable behavior patterns, sometimes teachers remove a learner for the purpose of placing him or her closer to the teacher's desk. This kind of move is designed to take advantage of the principle of proximity control. That is, a youngster seated closer to the teacher is less apt to misbehave than if seated at a point more distant from the teacher's desk.

Removing Physical Barriers.   Sometimes physical barriers in the classroom contribute to classroom control problems. A student teacher in a classroom once supervised by one of the authors experienced a great deal of difficulty in maintaining effective control over youngsters on one side of the classroom. A study of this situation revealed that a map stand in the front of the room prevented the teacher from moving easily to the side of the room where behavior problems seemed to break out too frequently. The map stand was removed, and the student teacher varied his movement patterns to ensure that the "problem" side of the classroom was visited as often as other parts of the room. As a result, incidences of misbehavior in this part of the room dropped off dramatically.

Box 11-5
Alternative Classroom Arrangements

1. Lecture on causes of World War I.
2. Demonstration of appropriate way of preparing a slide for use with a microscope in a biology class.
3. Work on dolls to be presented to mothers on Mothers' Day.
4. Group work on class safety poster.
5. Explanation of basic factoring using the chalkboard in an algebra class.
6. Small group work with teacher in reading groups in a grade 3 classroom.
7. Individual preparation of ceramic ashtrays in a crafts class.
8. Explanation of cooling line hoses in an automobile.

LET'S PONDER

Look at the list of classroom activities above. Then, respond to these questions.

1. For which of the above activities would you think a classroom arranged with learner seats in rows would be most appropriate? Why do you think so?
2. For which of the above activities would you recommend equipping the classroom with a number of tables at which learners could work? Why do you think so?
3. For which of the above activities would you like learners to move individual desks into small clusters? Why do you think so?
4. What other physical arrangements might work well with some of the above activities? Why do you think so?

Other physical barriers can cause problems as well. It is important that youngsters have a clear view of chalkboards and screens. Lecterns and other visual barriers need to be removed to ensure that views are unimpeded. Also, care should be taken to ensure that extremely tall learners seated at the front of the room do not block the views of those shorter youngsters seated farther back. Visual obstructions of any kind can break the attention of youngsters. When this happens, classroom control problems may develop. Teachers sensitive to this possibility are careful to remove physical obstacles that may divert the focus of learners to something other than the lesson.

Organizing Space Productively. Learning tasks of various kinds demand different types of physical arrangements to facilitate maintenance of the learners' attention and to optimize learning. For a short lecture, arrangement of youngsters in rows may work well. If the task involves cooperative work on a project, however, moving desks together or bringing in work tables will better support learning. Every effort should be made to establish a congruence between the physical arrangement of the classroom and the expected learning outcome. Such congruence enhances the likelihood that youngsters will succeed. And success (or at least potential success) acts to diminish control problems.

Beginning teachers sometimes overlook a critically important principle when they rearrange positions of youngsters in their classrooms for a special assignment. This principle has to do with light sources. It is imperative that learners never be seated in such a way that they face a light source directly. Such positioning results in physical discomfort, breaks concentration, and provides conditions that may well lead to classroom control problems.

Teacher actions related to classroom environments have as major objectives (1) maintenance of learner focus on assigned tasks, (2) creation of a learning context that will help youngsters to succeed, and (3) provision of space that will allow the teacher to move in an unobstructed way throughout the classroom. When these objectives are met, chances are good that classroom control problems will be less frequent than when these objectives are not achieved.

Actions Teachers Can Take to Deal with Significant Misbehavior

Despite their best efforts to prevent misbehavior and to deal with minor learner lapses from expectations, all teachers from time to time must deal with more serious learner behavior problems. When a given youngster persists in misbehavior problems after repeated attempts by the teacher to resolve the situation, it is time for the teacher to seek assistance from others.

Other Teachers and Counselors. As has been noted, sometimes misbehavior in the classroom is simply a reflection of serious problems a youngster is experiencing at home or in some other out-of-school settings. It may be that teachers who have worked with the youngster before may have information not available to the teacher presently working with the misbehaving learner. Counselors, too, may be able to provide information. Also, because of their specialized training, members of the school counseling staff may be able to suggest new approaches for helping the youngster develop more acceptable patterns of classroom behavior.

It makes good sense for a teacher to seek out assistance from other professionals when he or she is faced with a particularly difficult classroom control problem. These people can bring diverse perspectives and a strong collective expertise to bear on the problem. Furthermore, when others in the building are informed, a general familiarity with the situation develops that may prove useful should additional actions have to be taken at a later date.

Involving Parents. Certainly it makes sense to alert parents and to involve them when a youngster's behavior in class persists along unacceptable lines.

It may prove sufficient to talk to a parent by phone. On the other hand, many teachers find face-to-face discussions to be more productive.

In approaching parents, the teacher needs to outline the situation in the clearest language possible. The idea of involving the parents is to get the issue resolved, not to place the parents in a position where they sense either themselves or their youngster to be victims of an unjust attack. Ideally, the teacher and the parents will operate as a team working diligently to help a youngster develop more appropriate school behavior patterns. When this effort is successful, all three parties (teacher, parents, learner) emerge as winners.

Last Resort.   When other measures fail and a learner's problem behavior continues at an intolerable level, the case should be referred to school officials who are charged with handling severe discipline cases. This step should be taken only after other alternatives have been explored thoroughly.

In preparation for meetings with these school authorities, the teacher should be prepared to document specific incidences of unacceptable behavior and specific actions he or she has already taken to change this behavior. Any notes taken about particular classroom episodes; conferences with the youngster, and other evidence should be gathered and organized. The need for documentation suggests that when a teacher senses that he or she may be working with a youngster whose behavior may prove difficult to change, immediate action should be taken to start a file of notes indicating the nature of the problem, specific dates and circumstances when problem behavior has occurred, and particular actions taken to resolve it. School officials are reluctant to take action in the absence of such a solid evidentiary record.

In thinking about referring difficult cases to school officials, teachers must recognize that there will be times when these officials will not agree with the judgment of the teacher. They have legal obligations requiring them to protect youngsters' rights to due process. They must weigh evidence carefully and avoid any impression that they are making arbitrary judgments. This necessity reinforces the points that only the most persistent behavior problems should be referred to school disciplinary officials and that cases that are so referred must be backed by solid documentary evidence to support charges of gross misbehavior.

Classroom Management and Discipline: Some Final Thoughts

Classroom management and discipline problems are complex. There are no magic formulae that are guaranteed to produce classrooms full of highly motivated and easily managed youngsters. Every teacher should expect that, from time to time, he or she will have to deal with youngsters who misbehave. The diversity of the school population makes it inevitable that, on occasion,

"Do you have any 'We Promise Not To Do It Again' cards for a school bus driver?"

some youngsters will wish they were anywhere but in school. This will be true regardless of how hard a teacher may work to prompt their interest.

The issue, then, is not one of eliminating control and discipline problems entirely, but rather one of dealing with them as they occur and with a view to helping often-frustrated youngsters grow in terms of their personal control of their own behavior. By applying basic management and discipline principles, teachers can contribute to youngsters' learning in this important area. Instruction directed toward self-management is an important responsibility of every classroom teacher.

Recapitulation of Major Ideas

1. All teachers face challenges in the areas of classroom management and discipline. The diversity of the school population is tremendous, and this diversity all but guarantees that all teachers will have to deal with misbehaving learners from time to time.

2. A number of basic procedures have been found useful by teachers with successful records as classroom managers. Among these are (1) establishing rules and routines, and (2) coherent management of instructional lessons.

3. Discipline is an instructional responsibility of all teachers. It is directed toward helping learners develop patterns of self-control and acceptance of responsibility for their own actions.

4. A number of basic principles are associated with successful discipline programs. Among these are (1) respect learners' dignity, (2) provide chances for correct behavior to occur, (3) discover the nature of learners' "real" problems, and (4) use a variety of techniques.

5. In responding to inappropriate behaviors, teacher options might be thought of as scaled along a not-severe-to-severe continuum. Among these options are (1) taking action to support opportunities for youngsters to demonstrate their self-control, (2) the "cold, hard stare," (3) proximity control, and (4) verbal commands.

6. In diminishing potential control problems, some teachers have found the following actions to be effective: (1) changing the seat of a misbehaving youngster, (2) removing physical barriers that may be interfering with learners' attention, and (3) organizing classroom space to facilitate learning.

7. In dealing with severe and persistent behavior problems, teachers might confer with other teachers and counselors, make arrangements for conferences with parents, and, when other measures fail, seek out school district authorities with responsibilities for dealing with severe misbehavior problems.

Posttest

DIRECTIONS: Using your own paper, answer each of the following true/false questions. For each correct statement, write the word *true* on your paper. For each incorrect statement, write the word *false* on your paper.

1. Learner misbehavior occasionally occurs even in classes taught by very experienced teachers.

2. Classroom management and discipline are the responsibility of the school counseling staff, not classroom teachers.

3. Learners do not function well in classrooms where routines are well established; consequently, teachers in such classrooms tend to have many discipline problems.

4. A major purpose of discipline is helping learners develop a sense of self-control.

5. Creative teachers who avoid lesson planning probably experience fewer discipline problems than teachers who plan each lesson with care.

6. For any given learner misbehavior, there is a universally "correct" teacher response.

7. Because of the possibility of a court suit, a teacher ought to keep a written record containing information about a learner's misbehavior.

8. A major principle to be followed with a view to minimizing discipline problems is to respect the personal dignity of learners in the classroom.
9. Sometimes teachers need to change the nature of the physical environment as they work to improve the discipline climate within a classroom.
10. It is a sound practice for teachers to discuss with learners a set of rules describing appropriate patterns of classroom behavior.

Summary

All teachers from time to time experience problems associated with classroom management and discipline. The diversity of the school population virtually ensures that every single learner will not always appreciate school teachers and school classes. Though most teachers do not consider their classroom management and discipline responsibilities as among the aspects of teaching they enjoy most, they recognize these responsibilities as an essential part of their professional role as teachers.

Discipline properly is thought of as a part of teachers' instructional responsibilities. The goals of instruction in discipline are to help learners grow in terms of their abilities to manage their own behavior appropriately and in terms of their recognition of a personal responsibility for their own behavior.

Successful programs of classroom management and discipline are developed around several important principles. Among these are that learners value consistency, respect for their own worth and dignity, and good classroom and instructional organization. Teachers who attend well to these principles tend to have fewer difficulties in the areas of management and discipline than do teachers whose practices are inconsistent with these principles.

References

CHARLES, C. M. *Building Classroom Discipline: From Models to Practice.* New York: Longmans, Inc., 1981.

CHARLES, C. M. *Elementary Classroom Management.* New York: Longman, Inc., 1983.

DUKE, DANIEL LINDEN, AND MECKEL, ADRIENNE MARAVICH. *Teacher's Guide to Classroom Management.* New York: Random House, 1984.

ELAM, STANLEY M. "The Gallup Education Surveys: Impressions of a Poll Watcher." *Phi Delta Kappan* (Sept., 1983): 26–32.

EVERTSON, CAROLYN M., EMMER, EDMUND T., CLEMENTS, BARBARA S., SANFORD, JULIE P., AND WORSHAM, MURRAY E. *Classroom Management for Elementary Teachers.* Englewood Cliffs, N.J.: Prentice-Hall, 1984.

GALLUP, GEORGE H. "The 15th Annual Gallup Poll of the Public's Attitudes Toward the Public Schools." *Phi Delta Kappan* (Sept. 1983): 33–47.

MEDLAND, MICHAEL, AND VITALE, MICHAEL. *Management of Classrooms.* New York: Holt, Rinehart and Winston, 1984.

MENDLER, ALLEN N., AND CURWIN, RICHARD L. *Taking Charge in the Classroom: A Practical Guide to Effective Discipline.* Reston, Va.: Reston Publishing Company, Inc., 1983.

WEINER, ELIZABETH HIRZLER (Ed) *Discipline in the Classroom.* 2nd revised ed. Washington, D.C.: National Education Association Publications, 1980.

WOLFGANG, CHARLES H., AND GLICKMAN, CARL D. *Solving Discipline Problems: Strategies for Classroom Teachers.* Boston: Allyn and Bacon, 1980.

CHAPTER

12

Legal Concerns of Teachers

Objectives

This chapter provides information to help the reader to

1. Understand differences between certification requirements and graduation requirements.
2. Recognize several kinds of teacher contracts.
3. Point out characteristics of tenure and identify conditions under which tenured teachers can be dismissed.
4. Describe how due process applies to teachers.
5. Define academic freedom and explain its limitations.
6. Describe professional negligence or malpractice and identify the potential impact of malpractice suits on educational practice.
7. Describe several legal issues regarding the use of corporal punishment as a discipline device.

Pretest

DIRECTIONS: Using your own paper, answer each of the following true/false questions. For each correct statement, write the word *true* on your paper. For each incorrect statement, write the word *false* on your paper.

1. Teacher certification automatically accompanies qualification for graduation from a college or university.
2. It is legal for an interviewer to ask about the marital status of a candidate for a teaching position.
3. It is permissible for an individual to sign several teaching contracts and to choose to honor the one offering the best terms.
4. Tenure guarantees career-long employment.
5. Teachers can be dismissed for criticizing their employers.
6. "Reasonable suspicion" of immoral behavior is sufficient cause for teacher dismissal.
7. Academic freedom ensures the right of any teacher to discuss any topic in the classroom.
8. A basic test of negligence is whether a person with similar training would have acted in the same way.
9. Lack of student achievement usually is regarded as sufficient grounds for a malpractice suit.
10. Corporal punishment has been declared to be an illegal form of "cruel and unusual punishment."

Introduction

"Teachers are simply average citizens who enjoy all of the rights and responsibilities of any other citizens." Do you agree with this statement? Not everybody does. Consider this exchange between a superintendent and an interviewer:

Superintendent: "Teaching is a privilege, not a right. If one wants the privilege, he has to give up some of his rights."

Interviewer: "Just what constitutional rights does one have to give up in order to enter teaching?"

Superintendent: "Any right his community wants him to give up." (Fisher and Schimmel, 1982, p. 6)

Of course not everyone agrees with this view. Historically, however, some communities have placed severe restrictions on teachers' behavior. In more recent years, many of these have been rightfully challenged as being inconsistent with the constitutional guarantees that all United States' citizens enjoy. In general, there are fewer of these restrictions today than there were in times past. Even in the last decades of the twentieth century, however, guidelines specifying what teachers can and cannot do are not always clear. This chapter introduces some trends in legal thinking and identifies some issues that relate to such critical areas as conditions of employment, certification and contracts, teachers' rights and responsibilities, and teachers' malpractice and negligence.

Conditions of Employment

Teachers' Certification

Possession of a valid teaching certificate is a basic requirement for employment in public education. Teaching certificates are not automatically awarded along with college or university diplomas. Colleges and universities control requirements for diplomas. State governments control requirements for teaching certificates. Typically, though, colleges and universities with teacher preparation programs will organize courses in such a fashion that students will meet major certification requirements at the same time they meet graduation requirements. These circumstances vary somewhat from place to place, and students seeking teaching certificates should check carefully to determine exact procedures for qualifying for and applying for teaching certificates.

Teaching certificates have not always been required of individuals interested in teaching in the schools. They were established out of a belief that there was a need to set certain minimum standards of quality for individuals teaching in the schools. Mandatory teaching certificates were viewed as a

Box 12-1
Does Teacher Certification Ensure Quality?

The following editorial appeared in a local newspaper:

Teacher certification stands as the greatest barrier to improvement of instruction in the schools today. Certification is defended as a guarantor of quality. In fact, it is a guarantor of mediocrity.

Certification is rigidly controlled by the bureaucrats of professional education. It is used to protect enrollments in weak college of education courses. It is used to exclude from teaching the brightest and the best who have majored in more demanding academic areas and who resist the requirement to expose their intelligences to the soporific pap served up by education departments.

Today's youngsters deserve teachers who are intellectually alive and who are solidly grounded in strong academic disciplines. Teacher certification as it exists today is exclusionary. More importantly, its exclusionary bias is directed against the very kind of bright academic talent so desperately needed in the schools today. The perpetuation of mediocrity through the teacher licensing process must stop. It is time for the legislature to act.

LET'S PONDER

Read the editorial above. Then, respond to these questions:

1. What evidence is there that teacher certification weakens quality of teaching?
2. What advantages would you see if proposals to scrap teacher certification became law?
3. What problems might arise if teacher certification were abandoned?
4. What is your personal opinion on the issue raised in the editorial? Why do you feel this way?

means for upgrading the quality of teachers in the schools. Even today, not all people accept this view. Consider, for example, some of the arguments posed in Figure 12-1.

Certification is a function of state government. Each state legislature establishes standards for certification in its state. These standards change from time to time. Though there are similarities in certification patterns among the states, each state's certification requirements differ slightly from those of any other state. For specific information about the requirements in a state where you may be interested in teaching, you should write to the state department of education. (This information may also be available from officials in the education department on your own campus.)

Though each state has a unique set of certification requirements, this does not mean that you have to start all over again should you be certified in one state and wish to accept a job in another state. Most states have reciprocal certification agreements. This means that if you are given an initial teaching certificate in one state and wish to teach in another, the second state will ordinarily grant you an initial teaching certificate allowing you to teach in the schools of that state. This second state may require you to take one or more specified courses within a given period of time to maintain the validity of your certificate. Typically these course requirements are not oppressive. Very frequently, little is required other than a course in the history or government of the state in which you are teaching. Today there is a great deal of migration across state lines. Once you have your certificate, it is fair to say that you will not experience great difficulty in obtaining a certificate to teach anywhere in the country.

A teaching certificate is essentially a license. A certificate permits you to perform certain functions, but it does not confer an absolute right. This means that a state may legally alter certification requirements without having to worry about depriving an individual of a right without due process of law. In this respect, a teacher's certificate is somewhat similar to a driver's license. A driver's license gives the holder a right that is exercisable throughout a state, but the state may change its standards for licensing and require all drivers to meet these new standards. Similarly, qualification for a certificate at one time does not necessarily ensure that the certificate holder will not have to meet new requirements established at a later date. In practice, few substantial changes in certification requirements affect those with certificates in hand. For political reasons, state legislatures find it easier to pass changes in certification requirements by exempting those already holding certificates from many, if not all, of the new requirements.

Most states require individuals to possess a valid teaching certificate before they can be employed. In some states, if an individual who signs a teaching contract does not have a valid certificate, the district may be prohibited by law from paying his or her salary. A number of court cases have declared individuals who sign contracts without having proper certificates to be "volunteers" who have donated their services to the district. Such voluntarism can be a very expensive proposition, and the costs involved point up the extreme importance of meeting all certification requirements before contracting for employment as a teacher.

In many states, teaching certificates are issued for a given number of years. Various procedures are provided for renewal. Typically these require teachers to complete a certain number of professional development courses and to provide evidence of satisfactory performance. It is important to note the expiration dates of certificates. Signing a contract with an expired certificate is no different from signing a contract with no certificate at all. Generally school-district personnel offices, particularly in the larger districts, will provide the teacher with reminders when the expiration date of her or his certificate is approaching.

A number of benefits accrue to the holder of a teacher's certificate. Teachers with certificates receive either the state-mandated minimum salary or that salary plus any supplements provided for in the locally adopted teachers' salary schedule. The certificate provides the holder with an "assumption of competence." Thus a charge of incompetence must not be capricious and must be proved by any who makes the charge.

The assumption of competence provided by the teacher's certificate explains the great interest in the issue of standards of teacher preparation. Administrators, teachers' professional organizations, colleges and universities, and, indeed, the entire professional educational community are concerned that those certified as teachers will be able to perform their duties at a satisfactory level of competence. When certified teachers are found to be incompetent, the entire profession suffers. Concern about professional credibility prompts a great deal of interest in patterns of teacher preparation.

Across the nation, two common organizational arrangements for monitoring the quality of teacher preparation programs are in evidence. The first of these might be called the *program approval pattern*. Where program approval patterns are used, colleges and universities interested in teachers' education must develop a proposed program and submit it to the state department of education for approval. Typically the state department sends a team to visit these institutions to review the proposals. If the team approves of what is being proposed, a recommendation urging support of the proposed program(s) is made to the state board of education. If the board gives its approval, then the institutions have an "accredited" or approved teacher education program.

These institutions may then begin preparing individuals for careers in teaching. When an individual has met all program requirements, then the college or university "recommends" him or her for a teaching certificate. The certificate itself is awarded not by the college or university but by the state. Ordinarily, however, this is a routine matter once the recommendation has gone forward from the college or university.

In program approval arrangements, quality control is maintained by periodic visits of teams from the state department. Though times vary, a visit once every five years would be fairly typical. During these visits, members of the team attempt to determine whether the college or university is doing what it has been approved to do in its official teacher-education program. Some weeks or months after the team visit, an institution is reaccredited, put on probation, or denied authority to continue its teacher preparation program.

A second pattern of certification approval is represented by the *professional review board*. Under this system, students are not recommended by their individual institutions. Rather, they or their colleges and universities send all relevant materials to a central professional review board. Typically this board sits in the state capital. The review board examines all relevant materials and makes the decision to certify or not to certify. There is much less work for the individual college and university staff in this pattern. The colleges and universities do not themselves do a great deal of checking to see that "approved programs" have been completed and do not assume the respon-

Box 12–2
Certification and You

Certification is a function of the state. Though there is some commonality in practices among states, no two states have exactly the same set of requirements. Ordinarily, teacher certification requirements are mandated by the state legislature. Administration and enforcement typically is the responsibility of the state department of education.

LET'S PONDER

Consider the teacher certification in your state and find answers to the following questions:

1. What is the teacher certification agency in your state?
2. How does your college or university handle certification requirements?
3. What are the minimum professional certification requirements for your state?
4. Does your state have any personal standards that must be met? What are they?
5. Does your state administer any kind of an examination people must take and pass before qualifying for a teacher certificate?
6. Under what conditions can a teacher certificate be revoked in your state?
7. How have certification standards in your state changed in recent years? Are any other changes pending?
8. What kinds of certificates are there for teachers? How long is each type valid? What are the qualifications for each?
9. Are there provisions for renewal of teacher certificates? If so, what are they?

sibility of "recommending" people for certification. Rather, the colleges and universities simply act to funnel information about the students to the state professional review board, where the recommendation decisions are made.

In general, in areas where a program approval method is used, there are greater differences in teacher preparation programs among the individual colleges and universities. Each may propose a unique set of learning experiences for prospective teachers. If approved, a wide variety of individual programs may operate in a state. A student satisfying the requirements of any one of them will qualify for a certificate. In the model of the professional review board, all certification decisions are made by one central agency. All colleges and universities have to provide experiences that this board will find acceptable. Consequently there tends to be much less diversity among the programs at different colleges and universities in areas where certification is passed by a professional review board.

Certificates can be terminated for reasons other than simply expiring. The conditions under which certificates can be revoked vary considerably from state to state. Generally, conviction of crimes, public immorality, and extreme examples of socially unacceptable behavior are regarded as legitimate causes for the revocation of a certificate. State legislatures, reflecting the concerns of their constituents, have perceived teaching as a unique profession. Teachers, because of their contact with impressionable young people, are generally expected to adhere to higher standards of personal conduct than might be expected of the general population.

The Hiring Process

Prospective teachers need to know something about the legal aspects of interviewing and hiring. Today, there are numerous state and federal laws that govern the process of screening applicants for positions. Many of these laws address the issue of discrimination in employment. For example, the Washington State Law Against Discrimination (RCW 49.60) makes it an unfair practice for an employer of eight or more employees to use any form of application for employment or to make any inquiry in connection with prospective employment that expresses any limitation, specification, or discrimination as to age, sex, marital status, race, creed, national origin, color, or the presence of sensory, mental, or physical handicap, or any intent to make any such limitation, specification, or discrimination, unless based upon a bona fide occupational qualification.

In plain English, this statute means that questions asked applicants must have a demonstrated relationship to the job. For example, a question regarding a physical handicap would not be legal unless such a handicap would prevent the accomplishment of tasks associated with the position being sought.

Most states have laws similar to the Washington statute. Such legislation has placed many restrictions on the topics that school personnel people can raise during interviews with candidates for teaching positions. Though practices vary from place to place, questions regarding marital status, pregnancy, age, and religious preferences generally can no longer be asked. In addition, these statutes have led many districts to drop the formerly almost universal practice of requiring applicants to attach a personal photograph to their official application materials. A result of this legislation has been to force school districts to think through much more carefully the real demands of the positions for which they are seeking applicants. As a result, today's interview questions are much more focused on the demands of the position itself than on extraneous matters.

Some laws, such as Title VII of the Civil Rights Act of 1964, apply both to public and private educational institutions. Others relate only to public institutions. This area of the law is complex. For example, if a particular condition may be demonstrated to hinder the ability of a person to teach or to interfere with the mission of the school, it may be included as a condition for employment. In other words, a private religious school can legally give preference to individuals with a particular religious affiliation if such affiliation is required for the school to fulfill its stated mission.

Prospective teachers commonly are asked to prove they are free from serious medical conditions. Many states require, for example, that individuals working in the schools be certified free of tuberculosis. Other requirements relate to such issues as absence of a criminal record, appropriate scores on academic competency tests (tests over subject matter to be taught), and to other areas thought to be associated with "fitness" for the teaching profes-

---

Box 12-3
Legal Limits of Questions in Interviews of Teacher Candidates

Ms. Lee Jamison was being interviewed for a position as third grade teacher in a small rural community. A representative from the school district had come to her campus, and the interview was conducted in a room in the teacher placement center. Among others, Ms. Jamison was asked the following questions:

1. What kind of an approach do you recommend for your reading program?
2. How do you feel about corporal punishment and the whole general area of discipline?
3. How regular is your church attendance?
4. Would you ever buy beer or wine in a local grocery store?
5. If you were assigned to manage the playground, what would you do?
6. How could you improve relationships with parents of your youngsters?
7. If you have a boy friend, do you have any immediate plans of getting married?
8. How long do you expect to be a teacher?
9. We would like to start a laboratory program for part of third grade science. How would you feel about that?
10. Would you spend most weekends in our community or would you be more likely to drive to the city?

LET'S PONDER Consider the questions asked by the interviewer and respond to the following:

1. Are all of the above questions appropriate? Are all of them likely to be legal?
2. Which questions in the list above do you believe to be most legitimate? Why do you think so?
3. Which questions in the list above do you believe to be least legitimate? Why do you think so?
4. How would you respond to an interviewer asking questions that you felt to be inappropriate?

sion. Some districts even require candidates to formally declare that they are unrelated to any school board member.

When interviews go well and candidates meet all necessary requirements, they may be offered a teaching contract. The next subsection details several important contract types.

Teachers' Contracts

The teacher's contract is one of the most important documents a prospective teacher will deal with in his or her professional career. Contracts spell out not only salary levels, but other conditions of employment as well. It is essential that prospective teachers read contracts carefully before signing them with a view to understanding precisely what their responsibilities will be.

One item of interest should be the type of contract that is being offered. Generally a new teacher is given what is called a *term contract*. A term contract provides for employment for a specified time period, usually one year. At the end of the specified period, the teacher is reviewed and a determination is made either to offer a new contract or to terminate the teacher's employment. Under a term contract, both parties (school board and teacher) retain the right to negotiate new terms in any subsequent term contracts. Some states allow term contracts to be issued to all teachers. Others allow them to be used only for teachers new to the system until they have served out a prescribed probationary period (typically about three years).

A second type of contract is the *continuing contract*. Continuing contracts do not have to be renewed after a specified period of time. They normally continue automatically on a year-to-year basis until terminated by one of the contracting parties according to very explicit procedures. Today there are usually safeguards that protect teachers with continuing contracts from summary dismissal.

A third type of contract is the *tenure contract*. A tenure contract, similar to a continuing contract, stays in force from year to year. A tenure contract can be terminated only if a teacher violates provisions of state statutes governing the behavior and performance of teachers and only if the school board follows extremely strict procedures.

Tenure contracts have come under fire in recent years. Critics claim that tenure laws protect incompetent teachers. In part, these criticisms result from a misunderstanding of tenure laws. Tenure laws do *not* guarantee teachers lifetime employment. Typically, they specify a number of circumstances that allow for dismissal of a tenured teacher. These might include (1) evidence of gross incompetence, (2) physical or mental incapacity, (3) neglect of duty, and (4) conviction of crimes.

Basically, a district must "show cause" and be able to document charges before a tenured teacher can be released. Certain procedural steps must be followed. These include (1) early notification of the intent not to rehire; (2) a written statement of the reasons for this action, provided early enough to

"And now, the criteria for tenure. . . ."

give the teacher time to appeal; (3) a formal hearing where evidence is presented; (4) the right of the teacher to be represented by legal counsel; and (5) the provision for appeal and review of the entire proceedings.

It should be emphasized that tenure laws are not designed to protect incompetent individuals. Properly enforced, they should have the opposite effect. Today, much criticism centers on the capacity of tenure laws to protect teachers' rights to employment. Too often ignored are the very real safeguards built into most tenure legislation, which, when properly applied, can be used to monitor teacher performance and to weed out the unfit.

Regardless of the type of contract offered, each contract is a legally binding document. It sets forth the teacher's responsibilities and the school district's responsibilities. It places certain responsibilities on both parties. For example, in some places, a teacher who fails to report to honor a signed contract can be stripped of a teaching certificate.

Should you sign a contract and then receive a much more handsome offer from a second school district, it is a very poor practice to sign the second contract. To do so would put you in the illegal posture of being obligated to perform duties simultaneously in two locations. Should you really wish to accept the second position, the proper procedure is to call the first district and ask whether you might be released from your first contract "without prejudice." Though there is no guarantee that the district will honor your request, in most cases it will. The first school district, after all, is not likely to get a first-class effort from a teacher who really wishes to be working elsewhere.

Teachers' contracts are governed by state regulations. These laws specify, among other things, the party who represents the state in the agreement. That is, they indicate who contracts with the teacher for his or her services. Many beginning teachers mistakenly assume that the state has authorized principals or superintendents to be official representatives in the contracting process. They presume that once a contract has been *offered* by a superintendent (or by one of his agents, for example, a personnel director), the contract becomes *binding* as soon as the candidate signs it. In fact, the legal agent for

---

Box 12-4
To Tenure or Not To Tenure

It has been argued that tenure systems accomplish the following:

1. They encourage teacher creativity by allowing introduction of new materials and methods without fear of reprisal.
2. They help teachers keep free from intimidation by teachers' professional groups.
3. They insulate teachers from political pressures in the community.
4. They protect teachers from arbitrary actions of school board members who may have personal grievances against them.
5. They prevent wholesale firing of teachers after a school board election that results in a large number of new board members who may wish to employ their friends.
6. They allow teachers to maintain classroom control and to treat all youngsters the same regardless of the political influence of their parents.

LET'S PONDER

Look at the items above and respond to the following questions:

1. Do you agree with all of the items above? If no, with which items do you agree? Why? With which items do you disagree? Why?
2. Some have said tenure laws protect incompetent teachers? Do you agree or disagree? Why?
3. Were there no tenure laws, do you suppose there would be any difference in the kind of individual attracted to teaching? If yes, what would that difference be?
4. What is your personal reaction to tenure laws? Why do you feel this way?

the state in almost every case is not the superintendent but the school board. Generally the contract becomes binding only when the school board votes its approval. This is an almost automatic procedure once a candidate has been recommended by the superintendent's office, but if for some reason the board does not approve the contract, the contract, in fact, does not exist. The new teacher, then, needs to be sure that the board has acted favorably on the contract before she or he can be sure of the position.

Sometimes the issue of "oral" contracts arises. That is, sometimes applicants believe that a spoken offer of a position constitutes a binding contract. Legally the oral contract simply does not exist, so it is imperative that all terms discussed in an interview be included in the written contract that is approved by the school board. For example, if an interviewer suggests that the regular salary will be augmented by $700 additional compensation for bus supervision duty, the written contract must also contain this proviso. Otherwise, the district is under no legal obligation for the extra compensation. The teacher must read the contract very carefully to be sure that all special situations have been included before signing it and sending it on to the school board.

Teacher Dismissal and Due Process

Does a teacher have the right to challenge a nonrenewal of contract or dismissal? The question has no answer that applies in every case. The concept of due process as embedded in the Fourteenth Amendment of the United States Constitution is relevant to this important issue.

Due process requires decisions that affect the rights of people to be made fairly. Two basic types of rights are important. *Liberty rights* are rights freeing individuals from personal physical restraints and assuring them opportunities to engage in the common occupations of life. (*Meyer* v. *Nebraska,* 262 U.S. 390, 399, [1923]). The concept of liberty right suggests that no unconstitutional reason can be used to prevent a person from seeking certification and employment as a teacher.

Property rights are a second important type of rights. They ensure individuals' rights to present and future benefits of material and nonmaterial economic goods. Is teaching a property right? The courts have generally ruled that a person acquires a property right upon entering a profession. It might be concluded then that a teacher has a property right during the period covered by his or her contract. This may not be true, however, if some language in the contract specifically states that the contract may be terminated by the school board at any time. If a contract includes such language, the employed teacher enjoys no property right.

In summary, contracts *may* protect teachers from summary dismissal on constitutional grounds. However, many variables are involved in this issue, including types of contracts involved and specific language contained within individual contracts. In the next section, we will take a more general look at the entire issue of teachers' rights and point out some emerging trends.

Teachers' Rights

What *are* teachers' rights? Do they differ from those of other citizens? Can teachers be held to special standards of behavior? Can teachers legally criticize their employers without opening themselves up to the possibility of summary dismissal? These and other questions associated with teachers' rights focus on some difficult issues. A perhaps disappointing general response to all of them is "well, it depends." Court precedents do not provide absolutely consistent guidelines with regard to any of these issues. Though there are some general trends reflected in these decisions, still specific situations continue in large measure to be considered on a case-by-case basis.

Teachers' Private Lives

In times gone by, teachers accepted restrictions on their private lives that would have prompted militant action from other groups. In recent times, however, teachers have become increasingly willing to challenge restrictions on their private lives in courts. In many of these cases, teachers have contended that their private lives are their own business and that they should be held accountable by school authorities only for their performances in the classroom.

In responding to this position, school boards and administrators often have pointed out that school teachers occupy a unique position in our society. They work with impressionable young people. Hence, because of their function as adult role models for the young, teachers' behavior both in and out of the classroom is a proper concern for school authorities. One court decision that supported this view was *Board of Trustees* v. *Stubblefield* (*Board of Trustees* v. *Stubblefield,* 94 Cal. Rptr. 318, 321 [1971]). In this case the court declared that certain professions, such as teaching, impose limitations on personal action that are not imposed by other occupations.

A number of cases have come before the courts involving the issue of allegedly immoral behavior on the part of teachers. Typically the courts have dealt severely with teachers who have been found to be "immoral." The difficulty in these cases has centered on defining what constitutes "moral" and "immoral" behavior. The meaning of these terms has tended to vary over time, and the meaning certainly varies from place to place.

In dealing with the issue of teachers' moral behavior, the courts have tended to look at how the behavior in question influenced the effectiveness of the teacher's classroom performance and his or her credibility in the community. When the behavior has been viewed as violating prevailing moral standards and when the behavior has resulted in widespread public outrage, the courts have tended to support teacher dismissal decisions of school districts. However, when the behavior has not been demonstrated to have a clear and obvious impact on the school and community, courts have tended to uphold teachers' privacy rights. Discussions of several pertinent cases may help to bring this general issue into tighter focus.

In one case, a secondary school teacher was arrested for making a homosexual advance to an undercover police officer on a public beach. When his teaching certificate was revoked, the teacher brought the issue to court. He claimed that there was no connection between his behavior on the beach and his professional conduct in the classroom. The court disagreed. In the decision, it was noted that homosexual conduct was clearly contrary to the social mores and moral standards of the people in the community. Therefore, it constituted a violation of the morality standards as outlined in the education code of the district (*Sarac* v. *State Board of Education,* 57 Cal. Rptr. 69 [1967]).

In a second case in the same state, two teachers engaged in a brief homosexual affair. About a year later, one teacher reported the incident to the superintendent of the district where the second teacher was employed. In response to information from the superintendent, the school district took action to strip the teacher of his teaching credential. The teacher took the issue to court. The court ruled in favor of the teacher, noting that there was no evidence to indicate that his conduct had affected his performance as a teacher, to indicate that he had ever attempted to establish a homosexual relationship with a student, or to indicate that he had in any way failed to teach his students principles of morality as required by law (*Morrison* v. *State Board of Education,* 461 P. 2d 375 [1969]).

Box 12-5
Teachers and Profanity

Suppose a state department of education, in response to pressure from legislators, sent out a memorandum to all school districts in the state indicating that the following policy statement was to be placed in the *Teachers' Code of Conduct* manual in each district.

Any teacher found to use profanity in the classroom shall be deemed guilty of an infraction of appropriate moral behavior. Such an individual shall be subject to dismissal proceedings.

LET'S PONDER

Read the statement above. Then, respond to these questions.
Suppose a teacher was faced with dismissal based on the above regulation.

1. If the teacher sued, would it be likely the courts would consistently decide for the teacher or for the school district?
2. What kinds of issues might the courts have to consider in deciding these cases?
3. What special problems might courts have in making these decisions?
4. How would such a rule be accepted in the district where you graduated from high school?
5. What is your personal opinion of the rule? Why do you have this view?

In another case, a woman had taught successfully in a district for years. In their free time, she and her husband had become involved in a group that promoted deviant sexual behavior for members of the organization. At one point, the teacher and her husband appeared in disguise on a television program to discuss their unusual sexual preferences. Later, the teacher was arrested at a party in a private residence. The school district took action to have her teaching certificate revoked. The teacher appealed. In its decision, the court supported the school authorities. The court noted that unacceptable behaviors had occurred in the semipublic atmosphere of a party, had been witnessed by several individuals, had involved at least three different partners, and had displayed a notable lack of concern for the preservation of her dignity or reputation. All of this, in the court's view, added up to a clear violation of the minimum standard of propriety for a public school teacher (*Pettit* v. *State Board of Education,* 513 P. 2d 889 [Cal. 1973]).

In another case, a teacher began cohabiting with her boyfriend. Two

---

Box 12-6
Personal Standards of Teachers

Teachers are not like other people. Teachers are special. They work with our children. They provide models for our children. They suggest to our children what we hope they will become in the future. Truly, the teacher is a very special human being.

We do not want just anybody for a teacher. We cannot tolerate just anybody for a teacher. The teacher cannot be just "average" or "typical." We don't want teachers to simply mirror our society. We want them to be a beacon for children to guide them to a better future. Particularly, teachers' moral behavior has to be a step ahead of the "average." It should be impeccable. It should provide an inspirational model for our young people. An individual who is not willing to bear this moral burden has no business in teaching. If, despite our efforts, he or she *does* get into the profession, we should do all in our power to remove him or her from a profession that needs to set a standard for the future and not reflect an average of an admittedly deficient present.

LET'S PONDER

Read the paragraphs above and respond to the following questions:

1. How do you react to the general position taken in the paragraphs above?
2. Should higher standards for teachers be expected than for other professionals?
3. Do you think setting rigid behavior standards for teachers, even more rigid than they are today, would attract fewer or more people into teaching?
4. Should the society have any moral expectations of teachers at all? Why, or why not?
5. Do youngsters learn their moral standards from teachers? Why, or why not?

months later, the school administrators informed her that she could either resign or be fired. Ten days later, she married her boyfriend. She informed the school officials of this fact. Nevertheless, the district took action to suspend her on the grounds of immorality. The teacher took the case to court. The court upheld the rights of the teacher. In the decision, the court noted that before the teacher's dismissal most people were unaware that the teacher had been cohabiting with her boyfriend. The decision went on to point out that it had been unfair of the school district to make this situation public in order to generate a negative public attitude to support the dismissal decision. Furthermore, there was insufficient evidence to sustain the contention that the teacher's behavior had in anyway interfered with her effectiveness in the classroom (*Thompson* v. *Southwest School District*, 483 F. Supp. 1170 [W.D.M.O. 1980]).

Other issues in the teachers' rights area have focused on issues as diverse as drunk driving, using marijuana, attending church, and maintaining appropriate standards of personal appearance. In one state, dismissal of a teacher who had been convicted several times of driving while intoxicated was upheld. In another state and case, the court ruled in favor of the teacher.

Most cases involving use of marijuana have been decided by applying the criterion of "substantial disruption" of the educational process. That is, dismissals have been upheld when there was strong evidence to support the view that this behavior had a clear and negative effect on the teacher's credibility and ability to perform well in the classroom.

Attending church rarely emerges as an issue in teacher dismissal cases these days. There was a fairly recent case, however, involving an attempt to dismiss a divorced teacher. It was rumored that she was having an affair and that she did not attend church regularly. The teacher took the dismissal action to court. She not only won her case but in a later court action was also awarded a substantial financial damage settlement that had to be paid by the school district for wrongful dismissal.

Personal appearance is an issue that has been addressed in many court cases. Decisions have not reflected a particularly consistent pattern. But there has been something of a trend for courts to uphold the legality of grooming codes for teachers so long as they are reasonable and relate to legitimate educational concerns. In one case the court refused to sustain a district's decision not to rehire an overweight physical education teacher on the grounds that she was not a good "role model." The court noted that it is impossible for any teacher to be a perfect role model and that no evidence was introduced indicating that the teacher's weight had a negative impact on her teaching performance (*Blodgett* v. *Board of Trustees, Tamalpais Union High School District*, 97 Cal. Rptr. 406 [1970]).

Again, the criteria that have tended to be applied in all of these cases involve a limited number of general concerns. The courts want to know to what extent the behavior in question significantly disrupts the educational process or erodes the credibility of the teacher with students, parents, other teachers, and the community at large. The burden of proof lies with school authorities.

Teachers' Freedom of Expression

Freedom of expression is one of the rights guaranteed to citizens by the First Amendment to the United States Constitution. For many years, teachers' freedom of expression rights were quite limited. It was not uncommon for teachers to be dismissed who criticized administrators or general school district policies. The case of *Pickering* v. *Board of Education of Township School District 205* was a landmark case in the area of teachers freedom of speech rights. (*Pickering* v. *Board of Education of Township High School District 205, Will County,* 391 U.S. 563 [1968]).

Pickering, a teacher in this district, wrote a letter to the editor of the local newspaper criticizing allocation of school funds. The board of education was angered by the letter, claimed it contained untrue statements, and damaged the reputations of school administrators and the board of education. Consequently, the board dismissed Pickering. Ultimately, the case was heard before the United States Supreme Court.

The school district argued that a teacher has a duty as a public employee to support his superiors. The Court considered two major issues in its decision. The first was whether a teacher could be dismissed for making critical comments in public. The Court decided that teachers had the right to speak out on school issues as part of the general effort to provide for a more informed public. Second, the Court considered the issue of whether a teacher could be dismissed for making false statements. In reviewing the particulars of the case, the Court found only one false statement in Pickering's letter. In the absence of proof that the false statement had been included knowingly or recklessly, the Court decided against the school district and for Pickering.

In the *Pickering* case, the Court did not approve unlimited freedom of expression for teachers. The Court noted that there may be instances when teachers' free speech rights properly may be limited. The Court itself did not provide specific examples of these kinds of situations.

In another free speech case, a teacher was not rehired because she had made many private complaints to her principal. The principal claimed these had been made in a loud and hostile manner. In supporting its case, the school district authorities claimed that private expressions of opinion were not protected by the First Amendment. The Supreme Court disagreed, in effect supporting the teacher's claim of wrongful dismissal. The Court went on to explain, however, that a teacher's speech may be restrained or even punished if it hinders the performance of the teacher or generally interferes with the normal operation of the schools (*Givhan* v. *Western Line Consolidated School District,* 439 U.S. 410 [1979]). An implication of this decision is that teachers may make complaints, but they should be made at a proper time, in a proper manner, and in a proper place.

Teachers' Academic Freedom

Academic freedom refers to the idea that teachers and students should be able to inquire into any issues in the classroom, even those that may be perceived as extremely controversial by others. Issues centering on academic freedom involve a potential conflict between the right of the teacher to conduct a class according to his or her own best professional judgment and the responsibility of established educational authorities to ensure that the prescribed curriculum is being taught.

Court decisions regarding academic freedom do not reflect a clear and consistent pattern. Generally, though, decisions suggest that school authorities can impose some regulations on academic freedom, but guidelines provided must be defensible, specific, and clear. In general, school districts have been supported in efforts to insist that teachers teach toward established educational goals.

On the other hand, courts generally have decided that school districts cannot require teachers to avoid teaching controversial issues. Criteria applied in these cases generally revolve around relevance of topics to the approved school program, the teacher's purpose in exposing youngsters to the issue, the age and maturity level of the youngsters, and the degree to which the discussion did or did not disrupt the overall educational process.

In one case, an American history teacher used a simulation exercise that evoked strong student feelings on racial issues. The school board advised her to stop discussing controversial issues in American history. In spite of this advice, she continued to use the simulation exercise. As a result, her teaching contract was not renewed. She took the issue to court. The court ruled that the district had unjustly violated the teacher's constitutional rights of expression. (*Kingsville Independent School District* v. *Cooper*, 611 F. 2d 1109 [5th cir. 1980]).

In other cases, a teacher continued to teach sex-related issues in a health class because he believed the topic was of great interest to students, an art teacher taught her religious beliefs in class and actively encouraged youngsters to attend meetings of her religious group, and a mathematics teacher encouraged students to protest the presence of army recruiters through violent means. In each of these cases, the courts ruled against the teachers. Teacher actions were viewed as going beyond the reasonable limits of academic freedom.

A number of cases in this area have centered on the question of teachers' appropriate use of material thought to be "offensive" or "immoral." One teacher assigned students to read a book that school officials considered to be offensive and inappropriate. The teacher used the book anyway, and she was dismissed. She took the issue to court. The court ruled that the book was appropriate for use with high school students, that it contained nothing obscene, and that the rights of the teacher had been violated (*Parducci* v. *Rutland*, 316 F. Supp. 352 [M.D. Ala. 1979]).

In another case, several junior high school teachers distributed material about a movie. The material contained poems and pictures that school authorities determined to be offensive. Ultimately, the teachers took the issue to court. In its decision, the court ruled that the material was inappropriate for junior high school students. They noted that the movie had received an "R" rating and that it encouraged behavior that violated existing state law (*Brubaker* v. *Board of Education, School District 149, Cook County, Illinois,* 502 F. 2d 973 [7th Cir. 1974]).

In summary, decisions in the academic freedom area are very situation-specific in character. Teachers do have a right to deal with relevant topics in a fair and open manner, but teachers must exercise caution and common sense because the courts have decided that academic freedom does not imply a right for a teacher to do anything he or she wants in the classroom.

Teachers' Legal Liability

In recent years, the incidence of litigation against teachers has increased dramatically. Some believe that this increase has come about because of an erosion of public confidence in the schools. Others feel that it has resulted because schools have become larger. Large schools may make individuals feel that they are dealing with a cold and remote institution. For whatever reasons, teachers are being taken to court today in alarmingly high numbers.

In thinking about teachers' legal liability, two basic categories must be considered. The first involves *criminal liability*. Criminal liability involves criminal law and, for school personnel, might involve such issues as stealing school property. Most liability suits against teachers do not involve questions of criminal liability.

The second area of liability is that of *tort liability*. A "tort" is a civil wrong against another person that results either in personal injury or property damage. There are many types of torts, including negligence, invasion of privacy, assault, and defamation. Most liability suits against teachers involve issues of tort liability. Two areas in particular seem to attract large numbers of suits. These are negligence and excessive use of force when disciplining students. In the material that follows, we will examine each of these areas in some detail.

Negligence

Negligence is the failure to use reasonable care to prevent harm coming to someone. There are three kinds of negligence: (1) misfeasance; (2) nonfeasance; and, (3) malfeasance. "Misfeasance" occurs when an individual fails to act in a proper manner to prevent harm from coming to another. "Nonfeasance" occurs when an individual fails to act when it was his or his or her

Box 12-7
Teacher Liability: Some Issues

In the State of Washington, the Washington Administrative Code (Section 180-40-235, items 3–6) includes the following provisions:

(3) Corporal punishment shall be administered only in an office in some area outside the view of other students and only by a certificated employee. Such witnesses shall be informed beforehand and in the student's presence of the reason(s) for the infliction of corporal punishment.

(4) No cruel or unusual form of corporal punishment shall be inflicted on any student.

(5) Only reasonable and moderate force shall be applied to a student and no form of corporal punishment shall be inflicted upon the head of a student.

(6) Parents or guardians, upon their request, shall be provided a written explanation of the reason(s) for the infliction of corporal punishment and the name of the witness who was present at the time corporal punishment was administered.

LET'S PONDER

Look at the material above and respond to the following questions:

1. What reasons did the State of Washington have for adopting these measures, in your opinion? How do these rules relate to the issue of teacher liability? Are these rules too strict? Not strict enough? Why?
2. Do you think actions of courts and, perhaps, of state legislatures have placed too many restrictions on teachers' abilities to work with and manage youngsters in the classroom? Why do you think this way?
3. Think about the kind of classroom situation you hope to have when you begin teaching. What possible things might go wrong that could lead to a charge of teacher negligence? What kind of preventive action might you take?
4. What is your general reaction to corporal punishment? Do you believe it to be an effective control measure? Why, or why not?

(Extracted from Washington Administrative Code. Section 180-40-235, items 3–6)

responsibility to do so and when, as a result, harm comes to someone. "Malfeasance" occurs when an individual deliberately acts in an improper fashion and, as a result, harm comes to someone.

Misfeasance for teachers usually occurs when a teacher acts unwisely or without taking proper safeguards. The teacher may have had worthy motives but still have acted in a way that resulted in harm. For example, a teacher of very young children may ask a child to carry a glass container from one location to another. If the youngster falls and is cut, the teacher might be charged with misfeasance. The courts might deem it improper to ask a very young child to perform this kind of a task.

Nonfeasance cases frequently occur when something happens at a time at which a teacher is absent from his or her place of responsibility. For example, a student might be hurt when a teacher is out of the classroom and is not where he or she ought to be to supervise the behavior of youngsters under his or her charge. A teacher who fails to be present at his or her assigned area of the playground when a child is injured might also be charged with nonfeasance. Court cases tend to turn not so much on the issue of absence from the duty station as on the question of whether the absence was justifiable. If a teacher left the classroom to put out a wastebasket fire in a lavatory across the hall and, in his or her absence, a student was hurt in the classroom, the courts might well acknowledge that the fire situation represented a "reasonable cause" for the teacher's absence. In general, it is sound practice for teachers to be very cautious about leaving their assigned areas. There are relatively few excuses that courts will entertain as "reasonable cause" for teachers to be elsewhere.

Malfeasance cases often involve circumstances in which it is alleged that a teacher has acted deliberately and knowingly to do something resulting in injury to a youngster. For example, a litigant might contend that a teacher deliberately used too much force in breaking up a fight and that, as a result, a younster was hurt unnecessarily.

Basic legal tests often are used in deciding teacher negligence cases. In general, courts want to know (1) whether a reasonable individual with similar training would have acted in the same way, and (2) whether or not the teacher could have foreseen the possibility of injury. These tests suggest that teachers must exercise great care as they work with students to ensure that their actions (or inactions) do not result in harm or injury to the youngsters under their charge.

In general, misfeasance, nonfeasance, and malfeasance suits tend to address situations where, it is alleged, youngsters have suffered some kind of physical harm because of what a teacher did or did not do. An interesting new line of litigation is beginning to look as well at "academic damage" that may be the result of the behavior of the teacher. This area of "educational malpractice" is emerging as an area of concern for professional educators.

Educational malpractice suits have been based on the assumption that the schools have an obligation to provide professional educational services. Since children rarely have an option of selecting their teachers, school systems ought to be responsible for delivering high quality services that allow children to learn (Elam, 1978).

Critics of educational malpractice suits contend that the courts do not have the expertise to make decisions regarding what is and what is not responsible educational practice. Others point out that many variables other than actions

Box 12-8
Let's Sue for Malpractice!

The following letter to the editor appeared in a local newspaper:

"My nineteen-year-old son is lying around the house. He's bored. I'm frustrated. He's been to thirty-five firms looking for work. And these have *all* been outfits with advertised vacancies. No luck. No luck, anywhere.

Now you might think I blame the businesses. I don't. They've made a smart decision in not hiring him. To be blunt, he can't spell, and he can't figure simple math problems. His reading skills are pretty dismal, too. Beyond using him to haul things and follow verbal orders, what would a business do with him?

How did this happen? What went on during those twelve years we paid for his schooling? Not much, I can tell you. I don't know what he's going to do with his life now. If any of you out there are sharp lawyers, I'd like to know how to go about suing the teachers. As far as I'm concerned, their malpractice has robbed my son of thousands of dollars of earning power. It's a tragedy, and I'm fuming. Does anybody out there care?"

LET'S PONDER

Read the letter printed above. Then, respond to these questions.

1. To what extent is the son's problem the fault of the schools? Why do you think so?
2. What other variables might have contributed to the son's present deficiencies?
3. Does the parent have a right to be upset? Why, or why not?
4. What is your own reaction to malpractice suits against teachers? Why do you feel this way?

---

of teachers and schools contribute to determining how much an individual learns. For example, a failure to learn might be just as much attributable to a student's lack of study time at home, commitment to working too many hours outside of school, dietary deficiencies, and other variables as well as inadequacies in the school's instructional program. A number of court cases in this area have made this point in rejecting claims of student litigants that failure to learn was exclusively the fault of public education.

Today, there is great concern about the quality of educational services being delivered by the schools. Hence, it is probable that there will be larger numbers of educational malpractice suits as frustrated citizens attempt to bring into sharper focus the limits of responsibility of public school professionals. Certainly there is every indication that teachers who fail to make serious attempts to deliver to their learners the content for which they are responsible may find themselves challenged by learners and their parents.

Excessive Use of Force in Discipline

A number of court cases have considered issues focusing on the question of whether teachers have used too much force in disciplining youngsters. Physical punishment has been of special concern in many of these cases. In the case of *Ingraham* v. *Wright* (*Ingraham* v. *Wright,* 430 U.S. 651 [1977]), the Supreme Court ruled that teachers could use reasonable, but not excessive, force in disciplining a child. Furthermore, the Court declared that corporal punishment in the classroom did not constitute "cruel and unusual punishment" and, hence, was not a violation of a youngster's constitutional rights.

The *Ingraham* v. *Wright* case suggests a need to define the term "reasonable force." In general, the courts have come to consider several factors in deciding whether force applied in a given situation was "reasonable." Among these are (1) the gravity of the misbehavior, (2) the age of the learner, (3) the sex and size of the learner, (4) the size of the person administering the punishment, (5) the implement used to administer the punishment, and (6) the attitude of the person administering the discipline. With regard to this last category, courts have looked more favorably on disciplinarians who have not been in a state of anger or who have not been obviously seeking revenge at the time the punishment is administered.

"Mr. Jackson has got to stop reading court decisions in these teacher liability cases."

Most laws relating to corporal punishment are state and local school district regulations. Some states outlaw corporal punishment of some kinds. Currently two states, New Jersey and Massachusetts, forbid all forms of physical punishment. Even where corporal punishment is permitted, ordinarily there are strict and specific guidelines regarding how it is to be administered. Certainly teachers new to a district ought to take early action to familiarize themselves with these regulations.

Teachers need to understand that the simple legality of corporal punishment in a given state or district does not, by itself, protect a teacher from a suit brought by a learner or by his or her parents. Citizens have a right to sue for redress if they believe the teacher has used punishment carelessly or in any other way that exceeded the constituted legal authority to administer punishment.

In summary, corporal punishment in the schools remains a very controversial issue. Teachers who use it face the possibility of being taken to court, even in jurisdictions where rules and regulations permit the practice. Many teachers today feel that the risks associated with corporal punishment outweigh any supposed benefits.

Recapitulation of Major Ideas

1. A teacher's certificate is a basic requirement for employment in public education. Typically, certificates are issued by state governmental authorities. Certification and graduation requirements may be related, but they are not identical. Today, it usually is not too difficult to get certified in a state different from the one where the initial certificate was issued.

2. Numerous federal and state statutes govern hiring procedures. In general, questions asked candidates must have some logical connection to the demands of the position. There is an effort to ensure fairness in hiring practices.

3. Teachers' contracts spell out salary levels and other conditions of employment. *Term contracts* provide for employment for a specific time period. *Continuing contracts* normally continue automatically on a year-to-year basis until terminated by one of the contracting parties. *Tenure contracts* continue from year to year and can be terminated only if a teacher violates specific statutes governing the behavior and performance of the teacher and only then after due process procedures have been followed.

4. Teachers' contracts are legally binding documents. They become binding when approved by the school board of the hiring districts. It is not considered ethical for a teacher to sign more than one contract at a

time. In some states, teachers who do this may be liable to having their certificate revoked.

5. Many court cases have considered issues associated with teachers' private lives. In general, decisions to dismiss teachers because of out-of-school behavior have favored teachers when school administrations have been unable to demonstrate a connection between the behavior and negative performance in the classroom or loss of credibility with learners, parents, or the larger community.

6. Teachers' rights cases involve complex issues. Court decisions do not provide a clear set of guidelines that are universally applicable. Cases tend to be decided on the basis of variables unique to individual cases being litigated.

7. Many suits against teachers involve charges of negligence. Negligence can involve misfeasance, nonfeasance, or malfeasance. Negligence cases focus on situations where teacher actions or inactions allegedly resulted in harm to someone.

8. An emerging area of litigation is that of educational malpractice. Issues in this area focus on the extent to which teachers and schools can be held legally accountable for student learning. Some court decisions have suggested that there are many variables other than those associated with teachers and schools that influence youngsters' learning. More suits focusing on alleged malpractice are expected in the future.

Posttest

DIRECTIONS: Using your own paper, answer each of the following true/false questions. For each correct statement, write the word *true* on your paper. For each incorrect statement, write the word *false* on your paper.

1. Teacher certification automatically accompanies qualification for graduation from a college or university.

2. It is legal for an interviewer to ask about the marital status of a candidate for a teaching position.

3. It is permissible for an individual to sign several teaching contracts and to choose to honor the one offering the best terms.

4. Tenure guarantees career-long employment.

5. Teachers can be dismissed for criticizing their employers.

6. "Reasonable suspicion" of moral behavior is sufficient cause for teacher dismissal.

7. Academic freedom ensures the right of any teacher to discuss any topic in the classroom.

8. A basic test of negligence is whether a person with similar training would have acted in the same way.

9. Lack of student achievement usually is regarded as sufficient grounds for a malpractice suit.
10. Corporal punishment has been declared to be an illegal form of "cruel and unusual punishment."

Summary

The courts have played an increasingly important role in public education in recent years. Lawsuits have resulted in reexaminations of many educational practices. Schools have made adjustments to their practices in response to various court decisions.

Because of the more active role courts are playing in education today, prospective teachers need to familiarize themselves with legal issues relating to education. In particular, teachers must be familiar with legal aspects of contracting, preemployment interviewing, and the general issue of teacher liability.

References

ABEL, DAVID A., AND CONNER, LINDSAY, A. "Educational Malpractice: One Jurisdiction's Response." In Clifford P. Hodder (Ed.), *The Courts and Education.* The Seventy-seventh Yearbook of the National Society for the Study of Education. Chicago: University of Chicago Press, 1978, pp. 248–272.

ELSON, JOHN. "Pedagogical Incompetence and the Courts." *Theory Into Practice* (Oct., 1978): 303–313.

FISHER, LOUIS, AND SCHIMMEL, DAVID. *The Rights of Students and Teachers.* New York: Harper and Row Publishers, 1982.

FRANCIS, SAMUEL N., AND STACEY, CHARLES E. "Law and the Sensual Teacher." *Phi Delta Kappan* (Oct., 1977): 98–103.

HAZARD, WILLIAM R. *Education and the Law,* 2nd ed. New York: The Free Press, 1978.

JONES, THOMAS N., AND SAMLER, DAREL P., (Eds). *School Law Update—1982.* Topeka, Ks.: National Organization on Legal Problems of Education, 1983.

KEMERER, FRANK R. *Texas Teacher's Guide to School Law.* Austin, Tx.: University of Texas Press, 1982.

Cases

Blodgett v. Board of Trustees, Tamalpais Union High School District, 97 Cal. Rptr. 406 (1971).

Board of Trustees v. Stubblefield, 94 Cal. Rptr. 318, 321 (1971).

Brubaker v. Board of Education, School District 149, Cook County, Illinois, 502 F. 2d 973 (7th Cir. 1974).

Doe, P. W. v. San Francisco Unified School District, 31 Cal. Rptr. 854 (1976).

Givhan v. Western Line Consolidated School District, 439 U.S. 410 (1979)

Goss v. Lopez, 419 U.S. 565 (1975).

Ingraham v. *Wright,* 430 U.S. 651 (1977).

Kingsville Independent School District v. *Cooper,* 611 F. 2d 1109 (5th Cir. 1980).

Meyer v. *Nebraska,* 262 U.S. 390, 399 (1923).

Morrison v. *State Board of Education,* 461 P. 2d 375 (Cal. 1969).

Parducci v. *Rutland,* 316 F. Supp. 352 (M.D. Ala. 1970).

Pickering v. *Board of Education of Township High School District 205, Will County,* 391 U.S. 563 (1968).

Pettit v. *State Board of Education,* 513 P. 2d 889 (Cal. 1973).

Sarac v. *State Board of Education,* 57 Cal. Rptr. 69 (1967).

Thompson v. *Southwest School District,* 483 F. Supp. 1170 (W.D.M.O. 1980)

13

Teachers' Professional Groups

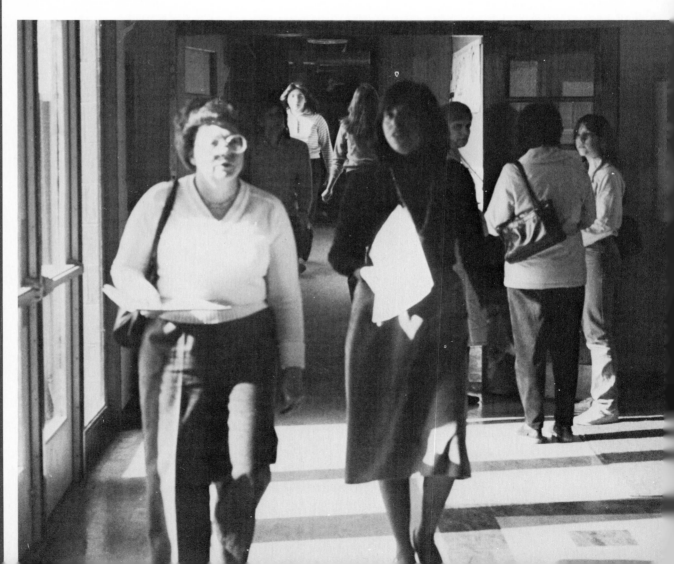

Objectives

This chapter provides information to help the reader to

1. Identify the major teachers' organizations and their basic orientations.
2. Describe the major episodes in the development of the major teachers' organizations.
3. Point out the arguments that have been made for and against the proposition that teachers should be regarded as professionals.
4. Differentiate between sanctions and strikes.
5. Suggest how teachers' organizations apply political pressures to the governmental authorities with responsibilities for education.
6. Note the patterns of conflict among the major teachers' organizations.
7. Recognize the role of teachers' organizations in winning for teachers a greater role in formulating basic school policies.

Pretest

DIRECTIONS: Using your own paper, answer each of the following true/false questions. For each correct statement, write the word *true* on your paper. For each incorrect statement, write the word *false* on your paper.

1. The American Federation of Teachers tends to be stronger in rural areas than in urban areas.
2. The sanction has been a tool used more frequently by the National Education Association than by the American Federation of Teachers.
3. The American Federation of Teachers is affiliated with the AFL-CIO.
4. The American Federation of Teachers has more members than the National Education Association.
5. The National Education Association has never approved the use of the strike as a bargaining tool for teachers.
6. The American Federation of Teachers and the National Education Association have been involved in a good deal of competition for members.
7. The American Federation of Teachers includes many school superintendents in its membership.
8. UniServ representatives provide services for members of the National Education Association.
9. The National Education Association has never established a formal affiliation with the American Federation of Labor–Congress of Industrial Organizations (AFL-CIO).
10. Generally, teacher members of the National Education Association have come to dominate the organization in recent years.

Introduction

Few topics stimulate as much debate among educators as those centering on the proper roles of teachers' organizations. Though there is some agreement on the idea that teachers are (or are striving to become) professionals, the consensus breaks down when individuals are asked to describe what a professional teacher is. Divisions between the two major organizations of teachers, the National Education Association (NEA) and the American Federation of Teachers (AFT), to a large degree reflect differing perceptions of teachers' professionalism. Because each of these major groups pursues policies consistent with its own (and inconsistent with the rival organization's) view of professionalism, the actions of both groups have always been a subject of high interest in America's faculty rooms.

Basically the philosophical differences between the NEA and the AFT result from differing perceptions of the nature of the teaching profession. In general, the NEA has taken the position that teachers have much in common with members of the medical and legal professions. Like doctors and lawyers, teachers go through a specialized preparation program. The state certifies their competence. They are charged with maintaining their level of competence through active participation in self-improvement programs and by study in organized professional-development courses. A code of professional ethics guides teachers' behavior.

Given this view of the nature of teaching, the NEA has pushed hard for programs that are directed to give teachers more control over their professional lives. The idea that teachers should be directly involved in decisions at all levels in the school results from the belief that, like doctors, teachers themselves ought to judge the adequacy of the professional environment in which they operate. Many of the NEA's efforts have sought to expand the range of teachers' control. These efforts are entirely consistent with a view of the teaching profession as a collection of skilled specialists who share the responsibility for maintaining the quality and the integrity of the profession.

The AFT has taken quite a different view of the teaching profession. In the view of the AFT, teachers are more like employees of large corporations than they are like lawyers and doctors, because teachers do not follow a lengthy preparatory program requiring years of work beyond the baccalaureate degree. Furthermore, many studies reveal that teachers are not perceived as having as high a social or economic status as lawyers and doctors. But the single most important difference is that large numbers of lawyers and doctors are self-employed. On the other hand, most teachers (indeed, nearly all of them) work for an institution. In many cases, school systems are large, and teachers have little contact with the individuals who are responsible for their continued employment. This situation, it is argued, tends to make teachers similar in many respects to employees of large corporations. Given this situation, the highest need of teachers is for a strong organization that can counterbalance the potential for often-distant administrative authority to be exercised arbitrarily.

This perception of the nature of the teaching profession has led the AFT to be most concerned with winning salary and working-condition benefits for teachers. The AFT has been much less concerned, generally, with increasing teachers' involvement in the governance of the entire school program than the NEA. Basically, the position has been simply this. There are two classes of educators: administrators, representing management, and teachers, representing labor. The interests of the two groups are fundamentally different. In a responsible teachers' organization, the primary effort should be to maximize the benefits for teachers and restrict arbitrary administrative power. But the right of administrators to manage what has been negotiated is recognized so long as that management remains consistent with formally adopted agreements. When administrative management is not perceived as consistent, then a pattern of teachers' organization–administrator arbitration based on traditional labor–management practices is seen as the most productive approach.

Regardless of their sympathy for either the NEA view or the AFT view of the nature of the teaching profession, most teachers share a common recognition of the need for some kind of a broad-based teachers' organization. This has not always been the case. In the early years of the twentieth century, for example, only a fraction of American teachers belonged to any professional group. A number of changes in the teaching profession have resulted in a dramatic upsurge in teachers' interest in large, nationally based organizations to represent their views.

Probably the biggest change in the teaching profession over the past hundred years has been the changing view of teaching as a permanent rather than a temporary employment situation. For many years, teaching required little formal training, paid little, and was regarded by almost no one as an occupation that would provide a fulfilling lifelong career. Teaching was regarded as a fallback profession that could tide an individual over until something better came along. Today, teachers regard themselves as being occupationally permanent. Given this perception, they have sought to improve their long-term expectations by supporting the organizations devoted to their own special needs.

Though there are more female teachers than male, many more men are in teaching today. This has meant that more individuals with the primary financial responsibility for their families are employed as teachers. These men, along with women who are heads of families, have seen a need to organize to achieve better financial rewards for teachers. In earlier days, when large numbers of teachers were single women or married women whose teaching salaries represented a second family income, teachers felt less need to join large professional groups.

Finally, the increase in the size of school districts (something that has been happening almost continuously since the early years of this century) has resulted in a depersonalization of teaching. In many districts, the administrators who make and implement policy affecting teachers have little or no personal contact with teachers. Often teachers in individual buildings have sensed themselves to be isolated and unable to communicate effectively with those at the top. Teachers' organizations have provided a collective voice for teachers through which the concerns of those in the classroom have been brought to the attention of central district administrators.

In the sections that follow, the development of the two largest teachers' organizations, the NEA and the AFT, will be traced. Though there are other groups, these two dominate American education today. Together, their histories and concerns represent a cross section of what teachers in this country have felt to be critical and important issues.

The National Education Association

Teachers' organizations have had a long history in the United States. Donley (1976) pointed out that the first recorded teachers' association in the nation was the Society of Associated Teachers of New York City founded in 1794. By the early 1800s a number of teachers' organizations had been established. Most of these groups were located in the major urban areas of the Northeast.

From these urban beginnings, teachers' organizations began to reach out for broader geographic bases. Between 1840 and 1860, sufficient numbers of local and county groups had been organized to provide a ground swell of interest in establishing state organizations. About thirty such groups were formed during this time.

In these early years, state organizations faced many significant problems. One of the most important of these had to do with what today we might call a "chicken–egg" problem. Teachers' groups of the mid-nineteenth century engaged in endless debates on the question of whether education would better be served (1) by increasing teachers' salaries and improving their working conditions to enhance the overall quality of the school program or (2) by working to enhance the overall quality of the school program and, by so doing, attracting more highly qualified individuals to the profession. Should teachers' money come first? Should money for other program items come first? Discussion of the responses to these questions was a regular feature of meetings of state teachers' groups during this period. Donley (1976) wrote of this situation as follows:

> Altruism accounted for much of the fluctuation of teacher groups between welfare concerns and the drive for better public education. Some members sincerely believed that advances for teachers would follow automatically when the public realized that it should support the schools more adequately. Only a few believed that higher pay for teachers could precede a great improvement in the

quality of teachers themselves. Did the appearance of the normal school with its better-trained product come first and persuade communities to pay higher and more equitable salaries? Or did the public first commence to pay salaries that justified the investment by young men and women in the longer normal school training?*

In the nineteenth century, the number of teachers in teachers' organizations remained very small. Most of the debates involved not classroom teachers themselves but superintendents, state school officials, and university people interested in education. Membership in a state teachers' association implied the kind of long-term commitment to education that many teachers at this time did not have. While school administrators and university professors would join a group willing to look at the improvement of education, many teachers perceived their time in the profession to be only "temporary." Many, consequently, took little active professional interest in the so-called teachers' organizations.

Despite their domination by administrators and university people, state teachers' groups continued to grow in the last half of the nineteenth century. A National Teachers Association was organized in Philadelphia in 1857. This group merged in the 1870s with the National Association of School Superintendents and the American Normal School Association (Donley, 1976). The new group was called the National Educational Association. The second word in the name, *educational,* was shortened to *education* in 1906.

In the early years of the twentieth century, the NEA was little concerned with teachers' benefits, in part because the percentage of members who were teachers remained very low, and in part because of the widespread belief that teaching was a "calling" almost in a religious sense and that it was not quite "proper" for teachers to be too concerned about financial rewards and working conditions. Realistically, the NEA was more of a forum for disseminating ideas about instruction and school management than a group interested in promoting teachers' welfare.

Nevertheless, some beginnings of attempts to improve teachers' working conditions occurred in these pre-World War I years. Before 1910, for example, efforts were begun to gather and report information about salaries and working conditions in school districts across the nation. From this time forward, the NEA began to report such figures consistently as part of the work of the organization.

The post-World War I inflation galvanized the NEA into paying more direct attention to teachers' welfare. One result was a dramatic increase in teachers' membership in the NEA. In the ten years following the end of the war, NEA membership increased fifteenfold. The major effect of this dramatic increase in teacher memberships was to involve teachers in influential

*Reprinted from Marshall O. Donley, Jr., *Power to the Teacher* (Bloomington: Indiana University Press, 1976), p. 9. Copyright 1976 by Indiana University Press.

Box 13-1
What Comes First, the Teacher or the School Program?

The issue of "Where should the money go?" has raged for years in public education. Some have suggested that increases in teachers' salaries should have first call on any new money. According to this argument, higher salaries will attract better teachers. This will result in better schools. Others have said that this approach is not a good one. Higher teachers' salaries take money away from modern textbooks, good laboratory facilities, and other elements of the school learning environment. It makes no sense, they argue, to pay teachers a high wage but to deny youngsters access to the most modern learning material available.

LET'S PONDER

Consider the issues raised in the paragraph above as you respond to the following questions:

1. Would a 10 percent increase in teachers' salaries result in a significant improvement in the quality of instruction in the schools? A 20 percent increase? Why?
2. What effect, if any, would you expect on the supply of teachers willing to work if teachers' salaries increased by 20 percent this year?
3. Would you expect there to be an immediate or a delayed effect on the quality of teachers' performance following a 20 percent raise in teachers' salaries? Why do you think so?
4. If a district had 30 percent increase in money to spend on education, how should this money be allocated between (1) teachers' salaries, and (2) instructional materials to produce the best net effect on learners?

roles in the organization for the first time. At this time, special NEA subgroups began to be formed that were charged with developing policies in areas of particular interest to teachers.

Despite the increasing teachers' involvement in the 1920s and 1930s, the NEA would certainly not be considered a militant group by today's standards. Still most of the program time at NEA conventions was devoted to issues having little connection with teachers' welfare. But the groundwork was laid during this time for a large teachers' organization that would be capable of making its pressure felt in later years when teachers' welfare commanded greater attention from NEA policymakers.

The potentials of teacher power began to be recognized after World War II. Again inflation had hit the teachers' pocketbooks with a vengeance. Teachers were simply finding it more and more difficult to meet their financial obligations. Large numbers were leaving the profession. By 1946, a critical shortage of teachers had developed. These conditions, well publicized through the publications of the NEA and other teachers' organizations, provided the backdrop for a large number of teachers' strikes in the postwar period. During much of this period, the NEA leadership opposed the use of the strike as a bargaining weapon. Part of this resistance came about because of a general reluctance of the middle-class membership of the organization to be identified with an approach typically associated with organized labor. Their conception of themselves as professionals did not square with the use of the strike as a bargaining tool.

Another factor contributing to the reluctance of the NEA's leadership to support the strike was a belief that pressure placed on Congress would lead to massive federal aid to education. This aid, it was reasoned, would provide the monies to improve teachers' salaries and working conditions. The leadership believed, and perhaps with good reason, that Congress would be much less receptive to voting federal funds for education if teachers were involved in large numbers of strike actions. For a variety of reasons, hopes for broad general assistance to the states failed to materialize during the later 1940s and through the 1950s. There was increased money after the Soviets launched *Sputnik,* but most of this was targeted for special programs to upgrade teachers' skills in the sciences and in languages. Little of this money became available to supplement teachers' salaries.

Though the NEA did not achieve a breakthrough on teachers' salaries by securing the passage of favorable federal legislation during this time, the organization continued to press its case by other means. A special group was formed within the NEA called the Teacher Education and Professional Standards (TEPS) Commission. The TEPS Commission worked nationwide for better teachers' salaries and working conditions. Frequent appearances were made before state legislatures to testify in behalf of proposals designed to improve teachers' working environment.

During the 1960s, the NEA worked hard to increase the political sophistication of its membership. Particularly effective were the "salary schools" that were sponsored by the organization to provide the membership with more sophisticated techniques for bargaining with school districts. Representatives from local and state units of the NEA attended national sessions and returned to lead similar programs at the state and local levels. As a result of exposure to skilled professionals in the area of bargaining, it became increasingly clear to large numbers of NEA members that legislation was needed to formalize bargaining relationships between teachers and school boards. Consequently a major effort was launched to secure the passage in every state of professional negotiations acts.

Large numbers of such acts were passed by state legislatures in the 1960s and 1970s. In general, such legislation guaranteed teachers some rights to negotiate salaries and working conditions with school boards. The specifics of individual laws varied greatly from place to place. Some states passed no

Box 13-2
Teachers' Strikes

Few issues have generated so much heat as that of strikes by teachers. Some have argued that this weapon undermines the image of the teacher as a professional. According to this position, teachers generally enjoy a positive image with the public as professionals who work hard and perform a difficult task well. When teachers strike, they say, there is danger that teachers will alienate the middle class and upper middle class who have been education's most ardent champions. The end result may be a dramatic reduction in support for funding of educational programs.

Others argue that the public is largely indifferent to many of the pressures under which teachers must labor. As evidence, they note the many conflicting pressures legislative bodies have placed on teachers. For example, teachers are expected to turn out learners who perform better than ever and to do so with little or no increase in funding. Supporters of teachers' strikes point out that the largest gains in teachers' benefits have come to teacher groups who have gone on strike to support a principle. While the public may say improvements in working conditions are needed, there is little evidence that much significant action has been taken in this direction when teachers have been unwilling to strike.

LET'S PONDER

Consider some of the arguments in the paragraphs above as you answer these questions:

1. Can a person be a professional and also believe in the use of the strike? Why, or why not?
2. How important is it for teachers to enjoy good relationships with middle class and upper middle class people who generally do not look with favor on strikes?
3. What validity is there to the argument that "strikes hurt the children?"
4. Do you think strikes have been overused or underused by teachers? Why?

laws of this type at all, but even in these states, there was an increasing tendency for teachers' advice and counsel to be sought on issues relating to their welfare and working conditions.

By the late 1960s, after a bitter fight, the NEA acknowledged that the strike was a legitimate bargaining weapon for teachers. Initially, attempts were made by the NEA leadership to soften the change in policy by avoiding reference to the term *strike*. "Withdrawal of services" was a code phrase that enjoyed currency for a time. However, as the number of teachers' strikes increased in the late 1960s, and as NEA surveys revealed increasing membership support for the strike as a bargaining tool, there was open talk of strikes and the phrase "withdrawal of services" tended to fade away.

Teachers' strikes came to be an almost predictable event of early fall by the late 1960s. There were 131 strikes during the school year 1968–1969 and 171 the following year (Donley, 1976). In many instances, the strikes were related to a situation that was created by many of the professional negotiation acts that had been passed. Many of these laws required school districts to identify one teachers' organization to represent all teachers in the district. This condition resulted in a great and often bitter competition for members between the NEA and the AFT. Ordinarily an election was held, and the group getting the most votes won the right to represent all teachers in a district. In an effort to win over new members, the leadership of both NEA and AFT affiliates accused one another of being "soft" and not aggressive enough in looking after teachers' interest. This competition resulted in a progressive escalation of rhetoric, inflated promises of what would be done to improve teachers' welfare, and generally inflammatory exchanges on a host of other issues. Not wishing to appear weak, whichever organization won the representation fight proved quite willing to recommend a strike to demonstrate its militance in defense of teachers. Quite possibly, had professional negotiations laws been written in a way that did not encourage open competition for the right to represent all teachers, the strikes may have been fewer in number.

Particularly in the late 1960s, the strike posed very real problems for teachers. At this time, teachers' strikes were illegal in every state. Thus teachers who participated took a chance not only of losing their jobs but also of breaking a law. Indeed, teachers and teachers' leaders in some areas did spend time in jail as a result of strike actions in the late 1960s and into the 1970s. Most frequently, however, settlements included amnesty provisions permitting teachers to return to work without fear that charges would be pressed because of their participation in an illegal strike. Still the possibility of prosecution for illegal strikes was a concern. Consequently the NEA in the 1970s worked hard to secure the passage of state laws making the strike actions of teachers legal. Some such laws were passed, but teachers' strikes continue to be illegal in many parts of the country.

Because of the difficulties associated with strikes, the NEA has favored putting pressure on states and school districts to deal fairly with teachers by threatening to impose (or by actually imposing) "sanctions." Sanctions involve the systematic dissemination of adverse information about a district or a group of districts to the entire national community of teachers. In essence, national sanctions tell teachers to "keep out—this is a very bad place to be employed." NEA members are urged not to seek nor accept employment in any district that is under national sanction. Such nationally distributed publications of the NEA as *Today's Education* and the *NEA Reporter* regularly include lists of districts under national sanction.

The "muscle" behind sanctions is districts' fear of adverse national publicity. When the word is out that there are severe problems in a community's schools, then doubts tend to be planted in the minds of business and other leaders in the community about the kind of negative image that might be being transmitted to outsiders. Frequently this concern translates to pressure to improve working conditons for teachers. When this happens, sanctions are removed and the adverse publicity stops.

Sanctions have proved most effective when a single school district or a relatively small number of school districts are involved. The limitations of sanctions as a weapon revealed themselves in 1967, when the NEA placed national sanctions on the entire state of Florida. Without going into the gruesome details, this effort resulted in relatively modest improvements in finances for schools, some teachers' losing their jobs, and an embittered relationship between many Florida political leaders and professional education people. The lesson of Florida was that a state represented too many people with too many diffuse interests for the "embarrassment" of sanctions to have the desired effect.

Reacting perhaps to the situation in Florida and other episodes, the NEA in the late 1960s and on into the 1970s moved to strengthen the hand of state and local associations. There was a tacit recognition that improvements in teachers' benefits—in many instances, at least—were to be won at the state and local level. But often the expertise needed to deal with sophisticated issues was not locally available. To remedy this situation, the NEA in 1969 began a program called *UniServ*. The idea was to place one highly trained NEA staff person in the field for every twelve hundred teachers who were members of the organization. A special Leadership Training Academy was established to provide the needed skills to UniServ representatives (Donley, 1976). These trained UniServ representatives set up shop in field offices throughout the nation. From these offices, they have provided needed support services to NEA affiliates in the local districts. The effect of the establishment of UniServ has been to make the resources of the NEA much more accessible to teachers.

NEA membership continued to grow in the 1960s and into the 1970s and 1980s. The effort to mount UniServ and other projects designed to increase the impact of the NEA at local and state levels resulted in a need for more revenue. Dues increases in the early 1970s resulted in a temporary flattening of the growth curve of NEA, but soon membership began climbing again. Part of this continued growth resulted from the push for "unification."

Unification, a long-standing objective of the NEA, means that an individual may not select membership in a local NEA affiliate, a state NEA affiliate, or the NEA itself without simultaneously joining all three groups. The battle for unification was fought primarily at the state level. State NEA affiliates sought the consent of their membership to unify or not to unify. By the mid 1970s, unification had carried the day everywhere. NEA affiliates throughout the nation had made the decision to require local and state NEA affiliate members to join the National Education Association as well.

The NEA reaped enormous financial rewards from the new members who joined the organization as a reult of unification. For example, when the state of Texas voted to unify in the 1970s, the NEA gained between thirty-five thousand and forty thousand new dues-paying members. These monies contributed significantly to the ability of the NEA to provide services throughout the nation.

The battle to achieve unification throughout the nation was not won easily. Arguments in many states were bitter. Members of many local groups did not object vehemently to the requirements that they now must join the state organization as well, but many were openly hostile to the NEA. A pattern in many states was for NEA–state–local membership to drop off immediately following a unification vote, but in time, membership tended to return to at least preunification levels.

In newly unified states, the NEA leadership, sensitive to the concerns of teachers in many local districts, typically attempted to become actively involved in supporting the passage of teachers' benefit laws by state legislatures. The general success of the unification effort is attested to by the more than 1 million teachers who belonged to the NEA by the early 1980s.

In the past fifty years, the NEA has evolved into an organization run by and for classroom teachers. Its publication arm, legal services operation, research division, and other components are all oriented toward serving the interests of teachers. A general thrust of the group in recent years has been centered on the belief that teachers should be more directly involved in school governance. *Governance* is a broad term, but generally the implication is that it encompasses those control points that have impact on the range of options given to teachers in the classrooms. Teachers represented by the NEA today are seeking more control over teachers' training, over curriculum decision-making, over extracurricular duties, and over a host of other areas that were once considered beyond their scope of responsibility. The eventual outcome of these efforts is by no means certain. Some of these proposals have generated heated opposition from universities and administrative groups. What does seem certain at this time is that the governance issue will be with us for some time to come and that the NEA will be vigorously representing the position of its membership.

The American Federation of Teachers

The American Federation of Teachers, a union affiliated with the AFL-CIO, has never enjoyed the numerical strength of the NEA. But the AFT has nevertheless had a great impact on education in this country. Much of this impact can be explained by the concentration of the AFT in large cities. Teachers' benefit packages won by AFT actions in cities such as New York and Chicago have greatly influenced teachers' groups throughout the country. Furthermore, because of the potential that the smaller organization has had for chipping away at the membership of the much larger NEA, the NEA has become much more aggressive in its support for militant teacher action. In the absence of a competing AFT, it is doubtful that the NEA would have recognized the legitimacy of the strike as a bargaining weapon as early as it did.

The AFT has always been strongest where organized labor in general has been strong. This accounts for the distinctly urban flavor that the group has always had. The AFT traces its roots to Chicago. The Chicago Teachers Federation was organized in that city in the late 1890s. A meeting of these Chicago-area unions and others from the industrialized sections of the Upper Midwest in 1916 resulted in the formation of the American Federation of Teachers.

Box 13-3
Teachers and Organized Labor

Is it desirable for teachers to be affiliated with organized labor? Arguments over this issue have consumed teachers for many years. Supporters of the proposition argue that organized labor represents a broad cross section of the American population. Union members range from unskilled workers to highly skilled airline pilots. All are joined together in a belief in economic equity. The breadth of union membership and the focus on basic economic welfare issues suggests that affiliation of teachers with organized labor makes very good sense.

Countering this argument, critics point out that organized labor is declining rather than expanding in influence. They note that the central areas of large cities, the traditional strongholds of organized labor, are in decay. Growth is occurring in the suburbs and in the small towns, areas traditionally unsympathetic to organized labor. Affiliation of teachers with organized labor, they argue, may well ``turn off'' people in the fastest growing parts of the country. Furthermore, affiliation with organized labor casts some doubts on teachers' professionalism. Professionals do not need to affiliate with nonprofessionals to achieve their objectives.

LET'S PONDER

Consider the arguments in the paragraphs above as you respond to the following questions?

1. Are the objectives of organized labor broader or narrower than the interests of teachers in the school? Does this have any implication for the desirability or nondesirability of teachers affiliating with organized labor?
2. Can a person be a professional and a member of organized labor? Why, or why not?
3. Are unions growing among other white collar groups? Which ones? Why?
4. Do you think teachers would be net gainers or losers if all had to belong to a group affiliated with organized labor? Why?

From the beginning, the AFT differed in two dramatic respects from the NEA. First of all, the organization sought members who were classroom teachers. It was never dominated by university people or administrators. Teachers played important leadership roles from the very first years. Second, the AFT had a primary concern about teachers' benefits right from the first. While the NEA in more recent years has been more concerned with teachers' benefits, for a long time the focus of this group was on a much broader array of educational themes.

The AFT's growth was not dramatic. By 1920, there were about ten thousand members. During the 1920s, there was a dramatic decline in membership. By the end of the decade, dues-paying members numbered only about five thousand (Donley, 1976). Much of this decline can be attributed to the general unpopularity of unions in the 1920s. Generally speaking, the economy was booming (until September 1929, at least). Government officials, the press, and other influential sources tended to brand unions in general, and teachers unions in particular, as aberrations from the American tradition.

The AFT experienced an enormous gain in membership during the 1930s. Clearly the glow had gone off the American economy. Passage of the Wagner Act and other legislation signaled that unions were viewed as "legitimately" American now. By 1940, close to forty thousand teachers belonged to the AFT. The important issues to union members during the 1930s were salaries and tenure. The focus on teachers' benefits had not shifted.

In the 1940s and 1950s, the AFT could fairly be described as in a static state. Membership grew only modestly. No hard-hitting leadership emerged to take the group in exciting new directions. Indeed, only minimal efforts were expended to build a national base for the union. Fundamentally, the AFT was a group of loosely aligned big-city locals. A few of these locals—for example, those in Chicago—continued to be very strong, but at the national level, AFT efforts to influence educational policy were weak during this period.

The AFT got a tremendous membership lift in the early 1960s as a result of certain developments in New York City. The AFT local there—the United Federation of Teachers (UFT)—and the NEA affiliate became embroiled in a contest for the exclusive right to represent the city's teachers as a bargaining agent. The UFT won the bargaining-agent election in a landslide. Along with this victory went the right to represent the interests of more than fifty thousand New York City teachers. This victory resulted in a tremendous increase in new union members.

The victory of the union forces in New York stimulated greater interest in teachers' unions in other large cities. Some of the stigma of union affiliation that had been felt by many teachers had begun to wear off. Many urban teachers, at least, came to accept the idea that one could be both a "professional" and a "union person." An analogy was made between teachers' situations and those of highly trained airline pilots, who felt no threat to their status by joining a union. Few denied the professionalism of the pilots.

Throughout the 1960s, the AFT's giant New York affiliate, the UFT, became involved in a series of bitter strikes. These strikes, directed in part toward New York's antistrike laws, generally resulted in higher teachers' salaries, better protection for teachers in the schools, and more involvement of teachers in curriculum decision-making. But they exacted a heavy cost. The union leaders spent time in jail. Many administrators with years of educational leadership experience resigned out of frustration. Community elements on both sides of the strike issues remained bitter long after agreements were hammered out.

From its successes in New York, the AFT expanded its activities in many other large cities throughout the country. Rights were won to represent the interests of teachers in Cleveland, Boston, and other major metropolitan areas. But these rights did not come without cost. In almost every case, a bitter and expensive fight with the NEA was involved. Sometimes teachers who voted in one year to have the AFT affiliate represent their interests would vote in another year to have the NEA affiliate represent their interests. Such switches in allegiance resulted in tremendous dollar losses for the "loser" organization. The AFT, with a much smaller membership, proved much less able to bear these losses than the rival NEA.

In 1968, the AFT was struck by a financial catastrophe. The United Auto Workers (UAW) under the leadership of Walter Reuther, severed its connection with the AFL-CIO. The UAW had been contributing millions of dollars to help the AFT keep its organizational campaigns in the major cities afloat. With disaffiliation from the AFL-CIO, the money from the UAW stopped coming. The AFT averted financial collapse only after a dues increase was approved by a narrow margin.

Another problem that faced the AFT at this time was the declining base of potential membership. The union had always been strongest in the central cities. These areas were losing population—and hence, teachers—to suburban areas. It was true that metropolitan areas were growing, but most of the increase was in the areas surrounding the traditional central city. People in the suburbs generally were not philosophically in sympathy with the union movement. Efforts to recruit members in the suburbs would require enormous expenditures of money, and the likelihood of success could not be considered high.

Given the financial difficulties of the organization and the erosion of the numbers of teachers who would be most attracted to membership, the AFT leadership began giving serious thought to the possibility of a merger with the NEA. The NEA now primarily a teacher-dominated group, had endorsed the use of the strike, and generally was not very distant from many positions being espoused by the AFT. A formal proposal to merge was made to the NEA, and a series of meetings were held. These broke down over the refusal of the NEA to merge with any group that would require affiliation with the AFL-CIO. NEA statistics revealed that tremendous numbers of NEA members would resign rather than have their dues go to a labor-affiliated organization.

"It's not fair for you to be so understanding during contract negotiations!"

What's Ahead for Teachers' Organizations?

Though speculating about the future is always somewhat hazardous, chances do seem good that these groups will continue to be very visible participants in the educational scene. Three general categories of pressure seem certain to continue to come down on teachers: (1) rising public expectations or "accountability," (2) the demand for "cost containment" in education, and (3) "legally mandated changes" in public education. In response to these pressures, teachers will very likely let their feelings be known through their professional groups. Each of the pressure categories presents teachers with problems that they find it difficult to repond to individually, but collective action may hold some promise.

In the area of rising expectations, or accountability, teachers find themselves confronted by a public that is alarmed by the decline in standardized test scores. This decline has resulted in increasing pressures on schools and teachers to "do better." In response, teachers argue that the sources for this decline may well go beyond what occurs in school. What students learn, they note, is only partly explained by the school program. If parents watch television more than they used to, then their youngsters are going to be less likely to spend their leisure time reading than in watching television. Although teachers are willing to be accountable for their own actions, they decline to be accountable for a failure of youngsters to learn everything that is presented to them. Too much evidence exists, teachers say, that youngsters' learning depends on many more factors than the quality of the teacher's performance. It is likely that teachers will increasingly wish their professional groups to speak up in support of this point of view.

Cost-containment efforts in education also give teachers cause for concern. As taxpayers themselves, they do not object to attempts to husband tax dollars. But they feel themselves caught in something of a bind between public demands to improve students' performance on the one hand and public demands to spend less money on the other hand. They feel that there is a basic incompatibility between these two public expectations. Through their professional groups, teachers seem certain to bring this inconsistency to the public's attention in the years ahead.

Legally mandated changes in education have placed great strain on teachers. Instructors report their frustration with new requirements to teach subjects in which they have received little or no formal training. Not many years ago, for example, elementary-school teachers in California found themselves faced with a requirement to teach Spanish, a language with which the vast majority were unfamiliar. In more recent years, many states have passed laws requiring that consumer-education or economic-education courses be taught (or at least that related content be introduced into existing courses). Lacking preparation in these areas, teachers have felt their professionalism undercut. How, they have asked, can we do a good job teaching something we don't know about? Probably the largest concern of all in this area came about as a consequence of the passage of federal "mainstreaming" legislation. This legislation introduced students into regular classrooms who had previously been taught by special-education teachers with professional training in this difficult area. Numerous teachers left the profession as a consequence of their inability to deal with this new situation.

Recapitulation of Major Ideas

1. In the years before World War I, few teachers belonged to the National Education Association. The group was primarily a forum for exchanging ideas about the entire field of education. Teachers' benefits received sparse attention. School administrators and university professors dominated the organization.

2. After World War I, many more teachers joined the NEA. Initially, the discussion of teachers' benefits was at a minimal, but beginning in the 1930s and continuing to the present day, such issues have been much more central to the purpose of the organization.

3. Today the NEA is run by and for teachers. The organization is dedicated to improving the lot of the classroom teacher in the United States. Services are disseminated through a large number of field offices as well as through the national office. As a mechanism for cementing its influ-

ence, the NEA requires members of affiliated state and local groups also to join the NEA.

4. Sanctions are a weapon developed by the NEA. Sanctions, imposed on a state, a number of districts, or a single district, tell the profession to "keep out—this is a bad place to work." Members are asked to refuse offers of employment from districts under national sanction. The strength of the sanction has been local communities' desire to avoid bad publicity.

5. The NEA is the largest teachers' professional group in the country. Dues-paying members number well over 1 million.

6. The American Federation of Teachers is affiliated with the AFL-CIO. This group, much smaller than the NEA, is strongest in New York, Chicago, and other urban areas. It enjoys little support in suburban and rural areas. Militant stands of the AFT have forced the NEA to become more aggressive in support of teachers' benefits.

7. Some attempts have been made to achieve a merger between the AFT and the NEA. To date, no merger has been consummated. There is great reluctance on the part of some NEA leaders to merge with any group that might require affiliation with organized labor. There is a fear of wholesale resignation of members should such merger terms be accepted.

8. Pressures on teachers seem to be increasing. Consequently, it is likely that national teachers' groups will be called on to represent teacher interests with great regularity in the future.

Posttest

DIRECTIONS: Using your own paper, answer each of the following true/false questions. For each correct statement, write the word *true* on your paper. For each incorrect statement, write the word *false* on your paper.

1. The American Federation of Teachers tends to be stronger in rural areas than in urban areas.
2. The "sanction" has been a tool used more frequently by the National Education Association than by the American Federation of Teachers.
3. The American Federation of Teachers is affiliated with the AFL-CIO.
4. The American Federation of Teachers has more members than the National Education Association.
5. The National Education Association has never approved the use of the strike as a bargaining tool for teachers.
6. The American Federation of Teachers and the National Education Association have been involved in a good deal of competition for members.

7. The American Federation of Teachers includes many school superintendents among its membership.
8. UniServ representatives provide services for members of the National Education Association.
9. The National Education Association has never established a formal affiliation with the American Federation of Labor–Congress of Industrial Organizations (AFL-CIO).
10. Generally, teacher members of the National Education Association have come to dominate the organization in recent years.

Summary

During its early years, the National Education Association had relatively few teachers as members. It was primarily an organization where general issues of interest to school administrators and university professors were discussed. Teachers did not start joining the organization in large numbers until the 1920s. These teacher members began to play a really influential role in the group beginning in the 1930s. Today it is fair to say that the NEA is run by and for its teacher members. The organization supports a broad range of programs with a general view to improving the lot of the classroom teacher. The largest teachers' organization in the country, the NEA today claims well over 1 million dues-paying members.

Never large in numbers, but often large in influence, the American Federation of Teachers was organized in Chicago. Its influence has always been strongest in major urban areas of the country, particularly in New York City and Chicago. The AFT is affiliated with the AFL-CIO. Unlike the NEA, the AFT from its inception was primarily interested in teachers' benefits. The AFT has not hesitated to use militant tactics to achieve its objectives. Some of the organization's successes were influential in moving the larger NEA into a more militant stance. In recent years, the AFT has run into some financial difficulties. Tentative approaches have been made to the NEA regarding a possible merger, but largely because of the AFT's AFL-CIO connection, to date nothing has come of these explorations.

Teachers today are coming under pressure from a number of sources. On the one hand, they are asked to produce evidence that learners are learning. On the other, they are asked to make do with little or no increase in funds for materials. Legislatures are placing requirements on teachers that, in many instances, involve them in teaching subjects or learners they have not been trained to work with. In short, many teachers feel themselves victimized by pressures that they do not feel they have created. These feelings suggest that they will be increasingly concerned in the years ahead about making their feelings known through the major teachers' professional organizations.

References

CALLAHAN, RAYMOND E. *Education and the Cult of Efficiency: A Study of the Administration of Public Schools.* Chicago: The University of Chicago Press, 1962.

DONLEY, MARSHALL O., JR. *Power to the Teacher: How America's Educators Became Militant.* Bloomington: Indiana University Press, 1976.

FLYGARE, THOMAS J. *Collective Bargaining in the Public Schools.* Bloomington, Ind.: Phi Delta Kappa Educational Foundation, 1977.

LIEBERMAN, MYRON. *Education as a Profession.* Englewood Cliffs, N.J.: Prentice-Hall, 1956.

WESLEY, EDGAR B. *NEA: The First Hundred Years.* New York: Harper Brothers, 1957.

14

Teachers and Other Professionals

Objectives

This chapter provides information to help the reader to

1. Recognize that professionals in education who do not teach may see their roles and responsibilities differently than teachers may see them.
2. Identify the roles and responsibilities of a number of nonteaching professionals in education.
3. Point out possible areas of conflict between teachers and certain other nonteaching professionals in education.
4. Note the kinds of support provided to teachers by nonteaching professionals in education.
5. Realize that the kinds and numbers of nonteaching professionals a teacher might encounter will vary enormously from situation to situation.
6. Differentiate among nonteaching professionals having "staff" as opposed to "line" authority.
7. Recognize the extent of and the limitations on help that teachers might expect from different nonteaching professionals in education.

Pretest

DIRECTIONS: Using your own paper, answer each of the following true/false questions. For each correct statement, write the word *true* on your paper. For each incorrect statement, write the word *false* on your paper.

1. The primary responsibility of a school psychologist is to provide teachers with a specific set of instructions regarding how a particular child should be treated.
2. Curriculum consultants and curriculum coordinators who work out of a district's central office more typically represent "staff" authority than "line" authority.
3. A secondary school is more likely to have an assistant principal or a vice-principal than is an elementary school.
4. University professors who visit public schools are more likely to be associated with student-teaching programs than with other specializations within colleges of education.
5. Today the school nurse usually does not have the authority to dispense medications to students from a supply owned by the school.
6. There is a fairly common pattern of hostility between teachers and counselors in many schools.

7. Principals always have to follow the suggestions made by curriculum consultants and curriculum coordinators who work out of the central district office.
8. It is a very common practice for principals in large high schools to sit in on classes.
9. In general, university professors of education today tend to have had more extensive and more recent classroom experience than was typical in the past.
10. There is a growing trend toward increasing the number of counselors in elementary schools.

Introduction

Many people with professional training who do not teach classes are involved in the operation of the public schools. All schools have principals. Large numbers have vice-principals and assistant principals as well. Guidance counselors work in virtually all secondary schools and in large numbers of elementary buildings. School nurses are attached to schools. University professors play a role. Specialists in various aspects of the school curriculum perform vital duties. Education, in short, is a sophisticated business, and highly trained specialists of many kinds contribute to the smooth functioning of the schools.

Not only are new teachers sometimes not aware of the numbers of these people, they tend to be even less well informed about their individual perspectives. Individual perspectives? Well, yes, individual perspectives. Because schools involve large numbers of youngsters and because the training of the various professionals in the school varies, it is only natural that what one individual sees as the reality of the school may be quite different from what another sees.

It is true that professionals within the same category tend to have some common feelings about what education is and what their role in education should be. Teachers, for example, generally agree that they have some responsibility for transmitting certain skills and knowledge to the young people in their classes, but even within a given professional category, such as *teacher,* enormous differences exist. An eavesdropper on conversations in any faculty room in the country would soon conclude that teachers disagree strongly about what it is they should be doing in the classroom. They disagree, too, on the nature of the youngsters in the school. Perceptions depend, to a large measure, on what the individual encounters personally in performing his or her role in the school.

Consider, for example, a high school French teacher who works primarily with interested college-bound students and a high school English teacher who works with "them all." Very likely, the French teacher experiences few motivational problems and suffers only occasional problems with classroom control. The English teacher, on the other hand, teaches a required course that all students must take to qualify for graduation. He or she might see motivation as a severe problem, and discipline or control problems might well be of great concern. Asked to comment on the general nature of the student body in the school, the two teachers probably would give dramatically different answers, and each answer would be "true" in terms of the experience of the individual responding.

Among administrators, differences in opinion about the nature of the student body are legendary among two common categories of high school vice-principals. These are (1) the vice-principal for discipline (sometimes euphemistically known by the title of "vice-principal for student affairs" or by some other less descriptive title) and (2) the vice-principal for curriculum. By whatever title he or she is known, the vice-principal for discipline spends the day working with students who are in trouble. He or she fields complaints from outside callers relating to students' behavior. Those students whom the vice-principal for discipline knows very likely do not represent a good cross section of the student body. Asked to describe a "typical" student, this vice-principal is quite likely to paint a rather gloomy picture.

On the other hand, the vice-principal for curriculum has much less contact with "difficult" students. Those students whom he or she does know may well be student representatives from the curriculum committee of the student council. They, in general, are likely to be reasonably articulate school leaders. Asked to describe a "typical" student, the vice-principal for curriculum may well describe a young person bearing scant resemblance to the pupil described by the vice-principal for discipline.

Differences in the perceptions of individuals *within* professional groups in education are very great indeed, but they do not begin to compare with the differences *between* groups of professionals who play a role in the schools. Because "reality" as experienced by such groups as nurses, teachers, administrators, counselors, and curriculum consultants is so different, it should not be surprising that the members of each group tend to have somewhat different perspectives on what goes on in the school. Differences in these perspectives not infrequently result in communications problems and interpersonal conflicts among members of these various groups. In the sections that follow, some dimensions of this situation are sketched, and particular attention is given to how teachers interact with the nonteaching professionals in the schools.

Education Professors and Teachers

During their undergraduate days, prospective teachers are generally favorably disposed toward their education professors. After all, these professors have been highly trained. Furthermore, most have actually experienced the demands of a profession that undergraduates have lived through only vicar-

Box 14-1
Perspectives of Three Different Ninth Grade Teachers

A. Mr. Bowen teaches a course called ''Practical Mathematics'' for ninth graders. He teaches five sections of the class every day. The course is for students who (1) failed algebra last year, (2) want to take only two years of high school mathematics and who do not plan to go on to college, or (3) experienced great difficulty in eighth grade mathematics and who were recommended for this course by their eighth grade teacher.

B. Ms. Scott teaches ninth grade orchestra. She has five classes a day. For two periods she meets strings. For two periods she meets brasses. For one period she meets the entire orchestra together. At this school, each student has two orchestra periods, either a string period or a brass period and a final period with the whole orchestra.

C. Mr. Lowery teaches ninth grade metal shop. The course is an elective. He has five classes every day. Students in his classes make items that the industrial arts club sells to raise money.

LET'S PONDER

Read the short paragraphs above relating to three different ninth grade teachers. Then, respond to these questions:

1. If teachers A, B, and C were asked to describe a ''typical'' ninth grade student, how might each respond? Would answers be similar, or different? If different, how would you explain responses of each?
2. If each of these teachers were asked, ''Is discipline a problem in your classroom?'' how would each respond? How would you account for any differences?
3. Would some students in the ninth grade likely be enrolled in classes taught by more than one of the above teachers? More than two? Explain your responses.
4. Which of the above teachers probably has to spend the most time preparing for classes each day? Which one spends the least? How did you reach these conclusions?
5. If you had to choose, which one of these teachers would you most like to be? Least like to be? Why?

iously through textbook accounts and, perhaps, a little on-site teachers' aide work. Having no real context for evaluating the merit of what the professor suggests to be "true" about education, most bow to the professor's experience and generally accept what he or she has to say.

The situation of the new teacher in the classroom is much different from that of the undergraduate student who is preparing to teach. The teacher experiences the "real world" of teaching. Given this exposure, the teacher has a context within which to evaluate the relative value of what he or she was taught by education professors in undergraduate classes. Not infrequently, the pressures and demands of the teaching situation are perceived as having sparse connection with the world of education as it was described in undergraduate education classes.

If this is the case, who is to blame? Should the professor have done better? Or is there something the matter with the teacher? There are no simple answers to these questions, but a case can be made for these problems' being primarily a result of differing perceptions of what the appropriate role of the education professor is.

The classroom teacher, particularly the new classroom teacher, tends to judge the education professor in terms of how well he or she provided solutions to problems that the teacher is facing in the classroom. Frequently, new teachers take the stance that undergraduate education professors should provide "site-specific" solutions to problems.

On the other hand, the university professor recognizes a responsibility to prepare students to qualify for a certificate that will enable them to teach in any area of any district in the state. Situations from school to school are viewed as being enormously different. Given this reality, the professor may well feel that there is no way to deal with issues other than in a rather general way. To provide "nuts-and-bolts" solutions to problems that might work beautifully in School *A* could prove a real disservice to the students who ultimately take jobs in School *B* where such solutions would not be effective at all. Many university professors, then, feel themselves compelled to deal with rather generalized responses to categories of teaching problems out of a recognition that the circumstances that the teachers will face are too idiosyncratic for a "sure-fire" answer that applies to every situation.

Though it would be a mistake to be too optimistic, some evidence does suggest that the "perception gap" between education professors and teachers may be narrowing. Two factors contribute to this improvement. First, college and university training programs are increasingly becoming performance-based or competency-based. Stripped of all the hoopla that sometimes accompanies these terms, this means simply that college courses increasingly seek to provide new teachers with the specific kinds of skills that they will need in the classroom. Certainly, for the reasons noted earlier, there is no attempt to suggest to new teachers that they are being provided with answers to every classroom problem, but there has been a serious attempt to orient courses toward providing new teachers with a more specific understanding of instructional skills than was formerly the case.

A second change may be seen in the professors themselves. Not many years ago, individuals who pursued doctoral work in education and became professors were drawn overwhelmingly from the ranks of school administrators.

Although many of these individuals had taught early in their careers, for large numbers this experience was ancient history. They tended to be much more familiar with the perspective of the administrator than with the perspective of the teacher. Although no one faulted their good intentions, some of these people simply lacked a feel for the kinds of specific information needed by new classroom teachers.

Today large numbers of classroom teachers who have never held administrative positions pursue doctoral-level work. Their interests center primarily on the needs of the classroom teacher. Given this orientation, they are able to frame courses that tend to respond fairly effectively to the day-to-day needs of beginning teachers. Although some "credibility gap" between these university professors of education and classroom teachers still exists, there has been great improvement with the entry into the university teaching ranks of people who have spent a good number of years in the classroom and who continue to identify closely with the concerns of teachers.

In the schools, teachers have most contact with those university professors of education who are responsible for managing the student-teaching program. Though patterns vary greatly from place to place, ordinarily these professors visit the schools periodically to arrange for the placement of student teachers, to chat with the teachers who are selected to work with student teachers, and to supervise student teachers. Sometimes new teachers are needlessly concerned that these university professors are critical of every move they make, a feeling carried over from their own student teaching, when their behavior in the classroom was being closely monitored. This issue should be of no concern at all to new teachers. First, the university professors are likely to be much too busy worrying about managing their own student teachers to become overly concerned with practices of others. Second, most of them have been around classrooms long enough to recognize that all teachers have splendid days as well as days that are better forgotten. Finally, university professors have no connection of authority with school district administration officials. Indeed, they function as guests of the district while visiting individual buildings. Consequently they are not at all eager to jeopardize their status as welcome visitors by making disparaging or critical comments about faculty members either to administrators or to colleagues back on the campus.

There has been a trend in recent years for the field experiences of prospective teachers to be greater in number and longer in duration than previously. At one time, few new teachers got into a school until they did their student teaching. Today many colleges and universities provide opportunities for their undergraduate education students to work in some capacity in schools very early in their program. This phenomenon has meant a great increase in the number of contacts between professors of education and classroom teachers. There is a growing awareness of the desirability of immersing prospective teachers in the reality of the school situation as much as possible. In some cases, university professors have even been assigned offices in public schools where they counsel the students who are working as teachers' aides and student teachers and where they conduct classes. A result of all this is that the university professor of education is coming to be a very familiar figure around public school classrooms. This familiarity provides the opportunity, at least, for the development of a close personal relationship between professor and teacher that can be valuable to both. When teachers and professors feel comfortable in exchanging their views candidly, conditions are excellent for the evolution of outstanding teacher-preparation programs.

In summary, new teachers need to remember two key points: (1) professors of education are strongly committed to improving school practices, and (2) teachers are strongly committed to improving school practices. Given their common commitment to this goal, there is no reason that teachers and professors cannot work comfortably together. Though they may bring somewhat different perspectives to the tasks, there is every reason to expect that out of a comfortable and candid exchange of views, the entire educational enterprise will profit.

Teachers and Administrators

The number of administrators with whom a new teacher deals varies greatly from situation to situation. It is true, however, that most elementary schools have fewer administrators than most secondary schools. The number is primarily a function of school size. Elementary schools tend to be smaller than middle schools, junior high schools, or senior high schools.

Many elementary schools have only a single administrative official in the building, the principal. The elementary principal is a very important figure. He or she is a "line" official. This means that the principal is in the chain of command that runs down from the superintendent's office. He or she has the authority to make and enforce the policy decisions that have been left to the principal's discretion by the superintendent. The opinions of principals are not simply advisory; the building principal has "clout."

Elementary teachers ordinarily have very frequent contact with the building principal. Few days go by when they do not see the principal at some time during the day. Particularly in the case of new teachers, the principal is likely to be an occasional visitor to the classroom. In the elementary school, too, the principal may make specific notes on what he or she observes and provide teachers with a critique of their performance after the observation. In addition to his or her responsibilities for school management, the principal tends to play an instructional leadership role in the elementary school.

Secondary-school teachers, particularly those teaching in large high schools, may well see the building principal as a more distant figure than do

Box 14-2
Moving the Education Professors to the Public Schools

Today, more than ever before, teachers are being trained in the classrooms where they will be working. Universities and colleges have recognized that it is not enough to talk about public schools. Texts and talk are fine, they have observed, but it takes a heavy dose of reality to convince new teachers of the serious challenges they will be facing in the classroom.

To provide this "dose of reality," universities and colleges are sending professors to the field. Many have offices in public schools. They work here, on site, with student teachers. They teach some of their methods courses in the very buildings where those methods will have to be used, for better or worse, by their students. The system provides prospective teachers with a solid understanding of what teaching really is and the professor with an opportunity and an obligation to provide students with insights that will have some real bearing on the problems they face in their public school classrooms.

LET'S PONDER

Read the paragraphs above. Then, respond to these questions:

1. Do you agree with the basic premise of this short article that sending professors to the field improves teacher training programs? Why, or why not?
2. To what extent is the training an individual might get in one field setting generalizable to another? Is there a danger that professors might learn how to teach teachers to work only in the public schools where they have their offices?
3. How do you think teachers would react if all professors of education had offices in school buildings? Who would be the major beneficiaries of this arrangement, teachers or professors? Why do you think so?
4. Should professors of education have to take leaves of absence occasionally to return to teach in the public school classroom? What advantages and disadvantages do you see for such a proposal?

their colleagues in elementary schools. Management tasks consume a great deal of the time of the high school principal. To assist in the governance of the building, the principal commonly has one or more associates. For example, a school might have a vice-principal for student affairs and a vice-principal for curriculum. In such an arrangement, the vice-principal for student affairs handles major student discipline problems, complaints about students from school patrons, relationships between legal agencies and students in the school, and a host of other student-related problems. This individual is unlikely to have much contact with individual teachers in the building unless some severe student problem is involved.

The vice-principal for curriculum is the individual most likely to have frequent contact with new teachers in a high school. This person is responsible for course scheduling and the general organization of the academic program. He or she needs frequent advice from teachers, particularly when new schedules of classes are being developed. In many buildings, this individual is expected to play an instructional leadership role as well. He or she may visit classes, particularly those of teachers new to the staff, to make formal observations and to evaluate performance. At the secondary-school level, however, classroom visitations by administrators tend to be much less frequent and systematic than at the elementary level. Some new secondary teachers may never receive a visit from a school administrator, not because of a lack of concern about how new teachers are getting along but because of the tremendous work load carried by administrators in large high schools. Sometimes, for all their good intentions, there simply is not time for secondary-school administrators to spend as much time working with new teachers as they would like.

Much more distant from the day-to-day lives of classroom teachers are the administrators who work in the central district administration offices. In small districts, superintendents may make regular visits to the schools. In some, too, superintendents do much of the interviewing and hiring of teachers. But in intermediate- and large-sized districts, many teachers may never have had a personal conversation with the superintendent. School management is big business. In addition to managing a very large personnel enterprise, the superintendent has many public relations tasks. As the official representative of the school district, the superintendent may be called on to testify before the legislature, respond to letters to the editor in the newspaper, and deliver talks before a host of important community groups.

FUNKY WINKERBEAN   by Tom Batiuk

(Funky Winkerbean by Tom Batiuk. © 1974, Field Enterprises, Inc. Courtesy of Field Newspaper Syndicate.)

The duties of school administration in intermediate and large districts far exceed the capacity of a single individual. Such districts typically have several deputy, assistant, or associate superintendents with specific responsibilities for managing such areas as finance, personnel, and curriculum. These individuals, too, generally spend little time in individual school buildings. Teachers' contacts with them will very likely be limited to service on district-level committees chaired by designated central office administrators.

Though these certainly do not offer occasions for personal contacts between teachers and administrators, many districts bring superintendents and teachers together at one or more ceremonial occasions during the school year. Frequently there is a "kickoff" program for the school year held early in the fall, to which all school personnel in the district are invited. Many school systems sponsor meetings in the spring to present awards to teachers and to otherwise provide a ceremonial capstone to the school year. For teachers in intermediate and large districts, it is possible that these special occasions will be the only times during the school year that they will see administrators from the central district office.

In summary, school administrators—superintendents and their deputies and principals and their deputies—represent line authority in districts. They are responsible for implementing and enforcing the policies of the school district. Their decisions are not simply advisory. Rather, these judgments provide a basis for action throughout that part of the district's operations over which they exercise control. Their contacts with teachers vary, depending on (1) the size of the school district and (2) the size of the school building. Generally, teachers have more personal contacts with school administrators in small school districts and in schools enrolling small numbers of learners.

Teachers and Counselors

Counselors have been part of secondary-school operations (particularly high school operations) for a number of years. Their arrival in large numbers on the elementary-school scene has been of relatively recent origin. The trend toward placing counselors in all elementary buildings seems to be accelerating, and the day may not be very far distant when nearly all elementary schools will have been assigned counselors.

To be candid, relationships between counselors and teachers, particularly in the secondary schools, are not always harmonious. Indeed, sometimes they are downright hostile because of dramatically differing conceptions of what the role of the counselor should be.

Counselors' training typically focuses on the individual. They are interested in helping youngsters come to terms with themselves. Counselors using what is styled a *directive* approach tend to take an active role in suggesting to youngsters how they might resolve problems that are bothering them. Counselors using what is styled a *nondirective* approach presume that individual youngsters carry within themselves the solutions to their problems. These counselors avoid making specific suggestions to learners and engage instead in procedures designed to help the youngsters themselves to recognize and identify their own solutions to difficulties. Although there are deep philosophical differences dividing directive and nondirective counselors, both groups focus on the individual learner. They see helping the individual as their primary responsibility.

Although teachers are certainly concerned about individuals, their role requires them to work with youngsters in groups. When they see a problem youngster, they tend to be as concerned about that individual's impact on the entire class as about his or her personal problems. When a teacher makes arrangements with a counselor to work with a disruptive student, that teacher is likely to expect the counselor to help that student "behave in class." The teacher, then, sees the student's behavior in the classroom as the most important dimension of the youngster's behavior. The counselor will very likely be concerned about the entire range of problems and behaviors of the youngster who is being counseled.

The teacher may expect the counselor to "do something" that will result in a quick turnaround of the classroom behavior of a given youngster. In the eyes of the teacher, the counselor's role is to prompt a relatively speedy correction of behavior that will permit the youngster to act in class in a way that is not disruptive to the instructional process. The counselor, on the other hand, who is more interested in establishing a long-term pattern of appropriate behavior, may be less concerned about achieving a dramatic turnaround in the youngster's in-class deportment. His or her inclination might be to undertake a program for the youngster that requires extensive counseling and a fairly long period of time for results to be noticed. Should a counselor exercise such an option, the classroom teacher may see few if any immediate changes in behavior. Because the youngster may continue to be a problem in class, the teacher may conclude that the counselor is not doing his or her job.

The differences in their understanding of what the outcome of counseling should be are a force that divides teachers and counselors in many schools. Both teachers and counselors find it difficult to appreciate each other's perspectives. Compounding the problem is a frequently felt, if rarely spoken, feeling that members of the "other group" have it "easy." Teachers note that counselors have few papers to grade at night and that they do not have to contend with disciplining large groups of youngsters. "How easy!" some of them reason. Counselors look at teachers and observe that they rarely take home extensive knowledge about the complex family and personal problems of individual students that they are bound by ethics to share with no others. "Teachers must sleep easy," they may reason.

Certainly we do not want to leave the impression that counselors and teach-

Box 14-3
Perspectives of a Teacher and of a Counselor

"Jane has been 'getting into my hair' since the beginning of the school year! I'm just not getting anywhere with this group of fourth graders. She simply *will not* stop talking. It disturbs the other children, and I feel they're being cheated. I've talked to her mother. I've tried to reward her for being quiet. I've tried keeping her in at recess. I've tried sitting down with her and putting together a little 'behavior contract.' *Nothing* works! I'm falling way behind where I should be, especially in math and reading. I hate to face these parents if our standardized test scores in these areas take a dip this year. If that's to be avoided, something has to be done about Jane."

LET'S PONDER

Assume the above statement has been made by an elementary school teacher to an elementary school counselor. Think about this situation and respond to these questions:

1. What is the primary concern of the teacher? How do you know?
2. What do you think the response of the counselor will be? Why?
3. What do you think should be done? What is the basis for your decision?
4. What kind of a decision in this situation would tend to make relationships between the teacher and counselor better?
5. What kind of a decision in this situation would tend to make relationships between the teacher and counselor worse?

ers are in hostile camps in all schools. This is not the case. In many schools, counselors and teachers enjoy excellent interpersonal-relations. It is probably accurate to say that most teachers and most counselors get along well, but of all the professional groups in the schools, misunderstandings seem most likely to arise between teachers and counselors. This situation is unfortunate in that both groups seek to help youngsters as they struggle toward maturity. It is not in the "ends" that there is disagreement but rather in the ways that those ends are best to be served.

Some efforts today are being undertaken to make both counselors and teachers more aware of the perspectives of the other group. At the undergraduate level, for example, many teacher preparation programs introduce future teachers to the counselor's role. Many students even take special courses in counseling as part of their certification program. In the schools themselves, administrators work hard to involve both counselors and teachers in the development and implementation of policies regarding the treatment of students. This kind of cooperative action is helpful in breaking down the barriers between the two groups. Although some conflicts between counselors and teachers will probably be with us always, there is hope that these can be minimized as members of each group come to understand more adequately the perspectives of the other.

Teachers and School Psychologists

Not all school districts have school psychologists, but they are becoming much more common in school districts across the country. They are much more common in intermediate- and large-sized school districts than in small school districts. Only rarely are they attached to individual buildings. Generally, school psychologists work out of the central district administrative offices. From these offices, they travel to individual schools as needed.

Occasionally difficulties arise in relationships between teachers and school psychologists. Not surprisingly, these problems result largely from conceptions of the "proper function" of the school psychologist that are at odds. In this respect, the situation between teacher and school psychologist is somewhat parallel to the situation between teacher and school counselor.

Most school psychologists view their role as being primarily diagnostic. They look at individual students, administer certain tests, and make judgments about the youngster being investigated. Their job is to provide as complete a description of the individual (and any problems he or she may have) that is consistent with the best scientific tools available.

Teachers, on the other hand, may have quite a different understanding of the role of the school psychologist. A good many of them see the primary responsibility of the school psychologist as being the provision of prescriptive as opposed to diagnostic information. That is, they expect more than a simple, complete, and scientifically grounded explanation of the youngster and the problem. The "more" that they often want is a set of specific directions regarding what should be done now. This prescription should accompany any diagnostic profile developed by the school psychologist, in many teachers' eyes.

In responding to requests for this kind of prescriptive information, school psychologists point out that it would be presumptuous for a single individual to suggest a definitive set of remedial procedures. This course should be the shared responsibility of teachers, the youngster, parents, social workers, administrators, and others. Prescriptions are just as much a responsibility of the teacher as of the school psychologist.

Part of the difficulty that teachers sometimes have in understanding the exact role of the school psychologist results from the rather limited opportunities they have to get to know one another well. Few schools are wealthy enough to have school psychologists in each building. Therefore, opportunities for informal contacts between teachers and school psychologists who

"Now, Jeff, tell me about this 'funny feeling' of yours."

work out of central district administrative offices are limited. Some districts attempt to overcome this difficulty by scheduling informal meetings between teachers and central office specialists, such as school psychologists, to promote better understanding of how members of each group view their roles and responsbilities. Such meetings can be very beneficial, but it is difficult, given the heavy time demands on school psychologists, teachers, and other specialists, to arrange for these meetings as frequently as might be desired. However, any meetings of this type at all are certainly better than none. It is likely that intermediate and large school districts will continue to work diligently on achieving a better understanding between teachers and central office specialists of all kinds.

Teachers and District Curriculum Specialists

In larger districts, it is common for specialists in various aspects of the school curriculum to be attached to the central district administrative offices. Typically such individuals are called *curriculum coordinators, curriculum directors, curriculum consultants,* or by some other title that suggests that they play a leadership role in the area of curriculum. When districts are not very large, these individuals may each be responsible for all subjects in a limited number of grades. For example, a district might have individuals filling such positions as director of primary education, director of intermediate education, director of junior high school education, and director of senior high school education. Somewhat larger districts, in addition to these specialists, will very likely also employ subject-matter specialists of various kinds. For example, a district might have such people as a social studies consultant, a mathematics consultant, a reading consultant, a science consultant, a language arts consultant, and a music consultant. Very large districts will have large numbers of these individuals. The kinds and numbers of these central office curriculum people vary enormously from district to district.

A new teacher who is interested in the priorities within a given district might look at a roster of curriculum specialists who work out of the central district offices. If, for example, there are large numbers of individuals who are science consultants and relatively few who are music consultants, the district may have made a decision to place more emphasis on science than on music. This could be good news for a teacher interested in science and perhaps not so good news for a teacher interested in music. The indication would be that a teacher interested in developing a first-class science program would very likely get more help from the central district curriculum staff than a teacher interested in developing a first-class music program. Certainly the number of subject-area specialists functioning as district-level curriculum people is not an infallible guide to a district's priorities, but it is an indicator that should be given some serious consideration by prospective teachers as they weigh the strengths and weaknesses of the districts where they might wish to work.

Central-district curriculum supervisors are generally responsible for planning many of the in-service activities for teachers in their area of specialization. Districts may have between four and ten days during the year devoted to special staff-development programs. Typically, district curriculum people arrange for noted authorities in the field to speak, for presentations by classroom teachers thought to have developed exemplary programs, and for round-table sessions where teachers in the district can exchange concerns and ideas. Nearly all teachers in districts with subject-area curriculum specialists have some contact during the year at these in-service meetings with specialists in their areas of interest.

Additionally, many subject-area specialists systematically visit the schools to work with the teachers. New teachers in some districts are regularly visited by a central-office curriculum supervisor. For example, a new third-grade teacher might be visited by someone such as the director of elementary curriculum or the reading coordinator. These visits are designed to assure new teachers that help is available from the central curriculum staff. These meetings, too, can give new teachers a feeling that they have some logical connection with the central-district administrative office and that somebody there "cares." The frequency of such visits varies tremendously from district to district. Indeed, some districts never ask their central-office curriculum people to go to the schools. As might be expected, relationships between classroom teachers and central-office curriculum people tend to be less cordial in these districts than in those where the central-office curriculum specialists are frequent visitors to school buildings.

Central-office curriculum specialists are "staff" as opposed to "line" officials. This means that their decisions tend to be advisory in nature. Their decisions are generally reported to a line official, such as a superintendent or a building principal. These decisions have the full force of adopted policy only when they have been approved and supported by people in line positions and those to whom these individuals might be accountable (in the case of superintendents, for example, these would be school board members).

The distinction between staff authority and line authority is an important one. Though the district-level curriculum directors may work out of the central district offices, they usually cannot be regarded as "outranking" the building principal. The principal is a line authority. Consequently, when situations arise where a district-level curriculum supervisor and a principal find themselves at odds over a particular matter of policy, it is ordinarily the principal's view that carries the day. Thus a teacher should understand that though principals and central-office curriculum specialists may disagree, it is the principal's decision that has the full force of school-district authority behind it. For the view of the curriculum specialist to prevail, he or she would have to convince the superintendent, another line official, of the merit of his or her position. In that case, the superintendent would direct the principal to adopt the position of the curriculum specialist. The principal would then agree to implement the policy of his line superior, the superintendent. It is important to note that he would react not to the staff wishes voiced by the curriculum specialist but to the line wishes of the superintendent, which, at this point, happened to coincide with the views of the curriculum specialist.

Generally, teachers enjoy quite good relations with curriculum specialists in the district. Curriculum specialists are ordinarily classroom teachers who have done advanced work to prepare themselves for the positions they hold. Most continue to identify closely with the concerns and needs of teachers. Many of these individuals have no aspirations to become principals or superintendents. Consequently they tend to think more like classroom teachers than like administrators. They tend to have relatively frequent contact with classroom teachers. They provide a conduit for teachers' views to become known to line officials working in the central-district administrative offices. Thus they provide a valuable service to superintendents as well as to classroom teachers.

Teachers and Selected Other Nonteaching Professionals

The School Nurse

The school nurse is a professional who is found in most elementary and secondary schools. In addition to providing regular vision and hearing checks and attending to other prescribed duties, the nurse provides first-line assistance in cases of emergency.

Many new teachers are surprised to learn that the kinds of services the school nurse can offer have been severely restricted in recent years as a result of court cases and other rules and regulations. With some few exceptions, the school nurse today is generally not permitted to administer medications to youngsters. The guidelines specifying exactly what nurses can and cannot do are quite detailed in many districts. Given their disposition to avoid litigation, school districts today are very concerned about what goes on in nurses' offices. This concern seems likely to be with us for a good many years to come.

The School Psychiatrist

Psychiatrists with direct connections to school districts are found only in the very largest school districts. With a few exceptions, they work for the district part time on a contractual basis. For example, the school psychiatrist may be available to work with school youngsters on Friday mornings. Given this schedule, school psychiatrists are able to work with only a fraction of the youngsters in the district. During an entire career, many teachers never meet a school psychiatrist.

The School Psychometrist

A psychometrist is a specialist trained in the preparation and administration of mental measurement tests. They tend to be found most frequently in very large school districts. Typically, psychometrists work in central-district administrative offices. They may be attached to a large "research division" or to the central-district guidance offices, often known as *pupil personnel services*. Many psychometrists have had little or no experience as classroom teachers. Many have a background in psychology and statistics. There tend to be few occasions when teachers and psychometrists in a district interact informally.

Recapitulation of Major Ideas

1. Many professionals who do not teach are involved in public education. Together with teachers, these individuals constitute the total professional staff of a school district. Each of these individuals provides a kind of expertise that is needed for the smooth functioning of the educational enterprise. The number of people and the range of their professional talents tend to increase as district size increases.

2. Teachers and other nonteaching professionals in school districts sometimes find themselves in disagreement on the basic issues because the members of each group tend to perceive their roles somewhat differently than those roles are perceived by members of other groups.

3. Teachers tend to come into most frequent contact with those professors of education who are responsible for managing student-teaching programs. In general, because of a new emphasis on field-based programs and because more professors of education have come directly to graduate work from teaching, relationships between teachers and professors of education seem to be improving.

4. Teachers deal directly with those administrators whose offices are in the schools in which they teach. Elementary teachers tend to have a great deal of personal contact with the principal. This is less so in secondary schools, primarily because they tend to enroll larger numbers of students than elementary schools. In large buildings, the classroom teacher is likely to have more contact with one or more of the vice-principals or assistant principals than with the principal himself or herself. Teachers tend to have limited contacts with administrative personnel attached to central district administrative offices.

5. The principal is an official with line authority. His decisions carry the full weight of the district's authority in those areas over which he has been given control. Curriculum specialists attached to the central district offices generally have only staff authority; that is, their decisions are advisory. Their decisions become mandatory only when they are backed by an administrator with line authority.

6. Conflicts between teachers and counselors are relatively common. Part of the difficulty stems from teachers' views of the counselor as someone who ought to be most concerned with an individual's behavior as it might influence the behavior of other youngsters in a classroom. Many counselors, on the other hand, feel a primary responsbility to the longer-term and broader problem of the entire repertoire of a youngster's behavior, both in the classroom and out. Teachers tend to want actions "now." Counselors tend to want a solution that may take time but that will be lasting.

7. Many teachers believe that school psychologists should provide solutions to problems experienced by the younsters who have been brought to their attention. Many school psychologists believe that their role is not to provide the solution but to diagnose the problem as precisely as possible. Because of these divergent views of the school psychologist's role, teachers and school psychologists sometimes have relationships characterized by more heat than harmony.

8. Central-office curriculum specialists are very common in intermediate- and large-sized districts. These individuals are responsible for planning in-service opportunities for teachers. They work fairly closely with the teaching staff. Many have had years of classroom teaching. Many tend to retain the perspective of the classroom teacher. They provide a valuable communications link between teachers and top-level district administrators.

Posttest

DIRECTIONS: Using your own paper, answer each of the following true/false questions. For each correct statement, write the word *true* on your paper. For each incorrect statement, write the word *false* on your paper.

1. The primary responsibility of a school psychologist is to provide teachers with a specific set of instructions regarding how a particular child should be treated.

2. Curriculum consultants and curriculum coordinators who work out of a district's central office more typically represent "staff" authority than "line" authority.

3. A secondary school is more likely to have an assistant principal or a vice-principal than is an elementary school.

4. University professors who visit public schools are more likely to be associated with student-teaching programs than with other specializations within colleges of education.

5. Today the school nurse usually does not have the authority to dispense medications to students from a supply owned by the school.

6. There is a fairly common pattern of hostility between teachers and counselors in many schools.

7. Principals always have to follow the suggestions made by curriculum consultants and curriculum coordinators who work out of the central district office.

8. It is a very common practice for principals in large high schools to sit in on classes.

9. In general, university professors of education today tend to have had

more extensive and more recent classroom experience than was typical in the past.

10. There is a growing trend toward increasing the number of counselors in elementary schools.

Summary

Many highly trained professionals who do not perform teaching roles are involved in the operation of the school program. The number of these individuals and the range of their specializations vary according to the size of the district. Large districts have many more specialists than small districts. In all districts, however, teachers have some contact with nonteaching professionals.

Relationships between teachers and members of other professional groups in education are not always harmonious. Most difficulties result from confusion about what roles are to be played by the various nonteaching professionals. Often teachers perceive the roles and responsibilities of these individuals quite differently than they are perceived by the individuals themselves.

In very rough terms, nonteaching professionals in school districts can be divided into the two broad categories of line officials and staff officials. Line officials, including superintendents and principals, have the power to enforce their decisions. Staff officials, including, for example, curriculum directors and consultants, have only the authority to advise. Decisions by staff people become enforceable only when they are embraced by appropriate line officials.

The operation of school programs demands a complex array of personalities and skills, particularly in large districts. These skills demand specialization, which, in turn, produces some differences in perspective that can interfere with open and comfortable relationships among all the categories of professionals. The problem is not a new one. School administrators have long worked to bring together teachers and other professionals in settings where views can be exchanged freely and mutual understanding can grow. These efforts seem likely to be a continuing feature of public education in this country in the years ahead.

References

Conroy, Pat. *The Water Is Wide.* New York: Penguin Books, 1970.

Lieberman, Myron. *Education as a Profession.* Engelwood Cliffs, N.J.: Prentice-Hall, 1956.

Nagi, Mostafah, and Pugh, Meredith D. "Status, Inconsistency, and Professional Militancy in the Teaching Profession." *Education in Urban Society* (Aug., 1973): 385–404.

STINNETT, T. M., AND HUGGETT, ALBERT J. *Professional Problems of Teachers,* 2nd ed. New York: Macmillan Publishing Co., 1963.

WILSON, CHARLES H. *A Teacher Is a Person.* New York: Holt, Rinehart and Winston, 1956.

WILSON, ELIZABETH C. *Needed: A New Kind of Teacher.* Bloomington, Ind.: Phi Delta Kappa Foundation, 1973.

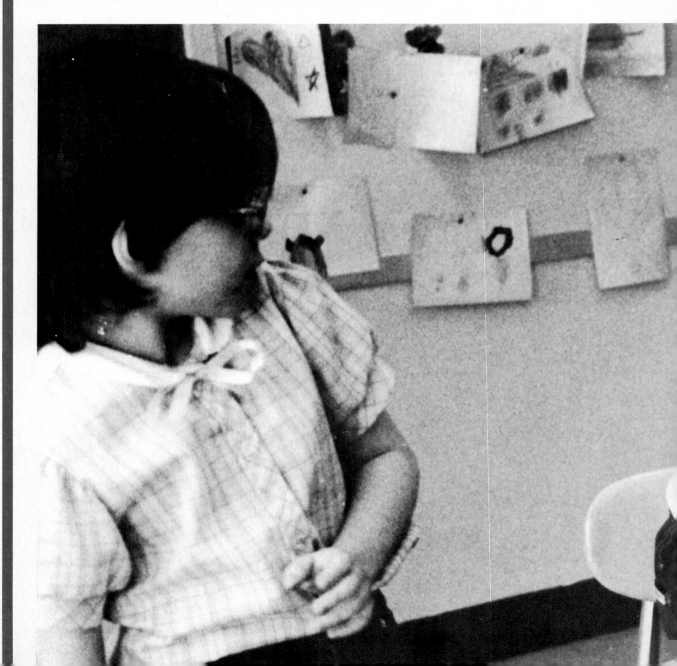

15

Learner Characteristics

Objectives

This chapter provides information to help the reader to

1. Recognize the diversity of youngsters in today's schools.
2. Note some trends related to achievement of different groups of youngsters as indicated by the National Assessment of Educational Progress.
3. Identify implications for teachers that arise from their having to work with youngsters who have such a wide range of individual differences.
4. Point out the major levels of Piaget's theory of intellectual development.
5. Describe characteristics of youngsters at different grade and age levels.
6. Cite kinds of problems often encountered by teachers at different grade levels.
7. Suggest teacher characteristics that seem to associate with success with youngsters at different grade levels.

Pretest

DIRECTIONS: Using your own paper, answer each of the following true/false questions. For each correct statement, write the word *true* on your paper. For each incorrect statement, write the word *false* on your paper.

1. There is evidence that there are fewer differences among youngsters in regular classrooms today than 20 years ago.
2. The National Assessment of Educational Progress tests the achievement of nine, thirteen, and seventeen-year-olds.
3. In 1990, it is likely that young people will represent a larger percentage of the total population than they did in 1965.
4. Youngsters at the "concrete operations" stage can use logic in arriving at solutions to problems.
5. All learners past the age of eleven can be expected to operate at the "formal operations" level.
6. At the end of this century, Spanish-speaking Americans may replace black Americans as the nation's largest minority group.
7. Teachers of kindergarten-aged youngsters need to be people who feel comfortable in giving positive approval to the children in their classes.
8. Physically, girls tend to develop somewhat faster than boys.
9. When there are not opportunities for active learning in primary-grades classrooms, children often develop nervous, fidgety habits.
10. Some problems we typically associate with adolescence may come about because of our cultural tendency to prolong childhood.

Introduction

Today's school youngsters are different from those in past years. Today's school youngsters are the same as those in past years. Strangely, both statements contain elements of truth. On the one hand, enormous changes clearly have occurred in the composition of the school population. There are more ethnic and language-minority children, more handicapped children, and larger numbers of younger children than there were a decade ago. On the other hand, basic characteristics of young people have remained the same. Patterns of intellectual, emotional, and physical development have stayed pretty much as they always have been.

Today's teachers face two major challenges as they prepare to work with school youngsters. They must understand both broad and common development patterns and take them into consideration as they develop lessons appropriate to the levels of readiness of their youngsters. Furthermore, they must prepare to deal with an extraordinary range of young people who come from homes characterized by a tremendous diversity of core values. In considering these challenges, let us turn first to the matter of the composition of today's school population.

Changing Patterns in School Classrooms

Advances in medical technology and changes in family patterns have had two important consequences for teachers. First of all, there are not as many school-aged youngsters as there used to be. Widespread availability of effective family planning information has contributed to a great decline in the American birthrate. Certainly, economic conditions have also played a role in encouraging smaller families. For the immediate future, at least, there appears little chance that schools will be pressed for classroom space as they were in the years after World War II when numbers of youngsters threatened to overwhelm available facilities.

In addition to there being fewer youngsters in the schools, most come from different kinds of homes than typified American families of a generation ago. Today, families where the father is the single breadwinner and where the mother stays at home to care for the children represent only a minority of the total population of families. Most youngsters in the schools today are either children of parents who both work or children of single parents. Large numbers of children in the schools spend a good many hours with babysitters and with day-care personnel. The quality of such care varies enormously. However, it probably is safe to suggest that youngsters get a good deal less personal attention in these situations than they do from their own parents. As a result, teachers today often find themselves dealing with information, especially in social and personal areas, that in previous times tended to be

Box 15-1
Changes in American Families

Today, fewer than 40 percent of American households have any children at all living in them. These numbers seem likely to decrease even more in the future. There is a definite trend for young people to stay single longer. And, of those individuals who marry, many more are making decisions to have no children at all.

LET'S PONDER

Read the paragraph above. Then, respond to these questions.

1. How do you react to the information that fewer than 40 percent of American households have children living in them? Does this figure seem high or low to you? What do you think the figure will be ten years from now? Why?
2. What factors do you think might be associated with people tending to marry later in life now than they used to? Is this a temporary trend, or is it a pattern that will be with us for a while? Why do you think so?
3. Do you see any connection between levels of employment or other economic statistics and the trend toward later marriages and smaller families? Would a change in economic conditions change these trends? What kinds of changes might you expect?
4. If there are fewer children in the future, will society look more favorably or less favorably on young people? Can you cite any evidence to support your opinion?

passed on to youngsters by parents in the home. This has been a source of conflict for many parents and teachers. The debate continues over where the dividing line lies that separates instructional responsibilities of home and school.

Certainly, there is no intent to suggest a return to the days when most women stayed home. Abundant evidence suggests that many women who work are happier than those who do not. Some studies indicate that a warmer mother–child relationship may develop in such situations. This seems to result from a realization that time together is limited and is, therefore, to be prized.

In addition to changes in numbers of youngsters and in their home situations, there is an unprecedented diversity within individual classrooms. Today's "typical" class may include an area of individual children representing all of the differences reflected in the larger society. Let us pause briefly to look at some of these groups of youngsters.

Language-Minority Children

During the 1970s and early 1980s, large numbers of families from other nations moved to the United States because of unsettled political and economic conditions in their homelands. Some came for other reasons. One result of this influx has been a dramatic increase in the number of youngsters who do not speak English as their first language. Vietnamese, Korean, Czech, French, Cantonese, Spanish, or any one of a number of other languages may be spoken at home. The largest number of these youngsters are native speakers of Spanish. Youngsters who speak Spanish at home, though found throughout the nation, are especially prevalent in the schools of California, Arizona, New Mexico, Florida, Texas, and New York City.

Some authorities believe that by the year 2000 Spanish-speaking Americans may be the largest minority group in the country. This information presents

---

Box 15-2
Make Them Learn English First

Recently, a letter to the editor, included these comments from a reader.

My father didn't speak a word of English when he got off the boat from Norway. Somehow, he got to Northern Minnesota. When he got there, he soon learned that like it or not, English was the name of the game here. He dug into the language in a hurry, and in two months time, he was reasonably fluent. He claims that he was even dreaming in English after a year.

I think there is a lesson in my father's experience that schools should heed. That is, English is the key to success in this country. Wouldn't it be much more efficient for us to insist that youngsters entering our schools pass a test in their understanding of spoken English *before* we let them enroll. We know that youngsters who come to school from Spanish-speaking homes don't do very well academically. It is clear to me that there is nothing wrong with their brains; they simply don't have a good command of English. If we insisted that they have good control of English as a condition for admission, they would do a lot better. And, in the end, we would all benefit.''

LET'S PONDER   Read the statement above. Then, react to these questions.

1. Are youngsters who are preparing to enter the first grade in a situation similar to the writer's father? Why, or why not?
2. Suppose you, as a School Board member, made a proposal to implement the program suggested by the writer. What do you think might happen?
3. What is your general reaction to the proposal?
4. How do you explain low scores on standardized achievement tests on the part of Hispanic children? What would you do to remedy the situation?

a real challenge to educators. Traditionally, children who are native speakers of Spanish have not scored well on tests over school content. For example, tests of nine, thirteen, and seventeen-year-olds conducted by the National Assessment of Educational Progress program consistently have revealed them to score below national averages in such areas as science, social studies, mathematics, and reading/literature comprehension (National Center for Education Statistics, 1982). Clearly, many school programs have not been serving these youngsters well, and teachers increasingly will be challenged to develop programs that respond more effectively to their needs.

Poverty and Children

A large portion of the total population falls below official government poverty levels. Not surprisingly, then, many children come to school from economically impoverished home environments. Such youngsters may not be receiving proper diets. For a variety of reasons, home situations may not be well-suited to supporting the school program. Many beginning teachers, for example, are startled to learn that many youngsters come from homes where no newspapers or magazines are delivered or read. Youngsters from such homes, consequently, are not nearly so likely to come to school valuing the skill of reading as are those from homes where adults regularly are observed reading for information and enjoyment.

In most areas of the country, the numbers of families defined as impoverished are increasing. In years ahead, many teachers will have even more youngsters than they now have from economically deprived homes. This reality obliges teachers to become informed about the culture of poverty. They need to be aware of the kinds of background experiences these youngsters bring with them to school. Particularly, teachers must take care to ensure that such youngsters are not asked to complete instructional tasks that demand resources that their homes simply are not able to provide. A failure to attend to special circumstances of these young people can place them in a situation where failure is foreordained. Teachers, as professionals committed to nurturing the maximum development of each youngster, should work hard to guard against programs that may defeat some youngsters even before their talents have had a reasonable chance to flower.

Very Young Children in the Schools

A dramatic change in family life has been the increase in the number of mothers who work. A result has been an increasing interest in enrolling youngsters in school at an earlier age. Traditional child-care facilities including private preschools and church day-care centers in many cases have been overwhelmed by increases in applications for admission to their programs. In fall 1980, 37.3 percent of all three-year-olds, 46.3 percent of all four-year-olds, and 84.7 percent of all five-year-olds were enrolled in school programs for very young children (National Center for Education Statistics, *Digest of Education Statistics*, 1982, p. 45).

One consequence of this trend has been increased pressure on public schools to increase the numbers of programs for very young children. Such proposals have not gone without controversy. On the "pro" side of this debate, supporters of expanded public school programs for the very young point out that some researchers have found that early childhood programs in the schools help young children develop positive self-images and good working relationships with others. As a group, youngsters who have experienced such programs tend to fit more smoothly into the routines of kindergarten and first grade than youngsters who have not had them.

On the other hand, critics worry that, in expanding early childhood programs, schools may be accepting responsibilities that properly belong to par-

---

Box 15-3
Is Early Childhood Education Compatible with Responsible Parenting?

"My child is one of a kind. My husband and I are unique individuals. We have certain strong values that we want our youngster to share. Because of my feelings, I have not worked since our child was born. I am a certified accountant and could get work anywhere. And we could really use the money. But I want my child to learn my family's values, not those of somebody in a day-care center or a public school. I realize many of these places are fine. I realize that some of the people who work there are sensitive individuals. But they are not *me*. Our child is precious to us, and we just won't risk letting the basic way she sees the world be shaped by a stranger."

LET'S PONDER

Read the paragraph above. Then respond to the following questions:

1. How do you react to this parent's concern about the values and attitudes she wishes to transmit to her child?
2. Do you find arguments presented by this individual valid? Why, or why not?
3. Is the solution taken by this individual one available to every parent? What limitations, if any, do you see regarding this solution?
4. To what extent do you think values and attitudes of young children in schools or day-care centers are shaped by the people who work there? Do you think influences of these people would be greater than those of the parent?
5. This parent seems to feel that the *quantity* of time she spends with her child is very important. Others have argued that it is the *quality* of time that is the key issue. What is your view?

ents. They believe that there could be bad social consequences if too many child-rearing responsibilities are turned over to public schools.

Today, those favoring expansion of public school programs for young children seem to be carrying the day. Economic pressures encouraging mothers to work are significant. Hence, teachers can expect a growth in the numbers of early childhood programs in the schools in the years ahead. This growth also suggests a general expansion of the public schools' child-rearing responsibilities.

Handicapped Youngsters in the Schools

Recently, there has been a great increase in concern about school programs for handicapped learners. Most notable has been an important attitude change. At one time, it was felt that such children should be kept apart from others in the schools. This was justified by an assumption that these children needed kinds of training that were not compatible with what occurred in "regular" classrooms.

Critics of this view argued that this isolation stigmatized these youngsters as something less than "real" students. In general, the views of these critics have prevailed. Increasingly, handicapped youngsters are becoming involved in all phases of classroom work alongside of so-called "normal" learners. Given this trend, individuals preparing to teach must learn as much as they can about working with handicapped learners. For more detailed information about this topic, see Chapter 16, "The Exceptional Learner."

Diversity within public school classrooms is greater today than it has ever been. Individuals preparing for the challenges of teaching must be intellectually and emotionally geared to deal with an incredible array of differences. At the same time, though, certain patterns of development persist that are quite similar for all youngsters. Some of these patterns are introduced in the next section.

Patterns of Children's Development

Ideas about how children develop influence ideas about how they should be educated. Today's teachers need to be certain that their procedures are based on up-do-date knowledge about human development, not upon outdated and now discounted views. Some historic views seem quite bizarre to us today.

One early view held children to be mindless creatures who were incapable of feeling or knowing anything. Profound educational implications flowed from this idea. For example, anyone wanting to spend money on early childhood education was unlikely to be well received. Formal education for young children was regarded as pointless. Adults' roles were limited to meeting youngsters' physical needs and to keeping them out of mischief.

Another historical view held children to be essentially miniature adults. Aside from their small size, children were seen as having adult characteristics. They only lacked knowledge and experience. If these could be provided, then they could perform adult roles at a very early age. Learning materials used by adults were seen as perfectly appropriate for use with children. If a child failed to learn, then he or she was lazy. It had nothing to do with the nature of what the child was being asked to learn. The tradition of punishing children for a failure to learn comes out of this view of childhood.

Still another historical perspective had it that children came into the world totally lacking any personalities of their own. They were simply so much animated clay or putty awaiting appropriate "modeling" by adults. There was an assumption that youngsters, appropriately guided, would turn into "good citizens." In the schools, this view resulted in educational practices that were exclusively planned by and delivered by adults. Youngsters' interests were considered to be of little importance.

Most of these historical views have not stood up well to the rigors of modern scholarship. Today, learning psychologists tell us that each child has unique qualities that affect his or her reactions to school. Though teaching might be simpler if youngsters were just so many "lumps of clay" awaiting our influences, that is not the way it is. Of course, many of us would be more than a little bored were we faced with the prospect of dealing with classrooms of passive youngsters every day. Today's teachers derive satisfaction from opportunities to respond professionally to the diversity that characterizes public school classrooms.

The Work of Jean Piaget

Today we know that children are neither lumps of clay nor miniature adults. Sigmund Freud was one of the first to recognize that childhood was an important and distinct stage of human development. He found experiences of childhood to have a profound influence later in life. More recently, the theories of Jean Piaget have had a tremendous impact on educational thought.

Piaget discovered that as children develop intellectually, they go through several stages. At each of these stages, the "thinking style" of the youngster is different from that of the earlier stage. In essence Piaget demonstrated that the modes of thinking of children are different from those of adults.

This means, for example, that no amount of threat or pressure can make a child think like an adult. It is not a matter of the child's unwillingness; it is a matter of the child's inability to do so. Piaget has outlined four different stages: (1) sensorimotor, (2) preoperational, (3) concrete operations, and (4) formal operations. Each successive stage builds on the one that precedes it. Piaget's stages have great implications for teaching youngsters of different age levels.

Piaget: Stages of Intellectual Development

Sensorimotor Stage (Birth to Two Years).   At this stage, much of behavior is reflexive. Intellectual activity is based primarily on immediate experiences that the child derives through his or her senses. The major intellectual activity is the interaction between the senses and the environment. With the development of language at about age eighteen to twenty-four months, the child begins mentally to manipulate objects and events. For example, words come to be understood as standing for concrete objects.

Preoperational Thought Stage (Two to Seven Years).   The most dramatic development during this period of time involves the use of language. The young child increasingly uses symbols to represent objects. A predominant characteristic of thought at this stage is that it is intuitive. At this age, the child is not concerned with precision. Youngsters at this stage have imaginary friends and are generally highly imaginative and freewheeling.

At this stage, youngsters tend to pay attention to only one characteristic of an object and to ignore others. As a result, their thought frequently appears illogical to adults. For example, they may insist that a tall, thin glass contains more water than a short one. Why? Because it's taller. No amount of demonstrating that two such containers may contain the same amount of water will convince them. They may recite what the adult wants them to say, but the understanding is not there. Children at this stage simply are not able to deal with abstract thought and logic. What they perceive to be true is what they believe to be true, even if it is a conclusion that makes no sense at all to the adult mind.

Concrete Operations Stage (Seven to Eleven Years).   At this stage, logic begins to emerge and to become stronger than simple perception. Increasingly, children begin using logic to arrive at solutions to concrete problems. Note, however, that the emphasis is on *concrete* problems. Children of this age experience difficulty in applying logic to abstract problems. For example, they might do very well with the water in the tall and the short glasses. They can see the objects, handle them, and have some kind of a direct (even a tangible) involvement with them, but, they have great difficulty in applying logic to problems presented in words or to problems dealing with the future.

Children of this age tend to be very literal-minded. They have enormous difficulty in detecting irony, sarcasm, and other "slants" in written materials. Indeed, once they have made up their mind about the literal meaning of something, they frequently refuse to change their minds even when confronted with conflicting evidence. In school, children at the concrete operations stage particularly enjoy activities that involve direct involvement with concrete objects. They want to solve problems that have definite answers. They are not comfortable with ambiguity.

Formal Operations Stage (Eleven to Sixteen Years). At the formal operations stage, young people can apply logical thought to all classes of problems, from the very concrete to the very abstract. Individuals at this stage have thought processes basically similar to those of adults. They are able to understand symbolic meanings. They can read stories and generalize the implications to situations beyond the stories themselves. They tend to rely on logic as the sole criterion of what is true or false, good or bad. Often, however, there is a failure during these years to differentiate between what is logical and what tends to happen in reality. As a result, many youngsters during these years are very idealistic.

In general, young people at the formal operations stage are capable of an adult type of thinking, but they lack experience. In part, their arrival at this stage explains the feelings of alienation that characterize many adolescents. The youngsters have moved out of the concrete operations stage, where, generally, they believed adults nearly always to be "correct." Now they find themselves burdened with an idealistic faith in logic as a method for explaining the world as it "should be" and the ability to understand that "reality" and the adults who have shaped it have frequently been "wrong." There is a tendency to dwell on the gap between what some adults say they believe and what they, in fact, do. Youngsters at this stage tend to generalize from these inconsistencies to conclude that many or even all adults are untrustworthy. Given this perception, they tend to be wary of lectures by adults who tell them to be "truthful," "responsible," and "law-abiding."

In a consideration of the formal operations stage, a caution should be noted. Though individuals at this stage may be *capable* of high levels of abstract thought, that does not mean that they always exercise this capability. Indeed there is some evidence that as many as 50 percent of the individuals in even the sixteen- to-twenty-year-old age group may not be fully utilizing the abstract thinking powers available to those at the formal operations stage.

Piaget's Stages: General Considerations

In looking over Piaget's stages, please note that the age ranges given for each represent only approximations. Different indviduals attain each stage at different times. Certainly, when a youngster has his or her eleventh birthday, it cannot be assumed that he or she automatically becomes capable of styles of thought characteristic of the formal operations stage. In any group of eleven-year-olds there will be youngsters who have already advanced to the formal operations stage as well as others whose thinking continues to be bound to the concrete operations stage. There is evidence that the rate of an individual's progress from one stage to the next is related to the quality of the experiences that he or she has had at the earlier stage. Sound instructional programs of an appropriate design can help youngsters get ready for the transition to the next stage. Though we cannot predict *when* a given youngster will pass from one stage to another, Piaget does tell us that all individuals move through these stages in the *same order*. That is, one begins at the sensorimotor stage, progresses to the preoperational thought stage, goes on to the concrete operations stage, and finally arrives at the formal operations stage. No steps are skipped.

The work of Piaget has important implications for those concerned about school programs. Piaget implies that as youngsters grow older, they tend to perceive reality in different ways. Consider, for example, the charge that the schools "stamp out youngsters' creativity" in the light of Piaget's work. Piaget notes that what many adults take for "creativity" in young children is nothing more than patterns of behavior associated with preoperational thought. Thus the decline in "creativity" comes not so much from something negative that the school has done as from youngsters' movement from the stage of preoperational thought to the stages of concrete operations and formal operations. At these stages, the thought patterns of youngsters "make more sense" to adults. Hence they tend not to be seen as so creative.

Physical Characteristics of Youngsters of Different Ages

Intellectual development represents only a single aspect of the changes that youngsters experience as they mature. Clearly the physical changes are equally dramatic and have implications for educational practice. Consider, for example, the physical characteristics of youngsters in a typical eighth-grade classroom. The differences among the youngsters in a given classroom are profound. Some youngsters will be small and immature in appearance and look as if they would fit in beautifully in a third-grade classroom. On the other hand, some youngsters may be as large and as well developed physically as the teacher. A few of the boys may even be sporting mustaches (much to the green-eyed envy of their smaller, less physically mature age-mates who have yet to have their adolescent growth spurt). These physical differences present problems related not only to youngsters' abilities to perform physical tasks but to their psychological and emotional development as well.

In the sections that follow, some general physical characteristics of youngsters of different ages are introduced. This information should be approached with the understanding that the differences within any given classroom are very great indeed. There is a significant definitional problem with the elusive term *normal school child*. Typically, *normal* is nothing but a statistical abstraction that does not apply to any specific youngster. Therefore a reading of the following sections should be tempered with the understanding that great variability is encountered in groups of youngsters of any age. Furthermore, this variability tends to increase as the age of the children increases. It is easier, for example, to characterize a kindergarten youngster than a senior-high-school student.

Box 15-4
Piaget's Stages and Junior High School Youngsters

It is known that teachers of junior high school youngsters face a greater challenge than teachers of elementary school youngsters or senior high school students. Many have a very difficult time in developing an instructional program that ''gets through'' to large numbers of youngsters in their classes.

LET'S PONDER

Think about what you know about Piaget's stages. Consider now the typical ages of junior high school youngsters. Respond to these questions.

1. Knowing what you know about Piaget's stages, what kind of thinking processes likely will be present in many junior high school classes?
2. Why do you think some teachers find it more difficult to design learning experiences for their junior high school classes than for classes of senior high school youngsters?
3. Given what you know about Piaget's stages, what kinds of things probably should be considered in developing lessons for junior high school youngsters?
4. Knowing what you know about Piaget's stages, what grade level or levels do you think would be most easy to teach? Why?

Characteristics of Preschool and Kindergarten Children

Children of preschool and kindergarten age are extremely active. They have quite good control of their bodies, and they seem to enjoy activity for its own sake. A student teacher once remarked on this phenomenon after spending an exhausting day with a group of lively youngsters in a kindergarten. She compared walking into the classroom to entering a world of moving, twisting worms.

Because of frequent bursts of energy-consuming activity, children at this age need regular rest periods. Unless these are provided, these youngsters are likely to become irritable. Some may become subject to emotional outbursts when confronted with even minor frustrations when they become overtired.

At this age, youngsters' large-muscle coordination is better developed than their small-muscle coordination. Consequently, tasks demanding small-muscle control can prove frustrating. For example, many youngsters at this age have trouble with shoestrings, buttons, and fine-motor tasks that slightly older children do with ease. Some youngsters in this age group may have eyes and eye muscles that are not yet fully developed. Consequently they may experience difficulty in focusing on small objects and in tasks demanding good hand–eye coordination.

Boys at this age tend to be physically a little larger than girls, but the girls tend to be ahead of the boys by nearly any other measure applied. This is particularly true in the development of fine-motor skills. During this period, girls, on average, are much more advanced in fine-muscle coordination than boys.

Teachers of preschool and kindergarten youngsters must be blessed with a tremendous reservoir of patience. They must be able to tolerate a lot of activity in the classroom. They must be people who understand that there are certain things that youngsters in this age group simply cannot do. They must be prepared to spend time tying shoes, mopping paint spills, and buttoning coats . . . and they must do so with a smile. Children at this age need and desire lots of affection. Teachers of these youngsters have to understand these needs and be very positive in their relationships with the children in their classes.

Characteristics of Primary-Grades Children (Grades One to Three)

The high need for physical activity characteristic of kindergarten carries through to the first year or two of the primary grades. The large muscles still tend to be more fully developed than the small muscles. Indeed, this large-muscle development gives youngsters at this age level a tremendous amount of confidence in the kinds of physical tasks they can accomplish. When a youngster of this age finds that he or she can climb a tree, the accomplishment is certain to be repeated (at least, when objecting parents or teachers are not on hand). Many youngsters at this age develop more confidence in their physical abilities than is warranted, and frequently the danger associated with a given physical task is underestimated. The accident rate among youngsters of this age is very high.

The early primary grades represent a difficult time for many youngsters. Many still have a very high need for activity, yet it is during this time that teachers being to expect more "in-seat" learning, a dramatic break from the non-stop activity routine of kindergarten. When there is too much forced sitting, many youngsters in this age group develop such nervous habits as pencil chewing, fingernail biting, and general fidgeting. These represent somewhat desperate attempts of the body to compensate for the lack of needed physical activity.

Typically the skill of handwriting is introduced during this period. This can be a very trying experience for a late-maturing child, who may still have very shaky control over the small muscles. Realizing that many youngsters may not be physically ready to do neat handwriting, teachers must be very sensitive in their comments to youngsters about their first efforts at cursive writing. If the small-muscle development is inadequate, no amount of admonishment will result in improved writing skills.

Experts tell us that in most people, the eyes do not fully develop until around age eight. Given this pattern, many primary-grades youngsters may have difficulty in focusing on small print or on small objects. This fact has enormous importance for educators. Reading is an important part of the primary grades curriculum, beginning in grade one. Teachers need to be sensitive to the possibility that a youngster having difficulty with reading may be having that difficulty because his or her eyes have yet to develop to the point where a focus on small objects can be maintained easily.

Youngsters who are slow to develop, in a physical sense, *do* catch up. If teachers have been sensitive to the physical basis of any learning difficulties they might have experienced, then they are generally able to catch up to others in the class with no particular problem. But if insensitive teachers have falsely attributed the problems they have been having to "laziness" or some other inadequate and inappropriate explanation, there is a good possibility that such youngsters may come to believe that they have no potential for success. When that kind of a self-image develops, youngsters are likely to stop trying. A pattern of failure established early could follow them through their entire educational program.

It is essential for teachers to recognize the very high need that primary-grades youngsters have for praise and recognition. They want to please the teacher and to do well in school. When youngsters get positive recognition from their teachers, they tend to adjust well to school. This adjustment sets a positive pattern for their entire school career. Because of their potential for affecting how youngsters are to view the educational program they will be in until high school graduation, many school systems place a high priority on finding especially talented teachers to work with first- and second-grade youngsters.

Characteristics of Upper Elementary Children (Grades Four to Six)

During the age period that covers grades four to six, most girls and a few boys experience a tremendous growth spurt. It is not uncommon for eleven-year-old girls to be taller and heavier than eleven-year-old boys. Many girls reach puberty during this period, and they tend to become very much interested in boys. Many boys, on the other hand, have little, if any, interest in girls.

By this stage of development, fine-motor control is quite good. Many youngsters at this age develop a great interest in applying their new ability to "make their fingers do what they're supposed to" by getting involved in crafts, model building, and other activities demanding fine-muscle control. The interest in learning how to play a muscial instrument, a task demanding good control of the small muscles, can be attributed in part to youngsters' growing confidence in their fine-motor skills.

Social friendships tend to divide along sex lines: boys tend to associate with boys, and girls tend to associate with girls. There is a good deal of competition between boys and girls. Insults are a common ingredient of interactions between groups of boys and groups of girls.

Teachers face a different set of problems in working with youngsters in grades four through six than do their colleagues who teach primary-grade youngsters. Teachers of these youngsters must concern themselves with the problem of motivation. Furthermore, they must develop ways of dealing with youngsters' emerging sense of independence.

Youngsters at this age tend to be perfectionists. Frequently they set unrealistically high standards for themselves. When they fail to perform up to these standards, many suffer extreme feelings of guilt. Teachers must be sensitive to this situation and must devise ways of letting youngsters know that they are developing in a satisfactory way.

Many teachers of youngsters of this age take a good deal of personal pleasure in watching youngsters begin to perform in some fairly sophisticated ways. Many youngsters' interests broaden tremendously, and some become voracious readers. Yet they still have about them an engaging air of innocence and trust. They tend to be extremely loyal to a teacher they like.

On the other hand, their misbehavior tends to be much more deliberate and certainly more challenging than the misbehavior of primary-grades youngsters. Increasingly, youngsters look to their peer group for guidance regarding "proper behavior" rather than to adults. This can prove very frustrating for the teacher. For example, the peer group may have decreed that "reading is boring." Given this dictum, the teacher is going to have a very difficult time motivating the class during the reading period. Teachers of youngsters of this age must become experts in group dynamics and keen observers of the patterns of interpersonal relationships in their classes. Armed with such insights, they can take actions to prevent the peer group from taking a negative position on important academic issues.

Teachers of these youngsters, like their counterparts working with primary-grades youngsters, need a healthy dose of patience. These youngsters still need a lot of positive support from the teacher. A heavy dose of teacher sarcasm can do a good deal of damage to a youngster's self-concept. Teachers must understand that youngsters of this age are just beginning to sense some independence. They make many mistakes. An understanding teacher allows youngsters the freedom to make mistakes yet maintains a reasonable and firm set of expectations. In this kind of atmosphere, youngsters make tremendous personal strides during these school years.

Characteristics of Junior-High-School Students (Grades Seven to Nine)

Many educators consider junior-high-school youngsters the most difficult age group of all to teach. There is evidence that it takes a special kind of teacher to be successful with this age group. Many individuals who begin teaching in the junior high school soon request a transfer to work with either older or younger learners.

Youngsters at this age level are incredibly diverse. Teachers find interesting mixes of maturity and immaturity within classrooms and even within individual youngsters. A given eighth-grader at one moment may appear to be the very image of sophistication and at the next little, if at all, different from a fourth-grader. Youngsters swing crazily back and forth between adult behavior and nonadult behavior.

In many societies of the world, particularly those that are less technologically developed than our own, the young are accorded full adult status at about age twelve. There is a recognition that at about this age, many individuals possess most of the adult physical characteristics. In our society and other more technologically advanced societies, a decision has been made to delay official adulthood for several years. In fact, our society does not have any official entry point that unequivocally says to a boy or girl, "Today you are an adult." The absence of any such specific time of passage from childhood to adulthood contributes to the role confusion of junior-high-school youngsters. They receive few cues from our society that as of a given moment, they are expected to act as adults.

During the junior-high-school years, most girls complete their growth spurt. For boys, the growth spurt may not be complete until the end of this age range or even later. Nearly all individuals, both boys and girls, will have attained puberty by the end of this period. There tends to be an almost universal concern about the physical and psychological changes associated with the coming of physiological maturity. Concerns about whether they are developing "properly" are rampant. Many youngsters become somewhat self-conscious during these years. Not a few become convinced that everyone is constantly looking at them and evaluating them. For many youngsters, the junior-high-school years are not a particularly comfortable time.

Teachers who experience success with junior-high-school students understand and are sensitive to the physical and psychological changes that these youngsters are experiencing. They are tolerant of the acting-out behavior and the occasional emotional outbursts displayed by individuals in this age group.

Regrettably the number of teachers who report satisfaction in working with junior-high-school youngsters is small. Survey after survey reveals that teachers of junior-high-school youngsters are much less satisfied with their professional role than either elementary or senior-high-school teachers. Particularly subject to feelings of unhappiness with their work are those teachers who are much in love with their academic specialization and who find lamentably few junior-high-school youngsters who share their interest and enthusiasm. Many of these individuals would be much happier working at the senior-high-school level. Indeed, many of them do transfer to senior high schools after a year or two of junior-high-school teaching.

Perhaps teacher preparation programs bear part of the responsibility for teachers' problems in working with junior-high-school youngsters. Very few people who work with this age group have had substantial course work directed toward the unique characteristics of junior-high-school students. Although some hasty mention in general secondary methods courses may be made of the necessity to adapt instruction to the special needs of junior-high-

DOONESBURY

by Garry Trudeau

school students, the treatment tends to be superficial in most such courses. Overwhelmingly the emphasis in the secondary-education program is the senior high school. Given this reality, it is perhaps no surprise that many teachers in junior high schools find themselves dissatisfied with their positions.

Clearly the need for sensitive, caring teachers at this level is great, but to date, no one has unlocked the secret of identifying and preparing large numbers of potential teachers who will be both successful and happy in working with this age group. Concern about junior-high-school instruction promises to be a problem that will continue to be a consuming interest of educators for a good many years to come.

The Adolescents: Characteristics of Students in Grades Ten to Twelve

Much has been written about adolescence. At this stage, the so-called generation gap seems to reach its peak. Parents frequently report great difficulty in communicating with their sons and daughters. The adolescents, too, find a great deal of frustration as they try to come to terms with their world. Several factors contribute to the difficulties experienced by the youngsters in this age group.

Erik Erikson (1968) pointed out that the major issue for people at this time of life is the search for personal identity. Young people seek to find a personal self that is distinct from that of either their father or their mother. They ponder such questions as "Who am I?" "Will I be successful?" "Will I be accepted?" In their attempt to assure themselves that they indeed do have separate identities, adolescents experiment with behaviors that they believe will show the world that they are "independent." They attempt to master their environment. At the same time, they desperately look for evidence that others are accepting them as individuals.

The problems of adolescents in this country result to some degree from our cultural view of youngsters in this age group. Consider that physically adolescents are for all practical purposes adults. Consider, too, that intellectually they have a near-adult capability of handling abstract thinking tasks. Yet we do not consider adolescents adults. What then is adolescence?

Some have suggested that adolescence is a cultural invention. It is something that has been devised to extend childhood beyond the limits imposed by many other cultures. Our culture simply is not prepared to absorb fourteen- and fifteen-year-olds into our technological economy. Therefore, some say, the concept of adolescence was invented to describe what is essentially a holding action until these young people can be absorbed into the work force.

Whether, indeed, adolescence is a "real" period in a physiological sense or not, certainly it is definitely a "real" period in terms of how young people at this age tend to feel about themselves and to behave. On the one hand, these youngsters have a desire to enjoy the benefits of adult status, and on the other hand, they fear the consequences of being an adult. Sometimes even adolescents' new-found ability to think abstractly produces unexpected side effects.

David Elkind (1970), a learning theorist, has suggested that youngsters may experience some problems as they begin to move into the formal operations (abstract reasoning) stage. With the new-found ability to think in abstract terms, many adolescents concern themselves with abstract notions of self and personal identity. Initially many adolescents, having developed the capacity to look at their own identity as an abstract idea, are unable to distinguish between what they think about themselves and what others think about them. Consequently a good many adolescents believe that all other people regard them as they regard themselves. Suppose a student is very concerned about some pimples; he or she may be utterly convinced that "everybody" is concerned about those pimples. Elkind wrote that this kind of thinking takes two forms: (1) the "imaginary audience" and (2) the "personal fable."

The imaginary audience results when adolescents are unable to distinguish between their own thoughts about themselves and those held by others. When this happens, adolescents tend to view themselves as perpetually "on stage." They are certain that everyone watches their every move.

The imaginary-audience concept explains much about adolescent behavior. Shyness, for example, is a logical result of feeling that any mistake made in public will be noted by others and evaluated critically. The slavish attention to dress fads results from an expectation that any deviation from an expected norm will be noted. For individuals for whom the imaginary audience is very strong, every minor blemish takes on the importance of a major flaw. Every action is taken in anticipation of the likely reaction of the imaginary audience.

Elkind's other variant is the personal fable. He pointed out that adolescents tend to become somewhat disoriented by the many physical and emotional changes that have taken place. At the same time, they find these changes utterly fascinating. Some come to believe that these changes and the accompanying feelings are so unusual that no one else has ever experienced them (particularly not parents or teachers). Many adolescents become so enamored of the importance of their own personal fable that they keep diaries that are written out of an unshakable conviction that future generations will be intensely interested in their "unique" feelings and experiences.

As adolescents have more and more experiences, the validity of the imaginary audience and the personal fable are tested against reality. In time, the imaginary audience gives way to the real audience. The personal fable is adjusted as youngsters' interactions with others reveal to them that their feelings and perceptions are not really significantly different from those of other adolescents.

Teachers of high school youngsters work with a population of students capable of quite abstract thinking. Yet they have personal characteristics that suggest that they are not yet college or university students or other adult learners, for whom exposure to the subject matter content may be enough. Adolescents do have emotional perspectives that demand teachers' attention. Successful high school teachers are able to strike a reasoned balance between concern about the psychological condition of their students and concern about providing them with a respectable grounding in the subject areas.

Box 15-5
The "Imaginary Audience" and the "Personal Fable"

David Elkind (1970) suggests that many adolescents construct an "imaginary audience" and a "personal fable" as they grow toward maturity. In time, most bring their perceptions more in accord with the adult view of the "real world."

LET'S PONDER

Consider the concepts "imaginary audience" and "personal fable" as you respond to the following questions:

1. How valid do you believe the concept of "imaginary audience" to be?
2. Can you cite some examples from your own adolescent days that might illustrate behavior indicative of a belief in an "imaginary audience?"
3. How valid do you believe the concept of the "personal fable" to be?
4. Can you cite some examples from your own adolescent days that might illustrate behavior indicative of a belief in a "personal fable?"
5. What sorts of personal experiences might you or your friends have had that tended to move you or them to a more adult view of reality?

Recapitulation of Major Ideas

1. Youngsters in the school today differ in many respects from those in schools a generation ago. For one thing, they are fewer in number. For another, the majority tend to come from homes with only one parent or from homes where both parents work. A result of these changes is that schools are being asked to assume greater responsibilities than ever before.

2. Many youngsters in schools do not speak English as their first language. Spanish-speaking youngsters represent the largest language minority in the schools. They are rapidly increasing in number. Recent tests reveal that Hispanic youngsters consistently have scored below national averages in such important areas as science, social studies, mathematics, and reading/literature comprehension.

3. There are many more handicapped children in regular classrooms today than there used to be. In part, this has resulted because of an important attitude change. Today, it is recognized that such youngsters, in many cases, can profit from instruction in classrooms where they sit side-by-side with so-called "normal" children. In former times, most handicapped children spent all day in classes filled only with other handicapped youngsters.

4. Throughout history, there have been varying attitudes about how children should behave and how they are transformed into adults. In former times, some people believed that youngsters were basically mindless creatures little different from animals. Other early views held that children were really miniature adults capable of thinking about the world much as adults do. Still others held children to be raw clay awaiting "proper" instruction from adults. In general, these early views today are largely discounted.

5. Jean Piaget found that youngsters pass through a series of mental stages enroute to maturity. Each of these stages, he noted, is characterized by a certain thinking style. An understanding of the characteristics of youngsters at each stage has implications for the kinds of instructional practices that will be most successful.

6. The intellectual, emotional, and physical needs of youngsters differ at various ages. Even within given age groups, differences among youngsters are profound. This is true because individuals' rates of development vary within broad ranges. Teachers need to consider these differences as they plan learning experiences for their youngsters.

Posttest

DIRECTIONS: Using your own paper, answer each of the following true/false questions. For each correct statement, write the word *true* on your paper. For each incorrect statement, write the word *false* on your paper.

1. There is evidence that there are fewer differences among youngsters in regular classrooms today than twenty years ago.
2. The National Assessment of Educational Progress tests achievement of nine-, thirteen-, and seventeen-year- olds.
3. In 1990, it is likely that young people will represent a larger percentage of the total population than they did in 1965.
4. Youngsters at the "concrete operations" stage can use logic in arriving at solutions to problems.
5. All learners past the age of eleven can be expected to operate at the "formal operations" level.
6. At the end of this century, Spanish-speaking Americans may replace black Americans as the nation's largest minority group.
7. Teachers of kindergarten-aged youngsters need to be people who feel comfortable in giving positive approval to the children in their classes.
8. Physically, girls tend to develop somewhat faster than boys.
9. When there are no opportunities for active learning in primary-grades classrooms, children often develop nervous, fidgety habits.
10. Some problems we typically associate with adolescence may come about because of our cultural tendency to prolong childhood.

Summary

Youngsters in the schools are diverse. They represent an incredible cross section of intellectual talent. They have vastly different personal and emotional problems. Yet for all these differences, there are broad patterns of behavior

"I'll probably never get rubbed out for knowing too much."

that in a broad sense typify many youngsters within a given age range. These characteristics need to be recognized by individuals preparing to become teachers.

More specifically, Jean Piaget has identified certain stages of intellectual development. These characteristics provide a basis for understanding the kinds of lessons likely to succeed with youngsters of different ages. Teachers who have some understanding of Piaget's stages of intellectual development and a general grasp of children's typical patterns of physical development have insights that allow them to respond professionally to the differing needs of individual youngsters.

References

AELIN, MARSHALL. "Teacher Responses to Student Time Differings in Mastery Learning." *American Journal of Education* (Aug., 1982):334–352.

BIEHLER, ROBERT T. *Psychology Applied to Teaching.* 2nd ed. Boston: Houghton Mifflin, 1974.

DEMAUSE, L. *The History of Childhood.* New York: Psycho-History Press, 1974.

ELKIND, DAVID. *Children and Adolescents: Interpretive Essays on Jean Piaget.* New York: Oxford University Press, 1970.

ERIKSON, ERIK H. *Identity: Youth and Crisis.* New York: Norton, 1968.

HAVIGHURST, ROBERT, J. (Ed). *Youth.* The Seventy-fourth Yearbook of the National Society for the Study of Education. Chicago: University of Chicago Press, 1974.

HENSON, KENNETH T. *Secondary Teaching Methods.* Lexington, Mass.: D.C. Heath and Co., 1981.

LEINHARDT, GAIE, AND PALLAY, ALLEN. "Sex and Race Differences in Learning Disabilities Classrooms." *Journal of Educational Psychology* (Dec., 1982):835–843.

NATIONAL CENTER FOR EDUCATION STATISTICS. *Digest of Education Statistics, 1982 Edition.* Washington, D.C.: United States Government Printing Office, 1982.

OVERTON, WILLIS F., AND MEEHAN, A. M. "Individual DIfferences in Formal Operational Thought." *Child Development* (Dec., 1982):1536–1543.

PIFER, ALAN. *Perceptions of Childhood and Youth.* Reprinted from the 1978 Annual Report, Carnegie Corporation of New York, 437 Madison Ave., New York, NY 10022.

SPRINTHALL, RICHARD C., AND SPRINTHALL, NORMAN A. *Educational Psychology: A Developmental Approach,* 2nd ed. Menlo Park, Calif.: Addison-Wesley, 1977.

WADWORTH, BARRY J. *Piaget for the Classroom Teacher.* New York: Longmans, 1978.

16

The Exceptional Learner

Objectives

This chapter provides information to help the reader to

1. Identify different kinds of handicapping conditions.
2. Take note of typical concerns teachers have about how to work with handicapped youngsters in the classrooms.
3. Point out a number of implications for classroom teachers of Public Law 94–142.
4. Suggest some general kinds of responses that classroom teachers can make to different handicapping conditions of learners.
5. Describe some problems for education that have resulted from legal mandates stemming from Public Law 94-142.

Pretest

DIRECTIONS: Using your own paper, answer each of the following true/false questions. For each correct statement, write the word *true* on your paper. For each incorrect statement, write the word *false* on your paper.

1. Today there is a trend, to the extent possible, to instruct handicapped youngsters in classrooms alongside nonhandicapped youngsters.
2. Most teachers serving in public schools have had little or no training during their undergraduate teacher-preparation programs that focused on working with handicapped youngsters.
3. According to federal laws in existence today, school districts are required to provide handicapped youngsters with a specially designed education at no cost to the parents.
4. Teachers' fear is one of the most significant problems associated with including handicapped youngsters in regular classrooms.
5. The "least restrictive environment" provision of Public Law 94-142 means that larger numbers of handicapped children will be spending more of their time outside regular classrooms in special-education facilities designed to meet the unique needs of the handicapped.
6. Many school districts are worried about the financial implications of Public Law 94-142.
7. As a result of Public Law 94-142, handicapped children are less likely than formerly to have educational programs tailored specifically to their own needs.
8. There is a good deal of uncertainty among educators about what the various provisions of Public Law 94-142 will mean in practice.
9. Massive in-service efforts have been mounted in many parts of the

country to help teachers understand how to respond to the requirements of Public Law 94-142.

10. Teachers are nearly universally agreed that their work load has not been and will not be increased as a consequence of the provisions of Public Law 94-142.

Introduction

Few federal laws affecting education have stirred the intense interest and often-heated discussion that has developed since the enactment of Public Law 94-142, the Education for All Handicapped Act. Though the act was passed in 1975, many provisions did not go into effect until the 1978 school year. Despite attempts to publicize the provisions of this legislation, many educators, did not begin to appreciate the implications of the act until the implementation date approached. Since the enactment of the legislation and especially since 1978, there has been wide-ranging public argument between proponents and opponents of the legislation. Much of this discussion has centered on the requirement to provide education for handicapped learners in the "least restrictive environment."

In practice, the "least restrictive environment" has been interpreted to be the regular classroom unless a compelling case could be made for providing instruction in a special setting because of particularly severe handicapping conditions. This has meant that for the first time, many youngsters who formerly spent the school day in special-education classrooms are spending at least part of the day in regular classrooms alongside nonhandicapped youngsters. This situation has resulted in great anxiety on the part of many teachers.

In large measure, this anxiety results because many regular classroom teachers received no formal preparation in dealing with handicapped youngsters in their teacher preparation programs. When they were trained, there was an assumption that handicapped youngsters would be segregated from nonhandicapped youngsters and taught in special classrooms. Certain teachers who wished to work with handicapped learners took special programs to qualify for special-education certificates. Most teachers who envisioned a professional career within education graduated from college or university programs without much course work that related to the special needs of handicapped youngsters. Therefore many teachers have become frustrated with the requirement that they must now deal with both handicapped and nonhandicapped youngsters. It must be recognized that the vast majority of these teachers by no means are antihandicapped. Rather, they feel they may be held accountable for dealing with a situation for which they have not been trained.

Proponents of Public Law 94-142 point out that many teachers' fears are unfounded. They note that the similarities of handicapped learners to so-called normal learners are much more pronounced than their differences. They contend that given some in-service training and good administrative support, most teachers should experience few real difficulties in working with handicapped youngsters. They note, too, that the social benefits to be gained by handicapped youngsters who spend at least part of the day in regular classrooms are considerable. Such youngsters see themselves as more "typical" human beings who can share many of the aspirations of their nonhandicapped peers. There is some sentiment for the view that the traditional practices of dealing with handicapped youngsters in isolated special-education classrooms may have had the unintended result of lowering handicapped youngsters' levels of self-esteem. Given this claimed psychological advantage, supporters of Public Law 94-142 suggest that the initial adjustment difficulties of some teachers may be more than compensated for by the improved emotional health of handicapped youngsters.

Before proceeding to a more specific consideration of the general question of educating handicapped youngsters, let us pause for a moment to discuss a term, *mainstreaming,* that is central to most (or at least to a great many) discussions of education for handicapped learners. *Mainstreaming* refers to the practice of, when possible, placing handicapped youngsters in regular classrooms. The idea is that they are to be mainstreamed except when compelling

evidence suggests an alternative course of action. Mainstreaming intends to infuse handicapped youngsters into the main arteries of the educational system in as many ways as possible, with a view to preparing them for the adult world much as nonhandicapped youngsters are prepared.

To summarize, the present state of education for the handicapped is confused. The passage of Public Law 94-142 introduced elements into the educational system that may have profound long-term effects on schools. In the sections that follow, some issues related to the education of handicapped youngsters are discussed in more detail. Specific attention is devoted to the provisions of Public Law 94-142, the range of handicapping conditions, the reactions of teachers to mainstreaming requirements, and the possible dilemmas facing the school districts as a consequence of federal legislation related to educating handicapped youngsters.

Public Law 94-142: Basic Provisions

The Education for All Handicapped Act, Public Law 94-142, was passed out of a concern that many handicapped youngsters were not being well served by existing educational programs. During hearings related to the proposed legislation, Congressmen learned that over half of the approximately eight million handicapped youngsters in the country had no access to appropriate educational services. About a million of these youngsters were found to be receiving no services from public schools. Testimony revealed the problem to be not lack of concern on the part of school people and of parents but lack of funds to do the job properly.

A number of provisions of the law deserve mention.

Federal Monies for Handicapped

Public Law 94-142 established a formula whereby federal aid goes to the states to provide educational services for handicapped learners between the ages of three and twenty-one. A mathematical formula based on a percentage of the average amount spent on each youngster's education in the United States and on the number of handicapped learners to be served was developed as a basis for determining the amount of money to be spent.

Obligations of the States

Each state was directed to establish specific policies for all handicapped children between the ages of three and eighteen by 1978. These policies were later extended to include those handicapped persons between eighteen and twenty-one and were a prerequisite for receiving the federal funds targeted for the program.

Individualized Instruction

An individualized instructional program must be established for each handicapped child. Furthermore, the law specifies that such a program must be developed and agreed to at a meeting that includes a representative of the school district, the learner, and a parent of the learner. The individualized education program must include (1) the present level of educational performance, (2) development of goals and short-term objectives, (3) a description of the specific services to be provided and the time required for each, (4) identification of a starting date and an estimate of the expected duration of services, and (5) the evaluation criteria to be used in determining whether the objectives have been achieved.

Least Restrictive Environment

In implementing Public Law 94-142, the states must ensure to the maximum extent possible that handicapped learners are educated with learners who are not handicapped. The assignment of handicapped learners to special classes, special schools, or other alternatives to the regular classroom must be undertaken only when the severity of the handicap is so great that education in regular classrooms with the use of supplementary materials and aids cannot be achieved satisfactorily.

There are a number of other provisions of Public Law 94-142. Those selected for mention here have prompted most of the debate regarding whether education for the handicapped—and, indeed, education as a whole—has been helped or hindered by this legislation. Much of the discussion of this law stems from some fairly new policy ground that has been broken with its passage. Traditionally, federal regulations pertaining to the public sector have been addressed more to the question of what should be done than to the question of how the task should be accomplished. Where education was concerned, this resulted in regulations requiring schools, for example, to achieve *X* percentage of desegregation by year *Y*. The *means* of accomplishing this objective were left to educators. The assumption was that their specialized knowledge would permit them to develop the best responses to meet the goal specified in the federal regulation.

Public Law 94-142 goes well beyond this traditional goal-setting behavior of federal authority. The law says not only that something must be done for the handicapped but also what that something ought to be. For example, individualized educational programs for each handicapped learner are mandated by the language of the law. Furthermore, these individualized educational programs are to be jointly developed by school representatives, parents, teachers, and the youngsters themselves. The *process* of meeting the needs of the handicapped has been legislated as well as the *goal* of meeting these needs.

A good deal of the debate surrounding Public Law 94-142 stems from concerns about the wisdom of some of the mandated processes. For example, not all professional educators are agreed that the needs of handicapped youngsters are best served through the development of individualized educational programs following the procedures mandated by the law. Yet the law provides no alternatives; these procedures must be followed. In large mea-

---

Box 16-1
Handicapped Education and the Federal Government

Speaker A: "The federal government is putting its ugly hand into every pie. Now the name of the game is 'help the handicapped.' For years we have paid millions of dollars to prepare highly trained specialists to deal with youngsters having physical, emotional, and other kinds of handicaps. We have fine specially prepared classrooms with the best equipment on the market there for these specialists to use with these kids. Now the federal people tell us we're all wrong. We've wasted all that money. The answer, they say, is to put these kids in regular classrooms. Hooey — what next from Fairyland-by-the Potomac!"

Speaker B: "If the federal government doesn't do it, it just doesn't get done. Public school systems are the worst of all. They are simply bastions of inertia. They do all right in taking care of the average youngsters, but give them anything different and they hide their heads in the sand. Look at this handicapped situation. For years, instead of trying to do something with these kids they locked them away in separate rooms and kidded us that they were providing these youngsters with a 'special education.' What they were doing is convincing these kids that they were less than acceptable young people . . . that they were kids that had to be hidden away. Lots of them didn't get any consideration from schools at all. In fact, some simply were kept away by disgusted parents. I say hurray for the feds and Public Law 94-142. It's about time!"

LET'S PONDER

Read the statements by the two speakers. Then, respond to the following questions:

1. What past experiences do you think lead Speaker A to his/her conclusion?
2. What past experiences do you think lead Speaker B to his/her conclusion?
3. Which speaker has the sounder arguments? Why?
4. Are there some elements of truth and some elements of untruth in the statement of each speaker? If so, can you point them out?
5. How do you feel about the issue the speakers are addressing?

sure, then, discussions surrounding Public Law 94-142 have been prompted not by any wish to do poorly by the handicapped but by concern about the professional wisdom of some of the responses to this need mandated by the federal legislation.

There is some danger in preparing a simple list of handicapping conditions. The danger lies in two areas. First, the general characteristics of individuals suffering from these conditions are just that: general. An incredible range of diversity is found among the individuals in any single category. Second, there is a tendency to overlook the possibility that many youngsters in the school fall into several categories simultaneously. Given these limitations, a brief description will be helpful of the kinds of handicapping conditions that teachers may expect to encounter as they work with youngsters in the classroom.

Physically Handicapped Learners

Physically handicapped youngsters may be characterized by a wide variety of different conditions. Among these learners, we would expect to find individ-

---

Box 16-2
Visually Handicapped Students

It is your first year of teaching. Two days before school starts your principal calls you into the office. You are told that you will have a student who is legally blind in your class. You are told that money will be available to buy any special equipment you might need. Also, a specialist on education for the severely visually handicapped will be available in the central district administrative offices to talk to you should you have some questions.

LET'S PONDER

1. What is your first reaction to this news? How do you feel about having a learner with a severe visual handicap in your room?
2. What kinds of special problems will this youngster likely have?
3. How will you attempt to respond to these problems?
4. What kinds of special equipment do you think you will tell your principal you will need?
5. When you meet with the specialist, on education for the severely visually handicapped, what questions will you ask?

uals who are (1) visually handicapped and blind, (2) auditorily handicapped and deaf, (3) orthopedically handicapped, and (4) characterized by one or more of a number of other physically related impairments.

Visually Handicapped and Blind Learners.   Evidence suggests that youngsters who are visually impaired or blind have excellent potential for competing with other learners in regular classrooms provided their communications skills are well developed. For blind students, it is essential that materials be available in braille. Some states—for example, Texas—have made available braille editions of regular adopted textbooks to teachers whose classes include severely visually impaired or blind learners.

Many blind learners find it convenient to communicate with a teacher using a typewriter. Early instruction in acquiring typewriting skills needs to be provided. Furthermore, the individual needs to know how to produce braille as well as how to read it. To acquire this expertise, the youngster has to have access to a brailler. A tape recorder also proves useful to the visually impaired and blind learner. Assignments can be recorded, as well as lectures and other comments from the teacher. Some teachers, too, find it useful to assign a sighted learner to serve as a reader for visually handicapped and blind learners. The reader can serve as another source of information for individuals having severe visual handicaps.

Auditorily Handicapped and Deaf Learners

Auditorily handicapped youngsters' most marked difference from so-called normal learners is their difficulty in producing speech and in acquiring language skills. Amplification through mechanical hearing aids can provide help for some. In order for a youngster to derive the maximum benefit from this special equipment, it needs to be in good working order. Teachers who have learners with hearing aids and other amplification aids need to know something about how the equipment works and what can be done when a problem develops.

Because many youngsters who are auditorily handicapped have learned to read lips, teachers should make a point to face the class when addressing groups that contain learners with severe hearing problems. There should be no exaggeration of speech patterns; lip readers learn to read lips when speech is being produced in a normal way.

When giving directions, it makes sense to supplement oral instructions with visual representations. For example, assignments can be written on the board, or better yet, an overhead projector can be used. Expository material presented during a class, can also be supplemented through some use of visual cues. For example, some teachers write a brief outline of their remarks on a roll of acetate on an overhead projector and refer to it as they talk to the class.

The following are some tips for teachers working with youngsters with severe hearing problems.

Arrange the teaching area so that the hearing imparied youngster has a clear view of the teacher.

The teacher should stand so that the light from the window falls on the teacher's face, not on the youngster's face.

The teacher should be sure that fancy hairstyles and mustaches do not hide the face or distract attention from the lips.

The teacher should signal the beginning of a new train of thought by using a clear introduction to each new topic.

Use of written tests rather than oral ones is recommended. The teacher can give multiple-choice and true/false tests by exposing one item at a time on an overhead projector.

Before showing a film, the teacher should provide the hearing-impaired with some supplemental written material.

Language

The teacher should teach the idiomatic meaning of words so that the learner with limited hearing does not take idioms literally.

Practice in writing reports and telling stories will help learners develop the correct use of idiomatic phrases, intonations, and question forms.

When possible, the teacher should use simple sentences that are easy to understand. Complex sentence structure may cause problems.

The teacher should acquaint the hearing-impaired with the use of the dictionary.

The teacher should include the hearing-impaired in all language activities.

Speech

The teacher should help the hearing-impaired to learn the differences between sounds and how to use sounds correctly by pointing out the differences and providing examples of correct use.

The teacher should help the learner hear sounds clearly in a normal tone of voice.

The teacher should discuss the learner's speech with the speech clinician to find out how skills the clinician is working on can be reinforced in class.

The teacher should try not to interrupt the learner to make corrections but wait until he or she has finished speaking before making these corrections.

The teacher should become familiar with the patterns of speech of hearing-impaired learners by engaging them in conversations. Such conversations make it easier for the teacher to understand these learners when they speak up in class.

Adapted from "Tips for Teachers in Programming for Learners with Problems," a Texas Learning Resource Center publication (Austin: Apr. 1978). Division of Special Education, Texas Education Agency.

Orthopedically Handicapped Learners. It is difficult to generalize about youngsters who are orthopedically handicapped. They may suffer from one of a number of conditions that limit their physical abilities. Clearly the classroom teacher has an obligation to learn the precise nature of the handicap and its implications for the instructional process before many specific responses can be formulated.

A number of pieces of special equipment may be required for classrooms that include some orthopedically handicapped youngsters. Wheelchairs, special typewriters, and standing tables are among the items that might be needed. Threats to the effective and safe use of this equipment must be taken into consideration. For example, highly polished floors that pose no problems for most youngsters can be very dangerous for youngsters who must use crutches to move from place to place. Care must be taken, too, to ensure that the possibility of tipping a wheelchair is minimized. Because learners who use equipment designed to enhance the mobility of the orthopedically handicapped generally cannot move as quickly as other youngsters, teachers typically make arrangements for them to leave classes early so that they may avoid congested halls and arrive at their next class on time.

A variety of aids to learning and retention may be necessary to assist the orthopedically handicapped. If there are problems with handwriting, typewriters might be provided. The necessity of taking elaborate handwritten notes can be avoided if youngsters have access to small handcarried cassette tape recorders. Other aids may be desirable, depending on the specific nature of the handicap.

Emotionally Disturbed or Behaviorally Handicapped Learners

A learner characterized by an emotional or behavioral handicap displays a "marked deviation from age-appropriate behavior expectations which interferes with positive personal and interpersonal development" (Turnbull and Schulz, 1979, p. 41). Given this definition, it should be remembered that the behavior expectations are keyed to those typical of the appropriate age-mates of a given learner. Behavior that would be considered inappropriate for a twelve-year-old might be considered nothing out of the ordinary for a six-year-old.

Emotionally disturbed or behaviorally handicapped youngsters are likely to come to a teacher's attention because of either (1) disruptive behavior in class, or (2) personality characteristics (for example, extreme withdrawal) that mark the youngster as somehow clearly "different" from his or her classmates. Teachers find it extremely difficult to work with emotionally disturbed or behaviorally handicapped youngsters, particularly those who disrupt classroom activities.

Many teachers report being torn between two conflicting goals when working with disruptive youngsters. On the one hand, they sense an obligation to meet the special needs of each learner, even the disruptive one. On the other hand, they sense an obligation to serve all of the learners in their class—something that is difficult to do when they are faced with a disruptive youngster. There is a real challenge involved in striking a reasoned balance between the needs of the individual and the needs of the class. It is the kind of decision almost no teacher looks forward to making.

Because the causes of emotional disturbance and behavior problems are so diverse, no list of possible responses for classroom teachers could ever be truly comprehensive. Sometimes teachers have been told simply that behavior problems would diminish if only they would do a better job of motivating youngsters. (For most teachers, such "solutions" are excess baggage. They *know* that motivation is a problem. What they do not know is *how* to achieve the objective, and given the complexity of the problem, neither do many of the people giving teachers advice.) Though the enormity of the problem sometimes does invite a sense of hopelessness, there are a few common threads that tend to recur in many emotionally disturbed or behaviorally maladjusted youngsters. Prominent among these is the idea that part of the difficulty these youngsters have results from their inability to function well when exposed to too many stimuli at one time. For youngsters for whom this is an adequate explanation of at least part of the difficulty, there are some specific things teachers can do. Teachers can arrange for such youngsters to do seat work in carrels or partially enclosed booths where extraneous visual stimuli are kept to a minimum. When appropriate (and provided the equipment can be had), extraneous sounds can be blocked by providing instruction to these youngsters via audio tapes to which they listen through headsets.

In working with many of these youngsters, the teacher will need to seek the help of other professionals in the building. Members of the counseling staff frequently will be involved. It may be necessary for a team of professionals to develop a systematic behavior-modification strategy designed to divert behaviors into more productive channels.

In summary, there are no quick and easy solutions for teachers who ask about procedures for working with emotionally disturbed or emotionally handicapped learners. These youngsters need to be approached sympathetically, but beginning teachers, in particular, need not delude themselves that working with them will be easy. They remain a frustrating challenge for many professional educators who bring years of experience to their tasks.

Mentally Retarded Learners

There are many reasons for mental retardation. Furthermore, there are many levels of retardation. In very general terms, youngsters who are mentally retarded have been categorized as *educable, trainable,* and *severely or profoundly retarded.* The majority of learners spending a part of the day in regular classrooms as a result of Public Law 94-142 are probably in the *educable* category, the group comprising those individuals deviating the least from the so-called normal range of mental functioning.

Educable youngsters are likely to have some language and speech deficiencies. In working with these individuals, teachers need to keep in mind that they may have relatively short attention spans, and therefore lessons should be short, direct, and to the point. Some tips for teachers working with educable youngsters include the following:

Working with Educable
Learners

The teacher needs to stress readiness activities by providing concrete examples and by dealing with relevant vocabulary before new material is introduced.

The teacher needs to illustrate with visuals or with actual concrete materials any items that are being introduced for the first time.

The teacher needs to supplement with oral information any material being introduced via reading.

The teacher needs to break tasks into small, sequential steps.

The teacher should consider assigning another learner to work with the educable youngster to be sure that tasks are being understood.

Adapted from "Tips for Teachers in Programming for Learners with Problems," a Texas Learning Resource Center publication (Austin: Apr. 1978). Division of Special Education, Texas Education Agency.

Recognition that teachers have needed help in adjusting to teaching some handicapped youngsters in their classrooms is nothing new. Indeed, Public Law 94-142 implicitly acknowledges this situation in its provisions for in-service training of teachers. The question is not so much of a nonrecognition of a very real problem as of a response to this problem. In surveying what has been done to prepare teachers to work with handicapped youngsters, Hyer (1979) noted that little attention has been given to specific procedures for working with these youngsters in classrooms. Rather, most of the effort has been directed toward promoting the acceptance of mainstreaming handicapped youngsters as a good idea. In Hyer's view, most teachers already accept the idea philosophically. Their concern stems from a lack of specific direction regarding how such youngsters should best be served.

In addition to their unease about having little specific background in working with handicapped children, teachers have many other concerns that have stemmed from the passage of Public Law 94-142. For example, teachers have always had many youngsters in their classes who found the work difficult. Such youngsters have demanded a good deal of personal attention. Even given this attention, many have experienced great difficulty in school. Some

Box 16-3
Working with Handicapped Youngsters in Regular Classrooms

You are a sixth grade teacher at a middle school. You find yourself caught in the middle between two different sets of very well organized parents. One group of parents has a high interest in developing solid academic skills in the areas of mathematics, science, English, and history. They expect their youngsters to attend a university with a reputation for academic rigor. They want you to spend sufficient time with their youngsters to ensure that these skills are mastered. A second group of parents has sons and daughters who are handicapped and who spend part of each day in your classroom as a result of the requirements of Public Law 94-142. They put pressure on you to ensure that you are spending time with their youngsters. They feel the school has shortchanged their children in the past, and they will not tolerate anything that they see as evidence their children are not being given the attention they need to succeed.

LET'S PONDER

Read the passage above. Then, respond to the following questions.

1. Do you see any incompatibility between the positions of the two groups of parents? Are members of each group after the same thing, or are they after something different?
2. Can you satisfy both groups, or will you have to make a decision?
3. Do you think these groups of parents have the same general goals for education or different goals?
4. Will you be able to keep good relationships with both groups of parents, or will you have to make a decision to keep one group happy and accept unhappiness on the part of the other?
5. Given this situation, what decision would you make?

teachers feel that the introduction of handicapped youngsters has placed a very heavy additional burden on their time. Though they are basically sympathetic to the plight of these youngsters, they recognize, too, that attending to their special needs (setting up carrels, turning on special equipment, locking wheels on wheelchairs, and so forth) takes time. This time, many feel, is given at the expense of time spent with other youngsters in the class. A large number of teachers express the concern that many youngsters who have experienced problems in school may have even greater difficulties when teachers' time has to be reallocated to serve the special needs of the handicapped youngsters.

It is possible that this situation will result in an undesirable confrontation between the parents of handicapped children and the parents of nonhandicapped children. Because the law so clearly specifies what must be done to serve the handicapped youngsters, some teachers feel that the parents of other youngsters may see their children as being shortchanged. This situation, some believe, has a dangerous potential for alienating many parents from the school.

The timing of the mainstreaming legislation bothers many teachers. They sense themselves caught between heated public arguments over education's ultimate purposes. On the one hand, there are people arguing that schools should be more academically rigorous and that teachers should be held strictly accountable for learners' achievement. On the other hand, there are individuals arguing that the schools should prepare youngsters for the world of work, for life's mainstream. Public Law 94-142 and its proponents identify with this latter view.

Many teachers feel that in the great national debate between the "basic-skills" people and the "life's-mainstream" people, the basic-skills faction is in the ascendancy. Large numbers of states have passed competency-testing legislation requiring certain minimal levels of academic performance for all high school graduates. Teachers increasingly sense themselves being pressured to produce youngsters who do well on standardized tests of achievement. Thus many feel that they have been put in a "no-win" situation by Public Law 94-142. They sense that the time required just to attend to overseeing the physical requirements of handicapped youngsters may take away valuable instructional time. Diminished instructional time may result in poorer learner achievement on standardized tests. Though teachers by no means speak with one voice on this issue, many feel that by serving the mandates of Public Law 94-142, they may be made to look bad because of the potential erosion of youngsters' scores on achievement tests. Certainly this issue is being widely discussed in many faculty lounges.

Additionally, many teachers find that whereas Public Law 94-142 provides substantial legal protection for handicapped youngsters and their parents, virtually none is provided for teachers. Regarding this situation, Anna L. Hyer (1979) has written, "It is possible that teachers may be legally responsible for implementing programs of instruction which they know from the beginning are destined to fail due to lack of adequate resources, support staff, and the like" (p. 135). Thus many teachers feel themselves not only professionally vulnerable in terms of complaints from parents that youngsters are not being adequately prepared, but also potentially legally vulnerable as well.

Perhaps impressions that may have been planted by information in the preceding few paragraphs ought to be tempered here with the observation that most teachers are making sincere attempts to work with handicapped youngsters. Indeed, many report that these youngsters fit in well with other learners. Happily, too, many strategies and techniques that these teachers have long been using with their regular youngsters have been found to work well with classes including some handicapped learners. As one teacher reported to one of the authors, "I was a bit nervous about this business at first. But these kids just aren't *that* different. Now I look at them just as some of the kids who come to school.''

School districts have been moving ahead with plans to provide inservice training to help their teachers become more familiar with ways of working with classes including handicapped learners. Hyer (1979) suggested that such programs might well provide such help as the following:

1. Basic information about what mainstreaming is should be included, especially information to teachers that *all* handicapped children are not going to be returned to regular classrooms from their special-education classrooms.
2. Specific role information about the duties not only of teachers but of administrators and support personnel needs to be included. It is especially important that lines of authority are clearly understood by all.
3. Collective planning strategies should be introduced. Mainstreaming requires a good deal of joint decision-making, and the dimensions of this practice need to be made clear.
4. Diagnostic techniques and behavior management techniques require emphasis. Many teachers have had little formal training in this area. Specific diagnostic techniques should be introduced, not simply the notion that diagnosis is a good idea.
5. Individualized instructional techniques require emphasis. As in the case of diagnosis, what is required are specific practical examples, not an intellectual case for individualization as a good idea.
6. Methods of preparing regular learners for the introduction of handicapped youngsters into the classroom are needed. Without such preparation, some children may make very insensitive comments to handicapped youngsters. Furthermore, they may resent the extra attention that handicapped learners get from teachers. Jealousy may result if some special audiovisual media equipment is provided for the exclusive use of handciapped youngsters.
7. Methods should be included for preparing handicapped learners for introduction into the regular classroom. Some handicapped youngsters, particularly the mentally retarded, may suffer motivational problems because of a feeling that they cannot compete successfully in classrooms with nonhandicapped learners.
8. Methods of evaluating handicapped learners ought to be provided. This frequently presents a problem for teachers because many handicapped youngsters cannot do the traditional paper-and-pencil tests. Additionally, attention must be given to breaking up content into short units and to establishing short-term rather than long-term learning goals.
9. It is important for teachers to know parent liaison techniques. Because of the direct involvement of parents in the instructional planning process that is mandated by Public Law 94-142, it is essential that teachers be familiar with procedures that can facilitate communication

with the parents. It is especially desirable that teachers learn techniques that can be used to reduce both their own anxiety and those of the parents.

Not all teachers are going to need instruction in all of these areas, but surveys do suggest that many of these topics are relevant to the concerns of many of them. The idea that some sort of systematic help for classroom teachers is needed is endorsed almost universally.

In summary, classroom teachers have many concerns about working with the handicapped learners who are now in their classes as a result of the passage of Public Law 94-142. Basically, these concerns flow from a lack of formal preparation for working with these individuals. With few exceptions, teachers support the idea of mainstreaming but feel uneasy about their ability to instruct the handicapped youngsters in their classes. Today intensive inservice training programs are under way to respond to some of these concerns. It is hoped that in time, these programs and college and university programs for new teachers will provide teachers with the kind of knowledge base they need to work productively and comfortably with handicapped youngsters in their classrooms.

School District Administrations and Public Law 94-142

The enactment of Public Law 94-142 has provided a number of new challenges for school district administrative officials. Generally speaking, administrative leaders have applauded the intent of the new law, but large numbers report frustrations in dealing with some of the implications flowing from the language of the legislation.

For example, there is a requirement to provide in-service experience for teachers to help them work more effectively with handicapped youngsters who are being mainstreamed into their regular classrooms. It has been very difficult for administrative people to find models of exemplary procedures to show to their teachers (not surprising, given that Public Law 94-142 represents a sharp break from former assumptions about how handicapped youngsters should be taught). Furthermore, very few individuals are available who have had long personal experience working with handicapped learners in regular classrooms and who can talk to teachers as credible peers.

Some administrators report that the passage of Public Law 94-142 has strained relationships between teachers and district administrative officials. Frustrated by a feeling of being unprepared to work with handicapped youngsters and somewhat shaky on the source of the mainstreaming requirement, in some districts teachers have lashed out at administrators for giving them responsibilities that they are not trained to handle. Administrative offi-

Box 16-4
Preparing Learners in Regular Classrooms for Handicapped Learners

You are a seventh grade teacher in a junior high school. Your principal has told you that, starting about the third week of school, you will have two physically handicapped boys in your second period class. One is confined to a wheel chair. The other walks with crutches and braces.

LET'S PONDER

Read the paragraph above. Then, think about what you would do to prepare youngsters in your class to accept these handicapped learners. Respond to the following questions.

1. What potential problems would you foresee?
2. How would you respond to each of these problems?
3. Specifically, what would you do to ''ease the entry'' of these youngsters on the first day of class?
4. Specifically what strategy would you suggest for getting the rest of the class to accept these learners as just other members of the class?
5. Do you think there are likely to be more difficulties in getting learners of this age to accept handicapped youngsters than would be true for learners of other ages? Why, or why not?

cials have had to work hard to explain that the specific conditions of teaching handicapped youngsters in the "least restrictive environment" were provided by federal legislation, not through state or district action.

While trying to appease frustrated teachers who have felt that mainstreaming was being introduced too precipitously, administrators have also had to deal with groups of parents of handicapped youngsters, very well organized in some communities, who have felt that the districts have been dragging their feet in their compliance with Public Law 94-142. Many parents' groups are very well informed on their legal rights under the law, and they have not been reluctant to sue school districts when they sensed that their youngsters were not getting their due as mandated by the law.

In addition to the squeeze between teachers' concerns and parents' concerns, district administrators in many places have found themselves in an insecure position in terms of the costs of the procedures mandated by Public Law 94-142. Although extra money is provided from federal sources to defray the expenses of providing educational services for handicapped youngsters under the new requirements of the law, it is unclear whether these monies will be sufficient to cover the added costs. The law is not very explicit in stating at what point the districts' responsibilities end in providing for the education of handicapped learners. Given this ambiguity, some groups have been pushing for an expansion of the districts' responsibilities, even to the point of having the districts pay for full-time custodial care of all handicapped youngsters in the district as well as for educational experiences for the handicapped. One district outside of a major metropolitan area reportedly expended $145,000 in a recent year just on services to benefit six profoundly handicapped youngsters. It is hoped that federal money will defray such costs, but the issue has yet to be decided. In the interim, financial concerns related to the various programs to serve the handicapped remain very real for school-district administrative personnel.

Recapitulation of Major Ideas

1. Passed in 1975, Public Law 94-142, the Education for All Handicapped Act, changed basic assumptions regarding the education of handicapped youngsters. Formerly it was assumed that handicapped youngsters should be taught primarily in special classrooms by specially trained teachers. Today it is assumed that as much education of handicapped children as possible should take place in a regular classroom alongside nonhandicapped learners.

2. A majority of teachers in regular classrooms received little or no training during their undergraduate teacher-preparation programs with regard to working with handicapped children in regular classrooms. Consequently large numbers of them have felt very uneasy about their ability to work with these youngsters.

3. Few models have been available regarding specific procedures for working with handicapped youngsters in regular classrooms, primarily because, traditionally, it was assumed that such learners would be educated exclusively in special classrooms. Because models of successful programs are few, districts have experienced difficulty in providing examples of procedures that have proved successful to their teachers at in-service training programs focusing on mainstreaming procedures and techniques.

4. An assumption behind the passage of Public Law 94-142 is that traditionally handicapped youngsters have not been well served by the American educational system. Large numbers were provided no services at all. Others developed unnecessary feelings of personal inadequacy because of a stigma attached to youngsters enrolled in "special classrooms."

5. Public Law 94-142 mandates an individualized instructional program for each handicapped learner. Parents, the learner, the teacher, and other district officials are charged with developing and approving such individualized educational plans. The law gives parents a participatory role in the development of educational plans for their youngsters.

6. Public Law 94-142 calls for handicapped youngsters to be educated in the "least restrictive environment." This means that to the extent possible, handicapped youngsters should be in regular classes with regular learners. This does not mean that special classes will disappear. For some handicapping conditions, special classes will be the "least restrictive environment."

7. There are large numbers of handicapping conditions. In a very general sense, these can be divided into the broad categories of physical handicaps, emotional or behavioral handicaps, and mental handicaps (retardation). Teachers must make special arrangements to deal with problems unique to the handicapping condition(s) of each handicapped learner.

8. Implementation of Public Law 94-142 has caused problems for many school-district administrative officials. They, as a group, tend to support the objective of improving education for the handicapped, but specific provisions of Public Law 94-142 have caused headaches. Among these have been concerns of teachers that they are unprepared to work with handicapped youngsters, concerns of parents of handicapped youngsters that districts are doing too little to help their children, and concerns about the ultimate costs of educating handicapped learners.

Posttest

DIRECTIONS: Using your own paper, answer each of the following true/false questions. For each correct statement, write the word *true* on your paper. For each incorrect statement, write the word *false* on your paper.

1. Today there is a trend, to the extent possible, to instruct handicapped youngsters in classrooms alongside nonhandicapped youngsters.

2. Most teachers serving in public schools had little or no training during their undergraduate teacher-preparation programs that focused on working with handicapped youngsters.

3. According to federal laws in existence today, school districts are required to provide handicapped youngsters with a specially designed education at no cost to the parents.

4. Teachers' fear is one of the most significant problems associated with including handicapped youngsters in regular classrooms.

5. The "least restrictive environment" provision of Public Law 94-142 means that larger numbers of handicapped children will be spending more of their time outside regular classrooms in special-education facilities designed to meet the unique needs of the handicapped.

6. Many school districts are worried about the financial implications of Public Law 94-142.

7. As a result of Public Law 94-142, handicapped children are less likely than formerly to have educational programs tailored specifically to their own needs.
8. There is a good deal of uncertainty among educators about what the various provisions of Public Law 94-142 will mean in practice.
9. Massive in-service efforts have been mounted in many parts of the country to help teachers understand how to respond to the requirements of Public Law 94-142.
10. Teachers are nearly universally agreed that their work load has not been and will not be increased as a consequence of the provisions of Public Law 94-142.

Summary

The passage of Public Law 94-142 in 1975 signaled a change in the basic assumption of what kind of education best meets the needs of handicapped learners. Practices in the schools before the enactment of this law were premised on an assumption that the handicapped were best served in special-education classrooms where they spent the day under the tutelage of specially trained teachers. Public Law 94-142 and its requirement for educating handicapped children in the "least restrictive environment" suggest a new assumption, that the handicapped, when possible, should be educated alongside so-called normal youngsters in regular classrooms.

The passage of the law, in part, resulted from concerns that traditionally many handicapped youngsters had not been well served. Of those who were in school, many, it was feared, had developed unnecessarily negative conceptions of their own self-worth and importance as a result of being isolated in special-education classrooms. The remedy, as reflected in Public Law 94-142, is a requirement that to the extent possible, handicapped learners should become members of regular school classrooms.

Public Law 94-142 and its accompanying introduction of handicapped learners into regular classrooms have prompted concerns among many teachers. Few teachers in regular classrooms received any training during their undergraduate years for working with handicapped learners. Many have been concerned that they now are being asked to do something for which they lack adequate preparation. Sensing the pressure to demonstrate the improvement of achievement levels of all youngsters, some teachers also have wondered whether others in the class may suffer academically because of the increased time that must be spent working with handicapped learners. These issues continue to be much discussed by professional educators.

Administrators, too, have faced problems in the wake of the passage of Public Law 94-142. In a general sense, they fear a serious erosion of the spirit of community in their districts as a consequence of the often-heated debates that have sprung up between the proponents and the opponents of Public

Law 94-142. More specifically, they have sensed themselves caught amid pressures coming from unhappy teachers, from unhappy parents of handicapped youngsters, and from still others who wonder what the costs of the new programs are going to be. These issues seem certain to be a primary concern of administrators for some years to come.

References

BERGESON, JOHN B., AND MILLER, GEORGE S. *Learning Activities for Disadvantaged Children.* New York: Macmillan Publishing Co., 1971.

BLATT, BURON. "On the Bill of Rights and Related Matters." In Robert Heinich (ed). *Educating All Handicapped Children.* Englewood Cliffs, N.J.: Educational Technology Publications, 1979, pp. 3–15.

BOGDAN, ROBERT. "'Does Mainstreaming Work?' Is a Silly Question." *Educational Leadership* (Feb., 1983): 427–428.

GIORDANO, GERALD A. Would You Place Your Normal Child in a Special Class?" *Teaching Exceptional Children* (Winter 1983): 95–96.

GLICK, HARRIET M., AND SCHUBERT, MARSHA. "Mainstreaming: An Unmandated Challenge." *Educational Leadership* (Jan., 1981): 326–329.

HYER, ANNA L. "The View of P.L. 94-142 from the Classroom." In Robert Heinich (ed). *Educating All Handicapped Children.* Englewood Cliffs, N.J.: Educational Technology Publications, 1979, pp. 131–151.

KIRK, SAMUEL A. *Educating Exceptional Children.* Boston: Houghton Mifflin, 1972.

L'ABATE, LUCIANO, AND CURTIS, LEONARD T. *Teaching the Exceptional Child.* Philadelphia: W. B. Saunders, 1975.

LEINHARDT, GAIE, AND PALLEY, ALLAN. "Restrictive Educational Settings: Exile or Haven?" *Review of Educational Research* (Winter 1982): 557–578.

LOVE, HAROLD D. *Educating Exceptional Children in Regular Classrooms.* Springfield, Ill.: Charles C Thomas, 1972.

MOSES, BARBARA. "Individual Differences in Problem Solving." *Arithmetic Teacher* (Dec. 1982): 10–14.

QUAY, H. C. "Special Education: Assumptions, Techniques, and Evaluative Criteria." *Exceptional Child* (Nov., 1973): 165–170.

SMITH, ROBERT M., AND NEISWORTH, JOHN T. *The Exceptional Child.* New York: McGraw-Hill, 1975.

STEARNS, MARIAN S., AND COOPERSTEIN, RHONDA ANN. "Equity in Educating the Handicapped." *Educational Leadership* (Jan., 1981): 324–325.

TEXAS LEARNING RESOURCE CENTER. "Tips for Teachers in Programming for Learners with Problems." Division of Special Education. Texas Education Agency, Austin, 1978.

TURNBULL, ANN P., AND SCHULZ, JANE B. *Mainstreaming Handicapped Students: A Guide for the Classroom Teacher.* Boston: Allyn and Bacon, 1979.

17

Learners' Rights
and Responsibilities

Objectives

The chapter provides information to help the reader to

1. Describe the historical development of learners' rights.
2. Define *in loco parentis* and suggest how the concept has been applied to educational settings.
3. Point out how court decisions have had an impact on rights of learners to a free and appropriate education.
4. Identify the factors that seem to play an important role in court decisions in corporal punishment cases.
5. Define *expulsion* and describe the required steps that must precede it.
6. Differentiate between the substantive principles and the procedural steps associated with due process.
7. Describe the implications of a number of court decisions for patterns of teachers' interaction with learners.
8. Point out present and probable future areas of litigation in the area of curriculum and instruction.

Pretest

DIRECTIONS: Using your own paper, answer each of the following true/false questions. For each correct statement, write the word *true* on your paper. For each incorrect statement, write the word *false* on your paper.

1. Schools may pass whatever rules they deem necessary regarding learners' behavior without having to worry about the rights guaranteed to adults by the U.S. Constitution.
2. Today most court cases involving learners' rights tend to strengthen the *in loco parentis* principle.
3. Schools cannot deny a child an education because of behavioral problems, learning problems, or handicapping conditions.
4. *Suspension* and *expulsion* are different words for the same thing.
5. Learners, because of their rights to due process, have a right to legal counsel in many hearings related to an alleged violation of school rules.
6. A girl may be suspended or expelled from school because she is pregnant.
7. In many cases, school officials have the right to search learners' lockers without permission.
8. At one time, many people regarded attendance at a public school as a *privilege*. Today there is a tendency to view a public education as a *right*.

9. Under the Family Educational Rights and Privacy Act, parents have a right to review the school's records of their children.
10. School administrators enjoy an absolute right to control the contents of school newspapers and other school publications.

Introduction

In times past, school principals and teachers exercised an authority over youngsters in their buildings that was challenged only rarely. They made the rules; the youngsters were expected to obey them. Those few young people who failed to conform could be dismissed summarily. In such cases, expelled pupils or students had no legal recourse. Unlike adults, who enjoyed certain constitutional rights, youngsters in the school (or parents acting in behalf of their children) could not demand a hearing or a review of an administrative decision by a school official.

This situation began changing rapidly during the 1960s, and these changes accelerated during the 1970s. As a consequence, by the early 1980s, youngsters in schools had come to enjoy many of the rights guaranteed to all adult citizens by the U.S. Constitution. This dramatic change in society's perception of the legal status of the child in the school came about as a result of a number of events that led Americans to question many traditional practices during this period. Some of these changes came about as a result of court decisions. Others resulted from the passage of new laws. Still others developed more informally as administrators and teachers, on their own initiative, began modifying some traditional patterns of dealing with youngsters who, for some reason or another, "did not fit" the expected pattern. If the reader is to understand the state of learners' rights and responsibilities today, a brief review of some historical trends should prove instructive.

Historical Changes in Society's View of the Child in School

The traditional legal doctrine governing the relationship of the school to the child was known as *in loco parentis*. According to this position, the school acted "in place of the parent." This meant that the school and its designated authorities (administrators and teachers) were free to treat children much as they could be treated by their parents. Common-law precedents relating to the parent–child relationship were extended to the school. For example, a child cannot take his or her parent to court and demand a hearing on the grounds of a disagreement over some parental directive. The parent is legally defined as having a custodial relationship to the child. Under *in loco parentis,* this same custodial responsibility was vested in the school. Given this legal doctrine, school officials did not have to justify actions taken against youngsters who were judged to have broken school rules and regulations. As the child could not sue the parent, so, too, under *in loco parentis,* the child (or those representing the child) could not sue the school.

The *in loco parentis* doctrine began crumbling in the early 1960s. A number of human and civil rights issues captured the public mind during this period. Efforts to extend full constitutional privileges to all racial groups prompted people to become increasingly interested in whether constitutional guarantees applied to everybody or only to "some everybodies." University groups, in particular, were quick to speak out against institutional practices that seemed to deny students the same constitutional protection they could enjoy were they not enrolled in institutions of higher learning. Finally, the increasing public suspicion that the government was not being responsive to the general will on the Vietnam war issue led to close scrutiny of all traditional sources of authority. In this context, it was only a matter of time before questions began to be raised regarding the *in loco parentis* relationship between school officials and youngsters in the schools.

The issue came to center on the question of the appropriateness of *in loco parentis* as a regulator of school–learner relationships in the latter part of the twentieth century. Some people said that changes in how society views children since the original formulation of *in loco parentis* had rendered the doctrine a very poor reflection of public attitudes and desires by the 1960s. A review of the historical roots of *in loco parentis* does reveal a dramatically different way of viewing young people than that prevailing today.

In assessing this change in perception, we must recall that the notion of children's being separate and distinct from adults is of relatively recent origin. In the past, children were often viewed only as miniature adults. Certainlly there was little conception of a long period when a person was something other than either an infant or a contributing member of the adult community. In times when all members of the family had to do some work to keep the economy of the family going, full adult rights were extended to children at a very young age.

As the years went by and Western societies changed in such a way that there was more lag time between infancy and a person's entry into the work force, the concept of *childhood* gradually emerged. With increases in technology, the span of years between an individual's birth and the time when he or she would assume the work burdens of an adult grew in length.

In a sense, the schools might be thought of as developing as "holding institutions" for young people who had no clearly necessary economic function to perform until they reached a certain age. These nonworking children could not be kept at home. To keep them there would be to interfere with the work efficiency of the adult members of the family. These youngsters could not go to work. There was no economically efficient return from the labor of unskilled, easily tiring hands in a time that was beginning to reward specialization and technical prowess. The solution, then, was to send the child to school.

But this school was very different from our public schools today. Schools were small. They were clearly creatures of the local community. The hiring and firing of the teachers by local community leaders ensured the congruence of instructional practices with local interest and values. Given the kind of individual likely to be hired as a teacher, parents were not at all reluctant to regard the school as a surrogate parent for their children. If the economics had been right, the parent would have enjoyed having their children at home as contributing workmates. But since the economics were not right, parents were willing to turn their youngsters over to the school and the school-teacher, an institution and an individual they expected to stand *in loco parentis.*

Given a perception of the school as a holding institution where youngsters could be sent until such time as they were physically mature enough to do some "real" work, public expectations of what the schools could do for youngsters were not high. Consequently teachers and administrators were more likely to be prized for their close reflection of community mores than for any substantial contributions they might make to youngsters' learning. Assuming youngsters had mastered a few basic survival skills, many people were not terribly concerned when youngsters dropped out of school. If long years of schooling were not expected to provide much of substance to those who attended, then those who dropped out were not viewed as having lost much of significance.

Given this view, no great efforts were expended to make special provisions to keep youngsters who were behavior problems in schools. Schooling was regarded as a "privilege" to be enjoyed by those who could live by the rules. It was not a "right" that society felt was owed to all young people. As schooling was not conceived of as a right, youngsters in schools were not perceived as having any legal recourse when they were removed from school for a violation of rules. Schools were thought of as substitute parents. A misbehaving learner could be "punished" by the school by being expelled with no more legal recourse than any child might have when punished by his or her parents for some minor infraction of household rules. The doctrine of *in loco parentis* gave youngsters no remedy to challenge decisions made by school officials.

The conception of schooling as a "privilege" rather than as a "right" that had tended to support the doctrine of *in loco parentis* began to unravel beginning in the late 1950s and early 1960s. Critics of the "schooling-as-privilege" position noted that literacy had become necessary for survival for nearly everyone in the society. Given the need for an educated population, it was illogical to argue that public schooling, the best available mechanism for promoting literacy, should be viewed as something other than a "right" to which all youngsters were entitled.

Given an increasing conviction that schooling was indeed a right, an ever-larger number of challenges to the *in loco parentis* doctrine began appearing on court dockets. In *Dixon* v. *Alabama State Board of Education* (294 F. 2d 150 [1961]), the court ruled that a tax-supported public education had become so fundamental that it should be regarded as a "substantial right." This important shift in the legal view of education as a right rather than a privilege carried important constitutional implications with it. The U.S. Constitution protects certain rights of citizens. Among these protections is a requirement that "due process of law" be observed in a situation that could result in the loss of a right. Due process includes such things as the right to know any charges, to be represented by counsel, to know the identity of any accusers, and other protections designed to ensure the fair adjudication of any dispute that could result in a citizen's losing a right to which he or she may be constitutionally entitled. Beginning with the *Dixon* case, there has been a continuing trend to extend due-process rights to learners in the school.

In addition to due-process guarantees, a number of other court decisions have had the effect of extending to school youngsters privileges granted to citizens under the Bill of Rights. An important landmark decision of this kind was the famous *Tinker* v. *Des Moines Independent Community School District* (343 U.S. 503 [1969]). In the *Tinker* case, the Supreme Court struck down a school district rule banning the wearing of armbands as a gesture of protest against the Vietnam war. Holding the rule to be an illegal restraint of freedom of speech, the court pointed out that constitutional guarantees do extend to learners in the school.

The decision in the *Tinker* case resulted in a great deal of debate among educators. Many identified closely with the minority opinion by Mr. Justice Black, who wrote, "One does not need to be a prophet or the son of a prophet to know that after the Court's holding today some students . . . in all schools will be ready, able, and willing to defy their teachers on practically all orders." Many teachers were greatly confused regarding exactly what authority did remain to them in the area of controlling learners. Many regarded the *Tinker* decision as an interference in the school management process that could have serious implications for the smooth functioning of the educational program.

But others drew somewhat different conclusions from their review of the *Tinker* case. In their view, the Supreme Court had done little to undermine the real authority of school officials. Rather, the court might be seen as confining its concern to the processes followed by school officials as they exercise their authority. In the view of educators taking a more positive view of the *Tinker* decision and other decisions having the effect of extending many rights enjoyed by adults to youngsters in the schools, these court decisions provided educators with an opportunity to develop sets of procedures that would build public confidence in the schools. Not only would these procedures be constitutional, but they would also blunt the criticism of those who felt that many actions of school authorities were irresponsible and taken out of a belief that they could not be held accountable for their actions. Some people are convinced that the general public will see schools and school officials in a more positive light when constitutional accountability is assured.

Arguments between those who support and those who oppose court decisions affecting education seem certain to continue in the years ahead.

At times throughout our history, schooling has been regarded as a privilege. Since a privilege is something that does not come to a person as a right but rather is something that is granted providing certain conditions are met, youngsters who were expelled from school when most viewed schooling as a privilege had little legal recourse.

Recently, there has been a tendency for the courts to define schooling as a right. Rights entitle the holder to certain legal protections. With regard to schooling, there has been a tendency to extend to youngsters the same constitutional protections enjoyed by all adults. This has meant that a decision to expel a youngster, for example, must be done in such a way that the youngster's due process guarantees are observed.

LET's PONDER,

Read the above paragraphs. Then, respond to the following questions:

1. Should schooling be regarded as a privilege or as a right? Why?
2. What problems do you see for teachers if schooling is regarded as a right?
3. What problems do you see for teachers or for parents if schooling is regarded as a privilege?
4. Do you think there should be some "outer limit" of educators' authority over youngsters in the school? If so, what should that "outer limit" be?
5. Twenty-five years from now, would you expect there to be more public sentiment for viewing schooling as a privilege or as a right? Why do you think so?

Because many of these decisions have important implications for teachers, it makes sense for individuals preparing to enter the profession to know something about what the courts have decided. A number of issues addressed by recent court decisions are introduced in the sections that follow.

Disciplining Learners

Classroom discipline or control issues have long interested professional educators and parents. Discussions related to these issues have often centered on the great difficulty teachers have in achieving a balance between two key needs. On the one hand, sufficient classroom decorum must be maintained to allow learning to go forward. On the other hand, care must be exercised so that disciplinary action directed toward a given youngster results neither in personal harm nor in a violation of his or her basic rights.

Box 17-2
Should Youngsters Be Classified According to Individual Differences?

In recent years, pressures have mounted to force schools to abandon attempts to attach labels to individual youngsters. Critics of labeling practices point out, for example, that some youngsters have been incorrectly diagnosed as mentally retarded early in their school careers. This mislabeling resulted in their receiving an education totally inappropriate to their real needs and abilities.

Supporters of labeling or classification of youngsters point out that youngsters' individual needs cannot be met unless there is some way of identifying what those needs are. Individual assessment and assignment of youngsters to certain categories is necessary if teachers are to have any way of knowing how a given youngster or group of youngsters should be approached. Furthermore, supporters of labeling point out that many federal funds are made available to schools only when youngsters have been sorted into categories according to such criteria as race, intellectual ability, economic status, and so forth.

Today, a number of court suits are in process that center around the general issue of labeling or categorizing youngsters. At this point, no clear trend of judicial opinion is available. Clearly, this issue is one that will be with educators for some time to come.

LET'S PONDER

Read the paragraphs above and respond to the following questions:

1. What specific advantages do you personally see for labeling youngsters?
2. What specific disadvantages do you personally see for labeling youngsters?
3. How do you think most teachers feel about labeling or categorizing youngsters? What is the basis for your opinion?
4. If you had a crystal ball and could forsee what educational practices would be in vogue twenty-five years from now, would you expect to see more or fewer instances of categorizing or labeling youngsters than we have now? Why?

Suspension and Expulsion

Traditionally, schools dealt with difficult youngsters by suspending them or expelling them from school. In recent years, courts have tended to define schooling as a right. Hence, public school authorities today must follow carefully established procedures before they can suspend or expel a youngster. If such procedures are not followed, these authorities may find themselves in court because of an alleged violation of a learner's due-process rights.

"Suspension" involves a mandatory separation of the learner from the school environment. There are three general categories of suspension. Procedures that must be followed to ensure that the due-process rights of learners are not violated vary according to whether a case involves (1) short-term suspension, (2) long-term suspension, or (3) indefinite suspension.

Short-Term Suspension. Due-process provisions associated with short-term suspension generally require the learner to be provided with either oral or written notice of the impending suspension. Furthermore, he or she is entitled to an explanation of the relevant evidence and to an opportunity to present his or her side of the story at an informal hearing. Typically the hearing procedure for a case of short-term suspension can be accomplished fairly quickly and, if warranted, the suspension can begin without much delay.

Long-Term Suspension. Typically, long-term suspension has a duration of more than ten days. A specific date for the youngster's return to school is indicated. A youngster facing a potential long-term suspension usually has his rights protected by somewhat more elaborate due-process provisions than when short-term suspension is being contemplated. For example, the violation must involve a written rule or regulation, witnesses must be identified, a public hearing may be held at the request of the youngster or his or her representatives, substantial evidence must support the charges, and legal counsel may be brought in to represent the youngster's interests if he or she so desires. Because there is a much greater possibility of a legal challenge to the school's authority by the parents or other representatives of a youngster given a long-term suspension, school districts tend to be very careful to preserve due-process rights in these situations.

Indefinite Suspension. When a youngster is given an indefinite suspension, he or she is required to stay away from school with no promise of a potential future return date. Ordinarily, indefinite suspension is used in situations where the presence of the youngster at school may endanger his or her welfare or that of others in the school. Indefinite suspension is often a short-term emergency measure taken to defuse a potentially dangerous situation. It is usually followed by either a short-term or a long-term suspension once there has been time to set up the process that ensures protection of the youngster's due-process rights.

Expulsion. Expulsion is more serious than any kind of suspension. It involves the removal of a youngster from school under conditions in which no opportunity for return is held out. Very stringent due-process protections must be afforded to any individual facing expulsion. Given that schooling has come to be defined as a basic right, youngsters facing expulsion essentially enjoy all the constitutional protections afforded any adult citizen. Expulsion is such a serious matter that only rarely can the final decision be made by a teacher or a principal. Ordinarily, once all due-process safeguards have been observed and overwhelming evidence seems to support the action, a final decision is made by the school board.

Due Process

Several references have been made during the discussion in this chapter to "due process." Although most people have a general feeling that due process is designed to ensure some kind of fair treatment in an adversary situation, the specific implications of due process are less well known.

In general, due process involves two basic components. The first, the substantive component, is the basic set of principles on which due process is based. The second, or procedural, consists of the procedures that must be followed to ensure that due-process rights have not been violated.

The Substantive Component

With the great emphasis placed on preserving the due-process rights of youngsters when they have been charged with important breaches of school rules and regulations, it is essential for teachers to be familiar with the fundamental principles associated with due process. The substantive component of due process can be thought of as including the following principles:

1. Individuals are not to be disciplined on the basis of unwritten rules.
2. Rules are not to be vague.
3. Individuals are entitled to a hearing before an impartial tribunal.
4. The identity of witnesses is to be revealed.
5. Decisions are to be supported by substantial evidence.
6. The hearing can be public or private, depending on the wishes of the accused.

In times past, educators tended to overlook a number of these principles. For example, some administrators failed to specify rules out of a fear that a set of written regulations would undermine their flexibility in responding to problem situations. Furthermore, many rules and regulations that *were* written were couched in such vague terms that an individual could not in every case judge whether he or she was in compliance.

In the days when the courts were not insisting on due-process guarantees for school children, there was a general reluctance to release the names of the witnesses to the individual accused of being in violation of school rules or regulations. There was a fear that such a release might lead to the intimidation of witnesses and might prevent people from coming forward with information in future cases.

There is little doubt that the growing insistence that schools protect youngsters' due-process rights has increased the work of school administrators and has reduced their flexibility to a degree. On the other hand, given the amount of documentation that now must support charges, probably there has been a healthy reduction in the number of miscarriages of justice in cases involving school youngsters and school authorities.

The Procedural Component

The procedural component of due process attends to the procedures that are to be followed to ensure that principles of due process will be observed. In general, the procedural component of due process includes the following set of actions:

1. Rules governing learners' behavior are to be distributed in writing to learners and their parents at the beginning of the school year.
2. Whenever a learner has been accused of breaking rules that might result in a due-process procedure, the charges must be provided in writing to the learner and to his or her parents.
3. Written notice of the hearing must be given with sufficient time provided for the learner and his or her representatives to prepare a defense. Usually the hearing must be held within two weeks.
4. A fair hearing must be held that includes the following:
   a. Right of the accused to be represented by legal counsel.
   b. Right to present a defense and to introduce evidence.
   c. Right to face accusers.
   d. Right to cross-examine witnesses.
   (Usually, it is recommended that adults who are unfamiliar with the situation sit as members of the hearing board. In addition, a transcript of the hearing is to be prepared.)
5. The decision of the hearing board is to be based on the evidence presented and is to be rendered within a reasonable period of time.
6. The accused is to be informed of his or her right to appeal the decision.

These procedures require a heavy investment of time by school administrators and teachers. Their very complexity probably has done a good deal to ensure that fewer capricious charges will be made against youngsters in the schools than were made in the days before due-process procedures had to be followed. Given the necessity to show evidence, provide witnesses, and be cross-examined by a youngster's attorney, it is clear that those cases that do go forward involve situations that are serious and well documented.

Marriage and Pregnancy

In addition to the interest in ensuring due process for youngsters charged with violations of school rules and regulations, there has been an additional effort in recent years to determine the legitimacy of specific school rules and regulations. Rules relating to pregnant youngsters have come under a great deal of scrutiny.

Until relatively recent times, schools routinely excluded pregnant youngsters, whether married or unmarried. One rationale for these policies was that teenage marriage ought to be discouraged and that the presence in

Box 17-3
Due Process and Problem Youngsters in Schools

In recent years, because courts have tended to define public education as a "right" rather than a "privilege," youngsters have come increasingly under the protection of the "due process" clause of the Constitution. This has meant that they are entitled to the same protections afforded an adult citizen when faced with a charge of a violation of a rule or regulation. For example, they have to be provided with a formal statement of charges, be provided a hearing to present counter evidence, be given an opportunity to face and cross examine witnesses, be afforded an option of engaging an attorney to represent them, and be provided a number of other protections to preserve due process rights.

LET'S PONDER

Read the paragraph above and respond to the following questions.

1. Some have said the courts' insistence on due process rights for learners has tied the hands of administrators. Because of the need for due process protection, principals are very reluctant to do anything about problem youngsters in the schools, it is alleged. How do you react to these allegations? On what do you base your reactions?
2. Others argue that extension of due process rights to school children has been the best thing ever to happen to education. For the first time, it is argued, youngsters do not feel they will be treated in an arbitrary or capricious manner. Consequently, attention to youngsters' due process rights has led to a reduction of problems in schools between learners and school authorities. How do you react to this position? On what is your reaction based?
3. Some people when they first read about "due process" in the schools say, "it certainly doesn't work that way in the school district I live in." How can it be that the courts generally have insisted on the provision of due process protection and yet, in some places, school officials do not seem to have paid any heed? What kinds of districts are likely to be most responsive to these court decisions? Least responsive?
4. Ten years from now, would you expect to see an extension or a reduction in the emphasis on learners' due process rights? Why?

school of pregnant married girls would promote an unhealthy interest in early matrimony. Some also felt that married girls might be prone to talk with others about the more intimate aspects of their relationship with their mates and have a "morally corrupting" influence on other youngsters. Of course, the moral-corruption argument was used, too, to rationalize the exclusion of unmarried pregnant girls from school.

In recent years, the courts have been moving in the direction of protecting the rights of all learners to complete an education. There has been a tendency

FUNKY WINKERBEAN

by Tom Batiuk

(Funky Winkerbean by Tom Batiuk. © 1973, Field Enterprises, Inc. Courtesy of Field Newspaper Syndicate.)

to suggest that school policies denying school attendance privileges to pregnant girls undermine their potential to develop the competencies needed to support themselves and their dependent children. Though practices still vary widely, most districts make provisions for pregnant girls to attend school today.

In general, the courts have taken the position that unless a school district can prove that the individual in question is morally corrupt and a detrimental influence on others, there is no basis for exclusion on the grounds of pregnancy. It has been held reasonable, however, for a pregnant learner to provide notification of pregnancy to her school administrator and to provide regular health statements from her doctor certifying that she is healthy enough to continue in school.

Freedom of Speech and Expression

A number of court cases have been filed focusing on freedom of speech and expression. The rule that the courts have followed in determining whether freedom of speech and expression may be abridged by school authorities seems to be that abridgment is proper only when such speech or expression can be shown to result in some serious disruption of the learning process.

For example, in one case, a school regulation banning the wearing of protest messages by youngsters was challenged. In this situation, because administrators and other witnesses were able to cite a number of specific incidences of violent disruptions involving fights between different ideological factions in the school, the court let the school regulation stand. The wearing of messages had been shown to be interfering with the school program, and the rule was regarded as a legitimate exercise of administrative authority.

A number of cases have focused on the rights of expression of youngsters writing in school newspapers and journals. Generally, student publications enjoy the same legal protections as the adult press. Numerous cases have come to court involving attempts of administrators to suppress the publication or distribution of school papers or journals because of the alleged use of "improper" language. Generally the rule here, too, has been one of establishing a convincing connection between the contents of the newspaper or journal and some documented disruption of the educational process. It is legal for administrators to screen content, provided they can prove that this screening is necessary to prevent disruption and that it is not simply used to suppress content that might prove politically embarrassing to the school.

A number of cases have been adjudicated concerning the school's right to prescribe the dress styles and hairstyles of youngsters. A review of the decisions in these cases reveals no single pattern. Some courts have upheld school dress codes and hair standards (these latter usually involve the length of hair for boys). Others have struck them down. Though certainly not a universal pattern, there has been a tendency for the courts to support regulations in this area that seem to be based on concerns about youngsters' health and safety. For example, one state court upheld a requirement that boys working on the lunch lines had either to cut their hair or wear a hair net while on duty. The regulation was upheld because of the possible health danger resulting from particles falling into food from long, uncontrolled hair.

Search and Seizure

The Fourth Amendment of the Constitution protects individuals against unreasonable searches and seizures. Since justices in the *Tinker* case decided that learners do "not leave their constitutional rights at the schoolroom door," courts have been challenged to further define the limits on school authorities to engage in activities that might be deemed search and seizure. Among issues that have come to court are those involving searches of lockers, desks, purses, wallets, automobiles, and learners' physical persons.

Court cases in this general area have not resulted in clear guidelines for school authorities. There has been, however, a trend for courts to consider the typical "expectation of privacy" an individual might associate with the place where he or she is either searched or seized. Some courts have held that learners have little expectation of privacy at school. Where this view has been taken, courts have tended to support the authority of school officials to engage in search activities.

Another issue the courts have considered is the "intrusiveness" of the search (Baker, 1982). For example, a strip search (a personal search where a learner is asked to remove all of his or her clothing) is very intrusive. Some courts have argued that such searches unconstitutionally infringe on learners' privacy rights. On the other hand, a desk search is not nearly so intrusive. Hence, some courts have been inclined to support school authorities who have sought to search desks.

Two general principles govern the right to search. These are "probable cause" and "reasonable suspicion." Probable cause means that suspicion of wrongdoing is sufficiently strong for a reasonable person to believe that a party is guilty of illegal behavior. Often "probable cause" requires the testimony of a reliable witness. Probable cause normally is required before authorities will issue a search warrant. Probable cause is a very strict standard. Today, only Louisiana requires it as a necessary condition before school searches are permitted.

Reasonable suspicion is a much less stringent standard. Reasonable suspicion requires only that there be some reasonable suspicion that someone is guilty of an offense. Typically, this is the standard that is applied when it is necessary to decide whether a search by school authorities is appropriate.

In summary, case law in the area of search and seizure does not provide clear-cut guidelines to educators. Given this situation, teachers probably should not attempt searches on their own initiative. Though their motives

---

Box 17-4
Hair Length and Dress Codes

The Supreme Court has never provided a definitive decision in a case involving hair length of males in public school classroom or in a case involving proper school attire. Consequently, regulations in these areas tend to vary widely. Some state courts have held on one side of these issues. Some state courts have held on the other side of these issues. No final solution seems in sight at this time.

LET'S PONDER

Read the short paragraph above and then respond to the following questions:

1. Should schools have strict regulations relating to dress and male hair length? Why, or why not?
2. Did schools you attended have such regulations? How were they received? How did you feel about them?
3. Should school people spend their time worrying about dress codes and male hair length? Why, or why not?
4. Courts seem to be judging many school rules and regulations in terms of whether such regulations are essential to the smooth functioning of the educational process. In your view, are dress codes and regulations relating to make hair length necessary to prevent disruption of the school program? Why, or why not?
5. What would you expect to see happening over the next 25 years to dress codes and male hair length requirements? Why do you expect such a trend to develop?

may be exemplary, they may find themselves in serious legal difficulties. Responsibility for initiating search activities should be left in the hands of school administrators. Administrators are in a position to check their legal position by calling upon legal counsel retained by the school district.

Grades, Diplomas, and Graduation

Not long ago, a high school teacher was called to the office of her school, where she was confronted by a student, the student's parents, and an attorney. They had come to inform her that they were initiating legal proceedings to challenge the grade that the student had received in her class. Fortunately this individual was able to document the basis for the award of the grade. Teachers who have less meticulous record-keeping habits might have found themselves in a very embarrassing position.

It should not be inferred from this episode, however, that the courts have proved themselves eager to get into questions involving the grading of youngsters in schools. Indeed, courts generally have been reluctant to hear such cases and to substitute their judgment for that of the teacher, but where such cases have been heard, there has been an insistence that the teacher provide some kind of objective criteria as a basis for grading. The need for objective criteria points up the necessity of teachers' developing an objective grading system and maintaining data to support the grading decision they make.

In addition to grading, another interesting area that has been subject to some litigation in recent years concerns school rules denying the award of graduation certificates, diplomas, or degrees for reasons not associated with academic performance. For example, some schools have had rules requiring that all library fines be paid before a diploma can be given. Generally the courts have held that graduation certificates, diplomas, and degrees cannot be withheld for disciplinary reasons or for nonpayment of fees, including fines. In the case of colleges and universities, however, individuals owing money can be prevented from registering for additional courses until such fees are paid.

Family Educational Rights and Privacy

Beginning in the 1960s and continuing into the 1980s, there has been a growing concern over the potential misuse of records of all kinds. With regard to school records, there was a feeling that a youngster who had had personal difficulties with a teacher in the elementary grades may have been stigmatized throughout his or her school career by a set of school records that introduced him or her to new teachers as a "troublemaker." This concern resulted in the passage of the Family Educational Rights and Privacy Act in 1974.

This act required that schools provide parents free access to any records on their youngsters. Furthermore, learners over age eighteen or students in postsecondary schools could view these records themselves. The act also places restrictions on schools regarding the distribution of these records. In times past, schools had customarily released these records on request to government agencies, law-enforcement agencies, and others. Because the dissemination of records without the knowledge or permission of a youngster (or his or her parents) could result in a distorted picture of that youngster, records may now be released only after very strict guidelines have been met.

The act provides that if parents or an eligible student makes a request to inspect school records, the school must respond within a reasonable period of time, usually within forty-five days. Furthermore, if requested to provide such an individual, the school must make available someone capable of explaining and interpreting the records. After an inspection of the records, a parent or an eligible student may request to amend the record if it is believed to be (1) inaccurate, (2) misleading, or (3) in violation of privacy rights. If this request is denied, a hearing may be requested. If the request is denied by the hearing board, the parent or eligible student may have a statement placed in the file disagreeing with the information perceived as being objectionable.

This act has implications for future teachers as they seek out initial teaching positions. Usually, in preparing placement papers for teacher candidates, people at the college or university placement center will ask whether individuals wish to have an "open" file or a "closed" file. If an open file is chosen, then the candidate has the right to read everything that goes into the file, including recommendations. On the other hand, if a closed file is chosen, the candidate waives his or her right to see what goes into it. Individuals writing recommendations are usually notified by the placement center whether a candidate has opted for an open file or a closed file. Some professors and others who write recommendations hestitate to provide them to undergraduates who have opted for an open file. Furthermore, some district personnel people tend to look differently at placement papers that are open and those that are closed. Rightly or wrongly, many feel that they get a more honest appraisal of a candidate's strengths and weaknesses in a closed file.

Curriculum and Instruction

School curricula and school instructional practices, though subject to a good deal of public scrutiny and discussion, have not been so frequently tied to the issue of learners' rights as have some of the other topics discussed in this chapter. Generally the courts have been very cautious about attempting to make judgments that place the legal system in the position of taking a stand on educators' traditional prerogatives to determine what constitutes responsible behavior in the areas of curriculum and instruction. Though court cases centering on these areas have not been numerous in the past, public demands for accountability may result in more suits in the future.

Box 17-5
The Impact of Open Records Legislation on Employment Practices

Open records legislation has been a giant step backward for the principle of equity. Strangely, these laws, by intent, were designed to preserve equity. Regrettably, despite these worthy intentions, the effect of their passage has been a net reduction of equity or fairness in employment practices. This is particularly true with regard to the employment of new teachers.

When future teachers establish their placement papers on an "open file" basis, employers recognize that the individual establishing the file may read everything in it. Furthermore, people writing recommendations for this person generally are alerted that their comments are going to be placed in an "open file." This results in either (1) a recommendation couched in such vague terms that the potential employer can make no reasoned decision about qualifications of the candidate, (2) a glowing recommendation including no reference whatever to weak points, or (3) a refusal to write a recommendation at all.

Given the lack of solid information in many such files, employers have had to turn to alternative ways of getting details regarding teacher candidates. This need has resulted in a reactivation of the deplorable "old boy" network. Essentially what happens is that employers get on the phone and try to contact someone who might have some real knowledge of the candidate and who is willing to talk "off the record" on the phone. Clearly this may result in a good deal of unrepresentative information about a candidate flowing to the employer. Some good people may be denied teacher positions because of this practice.

One reason professional files of a closed nature were established originally was to combat potential abuses of the "old boy" network. Ironically, recent open records legislation has led to a return to the very practice credentials files were created to replace. These laws should be replaced, at least so far as they apply to teacher placement files. The best protection for the teacher looking for a position is a credentials file where those preparing recommendations are confident in the security of their comments.

LET'S PONDER

Read the paragraphs above and respond to the following questions:

1. What is your general reaction to the position stated above? Why?
2. In particular, how do you react to the argument that "closed files" likely will serve the individual looking for a position better than "open files?" Why?
3. Is there anything really wrong with the "old boy" network system of identifying candidates' strengths and weaknesses? Why, or why not?
4. How would you feel if asked to recommend someone for an "open file" set of placement papers as opposed to a "closed file" set of placement papers?

One important challenge that has been brought in the curriculum and instruction area has related to allegations of sex bias. Traditionally, many courses and activities were open only to learners of one sex. For example, in many schools, auto mechanics courses were reserved for male students and home economics courses for female students. Court challenges of such practices have eliminated most sex-based barriers to enrollment in school courses.

An issue that is of great concern to educators today is "educational malpractice." A number of suits have taken teachers and school districts to court on the grounds that learners did not learn. These cases have generated a tremendous amount of interest among professional educators and the lay public as well. So far, the courts have generally held that schools do have an obligation to provide learning opportunities in a defensible way, but that they are not responsible for the actual learning a given individual takes away from his or her exposure to these opportunities. This conclusion seems to be premised on the view that too many variables beyond the control of the teachers and the schools influence whether a youngster profits from instruction. It must a recognized, however, that this issue is anything but dead. Many more court cases centering on the educational malpractice issue may be anticipated in the future.

Recapitulation of Major Ideas

1. Traditionally the doctrine of *in loco parentis* governed relationships between school authorities and youngsters in the schools. According to this doctrine, the school, legally, acted "in place of the parent." In recent years, this doctrine has largely been undercut by a series of court decisions. There has been a tendency to extend to youngsters in the schools the full protection afforded to adult citizens under the U.S. Constitution.

2. Over time, there has been a shift from viewing education as a "privilege" to viewing education as a "right." In part, the change in perspective has arisen because of a feeling that a public education is necessary for productive survival in a technological society.

3. With the redefinition of school youngsters as individuals whose rights enjoy many constitutional protections, there has come a heavy emphasis on protection of the due-process privileges of youngsters who are charged with violating school regulations. These due-process protections, though adding some complexity to the work of responsible school officials, provide some assurance that charges and actions against youngsters will not be taken in an arbitrary and capricious manner.

4. Court actions and recent federal legislation have gone together to ensure that every youngster in the schools will be afforded an opportunity for a free and appropriate education. Schools can no longer exclude youngsters merely because they have learning problems or handicapping conditions that are difficult to accommodate.

5. A number of suits have been brought because of actions that schools have taken to suspend or expel youngsters. In general, there must be strict adherence to procedures that protect the due-process rights of the youngsters involved. A sub-area of interest in this category has to do with the status of pregnant learners. In general, the courts have ruled that a school cannot use pregnancy as the sole criterion for excluding a youngster from school.

6. In suits relating to freedom of speech and other categories relating to learners' rights, the court has said that the school may impose and enforce regulations that preserve the integrity of the educational process. If challenged on these regulations, the school must be prepared to demonstrate that a violation will substantially disrupt the educational process.

7. There has been a great concern about the privacy of records in recent years. Court cases and federal legislation have greatly restricted what schools may and may not do with records. Generally, parents and youngsters over age eighteen have the right to demand access to school records and to question comments included therein. There also are restrictions on school officials related to the distribution of such records to other potentially interested parties.

8. An emerging area of litigation centers on the theme of "educational malpractice." To this point, the courts have held that school districts and teachers cannot be held liable for the failure of a given individual to learn. The logic underpinning these decisions has been that too many variables beyond the control of the school contribute to the learning or to the nonlearning of a given individual. More suits in this area may be anticipated in the years ahead.

Posttest

DIRECTIONS: Using your own paper, answer each of the following true/false questions. For each correct statement, write the word *true* on your paper. For each incorrect statement, write the word *false* on your paper.

1. Schools may pass whatever rules they deem necessary regarding learners' behavior without having to worry about rights guaranteed to adults by the U.S. Constitution.

2. Today most court cases involving learners' rights tend to strengthen the *in loco parentis* principle.

3. Schools cannot deny a child an education because of behavioral problems, learning problems, or handicapping conditions.

4. *Suspension* and *expulsion* are different words for the same thing.

5. Learners, because of their rights to due process, have a right to legal counsel in many hearings related to an alleged violation of school rules.

6. A girl may be suspended or expelled from school because she is pregnant.
7. In many cases, school officials have the right to search learners' lockers without permission.
8. At one time, many people regarded attendance at a public school as a *privilege*. Today there is a tendency to view a public education as a *right*.
9. Under the Family Educational Rights and Privacy Act, parents have a right to review the school's records of their children.
10. School administrators enjoy an absolute right to control the contents of school newspapers and other school publications.

Summary

In recent years, the traditional view of schools as acting *in loco parentis* ("in place of the parent") in their relationships with youngsters has been breaking down. Part of this change has resulted from a perception that today the completion of an educaton has become a necessity. Consequently schooling has come to be viewed as a *right* rather than a *privilege*. Courts have tended to extend to youngsters in the school many of the protections of the U.S. Constitution formerly reserved for adult citizens. Many student rights cases have been litigated, and a clear trend has emerged in support of the view that youngsters in schools do, indeed, enjoy many constitutional protections.

In general, school leaders have been forced to seriously delimit the scope of rules and regulations applying to the youngsters under their charge. In general, the courts have insisted that school representatives demonstrate how any violation of rules and regulations constitutes a severe threat to the educational process. When such a threat has been demonstrated to the satisfaction of the courts, the school rules and regulations have been allowed to stand. When no such connection has been made, the school rules have been declared an unconstitutional infringement of learners' rights.

Reference

BAKER, KELLEY. "An Overview of the Law Regarding Search and Seizure in Public Schools." In Thomas N. Jones and Darel P. Semler, (eds). *School Law Update-1982*. Topeka, Kansas: National Organization on Legal Problems in Education, 1983.
Baker v. *Owens*, 423 U.S. 907 [1975].
CONNORS, EUGENE T. *Student Discipline and the Law*. Bloomington, Ind. Phi Delta Kappa Educational Foundation, 1979.
Dixon v. *Alabama State Board of Education*, 294 F. 2d 150 (1961).
Doe v. *Renfrow*, 475 F. Supp. 1012 [N.D. Ind. 1979].
FISCHER, LOUIS AND SCHIMMEL, DAVID. *The Rights of Students and Teachers* New York: Harper and Row, 1982.

HAMMES, RICHARD R. "In Loco Parentis: Considerations in Teacher/Student Relationships." *Clearing House* (Summer 1982): 8–11.

HAZARD, WILLIAM R. *Education and the Law,* 2nd ed. New York: The Free Press, 1978.

HENSON, KENNETH T. "Emerging Student Rights." *Journal of Teacher Education* (July/Aug., 1979): 33–34.

HOOKER, CLIFFORD P. (Ed). *The Courts and Education.* The Seventy-seventh Yearbook of the National Society for the Study of Education. Chicago: University of Chicago Press, 1978.

MENACKER, JULIUS, AND PASCARELLA, ERNEST. How Aware are Educators of Supreme Court Decisions that Affect Them?" *Phi Delta Kappan* (Feb., 1983): 424–426.

State v. *McKinnon* (88 Wash. 2d 75, 558 P. 2d, 784 [Wash. 1977]).

STAUB, FREDERICK W. "What Would Ernie Say Is Fair?" *Theory Into Practice* (Oct., 1978): 329–332.

Tinker v. *Des Moines Independent Community School District,* 343 U.S. 503 [1961].

18
The Extracurricular/ Cocurricular Program

Objectives

This chapter provides information to help the reader to

1. Suggest the general role of the extracurricular/cocurricular program in the schools.
2. Describe examples of the extracurricular/cocurricular activities typically found at different grade levels.
3. Point out several teachers' roles in the extracurricular/cocurricular program.
4. Discuss general trends relating to remuneration of teachers for their involvement in extracurricular/cocurricular activities.
5. Describe the relative attractiveness of different kinds of extracurricular/cocurricular activities to the general population of learners.
6. Suggest the reasons that learners seek involvement in extracurricular/cocurricular activities.
7. Point out how learners' perceptions of extracurricular/cocurricular activities compare with objectives of extracurricular/cocurricular activities developed by professional educators.
8. Note potential problems relating to balancing the time that learners spend in the academic program and in extracurricular/cocurricular activities.

Pretest

DIRECTIONS: Using your own paper, answer each of the following true/false questions. For each correct statement, write the word *true* on your paper. For each incorrect statement, write the word *false* on your paper.

1. Most learners who involve themselves in extracurricular/cocurricular activities do so because they find fun and personal enjoyment.
2. There is likely to be a greater variety of extracurricular/cocurricular activities in a high school than in an elementary school.
3. "Development of citizenship" has been an argument used by educators to defend the inclusion of extracurricular/cocurricular activities in the schools.
4. Administrators have sometimes been concerned about the possibility that extracurricular/cocurricular activities take time away from the academic aspects of the school program.
5. It is more common for secondary-school teachers than elementary-school teachers to receive some pay for helping with extracurricular/cocurricular activities.
6. In high schools, students who work tend to participate less frequently in extracurricular/cocurricular activities than those who do not work.

7. In most schools, the extracurricular/cocurricular program is regarded as a legitimate extension of the academic program and a proper responsibility of the school.
8. There is little correlation between the interest and enthusiasm of a teacher sponsoring an activity and the interest and enthusiasm of the youngsters participating in the activity.
9. Of all youngsters participating in extracurricular/cocurricular activities, a very high percentage are involved only because they want to "serve the school."
10. The success of most extracurricular/cocurricular activities today can be attributed to certification standards that require special courses for nearly all teachers in managing the extracurricular/cocurricular program.

Introduction

The activities programs in American schools represent a feature of the educational system that is not found in all countries. The clubs, social organizations, and other groups that exist within the school testify to a conviction that education embraces more than simply academics. Although there certainly are exceptions, most educators today support the general idea that the activity program "belongs" in American education. However, there is debate over the relative emphasis on school activities as opposed to academics.

Those who see the activity program as less central to the main purposes of education and who see academics as much more important have generally preferred the term *extracurricular* activities. This term implies that, although legitimate, the activities program is basically something extra that the school makes available to learners over and above the academic subjects. Another group of educators contends that what learners take away from involvement in activities may be as important to them as what they learn in their academic classes. These people tend to see activities as "educational" in and of themselves. They prefer the term *cocurricular,* which implies that the activities program enjoys an important status and that it should not be regarded simply as an extra that has been added to the academic program.

Within any school, there are likely to be teachers favoring the extracurricular activites view and teachers favoring the cocurricular activities view. But regardless of how they are viewed, evidence suggests that there is little variation in the actual kinds of activities offered from school to school. Thus, as our focus is to be on the activities themselves, in this chapter the general term *extracurricular/cocurricular activities* will be used in our discussion of the activity program. The reader should keep in mind that in some schools, it might be a more common practice to refer to activities as *extracurricular* and others as *cocurricular,* but that this terminology does not imply any differences in the nature of the activities themselves.

Today extracurricular/cocurricular activities are found at all levels of public education. The kinds of activities vary with the ages and interests of the youngsters being served. Generally, the range of activities available increases as youngsters grow older. Typically high schools have much more extensively developed extracurricular/cocurricular programs than do elementary schools.

In the sections that follow, extracurricular/cocurricular programs are examined in terms of their problems versus their benefits. Additionally, the connections between teachers' interest and teachers' preparation and the success of the activities program are explored. Some considerations of the range of activities typically available at various grade levels is also provided.

Kinds of Extracurricular/Cocurricular Programs

In a very general sense, extracurricular/cocurricular programs can be thought of as varying along a continuum. At one end of the continuum are those activities that bear a direct relationship to the academic program. For example, science clubs frequently engage in activities that enrich learners' understanding of the topics introduced in regular science classes. At the other end of the continuum are activities that bear little or no direct relationship to the academic program. For example, members of the school pep club rarely get together to engage in activities that represent a direct extension of their work in the classroom. Their activities tend to be more social than academic.

In general, there is a tendency for extracurricular/cocurricular programs for younger learners to include a higher percentage of activities bearing some relationship to the academic program than is true of extracurricular/cocurricular programs for older learners. This tendency reflects the broadening horizons of older youngsters, whose needs run across a wider spectrum than those of elementary-school youngsters. These differences are reflected in the patterns of activities generally made available to the youngsters in elementary schools, junior high schools, and senior high schools.

Elementary Schools

Elementary-school youngsters require a good deal more direct adult supervision in the extracurricular/cocurricular program than do older youngsters. This reality places some limits on the number of such activities that can be offered in the elementary school. The number of activities cannot exceed the number of adults available to supervise them.

In addition to the question of supervision, there is another constraint on the elementary extracurricular/cocurricular program that is not typically found in the secondary school. Elementary-school youngsters are either in class, at recess, or eating lunch for the entire time they are at school. Unlike secondary-school students, elementary youngsters usually have no "free period" during the day when they might be involved in the extracurricular/cocurricular program, so that these activities have to be made available either before school or after school. This constraint places a burden on youngsters who live at some distance from the school and who must depend on the school bus for transportation. Frequently they do not have time to participate in activities either before school or after school.

Elementary-school activity programs generally tend to be closely connected with the regular program of courses. Frequently there are "clubs" organized to provide enrichment experiences for youngsters in such areas as art, science, and music. A number of schools involve children in creative dramatics as an adjunct to their language arts and reading training. Boys and girls of this age particularly enjoy opportunities to participate in organized games and other physical activities that might be thought of as logical extensions of the physical education program. Some school librarians organize groups of "library helpers" who engage in simple record-keeping and management tasks.

As noted earlier, elementary activities programs demand a good deal of adult supervision. In many districts, parent volunteers have been willing to spend some time working with youngsters both before and after school. In other places, the districts have employed paraprofessionals to supervise youngsters in various extracurricular/cocurricular activities. In spite of these efforts, the heavy dependence of these programs on the availability of adults to supervise the activities has tended to make the size of the extracurricular/cocurricular program in elementary schools relatively modest compared with those in secondary schools.

Middle Schools and Junior High Schools

Practices in middle schools and junior high schools vary enormously. In part, this diversity reflects the lack of consensus regarding whether middle schools and junior high schools ought to be organized more like elementary schools or more like high schools. Activity patterns in those organized more along elementary-school lines, not surprisingly, tend to be more similar to those found in elementary schools. As might be expected, those organized more along the lines of the senior high schools tend to feature extracurricular/cocurricular programs very reminiscent of those found in the high school.

Regardless of how they are organized, middle schools and junior high schools generally provide a wider array of extracurricular/cocurricular activities than do elementary schools, partly because of the widening interest of youngsters who are entering early adolescence, and partly because of scheduling patterns that tend to provide teachers with some time during the day to work with students outside of scheduled classroom activities. Teachers' planning periods are a much more common feature in middle schools and junior high schools than in elementary schools. In many schools, teachers devote at least some of their preparation time each week to working with student clubs and organizations.

Though patterns vary a good deal from school to school, there is a general tendency to handle a good deal of the extracurricular/cocurricular program in middle schools and junior high schools during the regular school day. This practice has several advantages. Students of this age do not have personal transportation. Consequently, because of their dependency on their parents and on various busing arrangments, many would be unable to participate in activities taking place after school hours. Therefore it is common for the student council and many other groups to have meetings during the school day. Some schools even provide a regularly scheduled "activity" period, during which all youngsters are encouraged to get involved in a school project or organization.

Supervision by adults is a real concern with active middle-school and junior-high-school youngsters. Activities held during the day at school can generally be organized in such a way that faculty, paraprofessional, or other adult supervision can be provided.

In general, extracurricular/cocurricular programs in middle schools and junior high schools represent a transitional phase between elementary-school and senior-high-school practices. Many activities continue to bear a close relationship to the academic program, but during these years, increasing number of activities of a more purely social nature begin to attract youngsters' interest.

High Schools

In most school districts, the extracurricular/cocurricular program reaches its highest state of evolution in the senior high schools. This is a natural reflection of the maturation process and the broadening interests of youngsters during their last public-school years. Not only are their interests broad during these years, but their social maturity, particularly during the junior and senior years, advances to the point where the students themselves can provide a good deal of leadership for the various activities in the school. Indeed, in many groups, adults play a role that is purely advisory. The great bulk of the decision-making responsibilities is borne by student leaders.

In high schools, a good number of extracurricular/cocurricular activities do not take place during the regular school day. Older youngsters frequently have their own cars, borrow those belonging to their parents, or find rides with friends. There is much less dependence on adults for getting to meetings and events that take place during the evening hours.

In general, the high school is a more supportive environment for the development of new extracurricular/cocurricular activities than the middle school, junior high school, or elementary school. Such activities tend to be much less demanding on adult time. Although adults continue to be involved, the level

FUNKY WINKERBEAN

by Tom Batiuk

(Funky Winkerbean by Tom Batiuk. © 1980, Field Enterprises, Inc. Courtesy of Field Newspaper Syndicate.)

of maturity of high school students tends to make this involvement much less intense and demanding than is the case when groups of younger children must be supervised. Furthermore, many high schools provide some monetary compensation for those faculty members who take charge of particularly large and active student groups. Finally, as has been noted, the students themselves are able to exercise a much higher level of personal leadership in the high school activity program than can be expected of younger children.

Because of the congeniality of the high school setting to the development of the activity program, the range of activities at a single school can be simply astounding. A quick review of almost any high school yearbook in the country will reveal page after page of photographs of students belonging to groups of every description. Indeed, were we to count the pages devoted to clubs and activities and those devoted to academics, we might well conclude that the activities program was what school was all about and that the "real" extra-curricular/cocurricular program is the academic program. Some critics have made just this observation. Given the proliferation of activities at the high school level, it is not surprising that where the extracurricular/cocurricular program has come under attack, the target has almost always been the program as it exists at the high school level. In the next section, we take a look at some of the criticisms of that program.

Criticisms of the Extracurricular/Cocurricular Program

Probably the strongest general criticism of the activities program is the allegation that it gives youngsters a false sense of priorities. Critics suggest that the allure of some activities is so strong that students all too willingly trade off important study time to pursue them. Particularly insidious, so some crit-

Box 18-1
Activities and Appropriate Age Levels

Look at the following list of school activities:

Butterfly Collectors Club
Football Boosters
Fly-Tying Club
Canoeing Club
Spirit Club
Chess Club
Photography Club
French Club
Future Teachers of America Club
Science Experimenters Club
Shortwave Listeners Club
Reading Club
Good Citizens Club
Playground Clean-Up Club
Dance Planning Committee
Distributive Education Clubs of America Chapter
Future Farmers of America

How would you answer these questions:

1. Which of the above activities would you be most likely to find in an elementary school?
2. Which of the above activities would you be most likely to find in a middle school or junior high school?
3. Which of the above activities would you be most likely to find in a high school?
4. Which of the above activities would require the most intensive adult supervision? Why? The least intensive adult supervision? Why?
5. Would you expect any differences in the above list if you were looking at activities from a school district in a rural area? A suburban area? An urban area? What might account for these differences?
6. If you had a chance to serve as a faculty sponsor for one of these activities, what would you choose? (If you don't like any of these on the list, suggest one of your own. Tell why you would like to sponsor this group.)

ics contend, are those activities that appear to be extensions of the regular academic program. These activities may *seem* to be promoting the development of academic talent, but, say the critics, though they may be good for the school's public relations and for the student's personal pride, they provide no serious intellectual challenges at all.

Activities that have come in for a good deal of criticism include those associated with athletics and with speech and debate. Although few deny that physical education is a necessary and proper part of the curriculum, critics point out that in some cases, the athletic program is mounted more to please the public than to educate the participating youngsters. Other, less costly physical conditioning programs could be installed, critics say, that would involve more youngsters and be more "educationally relevant" to the task of promoting physical growth and development. Similar arguments are frequently raised against speech and debate programs. Critics suggest that too much time is spent in practicing to win various contests and competitions and not enough in mastering the related academic material.

In addition to the problems that an overemphasis on some activities might pose for the students who are involved, the extracurricular/cocurricular program has been charged with adding to the heavy public relations problems of school administrators. Critics point to difficulties both within the school itself and with the local community.

With regard to personnel in the school, it must be noted that teachers and other school staff members are by no means in agreement on the value of each of the various activities included in the extracurricular/cocurricular program. Because activities are more diverse and numerous in high schools, the problems in staff relationships stemming from disagreements about the activity program are most pronounced at this level. Teachers are particularly sensitive about individual activity programs that result in (1) student absences from their classes, or (2) changed daily schedules resulting in a reduction of time for individual class periods.

Activity-associated student absences can bring the wrath of a good many teachers down on the principal and his assistants and on the teacher or teachers who act as sponsors of the "offending" activity. Principals frequently find their public relations skills taxed to the limit as they attempt to reconcile the differences among teachers who see no reason for justifying a class absence and teachers who support the activity in question and suggest that it might have a good deal of educational relevance for the youngsters involved.

A variant of the class-absence debate is the argument that rages in many schools over whether time is properly expended when daily class schedules are altered (usually resulting in shorter class periods) to permit students to attend assemblies, pep rallies, and other acitivities during regular school hours. Some teachers are particularly unhappy if administrators adopt a policy of scheduling events in such a way that one class period gets shortened more frequently than others. For example, if assemblies are regularly given

Box 18-2
Proper Priorities and School Activities

Jane Smith has won three county tournaments in debate and has placed second in a state tournament. She is a high school junior. Debate is her passion. She spends hours of her time in the public library and at the library of the local community college building sets of evidence cards and adding to her general level of understanding of this year's topic. In a competitive debate situation, she is poised, prepared, and confident. In school last term she received an *A* in debate, a *B+* in English, a *C−* in mathematics, a *C* in physical education, and a *C* in physics. She failed to attend her mathematics classes and her physics classes on ten different days last term. These classes are of little interest to her at this time.

LET'S PONDER

Read the paragraph above. How would you answer these questions?

1. In general, is involvement in the debate program a good thing or a bad thing for Jane? Why?
2. How do you explain the pattern of grades? Is this pattern in any way related to her interest in the debate program?
3. Jane attended the state tournament out of town last year. Is there any justification for students missing school to attend an activity function in another community? Why, or why not?
4. Would your reaction to Jane's involvement in debate be any different if you knew whether (a) she was intending to go to college, (b) she was intending to go to business school after graduating from high school, or (c) she was planning to get married after graduating from high school? If yes, what would your reaction be under each set of conditions?
5. Do you think, in general, Jane's involvement in debate tends to give her generally higher grades in school or generally lower grades? Why?

at the end of the day and most of the time for them is taken from the final period of the day, many teachers with classes meeting at that hour may feel frustrated as they attempt to stay on the instructional schedule they have set up. Significant numbers of such teachers may well feel moved to question the educational values of activity programs that cut severely into their instructional time.

Community relations problems frequently add to administrators' woes in dealing with the activity program in their building. Loud amplified music at dances may prompt angry phone calls from residents living close to the school. Overzealous editorializing by students in the school paper sometimes plants an impression in the minds of school patrons that "incompetence is everywhere." Parents concerned about the selection procedures used in selecting drill team, pep squad, or honors club members consume a good deal of administrators' time. Given the time involved, many administrators have questioned the value of the extracurricular/cocurricular program. Though the frustrations are certainly very real, most have concluded that the benefits of the program tend to outweigh the negatives.

Although some students doubtless do allocate time to activities that might be better spent in academic pursuits, others may get more directly involved in the academic program as a result of participation in the activities program. Certainly, for example, students who become active in science clubs, foreign-language clubs, and other such activities are likely to develop closer working relationships with their teachers and to develop higher levels of interest in those subjects than students who do not participate. Many youngsters, particularly in high schools, come to school with very little initial interest in the academic program. Were it not for the availability of the activity program, a good many would drop out of school. Significant numbers of these young people, in time, do develop an interest in the academic side as well as the activity side of the school program. Interest in athletic teams, on the part of both participants and nonparticipants, has been described as a potent force motivating youngsters who may have few academic interests to stay in school.

In addition to its impact on the attitudes of youngsters, most administrators recognize that the extracurricular/cocurricular program has positive community-relations benefits that generally outweigh the accompanying community-relations problems. Performances by the band at civic functions in the community present a very favorable image for the school. Groups of these generally well-scrubbed and talented youngsters tend to promote the idea that "They're doing a fine job out there at the school." School plays, speech contests, athletic events, and other occasions that bring patrons into close contact with the school support the development of a public feeling of "pride of ownership" in the school and the school district. These favorable impressions become critically important when school money issues are on the ballot. For these reasons, most administrators, though recognizing the inherent problems in activities programs, tend to support them out of a recognition that they have much to do with shaping public perception of how well the school is doing.

How Are Activities Programs Supposed to Benefit Students?

Professional educators have formulated a large number of reasons for including the extracurricular/cocurricular program in public schools. Though varying considerably in their specifics, generally these arguments center on a common theme of enriching the academic side of school life through the

activity program. Proponents have suggested a number of specific benefits alleged to accrue to youngsters who participate in school activities.

Some have suggested that participating in extracurricular/cocurricular activities helps youngsters to become "better citizens." The idea here is that academic courses in schools concentrate largely on fragmented specialties that do not help learners come to grips with the important skills of discussion, compromise, and sensitive interpersonal relations that characterize effective adult citizens. Though the school might have on a shelf somewhere a set of lofty goals suggesting that "good citizenship" is the aim of all school courses, an examination of the courses themselves reveals that little direct teaching of basic citizenship skills goes on. Given this reality, the activities program can be a natural vehicle for teaching youngsters to work together in groups while they learn important decision-making skills. These skills are not taught overtly. Rather, they are acquired as a natural by-product of youngsters' involvement in the activities of their own choice.

Another case that professionals have made for activities programs is that they help youngsters prepare for a vocation. This argument has been made most frequently when activities bearing a close relationship to some part of the academic curriculum have been under discussion. For example, science clubs are thought to help youngsters make a decision to pursue further study in science. Distributive-education clubs provide a forum for students interested in a business career and deal with issues closely related to contents of a good number of regular business-education courses taught as part of the curriculum. Writing clubs stimulate extra effort on the part of youngsters with future interests in journalism or in other professional writing fields. A good number of school activities have been defended on the presumed connection between the activities and youngsters' future vocational roles.

Still another argument for at least some activities programs has been that they give youngsters a larger stake in the operation of the school. Proponents of this view believe this to be a desirable condition in that youngsters who develop strong proprietary feelings about the school are likely to put forth better efforts in their classes as a result of their commitment. Their general level of motivation may well be higher. Activities generally related to school governance have been defended on the ground that they make youngsters more interested in solving the problems of the school because they tend to see the school's problems as their problems. Belief in this premise has resulted in an almost universal establishment of student councils in junior high schools and senior high schools. Many elementary schools have them, too. In the senior high schools, there may be elaborate class-government arrangements as well as schoolwide student councils. Most schools provide abundant opportunities for students to get involved in the legislative process. Whether this involvement really does lead to an increased interest in the problems of the school has never really been established, but actions taken in support of this belief have certainly provided youngsters with an opportunity to gain experience in collective decision-making.

Why Do Students Participate in School Activities?

Perhaps more interesting than the reasons that professionals put forward to explain why youngsters *ought* to become involved in the extracurricular/cocurricular program are the reasons given by youngsters for why they *do* become involved. Buser, Long, and Tweedy (1975) surveyed several thousand high school students regarding their involvement in school activities. Among other questions, these students were asked why they participated. Interestingly, very few students cited the reasons given by professional educators as the reasons that activity programs are important.

Box 18-3
Learners' Attraction to the Activities Program

Assume you were on a committee of teachers in a brand new high school who had been assigned to develop a number of suggested clubs and organizations for students. As a result of your work, you developed a list of potential clubs and organizations. Part of this list is reproduced below:

French Club
Pep Club
Tropical Fish Club
Literary Society
Experimental Science Club
Student Council
Class Councils

LET'S PONDER

Suppose you had the job of encouraging students to participate in these new organizations. Think about what you might do. Respond to these questions:

1. Would you use the same general approach for all of these organizations? What would this approach be?
2. Would you have more difficulty in developing interest in some of these groups than in others? If so, which ones? Why?
3. Excepting the student council and the class councils, these groups might be able to welcome all comers and not be concerned about growing too large. Which of these groups would you expect to grow the largest? Why? Which would you expect to be the smallest organization? Why?
4. If you were making an argument to a student you wanted to enroll in the experimental science club and to a parent of a student who might be thinking about joining, would you use the same line of logic? Why or why not? If not, what would you tell the student? What would you tell the parent?

Over 55 percent of the youngsters surveyed reported that they rated "fun, personal enjoyment" as "extremely important" reasons for participating. On the other hand, only about 19 percent rated "prepare for a vocation" as an "extremely important" reason. "Prepare to become a more effective citizen" was rated as "extremely important" by about 15 percent. Only about 8 percent rated "serve the school" as "extremely important."

Clearly, youngsters have much more immediate interests in mind when making a decision to participate in the activities program than do the professional educators who have speculated on the attractions of the activities program for learners. This finding is generally consistent with psychologists' findings that most people respond more readily to situations promising immediate satisfaction than to situations requiring that satisfactions be delayed.

The results of the survey by Buser, Long, and Tweedy (1975) have important implications for school planners of extracurricular/cocurricular programs. These findings suggest that the extracurricular/cocurricular programs cannot be "sold" to youngsters on the same basis that they might be defended to an audience of adults interested in the "educational" benefits likely to accrue to the youngsters who participate. Although there certainly may be some truly substantial educational benefits, evidence suggests that promoting programs to young people on this basis will bear little fruit. The findings of Buser, Long, and Tweedy would indicate that initial emphases on the recreational aspects of the extracurricular/cocurricular experience generally draw more "recruits" than an approach emphasizing longer-term benefits that— to the youngsters, at least—might not seem to provide much of a prospect for "personal enjoyment."

The Numbers of Learners in Activities Programs

A dilemma that has faced educators who believe that extracurricular/cocurricular programs enrich youngsters' experiences as they go through school has been the failure of these programs to attract very high percentages of learners in a school. Though, particularly at the high school level, every effort has been made to provide an extraordinarily large number of activity options, large numbers of youngsters still do not participate.

Additionally, those that *are* active in the extracurricular/cocurricular program tend to be involved in more than a single activity. This tendency sometimes distorts the picture when someone attempts to determine exactly how many youngsters are being served. It will not do, for example, simply to count the number of members of the chess club, the speech club, the French club, and the pep club to come up with a single total. Many individual students may belong to all four organizations. Thus, although this sort of a count may provide an illusion that large numbers of youngsters are being served, more careful analysis reveals that many fewer individuals are involved.

Another concern has been the kind of youngster attracted to the activity program. Many educators have supported extracurricular/cocurricular activities because of their alleged ability to promote the development of responsibility, to enrich youngsters' academic experiences, and to develop a wide range of "citizenship" skills. There is some question regarding whether these programs tend to attract the students who already have many of these characteristics and fail to attract the students who would most benefit from these activities. Research provides no clear answer to this general concern. However, Buser, Long, and Tweedy (1975) did report a slight positive correlation between higher grade-point averages and the likelihood of active participation in the activity program. This finding would seem to indicate a tendency for youngsters with high grades to be more frequent participants than youngsters with lower grades.

What Keeps Learners from Participating in the Activities Program?

Certainly the diversity among young people in the school is so great that it is probably idle to hope that even the most varied activities program will have something that will interest *every* youngster. But even admitting that we will probably have to settle for less than 100 percent participation, there is still concern that less than an optimal number of learners is being reached.

Not surprisingly, considering that the extracurricular/cocurricular program is larger in high schools than in junior high schools and elementary schools, most systematic investigations of youngsters' involvement in the activities program have been focused on older learners. A number of factors have been cited as tending to limit participation. One of these is access to personal transportation. Even in senior high schools, large numbers of youngsters ride school buses to and from school. Although some of these individuals may have occasional access to their parents' cars or be able to ride with friends, many find it difficult to involve themselves in activities that meet after school. Certainly there are some activities provided during regular school hours, but students with transportation problems find the range of options open to them much more restricted than do students who do not have transportation problems.

A second reason that many older youngsters do not participate is that large numbers of them work. Beginning high-school teachers are sometimes astonished at the large number of students who work twenty, thirty, and even forty hours a week while maintaining their status as full-time students. These young people simply do not have time to play an active role in more than a token number of school activities programs.

Buser, Long, and Tweedy (1975) found that many youngsters feel that

Box 18-4
Levels of Participation in Different School Activities

PERCENTAGES OF STUDENTS PARTICIPATING IN 12 TYPES OF EXTRACLASS ACTIVITY

		Participating		
Activity	Presently %	Formerly %	Never %	Total %
1. Intramural athletics	29.2	23.1	47.7	52.3
2. Class-related clubs	27.2	19.6	53.3	46.8
3. Interscholastic athletics	26.9	17.2	55.9	44.1
4. Music-related activities	22.0	19.9	58.1	41.9
5. Service-related clubs	23.0	18.5	58.6	41.5
6. Dramatics-related activities	16.6	14.7	68.7	31.3
7. School publications	9.7	10.3	80.0	20.0
8. Hobby-/leisure-related clubs	10.9	8.6	80.4	19.5
9. Honor clubs	12.6	4.1	83.3	16.7
10. Student council	6.3	9.1	84.6	12.4
11. Class officer	3.9	10.5	85.6	11.4
12. Cheerleading	3.3	4.9	91.7	8.2

(Table is reprinted with permission from Robert L. Buser, Ruth Long, and Hewey Tweedy. "The Who, What, Why, and Why Not of Student Activity Participation." *Phi Delta Kappan.* (October 1974), p. 125.)

LET'S PONDER   Look at the table above and respond to these questions:

1. How do you explain the popularity of intramural athletics?
2. What constraints are there on student participation that might explain the relatively small percentage of students involved in cheerleading?
3. What changes might be introduced to increase percentages of students participating in acitvities 10, 11, and 12 on the table?
4. If you were to look twenty-five years into the future, would you expect any changes in percentages of youngsters participating in these activities? If so, what would those changes be?

clubs and organizations in the school tend to be dominated by a cliquish "in" group. Though the door to involvement is technically open to all, many learners feel that the welcome mat really is out only to those "approved" by members of a rather close-knit leadership group. The tendency of many of the same youngsters to be active in numerous school organizations gives some credence to the possibility that there may be some bias against youngsters not perceived to be "acceptable" by club and organization leaders. This is an area that deserves some systematic investigation by educators interested in the operation of extracurricular/cocurricular programs.

Some youngsters who do not participate in activities simply do not find any of the options relevant to their own interests. It may be that activities programs are organized by well-intentioned individuals who mistakenly think that they have provided options broad enough to meet all youngsters' interests. Part of the difficulty, too, may relate to discrepancies between what faculty and adult sponsors see as the purpose of various school activities and what learners expect to do as participants in such activities. For example, if a youngster joins the French club thinking that he or she will go to lots of parties or learn how to prepare some interesting pastries and finds out, instead, that the meetings are devoted to members' tedious oral reports on the regions of France, he or she may well feel that the group is irrelevant to his or her needs. Clearly there is a need to find out what youngsters really expect to get out of their involvement in organizations. A simple collection of their favorable or unfavorable opinions about joining a given group will not provide this kind of information.

Finally, there is evidence that the level of learners' involvement in the extracurricular/cocurricular program relates closely to the interest and enthusiasm of the faculty sponsors. When the sponsoring teachers are enthusiastic about the activity, the youngsters involved tend to be enthusiastic. When the teachers simply go through the motions and signal to youngsters that their real interests lie elsewhere, the youngsters' enthusiasm is not kindled. The problem of the teacher's indifference to the activity that he or she is assigned to sponsor is likely when the sponsorship is not voluntary. In most schools, teachers are asked to volunteer for leadership positions. In a few, they are "volunteered" by administrators. Lamentably, few teachers have had any training in their undergraduate programs in working with school activities, so it is little wonder that teachers react negatively to coercion. Given a free choice, few teachers stick with an activity that does not interest them.

The Question of Teachers' Pay for Extracurricular/ Cocurricular Work

For many years, voluntary participation in leadership roles in the activities program was considered a regular part of the teaching job. In many districts, all teachers were expected to have some involvement with learners outside their normal classroom responsibility. Beginning in the high schools, and spreading to junior high schools and elementary schools, there has been a tendency in recent years for teachers to receive some extra remuneration for at least some positions of leadership in the activities program.

This trend has arisen because of a growing realization that although all teachers might have some involvement in extracurricular/cocurricular activities, the time and effort expended by the teachers filling the different leadership roles were by no means equivalent. For example, a teacher serving as faculty sponsor for a German club with perhaps six members faces responsibilities that are miniscule indeed compared with those of a teacher serving as faculty sponsor for the entire senior class. These differences, together with growing strength of teachers' professional organizations, have resulted in a tendency for at least some teachers with heavy responsibilities in the activities program to receive money over and above their regular salaries. Generally, more high school teachers receive these additional salary benefits than do teachers in junior high schools and elementary schools.

In school districts where some teachers do receive extra money for working in the extracurricular/cocurricular program, a number of plans have been worked out. There tends to be little uniformity in practices among districts. The amounts paid vary tremendously as does the classification of roles thought to merit the payment of extra salary. There have been some promising beginnings of attempts to rationalize this process.

Particularly notable has been an effort undertaken by the local school district in Longview, Washington, where extracurricular/cocurricular activities are evaluated individually in the light of eight criteria (Hendrickson, 1977):

1. Student contact hours required beyond the normal teaching day.
2. Average number of students per adviser/coach.
3. Degree of public exposure and public expectations.
4. Preparation time.
5. Equipment and materials management.
6. Assigned adults supervised on a regular basis.
7. Instructional and organizational skills necessary to conduct the activity.
8. Obligated travel supervision.

A given number of points is assigned to each criterion in this list. Then individual activities are examined and assigned a number of points for each of the eight criteria. The total of these points is believed to reflect the approximate difficulty, time, and responsibility associated with performing the leadership duties for each activity. A dollar value is determined for each point. The extra salary for each activity is computed by multiplying that dollar value by the number of points associated with the activity. For example, if it was determined that being adviser for the yearbook was worth 30 points and each point was worth $50, then the teacher serving as yearbook adviser would receive an extra $1,500 dollars (30 × 50 = 1,500) in salary.

Though large differences among districts in terms of their policies for paying teachers for helping out with extracurricular/cocurricular activities will probably persist, it is evident that the trend toward paying teachers for assuming these responsibilities is growing. But because of great variations among individual school districts, graduates of teacher education programs interested in extracurricular/cocurricular activities should take care to ask about the remuneration policies of those districts they are considering.

Recapitulation of Major Ideas

1. The extracurricular/cocurricular programs featured in American schools are unique. Though there are disagreements about the relative emphases given the activities program and the academic program, most educators agree that the provision of some extracurricular/cocurricular activities represents a legitimate function of the schools.
2. Extracurricular/cocurricular programs are found at all levels of public education. The programs tend to be most highly developed and diverse at the senior-high-school level. At the elementary-school level, the programs tend to have rather direct ties to the academic program.
3. Activities programs have been criticized because they take learners' time away from academics. Some have charged that these activities give youngsters a false sense of priorities. Critics have alleged that many activities are educationally irrelevant to learners' real needs.
4. Extracurricular/cocurricular programs have the potential to create problems for administrators. These problems can involve relationships with community members and with members of the teaching staff. On the other hand, some activities portray a very positive image of the school to the public. They also can be greatly helpful to some students who might otherwise not stay in school. On balance, most administrators would oppose any move to eliminate the activities program.
5. Professional educators have made a case for the legitimacy of the activities program by pointing out that involvement can promote the development of important citizenship skills and help give learners a sense of greater personal commitment to the school. Surveys of learners suggest that few participate because of the lofty motives suggested by professional educators. Most get involved for reasons of fun and personal satisfaction.
6. Though the range of activities available, particularly in the high school, is enormous, large numbers of youngsters still do not participate. Some have transportation problems. Others find the activities irrelevant. Others feel that organizations are dominated by unfriendly cliques. Still others are employed.
7. Few, if any, teachers receive any special training in their undergraduate preparation programs for assuming leadership roles in the activities

program. Nearly all training of this sort tends to be "on the job."

8. There is a trend toward teachers' receiving compensation for assuming the leadership in the more difficult and time-consuming areas of the activities program. Practices in this regard vary greatly from district to district. Generally speaking, more high school teachers receive this compensation than junior-high-school or elementary teachers.

Posttest

DIRECTIONS: Using your own paper, answer each of the following true/false questions. For each correct statement, write the word *true* on your paper. For each incorrect statement, write the word *false* on your paper.

1. Most learners who involve themselves in extracurricular/cocurricular activities do so because they find fun and personal enjoyment.
2. There is likely to be a greater variety of extracurricular/cocurricular activities in a high school than in an elementary school.
3. "Development of citizenship" has been an argument used by educators to defend the inclusion of extracurricular/cocurricular activities in the schools.
4. Administrators have sometimes been concerned about the possibility that extracurricular/cocurricular activities take time away from the academic aspects of the school program.
5. It is more common for secondary-school teachers than for elementary-school teachers to receive some pay for helping with extracurricular/cocurricular activities.
6. In high schools, students who work tend to participate less frequently in extracurricular/cocurricular activities than those who do not work.
7. In most schools, the extracurricular/cocurricular program is regarded as a legitimate extension of the academic program and a proper responsibility of the school.
8. There is little correlation between the interest and enthusiasm of a teacher sponsoring an activity and the interest and enthusiasm of the youngsters participating in the activity.
9. Of all youngsters participating in extracurricular/cocurricular activities, a very high percentage are involved because they want to "serve the school."
10. The success of most extracurricular/cocurricular activities can be attributed to certification standards that require special courses for nearly all teachers in managing the extracurricular/cocurricular program.

Summary

Extracurricular/cocurricular school activities appear to be here to stay. Though heated debate rages regarding the amount of emphasis that ought to be placed on these nonacademic aspects of schooling, there is general agreement that they do serve a useful educative function.

Extracurricular/cocurricular activities tend to be most numerous and most diverse at the senior-high-school level. Youngsters of this age have a range of interests that goes well beyond the limits of course offerings. Although many activities do bear a close relationship to courses, many others are more social in nature. The maturity and mobility of high school youngsters makes it possible for many extracurricular/cocurricular activities for learners in this age group to take place after school hours.

The activities program at the elementary level—and to some extent, at the junior-high-school level as well—tends to be closely tied to the subject curriculum. Activities for these younger children tend to require a great deal of adult supervision. This need puts some limits on the numbers of options made available to these younger learners. Also, because of transportation difficulties, nearly all school-related activities have to take place during those hours when the youngsters are at school.

Critics of activities programs have suggested that they take learners away from academic subjects, but others argue that these programs can enhance youngsters' interest in school. Many young people, it is alleged, would not stay in school were it not for the extracurricular/cocurricular program.

Although the number of activities options is very large, significant numbers of youngsters still go through school without ever getting involved in any extracurricular/cocurricular programs. Some find their interests not to be served by these activities. Others have after-school jobs that limit their time. Still others fail to get involved because of a belief that clubs, organizations, and other school groups are dominated by small, cliquish clusters of students who do not really welcome participation by everyone.

In recent years, there has been a recognition that the teachers who supervise various school activities put in a tremendous amount of personal time and effort. Increasingly, those teachers who bear the responsbility for sponsoring the more demanding activities are being paid a salary supplement. Practices in this regard vary greatly from district to district. Generally teachers in high schools who sponsor activities are more likely to receive extra compensation than teachers in junior high schools and senior high schools.

References

BUSER, ROBERT. "What's Happening in Student Activities in the Schools of the Seventies?" *NASSP Bulletin* (Sept., 1971): 1–9.

BUSER, ROBERT, LONG, RUTH, AND TWEEDY, HEWEY. "The Who, What, Why, and Why Not of Student Activity Participation." *Phi Delta Kappan* (Oct., 1975): 124–125.

EMMINGHAM, ROBIN. "Let's Not Fool Our Prospective Teachers." *Educational Leadership* (Dec., 1981): 219.

HENDRICKSON, GRANT. "Establishing Salary Schedules for Supervising Extracurricular Activities." *NASSP Bulletin* (Feb., 1977): 14–19.

ROBBINS, JERRY H. "'Hot Spots' in Student Activities: How to Deal with Them." *NASSP Bulletin* (Sept., 1971): 34–43.

SAPP, GARY L., CLOUGH, JENNIFER O., PITTMAN, BETSY; AND TOBEN, CAROLYN. "Classroom Management and Student Involvement." *The High School Journal* (March, 1973): 276–283.

Professional Considerations

19

Getting a Job

Objectives

This chapter provides information to help the reader to

1. Identify the procedures followed in many school districts with regard to hiring teachers.
2. Prepare letters of inquiry.
3. Develop professional résumés.
4. Become acquainted with the process of job interviewing.
5. Recognize the services typically rendered by college and university placement offices.
6. Consider the variables to be weighed in deciding which people to ask for letters of recommendation.

Pretest

DIRECTIONS: Using your own paper, answer each of the following true/false questions. For each correct statement, write the word *true* on your paper. For each incorrect statement, write the word *false* on your paper.

1. One important source of information about vacancies in school districts is the district itself. Such information can be obtained directly by a candidate who writes a letter of inquiry.
2. It is probably true that a high percentage of school personnel-office officials have a rather conventional outlook regarding the kinds of dress and the patterns of speech that are "appropriate."
3. When going for an interview, it is a good idea for the candidate to prepare in advance a number of questions to ask about the district.
4. When thinking about getting people to write recommendations for inclusion in the credentials file, it is a sound practice to talk to the people first before making the request.
5. In writing a district about a potential teaching vacancy, it is better to write a brief note on a postcard than a formal letter.
6. It is always a mistake for a candidate for a teaching job to ask questions about the district. It is the candidate's role to answer the questions of the interviewer, not to ask questions.
7. Most school districts require individuals seeking employment as teachers to complete a formal application form.
8. It is possible, in most cases, for teachers to add material periodically to their credentials files at university placement centers even after they have graduated.

9. Few districts hire schoolteachers without first having a face-to-face interview.
10. Because of their experience in working with youngsters in the classroom during student teaching, few prospective teachers are anxious as they approach their first job interview.

Introduction

As the end of their undergraduate programs becomes a reality, the concerns of future teachers increasingly shift from worries about academic matters to worries about finding a job. Typically, a serious effort to land a teaching position begins during the last year in undergraduate school. This effort tends to heat up considerably during the spring. During this time, many school districts regularly send interviewers to the campus to interview prospective teachers. During this time, too, many education majors are engaged in a feverish campaign of letter writing to districts in which they have an interest. It is a time of frenzied activity, and it is a time of tense waiting. Though districts begin screening candidates for teaching positions in the spring (sometimes even earlier), many defer making hiring decisions until midsummer or even later. The days that pass between an interview that seemed to go well and an official contract in the mail with a job offer from a district seem agonizingly slow. But prospective teachers can take some solace in the knowledge that this rite of passage from college or university student to classroom teacher has been weathered successfully by all who teach in the public schools today.

There is a certain system to this effort of securing an initial teaching position. Basically nothing terribly complex is involved. It is a matter of following a few simple rules and of using some common sense. A failure in this latter category tends to jeopardize the "hireability" of individuals seeking teaching positions more frequently that it should. For example, it should seem clear (and it *is* clear to most who prepare to teach) that behavior during student teaching is going to have some bearing on future employment. Considering this reality, it makes great sense for prospective teachers to attend well to their public relations roles during this time. Two examples drawn from the experiences of the authors will illustrate the consequences of not following this advice.

A student teacher in an elementary school had been doing a reasonably effective job with her fourth-grade youngsters in a nice suburban district outside a major West Coast city. She happened to have in her class the daughter of the superintendent of schools. On one particularly trying afternoon, the superintendent's daughter and some other youngsters were doing more talking than productive working. Tired and frustrated, the student teacher let fly with this verbal blast directed toward the superintendent's daughter: "I know the rest of the teachers in this building are afraid of your old man, but I'll tell you I'm not. Now you shut up, and I mean *now!*" In addition to the inelegant phrasing of these sentiments, the message proved to be an utter disaster for the student teacher. She had hoped to get a job in this district, but the story of her behavior quickly reached the personnel office, and she was given no consideration. One suspects, too, that the personnel people from other districts who read the comments of people who had worked with her during her student teaching also picked up some signals that there were concerns about this person's behavior.

In another incident, a young man who had been assigned to student teach in a small, conservative, rural community rented a trailer house and moved, along with his female companion, onto a vacant lot across the street from the school where he had been assigned to teach. Unmarried couples in the community surrounding his urban campus were so common as to be unworthy of even a yawn, but the citizens in this small town were scandalized. The young man was allowed to finish his student teaching (although there were angry calls from parents requesting his removal), but he stood no chance of getting a job in that community.

The point of these illustrations is that getting a job in teaching requires the establishment of a set of priorities. If the highest priority within this set is getting hired then certain other preferences, habits, or dispositions may well have to take a back seat. Getting a job implies a need to convince others that (1) one has the competence to do well in the classroom, and (2) one's style of life is reasonably compatible with that of the mainline elements of the community. Given these conditions, those who are successful in getting initial teaching positions may well be those who, as much as anything else, are able to convince the representatives of the school district that they are the "kind of people" whom the citizens of that community want working with their youngsters in the schools.

In sections that follow, information is provided relating to finding out about job vacancies, corresponding with school districts, completing application forms, preparing résumés, and going through the interviewing process.

Finding out About Teaching Vacancies

There are many sources of information about teaching vacancies. Sometimes vacancies become known to student teachers by word of mouth in conversations with other teachers in the faculty lounge. Occasionally school districts take out advertisments in local newpapers. (This tends to occur only rarely. Ordinarily this is done only when a district is experiencing great difficulty in finding a teacher for a specialty where teachers are in extremely short supply). Probably the most common source of information about teaching jobs is the college or university placement service.

Most colleges and universities have placement services that are charged with helping graduates find initial positions. At larger institutions, there may even be placement services responsible for working only with people seeking teaching positions. Typically, the placement services are notified by the school districts when they have vacancies. Most of these services regularly collate and publish lists of these vacancies. Ordinarily these lists include the specific nature of the vacancy and the name and address of the individual who should be contacted by those interested in making a formal application. Some placement services simply post these lists at central locations on the campus. Others do this and also regularly mail them to individuals who have registered for this service (some charge a small fee to those who receive these mailed lists).

Generally speaking, the largest number of vacancies coming from a placement center on a university or college campus are from school districts in the state where the college or university is located. Some vacancy notices are received from other states, but these tend to be limited in number. Individuals interested in teaching vacancies in other states frequently must write to a placement center located in the state in which they are interested and pay for the vacancy lists printed and distributed by that placement facility.

In addition to information from placement centers, job information can be had from the individual school districts. Generally speaking, it is better to request vacancy information in a letter than to telephone. A busy administrator might not have time to make an immediate check of potential openings in response to a telephoned inquiry. A request for information coming in a letter allows the responsible school official to seek out the requested information at a time that might prove more convenient. Furthermore, a letter from an individual requesting vacancy information is ordinarily kept on file and represents some record of contact with the school district.

Requests for information about potential vacancies should be sent to district personnel directors in large and intermediate-sized school districts and to superintendents in small districts. Generally speaking, these school officials have more reliable information about potential vacancies in the springtime than in the fall. Many teachers who do not plan to return will not have made their intentions known to the administration until sometime in the spring.

In preparing to write to individual school districts, one needs their addresses. Placement centers at most universities and colleges maintain address lists of most school districts in their own state. Information regarding the addresses of school districts in other states can ordinarily be obtained (by letter) from the state department of education in the state capital. Many state education departments distribute the available lists either free or for a nominal fee.

Once one has the general vacancy information and decides to apply for a

Box 19-1
Freedom of Personal Behavior and Finding a Teaching Position

You just would not *believe* this creature who interviewed me. You just would not *believe* him. I mean, really, now, a duck-tail haircut in the 1980s! He was one of those birds who thinks double-breasted polyester suits, patent leather white shoes, and a wide white belt represent the height of sartorial elegance. And then he began by asking me whether I was active in either Kiwanis or Rotary . . . can you *believe* that. I'm still a little shaky from the experience . . . I thought that world only existed on "Happy Days."

Anyway, he asked me about my philosophy of education. I started off on my little rap on existential dilemmas but cut it short when he told me he'd not read *The Stranger*. In fact, I was only half-through my explanation of educational implications of *No Exit* when his eyes began to glaze. At that point he shifted gears on me. He started asking me about discipline and classroom control and all of that. He didn't seem much interested in what I had to offer kids. In fact, I think I would have really impressed him if I had come down four square for cattle prods as a disciplinary measure of last resort. Weird. He'd sure never have hired Jean Jacques Rousseau. He didn't seem too impressed with me either.

Statements from a teacher candidate just returned from a job interview:

LET'S PONDER

Read the paragraphs above. Then, respond to the following questions.

1. What does the description of the interviewer suggest about possible values of the community and the school leadership from which he comes? Is he unusual? Why, or why not?
2. Do you think school district personnel, particularly those charged with interviewing prospective teachers, tend to be at the forefront of social change? Why, or why not?
3. How do you react to the general attitude of the individual who was interviewed? Do you think the reactions of this individual are typical? Why, or why not?
4. To what extent should an individual seeking a teaching job keep quiet about his own convictions and appear to accept those that he believes to characterize the interviewer? Is there a line between "selling out" and being "sufficiently prudent" to ensure that the possibility that a job will be offered remains open?
5. If you were to give some advice to the individual who made the statements in the above paragraphs, what would that advice be?

position, a number of steps may follow. A more formal letter of inquiry may be needed. A professional résumé may have to be prepared and submitted to the district. A placement file may be requested from the college or university placement center. An interview may be scheduled. And other things may have to be done. A number of the more common chores that go along with finding a teaching position are detailed in the sections that follow.

The Letter of Inquiry

School-district personnel offices must deal with a tremendous volume of mail coming in from individuals inquiring about potential staff vacancies. One district with whom two of the authors were once associated had a total teaching staff of around 225 and usually had from 15 to 20 vacancies annually. The personnel office in this district averaged between 2,500 and 3,000 letters of inquiry per year from individuals interested in information about teaching positions. Given this volume, it is essential that care be taken in the preparation of the letter of inquiry to simplify the work of the personnel people who must deal with this very heavy volume of correspondence. Some important considerations are detailed in the following subsections.

Your Position Preference

Good letters of inquiry are characterized by very specific reference to the grade level and subject that the writer is interested in teaching. It is much better to express an interest in "teaching third-graders in an open-space school" than to express an interest in "anything you might have available." Clearly, an individual looking for a teaching position cannot seriously have an interest in "any" vacancy. When his or her specific interest is not mentioned, the personnel office must write a letter requesting more precise information. Sometimes, given the press of paperwork in personnel offices, this letter does not get written. Certainly a request for information about potential vacancies of a specific kind will make a better impression on personnel-office staff people than a vague and general query for information about vacancies.

Your Availability

A letter to a personnel office should include information relating to two separate kinds of availability: (1) legal availability, and (2) temporal availability. Districts cannot hire just *any* certified teacher to fill a vacant position. Rather, they must follow strict state requirements regarding the kinds of teaching permitted to holders of various types of teaching certificates. Consequently the personnel office is very much interested in knowing exactly what a candidate for a position is legally qualified to teach. A letter of inquiry should always include information about teaching certificates held (or, if they are not yet in hand, when they will be issued), the subjects for which they are valid, any grade-level restrictions, and the dates of expiration, if any.

Second, it is important that information be provided about when a position can be assumed, if offered. Usually a phrase such as "I will be available to begin teaching as of August 15" will suffice. Districts need to know whether a candidate is looking for a position to begin at the beginning of the year, at mid-year, or at some other date.

Your Student Teaching

It is well to include a few brief comments about student teaching in a letter of inquiry. Many personnel directors consider student teaching the most important part of the preservice teacher-education program. Frequently a special effort is made to contact individuals who worked with prospective teachers during the time of their student teaching. Given this interest, it makes sense to include the dates and places of student teaching (include the relevant addresses) and the names of the supervising teachers and the building principal.

Your Address and Phone Number

No letter of inquiry should be sent without the writer's address and phone number. Sometimes vacancies develop late in the summer that have to be filled in a hurry. A busy personnel office will not spend time looking up the addresses and phone numbers of individuals who have been in contact with the district about possible teaching positions. Rather, they will go to the file of letters that have been received and take phone numbers and addresses directly from the letters. Clearly, a candidate who has failed to provide this information has diminished greatly his or her chances of being contacted.

Sometimes people fail to include phone numbers and addresses because they contemplate a move. This is a mistake. An address and phone number of a parent, other relative, or friend who is likely to know the whereabouts of the individual seeking a teaching position should be included. If a move is contemplated at a future date and a new address and phone number are known, a phrase such as the following ought to be included: "Until June 4th, I will be at 603 Maple Drive, Falls City, Texas 77899 (phone: 713-865-9987). After that date, I will reside at 11186 Gulfplace South (phone: 713-889-9007)."

Other Considerations

Inquiry letters should not be too long, certainly no more than two pages. If space permits, some mention can be made of cocurricular and extracurricular activities that the writer might be interested in supervising. Any previous experience in handling activities of this type could be mentioned. Additionally, any other nonteaching kinds of experiences involving leadership of young people might be included.

The successful letter of inquiry must be prepared in accordance with sound standards of English usage and ought to have a professional appearance. District personnel officials despair over the number of letters they receive that are shot through with misspellings, tortured grammatical structure, and aimless point-by-point development. Proofreading letters of inquiry is critically important. Until such time as a personal interview may be scheduled, the impression that a district gets of a candidate is based almost entirely on his or her letter of inquiry. A shoddy letter may ruin chances for serious consideration.

In times past, some districts preferred to have teaching candidates submit letters of inquiry in their own handwriting (this particularly tended to be true when elementary-school teachers were being sought). The idea was that the quality of the handwriting in the letter could suggest something about how well a prospective teacher might model good handwriting for youngsters. Today, because of the quantum jump in the number of letters of inquiry that many districts receive, the issue of easy readability has become more important to most district personnel officers. If handwriting is exceptionally legible, certainly it is still all right to submit handwritten letters of inquiry, but for most people, typewritten letters represent a better choice. Furthermore, given the volume of mail that must be read, it represents a good investment for candidates who are not good typists to have letters typed professionally on machines using carbon-coated plastic ribbon. These machines make exceptionally readable copy, which will be appreciated by personnel office people. Applicants who type their own letters should see that the letters on their machines are clean and free of ink.

Letters should be prepared on a heavy stock paper, preferably 20-weight. Onion skin should be avoided. Also, any paper that is not cut to a standard 8½-inch × 11-inch size should not be used. Inquiry letters get filed in standard file folders. In time, a thin paper such as onion skin, will fall to the bottom of the folder and may become lost. The possibility of loss also recommends against the use of nonstandard-sized papers.

Though there may be a few personnel directors who feel differently, most do *not* appreciate receiving letters of inquiry on postcards. First of all, the size of a postcard does not allow the candidate to be specific about the kind of position desired, certificates held, cocurricular interests, address and phone number, and so forth. Second, a postcard gives the impression of someone seated at a table somewhere behind a stack of a hundred postcards and a list of school district addresses who is requesting vacancy information from everywhere. It is easy for a district personnel official to conclude that someone who sends in a postcard has no very serious interest in the district that receives it. Finally, postcards tend to become buried at the bottom of personnel file folders.

Every letter of inquiry should be written by the individual seeking the teaching position. Many district personnel people gnash their teeth when

Box 19-2
Letter of Inquiry

Ms. Pricilla Wichner
Personnel Director
Forestwood Centre Public Schools
Forestwood, Indiana

Dear Ms. Wichner:

I am majoring in cirriculum and instruction. I might decide to teach when I'm through. My parents say I would be a good teacher. And, I have done alright in my college classes.

I need to know immediately the various jobs I could get in your district. Hope to get to meet you personaly sometime real soon.

Thanks alot,

J. C. Smithers

J. C. Smithers

LET'S PONDER

Read the letter above. Then, respond to the following questions.

1. What are your general reactions to the letter?
2. What grammatical problems do you note?
3. Are there any informational problems in the letter? Are some essential elements missing?
4. How would a school district personnel official likely react to this letter? What kind of a response do you think would be forthcoming from the school district?
5. If you had a chance to talk to J. C. Smithers, what kind of advice would you provide regarding how the letter might be improved?

they get a letter reading something like this: "My husband will be finishing up his education program this spring. Please send us any information you might have about openings." A letter on behalf of someone else flashes a message to the district personnel staff that the "someone else" must have precious little interest in a position to allow another person to assume his or her responsbility for making job contacts. Letters written by others have a high likelihood of leaving a negative impression on personnel officials.

The following points should be kept in mind about the letter of inquiry.

References should be made to:

1. Specific position desired.
2. Kinds of certificates held.
3. When a position could be assumed.
4. Place of student teaching and people involved.
5. Address and phone number.

Letters should be typed (unless handwriting is outstanding) on heavy (preferably 20-weight) bond paper of a standard size (8½-inch × 11-inch).

The Résumé

Résumés are known by a variety of labels in education. A résumé prepared by a university-level professional, for example, is usually termed a *vita*. Other terms that are more or less synonymous with the term *résumé* are *dossier* and *personal data sheet*. By whatever label it is known, a résumé represents a very compact summary of a number of details respecting a single individual. Rarely very long, résumés are designed to provide those who read them with a quick impression of the characteristics and qualifications of the individual described.

Occasionally résumés are sent to school districts as attachments to letters of inquiry. School personnel officials with whom the authors have chatted are divided on the merits of this practice. Although none has said that a résumé is regarded negatively; some have said that, given the volume of mail that must be processed, résumés may be given scant attention. Other personnel people, however, suggest that they appreciate having the résumé available for quick reference should an unanticipated vacancy develop. Almost always, a résumé of some kind will be placed in professional files established by most teaching candidates at their college or university placement offices.

Good résumés communicate clearly and efficiently. This kind of communication requires a systematic organizational format. Furthermore, it requires careful proofreading to ferret out spelling errors and typographical errors (résumés *must* be typed) that may leave a negative impression with the reader. Typically, a résumé provides specific information regarding such areas as the following:

1. Personal data.
2. Educational background.
3. Teaching certificates held.
4. Experience.
5. Honors.
6. Professional memberships.

Descriptions of the kinds of information typically included under these headings are provided in the following subsections.

Personal Data

This section includes an address and a telephone number where the candidate can be reached. Additionally, information is typically provided regarding such things as date of birth, marital status, and military service experience.

Educational Background

In this section are included the names of the elementary and high schools attended. The dates of high school and college or university graduation are specified. The names of the degrees received (or anticipated) are noted as well. If there have been other educational or training experiences, perhaps obtained while on active military duty, these may be included.

Teaching Certificates Held

In this section, the names of the teaching certificates held (or about to be held) are listed. If there are expiration dates attached to these certificates, this information is also provided. Finally, the subjects that the certificates authorize the candidate to teach are generally listed in this section.

Experience

All employment experience is listed under this heading. Names of employers, names of immediate supervisors, and dates of employment are typically included. Additionally, any experiences involving work with youngsters—particularly where a leadership role was involved, even of a voluntary nature—can be included here. For example, service as a Sunday-school teacher or as a counselor at a scout camp would be perfectly acceptable entries in this section.

Honors

Scholarships, awards, prizes, and other recognitions can be included in this section. If there are a wide number of these from which to choose, those with the clearest relevance to education should be selected for inclusion.

Professional Memberships

This section is reserved for information regarding memberships in organizations that have a clear relevance to professional education. Positions of leadership, if any, in any such organizations should be noted also. Work in student education societies and in such national groups as Kappa Delta Pi can be included in this section of the résumé.

Some artistry is involved in preparing a résumé. The six categories listed above are not mandatory for *all* résumés, though most will probably include

Box 19-3
A Sample Résumé

ERIC CARLETON ROGERS

1. PERSONAL INFORMATION

Year of Birth: 1961
Marital Status: (Wife: Sue Ann. No Children)
Military Service: U.S. Army Signal Corps, 1979-1981
Address and Phone Number: 800 West 14th Avenue
　　　　　　　　　　　　　　　Spokane, Washington 99204
　　　　　　　　　　　　　　　(509) 696-0987

2. EDUCATIONAL BACKGROUND

Roosevelt Elementary School, Spokane, WA, 1967-1973
Sacajawea Junior High School, Spokane, WA, 1973-1975
Lewis and Clark High School, Spokane, WA, 1975-1979 (diploma 1979)
Western Washington University, Bellingham, WA, 1981-1985 (Bachelor of Arts
　　degree in English, 1985)

3. TEACHING CERTIFICATES HELD

Provisional Secondary (State of Washington), expires 1988.
　Authorized Teaching Fields: 1. English ; 2. French

4. EXPERIENCE

Junior Assistant Scoutmaster, Troup 31, Spokane Area Boy Scouts of
　　America, 1978-1979
Instructor - Basic Signal Course, Fort Devens, Massachusetts, 1980-1981
Counselor, State of Washington "Boys' State" Program, summer, 1982
Student Teaching - Auburn Senior High School, Auburn, Washington, spring,
　　1985. (Supervising Teacher: Mrs. P. Drehr. Principal: Mr. Amos Grant.
　　　Address: Auburn Senior High School, 4th Avenue East, Auburn, WA 98002)

5. HONORS

6. PROFESSIONAL MEMBERSHIPS

National Student Education Association (President, Western Washington
　　University Chapter, 1984)

them. There may be some value in an individual situation to adding other categories that provide additional information that might prove of interest to someone considering the qualifications of candidates for teaching positions. In some situations, too, it may be advisable not to list one of the six categories mentioned above. A reason for not including something will become clear from an examination of a real résumé. Spend a few moments looking over the résumé for Eric C. Rogers in Box 19-3.

Basically, the Rogers' résumé suffers from no serious deficiencies. It is concise, the headings are clear, and the general physical appearance is good. It probably would have been a good idea for this individual to delete the section on honors. As there is nothing to list in this category, there is no point in including it in the résumé. Indeed, to some eyes, the blank space may seem to make a negative statement about the individual.

Applications

The vast majority of school districts, assuming some vacancies are anticipated, will respond to a letter of inquiry from a prospective teacher with both a short letter and a formal application form. Though application forms have been greatly streamlined in recent years (in large measure, because of the heavy volume of paperwork that today's personnel offices must process), still they can be intimidating to prospective teachers. Each application form has a few individual quirks of its own, but some features tend to appear in nearly all of them. Many request information such as the following:

1. Name, address, and phone number of the candidate.
2. Specific teaching position desired.
3. Specific date on candidate availability.
4. Teaching certificate(s) held and subjects authorized to teach.
5. Coaching capabilities (if any).
6. Extracurricular interests.
7. Details regarding student teaching.
8. Reasons for applying to this district.
9. Candidate's philosophy of education.
10. Credentials from candidate's placement center.

Applications must be completed carefully. Most are accompanied by rather explicit instructions about how this is to be accomplished. If the instructions say that the form is to be handwritten, then it must be handwritten. Otherwise it is better to type the form. The responses expected in most categories can be discerned fairly easily from the questions asked. However, some candidates are bothered by the usual request for an explanation of their philosophy of education. (On many application forms, this question is followed by an ominously long blank space that may take up as much as an entire page.)

Personnel directors report that, although they do have some interest in the philosophical positions of teaching candidates, they are also interested in how these candidates express themselves in writing. The "philosophy-of-education" question provides personnel staff people with an opportunity to identify efficiently candidates who are extremely deficient in written communication skills. Considering that clarity of expression is the real interest of those who will be reading the responses to these questions, the responses on this section of the application must be prepared carefully. Certainly a professional job of proofreading is a must.

Once an application is completed, a copy should be made for the candidate's own files. Should an interview be scheduled as a result of a district's review of the application, the candidate can review the copy to refresh his or her memory regarding the kinds of responses that were prepared for the various questions on the form. Additionally, the copy can prove useful when completing applications from other districts. Because many questions on application forms from different school districts are the same, if a completed copy of one application is kept it can be referred to as a source for responses when similar questions are encountered on other applications.

Placement Centers

Nearly every college and university has a placement office of some kind dedicated to helping graduates find initial employment. At large institutions, there typically are individuals in these placement offices who work exclusively with teacher placement. In a few colleges and universities, there are entire educational placement offices that are physically distinct from the placement offices serving graduates in other areas.

Placement offices provide a number of services. As noted previously, they serve as a clearinghouse for information regarding job vacancies. Frequently, lists of such vacancies are mailed to individuals who are registered with the office, and they are posted in various places around the campus. Many placement offices update these lists at least monthly, and even more frequently during the prime hiring period from February through August.

Placement offices arrange for interviews between prospective employers and teaching candidates. Typically, the representatives of school-district personnel offices are invited to the campus to interview the candidates. When a visit is about to occur, the placement office makes known the date or dates that the interviewer will be on campus. Individuals interested in interviewing are asked to sign up for an appointment with the placement office. Most placement offices have interviewing spaces within their own facilities. In large colleges and universities, where numbers of interviewers may be on campus at the same time, large numbers of interviews may be scheduled at one time. The Educational Placement Center at Texas A & M University, for example, reports that on some occasions nearly forty interviews may be going on at one time.

Most placement offices require teaching candidates to go through a formal registration process. Typically this involves the payment of an initial fee. Frequently, too, small annual fees are required for individuals who wish to be kept on an "active" list, that is, to have the right to take advantage of the services offered by the placement office. Part of the registration at a placement office involves the preparation of a set of materials known as a *credentials file.* (This term is not used uniformly. At some institutions these papers are known as *professional dossiers, placement papers, professional files,* or by some other term. There tends to be a great similarity, however, in terms of what these sets of papers contain, regardless of the term used to describe them.)

The Credentials File

The credentials file is a collection of specific information about an individual teaching candidate. Typically, such a file contains the following components:

1. A résumé.
2. A list of the courses taken.
3. Letters of recommendation.

When a candidate makes a request to the placement office or when a request comes to the placement office directly from an interested school district (provided that the candidate has given the placement office permission to release his or her files on request by a district), the placement office makes a copy of the complete credentials file and sends it to the personnel office of the school district. Thus, once a credentials file has been established, the candidate is free from the chore of gathering together this information each time he or she wishes to send it to a school district. Ordinarily a call or a letter to the placement office results in the credentials file being expeditiously copied and mailed. Sometimes there is a small fee for this service. A few placement centers around the country make no charge for mailing out credentials files up to a given number per year. (For example, there might be no charge as long as no more than ten requests are made in a calendar year.)

Many teachers continue to work with the placement office at the college or university from which they graduated for years after the completion of their program. For example, the wife of one of the authors has maintained a credentials file at the University of Montana, where she was intially certified to teach, even though she has never taught in the state of Montana. As credentials files can be mailed anywhere, it makes little difference where they are kept. The files can be updated periodically by teachers who are employed. This involves adding new recommendations and other information relating to employment experience. Most placement offices have special updating forms that they send on request to the people whom they serve.

Though requirements vary considerably from placement office to placement office, generally about three or four recommendations are required when a credentials file is being established. Ordinarily one of these recommendations must come from the teacher who supervised the candidate during his or her student teaching. Other recommendations might be requested from education professors, professors in subject areas, employers, and others who can attest to the candidate's talents and character.

In the selection of individuals to write recommendations, several considerations should be borne in mind. First of all, individuals should be selected who are capable of providing information about a candidate of a type that would be of real interest to a school-district personnel official. Clearly, those individuals who have observed the candidate working with youngsters, for example, can speak to issues likely to be of more interest to an employer of teachers than the comments of individuals whose only contact with the candidate has been in other situations.

A surprisingly large number of candidates make the mistake of sending a recommendation form to someone whom they have not asked to complete a recommendation. Aside from the violation of common courtesy, such a practice can result in a recommendation that is lukewarm at best. Almost always, a recommendation will be better if the candidate takes the time to ask the individual who is to write it whether he or she would be willing to do so. In addition to making a positive impression, this practice can provide an oppor-

''Have you had any experience working with children?''

tunity for a discussion between the writer and the teaching candidate that may well refresh the memory of the writer regarding some things that might be included in the written recommendation.

In summary, placement offices play a very important role in helping prospective teachers find their initial teaching position. People who work in these offices know their territory well. They are an excellent source of information regarding the demand for teachers in various fields and at various locations. Happily, too, most tend to be "people-oriented" individuals who recognize the anxieties of teaching candidates as they begin preparing to go after their first teaching position. The kindness and good listening skills of these people are treasured memories of many teachers working in classrooms today.

The Interview

Almost no teachers are hired without a personal interview. Indeed, in some districts, several interviews may be required. For example, in one suburban district outside Houston, where team teaching is featured in the schools, teaching candidates are interviewed three times. They begin with an interview by the district's personnel office; then they are interviewed by a building principal; then they are interviewed by other members of the teaching team to which they might be assigned.

Many prospective teachers approach interviews with a very high level of anxiety. This is certainly to be expected since a successful interview is a necessary preliminary to an offer of a teaching position. Although not all anxiety can be eliminated, still there are things about interviews that teaching candidates should know that can keep the degree of unease at a manageable level. (It should be noted here that most interviewers recognize that candidates may be somewhat nervous initially. Most are very skilled at making the people they are interviewing feel at ease. One teaching candidate, reported that as the interview went forward, he sensed his anxiety slipping away like "air escaping slowly from a loosely tied balloon.")

Interviews provide an opportunity for two kinds of information. They serve as opportunities for school representatives to supplement the information they may have discerned from the credentials file about the candidate's likelihood of success as a teacher in their district. They also provide a chance for the candidate to "interview" the district, that is, to ask questions related to the kind of environment he or she might be expected to confront should a position be offered and accepted.

What Interviewers Tend to Ask

Though there are obviously differences in interviewing style among the thousands of representatives of school districts who interview prospective teachers, still there are patterns that characterize large numbers of interviewing

Box 19-4
Selecting People to Write Recommendations

1. A minister who knows you
2. The teacher who supervised you during student teaching
3. Your freshman English instructor in college
4. Your favorite professor in your academic specialization
5. Your uncle
6. The principal of the school where you did your student teaching
7. Your father's employer
8. The administrative head of the youth agency where you worked as a volunteer counselor last summer
9. Your shift boss at McDonalds
10. Your education advisor
11. A teacher you had in high school
12. The principal of the high school you attended
13. A teacher of an education methods course
14. Your drill sergeant from basic training

LET'S PONDER

Suppose you were preparing to put together your credentials file at the placement office on your campus. Your placement center wants you to get recommendations from at least three people. A special form has been provided that you are to give to the three people you select. You have developed the above list of fourteen people whom, possibly, you might ask. Look at this list as you respond to the following question.

1. Which of these individuals would be able to provide the most specific information about your ability to work with young people? Which individuals would have no information about this subject?
2. Which of these individuals would be able to provide the most specific information about your grasp of your subject area? Which individuals would have the least information about this subject?
3. Which of these individuals would be able to provide the best information about your ability to get along with other adults? Which individuals would have the least information about this subject?
4. Which of these individuals could best attest to your general "character?" Which individuals would have the least information about this subject?
5. Given this list, which three individuals would you choose? Why?

sessions. It is very common, for example, for an interview to begin with a warm greeting and some general questions to the candidate about his or her personal background. Frequently there will be queries about parents and other family members. Interviewers typically have little interest in specific responses to these kinds of questions. They are asked primarily to relax the candidate and to get the candidate used to responding to the interviewer's questions.

Once an easy climate of communication has been established, the interviewer begins to turn to more substantive issues. Nearly all school districts are concerned about the capacity of new teachers to control the youngsters in their charge. Questions related to classroom management and discipline crop up in many many interviews. Candidates need to be prepared to respond to questions regarding their approach to maintaining decorum in the classroom.

Questions concerning the organization of instruction occur with a good deal of frequency. There is some suspicion among public school people that many beginning teachers think that they can teach the subjects they learned in college with very little adjustment of their college class notes. Specific questions about topics and methods of presentation uniquely suited to the special needs of public school youngsters may be asked as the interviewer attempts to probe the extent to which the candidate has thought about the issue of adjusting the sophistication of his or her program to an appropriate level.

To determine the extent to which a prospective teacher has taken the time to become familiar with the instructional materials published for public school youngsters, interviewers sometimes ask candidates about the titles of textbooks (for school use) in their subject areas with which they are acquainted. It makes sense for candidates to make a special effort to learn something about the range of such materials well in advance of the interview.

At all levels of public education, there are concerns about the reading difficulties being experienced by learners in the schools. Given this situation, even those teaching candidates interviewing for high school positions may get questions about how they would deal with youngsters who have severe reading problems. Candidates who can speak with some degree of specificity about readability formulae, Cloze tests, and the other devices used to diagnose reading difficulties will make a positive impression on interviewers. This is particularly true when the candidate is a secondary-education person who would not automatically have been exposed to such information in most teacher preparation programs.

Generally, questions relating to interests in working with athletic teams and with other extracurricular/cocurricular activities may be expected. School administrators need teachers who not only can do an adequate job of working with youngsters in classrooms but will also lend a hand with the many other responsibilities assumed by schools that provide a comprehensive educational experience for youngsters. Teaching candidates who can demonstrate some experience and some interest in dealing with youngsters in out-of-the-classroom settings will very likely prompt a good deal of interviewer interest.

Finally, in almost all interviews, opportunities are provided for candidates to ask questions about the district. Invitations to do so may come at various points throughout the interview, or they may be offered toward the end of the session. When invitations to ask questions are extended, the candidate should have some questions in mind. Most interviewers are not impressed by individuals who have not thought enough about the position they are seeking to have formulated any questions.

What Kinds of Questions Should Candidates Ask Interviewers?

Teaching candidates should go into an interview with a number of questions in mind regarding the school district and the school in which they might be teaching. Interviewers expect such questions. Furthermore, if hired, the candidate is going to be spending a significant portion of his or her life working as a teacher. A decision to commit oneself to this kind of an obligation should be taken only when as much evidence as possible about the employment environment is in hand.

Questions about the community certainly are in order. Are the parents supportive of the schools? What is the percentage of college graduates? How are the working relationships between the parents and the teachers? What happens to most of the youngsters when they finish high school? These questions and others of this type are legitimate concerns of beginning teachers. Teaching candidates should not hesitate to ask about these matters during an employment interview.

Questions about organizational arrangements in the schools are also appropriate. Some individuals seeking teaching positions do not wish to work in a team-teaching situation. They need to find out from their interviewer whether they would be obligated to work as a member of a teaching team, if hired. Are any of the buildings constructed on an open-space plan? What administrative arrangements characterize the high schools? The elementary schools? What is the school calendar like? These and other questions relating to organizational matters might well be asked.

Beginning teachers often have concerns about how well they are doing their jobs. Sometimes, too, they have ideas but are not quite sure they will work. In thinking about potential concerns regarding teaching their subjects, teaching candidates should be prepared to ask interviewers about the kinds of support services that the district offers to teachers. Are there, for example, central-office curriculum specialists in all subject areas? Are these people willing to come out to individual buildings and work with the teachers? How about instructional-materials resources? Is there an adequate media center? Are the laboratories well equipped?

Questions about the school day represent another legitimate concern. Do all teachers have a planning period? How long is it? Are the teachers expected to supervise in the lunchrooms? Who is responsible for the youngsters' being loaded on buses at the end of the day? Do the teachers patrol the playground?

Do the buildings have teachers' lounges? What kind of parking facilities are there for teachers at school? What kind of cocurricular/extracurricular responsibilities and opportunities do the teachers have?

Finally, it is important for prospective teachers to know something about the relative level of teachers' involvement in the decision-making process in the district, particularly as it relates to the curriculum. Is there a central-district curriculum committee that includes teachers? Are there curriculum committees in individual schools? Who decides what textbooks are used? Do the teachers have some discretionary money in the school budget with which to order materials for their own classes? Can the teachers recommend the purchase of films and other instructional resources? All of these questions are important. The answers can suggest a good deal about how a district perceives its teachers.

Most interviews do not last long. Though times vary greatly, probably about twenty minutes is an average. Interviews that take place in placement offices generally tend to be shorter than those set up for a candidate in a school district office. The reason is the necessity to schedule a number of teaching candidates to see an interviewer whose time on the campus is limited.

It should be recognized that actual employment contracts are offered only rarely at the conclusion of an interview session. Typically, interviewers take notes on what has transpired and discuss the interviews later, perhaps with school administrators and others in the personnel office, on their return to the district. When a decision is made to offer employment to a candidate, a contract will arrive by mail stating all the conditions of employment. Should the candidate find these satisfactory, he or she signs the contract and mails it back to the district. Usually, when this has been done, the candidate can rest assured that he or she has been hired. Legally the contract does not become official until it is received by the district, presented to the school board, and voted on by the school board. Practically speaking, except in the rarest of cases, the school board automatically votes approval of all teachers' contracts forwarded to it for action by the district administration.

In summary, the interview represents a very important link in the process of changing one's status from that of teaching candidate to that of teacher. Successful interviews demand careful preparation. Candidates need to be prepared to ask questions of their own as well as to respond to the questions put to them by the representatives of the school districts who are looking for teachers.

Recapitulation of Major Ideas

1. Most people preparing for careers in teaching begin serious planning for job hunting during the final semester of their preservice training program at their college or university. Districts tend to begin considering candidates shortly after the beginning of the new year.

Interviewing activity accelerates dramatically during the months of mid and late spring. Most actual hiring is done from mid spring through August.

2. Securing a teaching position involves a certain sensitivity to public relations issues. Those who are hired tend to be people who, in the eyes of the district professionals responsible for personnel selection, reflect standards of conduct consistent with community standards.

3. There are numerous sources of information about teaching vacancies. A good deal of this information gets passed informally from individual to individual. Many student teachers learn about potential vacancies from casual conversations in teachers' lounges during their student-teaching experience. Another very important source of such information is the university or college placement office. The placement office typically receives notifications of most vacancies occurring in the state in which the placement office is situated. It also gets some information from other states. Teaching candidates wishing to teach in states other than that in which they were trained frequently find it profitable to contact university or college placement centers in those states in which they have an interest in teaching. Other vacancy information can be had by writing letters of inquiry directly to school districts.

4. Letters of inquiry to school districts need to be both brief and specific. They should alert district personnel officials to (1) the position being sought, (2) the credentials in hand, (3) address and phone number, (4) the date of earliest availability, and (5) other specific information clearly tied to competencies characterizing successful classroom teachers.

5. Résumés are compact collections of information about a given individual. Rarely do they run to more than a few pages in length. Their purpose is to give a great volume of information about a given individual in a very brief space. Résumés are occasionally included in letters of inquiry to school districts. Almost always, they become part of a candidate's professional credentials file.

6. Almost all school districts require candidates for teaching positions to complete a formal application form. These forms, though displaying some differences from place to place, tend to be quite similar for most districts. A frequent question asked on such forms is "What is your philosophy of education?" Though there is some interest in the substance of this response, it more commonly serves the purpose of helping personnel people assess the written communications skills of the candidate.

7. Nearly every college and university has a placement office. The placement office (1) arranges for interviews, (2) prepares and distributes copies of professional credentials files, and (3) alerts registrants to teaching vacancies.

8. Very few teachers are hired without a personal interview. Indeed, some

Box 19-5
Questions for Interviewers

1. How much can I be making in ten years?
2. Do you have any math supervisors in your central office?
3. Do teachers have to stay after school to help out with activities?
4. Will I be able to use some of my own ideas about teaching math?
5. Do I have to go to the football games?
6. Who will be my immediate supervisor?
7. About how many students might I expect in a class?
8. Do most people who graduate go on to college?
9. Is housing that teachers can afford available within a reasonable distance of the school?
10. Do teachers have to take inservice courses to keep in good standing with the district?
11. Are there other young teachers in the school?
12. Do teachers have to live in the school district?
13. Can married teachers teach in the same building?
14. Who evaluates teachers' performance?
15. Do teachers ever have a chance to request a transfer to another building?

LET'S PONDER

Suppose you were preparing to interview for a teaching vacancy and were preparing a list of some questions you might ask the representative from the personnel office of the school district. Look at the questions listed above as you respond to the following questions.

1. Which one of these questions would you ask first? Why?
2. Would any one of these questions be an especially poor choice as a first question to ask? Why do you think so?
3. If you were to identify the five best questions from this list, what would they be? What makes these questions better than the others?
4. If you were to identify the five worst questions from this list, what would they be? What makes these questions worse than the others?
5. Selecting some of these questions if you wish and developing others of your own, prepare a list of ten questions you would like to have answered in an interview with a representative of a school district. List questions in the order in which you would ask them. What reasons do you have for selecting this order?

districts require multiple interviews. Interviews provide districts with information about the teaching candidate. As importantly, interviews can provide the teaching candidate with information about the school district.

Posttest

DIRECTIONS: Using your own paper, answer each of the following true/false questions. For each correct statement, write the word *true* on your paper. For each incorrect statement, write the word *false* on your paper.

1. One important source of information about vacancies in school districts is the district office itself. Such information can be obtained by a candidate who writes a letter of inquiry.
2. It is probably true that a high percentage of school personnel-office officials have a rather conventional outlook regarding the kinds of dress and patterns of speech that are "appropriate."
3. When going for an interview, it is a good idea for the candidate to prepare in advance a number of questions to ask about the district.
4. When thinking about getting people to write recommendations for inclusion in the credentials file, it is a sound practice to talk to the people first before making the request.
5. In writing a district about a potential teaching vacancy, it is better to write a brief note on a postcard than a formal letter.
6. It is always a mistake for a candidate for a teaching job to ask questions about the district. It is the candidate's role to answer the questions of the interviewer, not to ask questions.
7. Most school districts require individuals seeking employment as teachers to complete a formal application form.
8. It is possible, in most cases, for teachers to add material periodically to their credentials files at university placement centers even after they have graduated.
9. Few districts hire schoolteachers without first having a face-to-face interview.
10. Because of their experience in working with youngsters in the classroom during student teaching, few prospective teachers are anxious as they approach their first job interview.

Summary

Most prospective teachers begin thinking about finding an initial teaching position during the last part of their preservice preparation program. Typically, during this time, they prepare résumés, send letters of inquiry to districts that may have vacancies, establish a credentials file with the college or university placement office, and try to arrange for interviews with school-district personnel people.

In general, preparing for the task of securing employment requires careful attention to detail. Communications with school districts, for example, must be error-free from a grammatical point of view and must be written with a clarity sufficient for school district officials to determine whether or not any vacancies in the writer's area or areas are anticipated. Furthermore, in working indirectly and directly with school district officials, a rule of common sense applies regarding such things as dress, manners, and patterns of speech. School districts operate in a political milieu, and consequently those officials responsible for hiring new teachers try to find people who will fit smoothly into the style of life characterizing the community. Some beginning teachers find that they have to compromise a few of their own personal convictions initially as a trade-off for securing employment.

References

ADDAMS, H. L. "Preparing Résumés and Letters of Application." *Business Education Forum* (March, 1978): 29–30.

BOLLES, RICHARD N. *What Color is Your Parachute?* rev. ed. Berkeley, Calif.: Ten Speed Press, 1982.

COCHRAN, J. "Self Appraisal: Introduction to the Job Search Process." *Journal of Business Education* (Jan., 1983): 141–144.

GOODLIN, E. H. "Job Interviews: From Stress to Success." *Business Education Forum* (March, 1982): 7–8.

KING, M. R., AND MONSTER, G. J. "Body Image, Self-Esteem, and Actual Success in a Simulated Job Interview." *Journal of Applied Psychology* (Oct., 1977): 589–594.

KREIDER, PAUL T. *The Interviewing Handbook for College Graduates.* San Anselmo, Calif.: KCE Publishing, 1981.

MAHONEY, ERIKA. "Seeking a New Teaching Job? Be Prepared for the Big Interviews!" *Instructor* (April, 1978): 21.

ORNSTEIN, ALLEN C. "Baby Boom: Bad News for City Schools." *Principal* (Nov., 1982): 8–15.

PETTUS, THEODORE. *One on One: Win the Interview, Win the Job.* New York: Random House, 1981.

ROSSON, J. "Credentials: A Game Teacher Applicants Play." *Journal of College Placement* (Winter 1978): 28–30.

SHROYER, G. "Getting the First Position." *Physical Education* (March, 1978): 15–16.

TRAVERS, P. "Seeking Teacher Employment." *Clearing House.* (Feb., 1983): 275–277.

STEIN, HARRY, AND BEYER B. K. "Ivan the Terrible Writes His Resume." *Instructor* (Oct., 1982): 46–47.

20
TEACHING AND YOU

Objectives

This chapter will help the reader to

1. Identify personal values.
2. Clarify the relationship between personal values and the role of the teacher.
3. Identify factors that are rewarding and frustrating in teaching.
4. Make a decision regarding education as a career.
5. Identify the types of settings where he or she would like to teach.

Values Inventory

DIRECTIONS: In place of the usual pretest, this chapter has a values inventory. Read through each of the items listed below and check whether or not that particular item is of very high priority for you, of high priority, of intermediate priority, of low priority, or of very low priority. Be completely honest in your response to the items.

	Very High	High	Intermediate	Low	Very Low
1. I have a desire to make a contribution to society.					
2. I want to work in an environment where I have a great deal of freedom to be myself.					
3. I want to communicate the excitement of some of the ideas in my subject area.					
4. I like to help individuals deal with problems.					
5. I want a job that is considered important by others.					
6. Economic security is an important goal for me.					
7. I want a job that provides a great deal of stability.					
8. I want a job that is relatively free from continual evaluation by individuals external to my profession.					

9. I would like a job where good performance is recognized and reinforced.
10. To me, a job is only of secondary importance. The main thing is to enjoy life.
11. I want a job where working conditions are pleasant and nonthreatening.

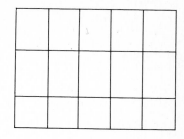

Do You Really Want to Teach?

As we near the conclusion of this book, you should be doing some very serious thinking about one of the most serious decisions you will ever make? Should you choose teaching as a career? Or should you do something else?

In writing this book, the authors have attempted to present an honest and balanced view of teaching. We have examined the problems and frustrations of teaching along with its rewards. Certainly any decision about a career should be based on a full knowledge of the pluses and minuses rather than on "romantic" notions that may be far from reality.

Every year, many teachers in this country decide that teaching is not for them. Although some turnover is certainly to be expected in any occupation as people's interests and priorities change, still some of these people leave because professional education failed to live up to their erroneous preconceptions of what teaching is all about. To some degree, at least, erroneous impressions result from the mistaken notion that many beginning teachers have that they "know all about teaching" because, after all, they were once learners in schools.

It is all too true that many aspects of teaching are "invisible" to the learner in the classroom. Few learners, for example, have opportunities to witness their teachers spending long hours preparing for lessons and grading papers on weekends. Learners rarely see teachers pick up their checks, scan the disappointingly small total that remains after deductions, and wonder whether the rewards are a fair measure of their effort. Few learners, too, have recognized the questions that many teachers ask about their own competence when they hear critics assail their performance.

Prospective teachers need to recognize that there are dimensions to teaching that they, as learners, never understood. For large numbers of teachers, these frustrations are simply "part of the territory." These pressures do not diminish their enthusiasm for teaching one whit. The authors of this text, for example, remember their public-school teaching days with great satisfaction. Though each had days that might best be described as eminently forgettable, still, on balance, we found teaching a personally rewarding experience. It must be recognized, however, that there are individuals who, exposed to the same demands, find little to be happy about in the world of the teacher. Certainly there is nothing at all "wrong" with these people. They are simply oriented in ways that prevent them from being completely fulfilled as human beings by serving as schoolteachers.

Because happiness in teaching is so tied up with how people see the world, it perhaps is desirable at this time for you to begin thinking both about what you find important in life and about what the real demands of teaching are. You might wish to review your responses on the checklist at the beginning of this chapter. Taken collectively, what do your responses say about your priorities? What things in life are most important to you?

Having thought through your responses to these questions, you need next to take a look at your own personality and decide how compatible it is with the world of teaching. The previous chapters of this text have provided a good deal of information regarding the dimensions of teaching. How does this information square with your own set of personal values? For example, if you prize financial security, does the available information suggest that you would be happy in teaching? Why, or why not? If you have a high need to work in a high-status profession, is teaching the answer? Why, or why not? You might wish to consider a number of such questions as you begin working toward an answer to the question of "Should I teach, or should I do something else?"

Many people who go into teaching have not taken the time to do a serious self-analysis. They have not examined their basic values and thought through the issue of whether teaching was really right for them. A number of teachers have entered the profession motivated by reasons that may not be sound. A number of these reasons are described in the sections that follow.

"I Don't Know What Else to Do!"

Although they are reluctant to admit it, many people seem to choose teaching by default. They are simply unaware of other career options. This tends to happen frequently when an undergraduate is attracted to a subject field that seems little connected to the demands of the career world beyond the baccalaureate degree. Some may ask, for example, "What does a person with a degree in history do except teach school?"

The "I don't know what else to do" argument is rarely a sufficient reason for choosing teaching as a career. Many who go into teaching motivated only by an interest in their academic subject become very frustrated when they begin teaching. They soon discover that many learners do not share their enthusiasm. Indeed, many may dislike those subjects that the teachers find intensely interesting and exciting. A teacher with a great love of literature may soon be disillusioned as he or she finds that a typical day is filled with paperwork, the disciplining of learners, and committee meetings rather than with exhilarating discussions centering on the subject matter. Although there are certainly moments when groups of youngsters really get "turned on" to academic content, teachers simply cannot count on this kind of reinforcement to be always available to compensate for the other demands made on them during a typical teaching day. If there is no satisfaction at all derived from the nonacademic side of teaching, then there is high potential for frustration and unhappiness.

How do you feel about your own motives for teaching? Are you interested in teaching only because of an abiding love of your subject matter and some concern that there may be nothing else you can do with your degree? If so, you might do a few things before you definitely commit yourself to teaching. First of all, you should visit the placement office on your campus. Professionals there will be able to discuss with you the career alternatives for individuals with academic majors in your area.

After chatting with a placement center counselor, you might look at the vacancy listings for people who will be graduating with your major. What kinds of jobs are available? What are the demands? What are the starting salaries?

Next, you might check the list of available teaching positions to get some feel for the relative demand for teachers in your academic specialty. Are there, for example, large numbers of school districts looking for English teachers? If so, are they looking for individuals to teach literature courses or to teach courses in grammar and composition? How do these teaching-position vacancy lists look to you? Do the positions look interesting or not?

Finally, you might schedule a personal visit to a school classroom of a teacher in your own area of specialization. Ask the teacher about the rewards and frustrations in teaching. Observe the amount of time spent on teaching the subject, the motivational level of the class, and the depth of treatment of individual topics. Are these as you would have anticipated? Is this what you would want to do?

After you have seriously considered alternatives to teaching and teaching itself, you need to do some serious thinking. What are your options? What are the advantages and disadvantages of each? Which option seems to fit in best with your own personal goals and values?

"Teaching Isn't Intellectually Demanding!"

Though few say so publicly, there are a number of individuals who, when pressed, admit that they were initially attracted to teaching because they felt that the preparation program was not intellectually demanding. This perception—in some instances, at least—has been fostered by practices of colleges of education that have allowed students to progress through programs and be certified with little attention to intellectual rigor. When this has happened, it has been only natural for undergraduates to presume that education represents a convenient path to a degree for those who do not wish to be intellectually taxed. This attitude was reflected in a student's comment to a professor at one institution where education was viewed as "academically soft." When confronted with the possibility of being dropped from the education program because of low grades, she responded, "All I want to be is a teacher."

Fortunately, this kind of teacher preparation program is on the decline. With increasing public calls for teacher accountability and a heavy public focus on the quality of teacher preparation programs, there has been a conscientious effort in the last ten years to upgrade the quality of teacher preparation programs across the country. Many institutions are developing and instituting competency tests to ensure that teachers have a sure grasp on fundamental knowledge and skills before they are recommended for certification. School districts, too, are demanding teachers who are well grounded intellectually.

Rather than being an intellectually shallow profession, teaching demands a depth of academic preparation in a number of areas. Perhaps most beginning teachers are aware that teachers must have a good grasp of the subjects they are to teach, but instructional effectiveness demands as well teachers who have an understanding of such diverse and sophisticated topics as the physiological and psychological development of children, the structural elements of knowledge, and the systems approach as it is applied to curriculum development and instructional design. Some familiarity with philosophy, law, human relations, and other areas is expected as well.

FUNKY WINKERBEAN   By Tom Batiuk

(Funky Winkerbean by Tom Batiuk. © 1974, Field Enterprises, Inc. Courtesy of Field Newspaper Syndicate.)

People who think that education is an easy field ought to reexamine their choice of teaching as a career. How about your own feelings in this regard? Are you prepared to commit yourself to the study necessary to become a quality teacher? Would you be comfortable entering the field without a solid knowledge base? Would it be fair to your students if you were not "academically sound"? You need to think about these questions as you make decisions about your own willingness to commit yourself to the task of striving for the sort of intellectual excellence that characterizes good teachers.

"Several of My Relatives Are Teachers. . . ."

Amazingly, many individuals decide to go into teaching based on no more thoughtful reason than having a relative who is a teacher. When asked about their choice, these people frequently say something like this: "Well, my mother is a teacher, and it just seems like the natural thing to do." It may be true that individuals who have relatives who are teachers may have a broader picture of what the teacher's life is than people who have not been closely associated with teachers outside the school, but it does not follow that teaching skill passes automatically from generation to generation.

Many students who go into teaching because of an initial interest sparked by a relative who is a teacher do well. However, if their choice is made without serious reflection concerning alternative career choices, these students may be making a mistake. For a moment, think about your motivations for thinking about a career in teaching. Are you choosing teaching because you believe it will please your parents or because it has always been "expected" of you? If so, do you really want to be a teacher? Have you seriously thought about alternative careers? If you have not given careful consideration to your motives for going into teaching and have assumed that it is simply "the thing to do," you should take a serious look at the demands of the profession. It may be that you will decide that teaching, indeed, is exactly right for you, but this choice ought to be made on the basis of some hard-headed analysis.

Sometimes students go into teaching because they have heard that it is a good career to have while rearing a family. There is some logic to this conclusion. Teachers, after all, do have holidays and vacations at the same times as their children. There is reason to question, however, whether this is a sufficient reason for choosing teaching as a career. Choosing teaching because it is compatible with rearing a family seems to suggest that teaching does not demand a total commitment. The increasing pressures being put on teachers today suggest that like doctors and lawyers, professional teachers are expected to work hard and devote long hours (certainly beyond a simple eight-to-five day) to their career. Education today has moved beyond a time when it could be regarded as something less than a full-time profession where something less than total commitment of its practitioners would suffice.

"I Like the Autonomy of Teachers"

Some people say they are going into teaching because they are attracted by teachers' freedom of action. Certainly teachers do enjoy a certain amount of autonomy that many people find attractive. Rarely do teachers have a supervisor looking over their shoulders all the time to make sure that they are working properly. They enjoy a great deal of flexibility in planning individual lessons and designing instructional approaches to meet the special needs of the youngsters in their classrooms, and they have opportunities to express their personal creativity. Even though teachers do have a large amount of latitude, it must be recognized that there are restraints on their actions, and evidence suggests that teachers' freedom of action may be in a decline because of increasing public concern over the declining scores of learners on standardized achievement tests.

With an increased emphasis on the idea of accountability and the introduction of competency tests, more and more school districts are prescribing what content is to be taught, and even, in some cases, how. These trends suggest a reduction in the range of choices that teachers can make in planning and implementing their own instructional programs. Furthermore, to ensure that district-mandated procedures are being followed, there has been a general increase in recent years in the frequency of observational visits to teachers' classrooms by administrators and instructional supervisors. The bottom line of all this is that although teachers retain a good deal of freedom of action, they are still probably less autonomous today than they were ten or twenty years ago.

As you contemplate a possible future as a teacher, you need to recognize that teachers are being held accountable for their actions as never before. It is likely that a good deal of what you teach (and even how you teach it) is going to be prescribed by others. You need to ask yourself whether these conditions are acceptable to you. For many people, the answer is yes, but others may well conclude that today's classrooms do not provide the kind of personal autonomy they desire in a career.

"I Like Working with Youngsters"

It is certainly to be hoped that teachers enjoy working with young people. If they do not, they are bound to become very unhappy after a year or two in education. It must be recognized, however, that liking young people, by itself, does not mean that teaching is an appropriate career choice, given the special relationship between the teacher and the learners whom he or she works with in the classroom.

It is one thing to enjoy young people in informal settings: at the playground, at home, while baby-sitting, and at a circus. It is quite a different thing to be responsible for a class of twenty-five to thirty children who are supposed to attend to prescribed tasks and learn something. Nearly all children on a playground enjoy being where they are. In classrooms, some youngsters may be uninterested and even hostile. On occasion, teachers must enforce certain standards of behavior and discipline. As you think about a possible career in teaching, how do you react to the likelihood that you will have to exert strong personal leadership? Does your enjoyment of children go beyond the sort of casual relationship possible on informal and social occasions? These questions demand careful reflection.

As you think about these issues, you might consider the sources of your enjoyment of young people. Do you enjoy them because of their freshness and openness? Do you enjoy their energy? Or—and here is an "enjoyment" that too many insecure and ineffective teachers rarely admit to—do you enjoy them because of the sense of power you get from having young people do what you ask them to do? Is your enjoyment a product of personal insecurity? There is evidence that some individuals overcome their own personal self-worth problems by assuming positions where they can successfully control others over whom they are given authority—for example, children who are smaller and younger than themselves.

The issue of personal insecurity on the part of teachers is one that the profession has been reluctant to face. Some of these people are drawn to young children because youngsters often are friendly and willing to show affection. These behavior patterns can be tremendously appealing to someone who finds these things missing in his or her interactions with adults. The difficulty arises when individuals go into teaching expecting a continual flow of positive reactions from learners. When youngsters do not react as expected, these teachers frequently suffer increased feelings of self-doubt, anxiety, and professional dissatisfaction.

Problems of this sort frequently surface when a teacher is confronted by a class of youngsters who are not very excited about being in school. These youngsters fail to provide the reinforcement that the teacher needs. Frequently such youngsters challenge the teacher ("Why do we have to do this boring stuff all the time?"). Insecure teachers may well respond with negative comments that make the reactions of the youngsters even worse. A typical statement of teachers suffering from this problem is "How could they do this to me when I've tried to do so much for them?" The real issue here is troubled teachers who are psychologically insecure because of their inability to fulfill their own needs by developing warm working relationships with youngsters.

Although we have sketched some general problems of individuals who enter teaching almost exclusively because of a feeling that their personal needs can be met through interactions with youngsters, we do not want to leave the impression that good teachers do not need and desire positive reactions from their learners. Clearly they do. But the need for positive reactions from youngsters must be kept in perspective. It is not a sufficient motive, in and of itself, for electing a career in teaching. Those who go into teaching thinking that work with young people, alone, will provide therapeutic relief for personal problems will be disappointed.

"I Want to Make a Contribution to Society. . . ."

Many teachers are motived to enter the field by a feeling that they will be doing something "important." Certainly society does consider education a worthy enterprise. Vast resources have been expended on teaching youngsters over the years, and a large and diverse American population has been educated to levels unequaled in history. American youngsters compare quite well with their counterparts in other countries.

Despite these accomplishments, the feeling that education is an "important" undertaking is not universal. For example, a significant portion of the American population holds teaching to be a low-status occupation. Many people do not believe that teaching requires any special and sophisticated body of knowledge and skills. Some see teaching as a minimally demanding job that is selected by people who lack the intelligence or drive to succeed in such fields as medicine, law, or business.

The teacher who sees his or her role as significant and important may be discouraged in still another way. Such a teacher may well believe that he or she can "make a difference" if only the proper conditions are provided, yet very frequently, these conditions are not available. Many school decisions are based not on the criterion of educational excellence but on the criterion of keeping costs down. When legislatures meet, they frequently look at expenditures for education as a place to contain costs.

There is a need, too, to think through the view that a teacher can derive satisfaction from seeing youngsters change for the better. Certainly these changes do occur, and they do provide a great deal of pleasure for teachers, but many beginning teachers expect these changes to take place much faster than they do. Rarely do the attitudes and behavior of youngsters change overnight. Teachers who, with college degree and teaching certificate newly in hand, burst on education with a missionary zeal to see dramatic changes overnight find disappointment sooner than revolutionary change. Sometimes it takes years for the cumulative impact of a number of teachers to show itself in the changed behavior pattern of an individual learner. Those who have been teaching for some time have witnessed these transformations. Many impatient newcomers quit teaching after a year or two out of a mistaken impression that they are having no influence on youngsters.

In thinking about a career in education, it is well to keep in mind that teaching *is* an important job, but this recognition must be tempered by a further recognition that not all people in our society see it that way. Teachers must be strong individuals who can "keep the faith" even though many other

Box 20-1
Do You Really Want to Teach?

LET'S PONDER

1. As you think about your choice to enter teaching what were the things that influenced your choice?
2. Did you really choose teaching or was it something that just sort of happened?
3. Have you considered other alternatives to a teaching career? If so, what are they?
4. What are the advantages and disadvantages of these other options?
5. Are you proud of your choice to become a teacher? Do you readily admit to new acquaintances that you want to teach?
6. How much are you willing to commit in order to become a good teacher? What are you willing to do in order to prepare yourself?

people in our society do not see in education the significant undertaking that they do. As you think about a career in education, you need to ask yourselves several important questions about your ability to tolerate appreciation for your work that may be less than you think it should be. Does it bother you that some people do not hold teachers in particularly high regard? Can you live in an atmosphere where the kinds of materials you feel you need to do a good job are not available? These are serious questions. They should be faced squarely before you make a firm commitment to enter the teaching profession.

Let's assume that you have considered carefully all of the questions that have been raised in the previous sections. Let's assume, too, that you have decided that a career in education is definitely what you want to pursue. The next decisions you might wish to make regard the specific age group that you might like to work with and the kind of teaching environment you would prefer. These decisions should be made after careful consideration of your own strengths, weaknesses, and preferences.

Learners in the early elementary grades tend to show much more personal excitement about what goes on at school than do older youngsters. Typically most of them will do what the teacher asks without question. Many teachers find their freshness and openness to be appealing characteristics. The discipline problems encountered in this age group rarely pose severe challenges to the teacher's authority. Almost never are they personally threatening to the teacher. The discipline problems tend to center on self-control difficulties and limited attention spans, which make it difficult for some youngsters to attend to an assigned task for any great length of time.

Learners in the early elementary-school grades tend to be very dependent on the teacher. They require a maximum amount of guidance. Primary-grades teachers tend to be in motion almost continually, as they work hard to help individual youngsters and keep them productively engaged. These teachers must be able to break instructional tasks into numerous small pieces and to design learning experiences that are very activity-oriented. At this level, teachers cannot plan on giving extended oral presentations or asking youngsters to do extensive assignments in textbooks.

Youngsters in the early elementary grades cannot delve deeply into academic subject matter. They are not ready to deal with ideas that are very abstract. Most instruction must be supported with many concrete examples. The inability of learners in the primary grades to deal with deep and complex academic subject matter by no means suggests that teachers at this level need to know less than their colleagues who work with older children. They need to know a great deal about child growth and development. They must be well versed in numerous diagnostic techniques. They must be proficient in the use of a great variety of instructional techniques. They must be extremely skilled in designing systematic programs of instruction for youngsters who bring little prior learning to their tasks and who have very short attention spans. In short, teachers at this age level must be very well prepared if they are to do well with these children.

Teachers of children in the upper elementary grades face a different set of challenges. Learners in this age group continue to be generally positive in their attitudes toward school. They are beginning to be less dependent on the teacher than they were during the early elementary grades. They can perform tasks with less direct guidance. But the instruction still needs to be buttressed with large numbers of concrete examples, and teachers need to plan instruction to include a good sprinkling of activity-oriented experiences.

Discipline problems with youngsters in this age group begin to include some challenges to the authority of the teacher. As youngsters become increasingly aware of their peer group, some attempt to achieve status by openly opposing the teacher. Increasingly youngsters are likely to question rules and see "how far they can go."

The spread of intellectual ability among youngsters becomes much more pronounced among older elementary children than it is among early elementary children. By the fifth and sixth grades, some youngsters are able to deal with some rather abstract concepts, whereas others find learning difficult unless it involves things that are elemental and concrete. Teachers at this age level find their abilities stretched to the maximum as they attempt to provide learning experiences that will challenge their brighter learners at the same time that they are designing learning experiences appropriate to the abilities of their slower learners.

Teachers of the upper elementary grades need a good grasp of the physical and psychological development of children. Additionally, they require a fairly solid grounding in the various subjects of the curriculum. They need to be proficient designers of alternative instructional experiences to meet the great diversity of intellectual development likely to be found in upper elementary youngsters.

It is widely held that, of all age groups, the one that presents the most challenges to teachers is the junior-high-school group. Youngsters of this age are undergoing tremendous physiological changes, which frequently have great impact on their behavior in school. Successful junior-high-school teachers are well versed in the nature of these changes and understand the difficulties that these youngsters experience as they flip-flop back and forth between desires to be independent of adults and desires to be dependent on them.

One reason that the junior-high-school age vexes so many teachers is that the teachers of these youngsters are expected to have substantial preparation in one or two major academic areas. The time required to get this preparation frequently leaves sparse additional time to become well acquainted with the psychological and physiological makeup of youngsters of junior high school age. Many new junior-high-school teachers have no more than one or two undergraduate courses intended to provide them with these essential perspectives. Consequently a good many beginning junior-high-school teachers find themselves faced with acquiring this information during their first year or two of teaching.

Discipline problems with junior-high-school students can be severe. There is more likely to be violence, or at least the threat of violence, associated with discipline problems at this age level than with younger children. Part of the discipline problem stems from the unpredictability of learners in this age group. At one moment, they seem terribly sophisticated and mature. At another, their behavior seems incredibly immature. Teachers at this age level must work hard to maintain the kind of relationships with youngsters that can stop severe discipline problems before they start. The task is made especially difficult in that most junior-high-school teachers see a given student only once a day for a period no longer than fifty-five minutes. There is not the kind of continuous contact that can be used to bridge over differences that is enjoyed by many elementary-school teachers.

High school teachers must have a great deal of background in one or two academic subjects. This required depth of understanding provides both rewards and frustrations for high school teachers. Many high school teachers derive considerable personal pleasure from being able to concentrate on a single subject or two that they find personally interesting and exciting. On the other hand, many are distressed, particularly during their first few years of teaching, to learn that a good many students do not share their enthusiasm. Many beginning high school teachers report frustration because they

Box 20-2
Choosing an Age Level

1. Is there a particular subject area that interests you?
2. How would you react to a towering sixteen year old who tells you he is not going to do what you asked?
3. Do you get bored if forced to be repetitious and go very slowly?
4. How do you react to the immaturity and high dependency needs of young children?
5. Do you have a need for learners to demonstrate overt approval of you?
6. What age level would you like to teach? Why do you make this choice?

cannot begin to cover topics with the attention to depth and detail that characterized their college and university courses. Frequently, new teachers report shock at the lack of knowledge of high school students.

In terms of interpersonal relationships, high school teachers, to all intents and purposes, are working with young adults. Teachers who talk down to high school students or in any way seem to regard them as children are asking for trouble. But this does not mean that simply treating students as adults will solve all of the problems. Many high school youngsters are not terribly interested in a number of the subjects they are required to take, and high school teachers spend a good deal of time working on ways to motivate students. This task is a difficult one because, unlike younger children (especially those in the elementary schools), these youngsters are not always disposed to presume something is important simply because the teacher says that it is important.

High school teachers can have a great impact on the future lives of their students. Perhaps more than at any other level of public education, high school teachers can see the results of their efforts. Often, only a few years after high school, teachers are rewarded by seeing their former students moving into responsible community positions or otherwise giving evidence that they are going to "make it."

The role profiles sketched in this section about teachers who work with learners of different ages have been generalized. Certainly there is a tremendous diversity of experience for teachers at all levels, but we believe that at least some of the characteristics of teaching at these levels remain fairly constant from place to place. As you think about making a decision about the age level that you would like to work with, you should think about the nature of youngsters and teaching at each of these levels. How do the demands of teaching at each level fit in with your own personality and priorities? What age group would you like to teach?

Some Final Thoughts

As we approach the conclusion of this chapter, you might wish to review your responses on the attitude inventory presented at the beginning. Thinking about the pattern of your check marks and about the real demands of the teaching profession, what do you conclude? Is teaching, indeed, for you? If the answer to this question is yes, we are happy for you. The authors have always felt good about their own choice of careers in education. If your answer to this question is no, we are also happy for you. There are many ways to make a productive contribution in this world. If your way does not happen to be education, that's fine. We wish you all the best in whatever you do.

Our real concern is that those who *do* choose education make this decision based on a full understanding of what teaching is. It is our belief that people who opt for education after considering both the negative and positive aspects of the profession will be prepared to deal with education's problems as well as welcome education's rewards. It is, in our view, precisely this kind of clear-headed professional that education so desperately needs today.

Recapitulation of Major Ideas

1. Many people who enter teaching do not stay long. In many cases, they leave because they had an erroneous impression of the real nature of teaching. Individuals who contemplate a career in teaching would do well to learn as much as they can about what teaching really entails before making a firm commitment to the profession.
2. Many students enter teaching because they simply do not know what else to do, given their undergraduate major. In fact, there are other employment and career alternatives. A visit to a college or university placement center can provide information regarding a large number of alternatives.
3. Some undergraduates claim that they are going into teaching because the preparation program is not intellectually demanding. In fact, the requirements are stiffening everywhere. Schools also are becoming much more rigorous in their expectations of teachers. Ill-prepared teachers will not survive long in first-class school districts today.
4. Large numbers of undergraduates choose a teaching career because they have a relative who is a teacher. There is nothing about teaching that suggests that it is a competence that is passed from relative to relative. While it is reasonable that an interest in teaching could be sparked because of an admired relative who teaches, having a relative who is a teacher is not, of itself, a sufficient reason for committing oneself to a career in teaching.
5. A good number of prospective teachers are attracted to the profession

because of teachers' freedom of action. It is true that teachers do enjoy a good deal of autonomy, but it should be recognized that with the current pressures on school districts to demonstrate evidence of academic progress on the part of learners, there is a growing trend to make more and more decisions about what teachers can and cannot do at the central-district administrative offices. Teachers today are not as free to operate in their own classrooms as they were ten and twenty years ago.

6. Many teachers say that they chose their profession because of a love of young people. Certainly one would hope that teachers enjoy working with youngsters, but prospective teachers who are strongly motivated to go into teaching because of a "love of children" need to examine themselves carefully to determine whether the motive is really love of children or obtaining self-fulfillment by being in a position to exercise control over children.

7. Large numbers of prospective teachers say they want to become teachers because they will be doing something important. Certainly this is true, but teachers need to be strong individuals who can live comfortably in a world where many people do not think that teaching is terribly important or that teaching is a particularly prestigious occupation.

8. Demands placed on teachers vary considerably from one grade level to another. In deciding which age level to teach, prospective teachers need to examine their own strengths, weaknesses, and personal priorities.

9. Teaching is a profession that demands a special set of talents and commitments. It is not a profession that will satisfy everybody. Those who decide to pursue teaching should do so with a full knowledge of the pluses and minuses associated with the teacher's role in American society today.

Postexercise

Force-Field Analysis

DIRECTIONS: The force-field analysis is a technique that can help you identify the variables associated with a given issue or problem. On a separate piece of paper, prepare a diagram similar to the one printed below.

In the left-hand column list all the forces *favoring* your choice of teaching as a career.

In the right-hand column list all of the forces *opposing* your choice of teaching as a career.

When you have finished your lists, rank the forces in each column from *most important* to *least important*.

Forces Supporting My Choice of Teaching as a Career	*Forces Opposing My Choice of Teaching as a Career*

Now, look at your list and your rankings. Think about and respond to the following questions:

1. What do your rankings tell you about your own set of values?
2. Do you have more forces "supporting" or "opposing?" Does this information tell you anything?

Next, identify the three most important "supporting" forces and the three most important "opposing" forces. Gather as much additional information as you can about these forces and respond to these questions.

1. Does the information you found tend to make each force stronger or weaker? Why?
2. What chances do you see of overcoming the "opposing" forces?

Finally, weigh all of the evidence and respond to these questions.

1. Do you wish to commit yourself to a career in teaching?
2. What specific evidence supports the decision you have made?

Summary

Frequently, undergraduates decide to pursue a program leading to teachers' certification for very superficial reasons. A good deal of the unhappiness of teachers in the field stems from their inadequate understanding of the "real world" of teaching before they made a firm decision to become a teacher. There is a need for prospective teachers to weigh all the available evidence regarding the teacher's role and regarding alternative career options before making a final decision to go into professional education.

Once the decision has been made to become a teacher, undergraduates should give serious thought to the age group that they would prefer to teach. The characteristics associated with each age level tend to be fairly consistent from place to place. Future teachers should weigh carefully their own interests, personalities, and preferences before making a final decision about the age level with which they would like to work.

Finally, teaching is not for everyone. For some people, teaching can be a rewarding and richly satisfying profession. For others, it can be a source of personal pain, frustration, and unhappiness. The decision to teach or to do something else should not be taken lightly. Education is better served when those who are committed to it teach and those who are not do something else.

References

BORTON, TERRY. *Reach, Touch, and Teach*. New York: McGraw-Hill, 1970.

CURWIN, L. *Discovering Your Teaching Self*. Englewood Cliffs, N.J.: Prentice-Hall, 1975.

DISIBIO, ROBERT A. *"Teaching: Is It for Me?" College Student Journal* (Summer 1981): 170–171.

GREER, MARY, AND RUBENSTEIN, BONNIE. *Will the Real Teacher Please Stand Up?* 2nd ed. Santa Monica, Calif.: Goodyear Publishing, 1978.

HALLIHAN, WILLIAM P. "Should I Become a Teacher?" *Teacher Education* (Summer 1982): 16–18.

ORNSTEIN, ALLEN C. "Motivations for Teaching." *Viewpoints Teaching and Learning*. (Summer 1981): 65–75.

STUART, JESSE. *To Teach, To Love*. New York: Penguin Books, 1973.

Answers to Pretest/ Posttest Questions

CHAPTER 1

Pretest on page 4.
Posttest on page 20.

1. false
2. false
3. false
4. true
5. false
6. false
7. false
8. true
9. false
10. false

CHAPTER 2

Pretest on page 25.
Posttest on page 43.

1. true
2. true
3. false
4. true
5. false
6. false
7. true
8. true
9. false
10. false

CHAPTER 3

Pretest on page 47.
Posttest on page 68.

1. false
2. false
3. true
4. true
5. true
6. true
7. false
8. true
9. true
10. true

CHAPTER 4

Pretest on page 72.
Posttest on page 90.

1. false
2. true
3. true
4. true
5. true
6. false
7. true
8. false
9. true
10. true

CHAPTER 5

Pretest on page 93.
Posttest on page 111.

1. true
2. true
3. false

4. false
5. false
6. true
7. true
8. false
9. true
10. true

CHAPTER 6

Pretest on page 117.
Posttest on page 138.

1. false
2. true
3. true
4. false
5. false
6. true
7. false
8. false
9. true
10. true

CHAPTER 7

Pretest on page 144.
Posttest on page 163.

1. true
2. false
3. true
4. true
5. true
6. false
7. false
8. true
9. true
10. true

CHAPTER 8

Pretest on page 167.
Posttest on page 184.

1. false
2. true
3. false
4. true
5. true
6. true
7. true

8. false
9. false
10. false

CHAPTER 9

Pretest on page 188.
Posttest on page 207.

1. false
2. false
3. true
4. true
5. true
6. true
7. false
8. true
9. false
10. false
11. false
12. false
13. true
14. false

CHAPTER 10

Pretest on page 210.
Posttest on page 232.

1. false
2. true
3. true
4. false
5. false
6. true
7. false
8. false
9. true
10. true

CHAPTER 11

Pretest on page 235.
Posttest on page 253.

1. true
2. false
3. false
4. true
5. false
6. false
7. true

8. true
9. true
10. true

CHAPTER 12

Pretest on page 257.
Posttest on page 281.

1. false
2. false
3. false
4. false
5. false
6. false
7. false
8. true
9. false
10. false

CHAPTER 13

Pretest on page 285.
Posttest on page 301.

1. false
2. true
3. true
4. false
5. false
6. true
7. false
8. true
9. true
10. true

CHAPTER 14

Pretest on page 305.
Posttest on page 323.

1. false
2. true
3. true
4. true
5. true
6. true
7. false
8. false
9. true
10. true

CHAPTER 15

Pretest on page 330.
Posttest on page 349.

1. false
2. true
3. false
4. true
5. false
6. true
7. true
8. true
9. true
10. true

CHAPTER 16

Pretest on page 353.
Posttest on page 371.

1. true
2. true
3. true
4. true
5. false
6. true
7. false
8. true
9. true
10. false

CHAPTER 17

Pretest on page 375.
Posttest on page 393.

1. false
2. false
3. true
4. false
5. true
6. false
7. true
8. true
9. true
10. false

CHAPTER 18

Pretest on page 397.
Posttest on page 415.

1. true
2. true.
3. true
4. true
5. true
6. true
7. true
8. false
9. false
10. false

1. true
2. true
3. true
4. true
5. false
6. false
7. true
8. true
9. true
10. false

CHAPTER 19

Pretest on page 422.
Posttest on page 445.

CHAPTER 20

There are no pretests/posttests for this chapter

Name Index

Abel, David A, 282n
Addams, H. L., 446n
Aelin, Marshall, 351n
Amidon, Edmund J., 233n
Anderson, Ronald, 113n
Andrew, Michael D., 233n
Aristotle, 6

Baker, Kelley, 387, 394n
Barr, Robert, 139n
Barry, Joseph E., 70n
Barth, Roland, 165n
Becker, Henry J., 113n
Bell, Terrell H., 130
Bender, Hilary, 208n
Bergeson, John B., 373n
Beyer, Barry K., 446n
Biddle, Bruce J., 165n, 185n
Biehler, Robert, 22n, 351n
Blatt, Buron, 373n
Bogdan, Robert, 373n
Bolles, Richard N., 446n
Borton, Terry, 165n, 464n
Bowman, Richard F., 113n
Branan, Karen, 113n
Brandt, Anthony, 8, 22n
Brophy, Jere E., 165n, 185n
Broudy, Harry S., 91n
Bruner, Jerome, 91n
Burke, Daniel, 139n
Buser, Robert, 408–410, 411n, 416n
Butler, Donald J., 208n
Butts, Freeman, 17, 22n, 45n

Callahan, Raymond E., 303n
Charles C. M., 254n
Clements, Barbara S., 254n

Clough, Jennifer O., 417n
Cochran, J., 446n
Conner, Lindsay A., 282n
Connors, Eugene T., 394n
Conroy, Pat, 324n
Cooperstein, Rhonda Ann, 373n
Cordasco, Francesco, 45n
Cornelius, Richard, 113n
Cox, C. Benjamin, 45n
Cremin, Lawrence, 45n
Curtis, Leonard T., 373n
Curwin, Richard L., 255n, 464n

Daimler, George, 94
Daneliuk, Carl, 99, 113n
Davis, O. L., Jr., 45n
Demause, Robert T., 351n
Dewey, John, 6, 22n, 36, 39, 86, 199–200
Dillon, Jacqueline, 165n
Disibio, Robert A., 464n
Doll, Ronald C., 91n
Donley, Marshall O., 288–289, 293–294, 297, 303n
Duea, Jerry, 10, 22n
Duke, Daniel Linden, 254n
Dyrli, Odvard Egil, 113n

Egan, Gerard, 233n
Elam, Stanley M., 236, 254n, 277
Elkind, David, 22n, 347–348, 351n
Ellenwood, Stephan, 208n
Elson, John, 282n
Emmer, Edmund T., 254n
Emmingham, Robin, 417n
Erikson, Erik H., 22n, 346, 351n
Evertson, Carolyn M., 254n

Felker, D., 233n
Fisher, Louis, 282n, 394n
Flanders, Ned A., 233n
Flavell, John H., 91n
Flygare, Thomas J., 303n
Ford, Henry, 94
Ford, Paul L., 6, 22n
Francis, Samuel N., 282n
Franklin, Benjamin, 31, 201
Frazier, Calvin M., 70n
Friedenberg, Edgar Z., 91n

Gallup, George H., 10, 22n, 236, 254n
Georgiades, William D. H., 165n
Gilstrap, R., 233n
Giordano, Gerald A., 373n
Glick, Harriet M., 373n
Glickman, Carl D., 255n
Goldhammer, Keith, 61–62, 70n
Good, Thomas L., 165n, 185n
Goodlad, John I., 91n
Goodlin, E. H., 446n
Greer, Mary, 165n, 464n
Greth, Carlos Vidal, 113n
Gross, Beatrice, 233n

Hallihan, William P., 464n
Hammes, Richard R., 395n
Havighurst, Robert J., 91n, 351n
Hawley, Richard A., 233n
Hawley, Willis D., 91n
Hazard, William R., 56, 70n, 282n, 395n
Heinich, Robert, 373n
Hendrickson, Grant, 413, 417n
Henson, Kenneth T., 22n, 165n, 351n, 395n
Higgins, James E., 165n
Hitler, Adolf, 196
Hodgkinson, Harold L., 7–9, 22n, 169, 185n
Hooker, Clifford P., 395n
Huggett, Albert J., 325n
Hunkins, Francis P., 91n
Husen, Torsten, 139n
Hutchins, Robert, 17
Hyer, Anna L., 364, 366–367, 373n

Jarolimek, John, 6, 13, 22n
Jarvis, F. Washington, 233n
Jefferson, Thomas, 6, 22n, 31–32
Johnson, David, 113n
Johnson, Lyndon, 123
Jones, Thomas N., 282n, 394n

Kemerer, Frank R., 282n
Kennedy, John F., 6, 22n
King, M. R., 446n
Kirk, Samuel A., 373n
Klossen, David, 113n
Kneller, George F., 208n
Koerner, J. D., 70n
Kreider, Paul T., 446n
Krist, Michael, 139n
Krug, Edward A., 8, 22n

L'Abate, Luciano, 373n
Lapp, Diane, 208n
Lavassor, Emile, 94
Lean, Arthur R., 6, 22n
Leinhardt, Gaie, 351n, 373n
Levin, Dan, 113n
Lieberman, Myron, 303n, 324n
Long, Ruth, 408–410, 411n, 416n
Lortie, Dan C., 10, 22n
Love, Harold D., 373n

McDonald, Dianne H., 113n
Mace, Jane, 229, 233n
Mackey, Maureen, 113n
McNeil, J. D., 91n
Mahoney, Erika, 446n
Mann, Horace, 32–34
Martha, John, 208n
Martin, W., 233n
Martorelli, Debra, 165n
Meckel, Adrienne Maravich, 254n
Medland, Michael, 254n
Meehan, A. M., 351n
Menacker, Julius, 395n
Mendler, Allen N., 255n
Miller, George S., 373n
Monster, G. J., 446n
Moses, Barbara, 373n

Nagi, Mostafah, 324n
Neisworth, John T., 373n

Ornstein, Allen C., 45n, 208n, 446n, 464n
Overton, Willis F., 351n

Pallay, Allen, 351n, 373n
Pandy, Siddheshwar Nath, 208n
Panhard, Rene, 94
Pascarella, Ernest, 395n
Peirce, Neil R., 131, 139n
Perkinson, Henry J., 13, 22n, 45n
Pettus, Theodore, 446n
Piaget, Jean, 84–85, 337–340, 351
Pifer, Alan, 351n
Pittman, Betsy, 417n
Pitts, Marcella R., 113n
Pugh, Meredith D., 324n

Quay, H. C., 373n

Reagan, Ronald, 41
Richey, Robert W., 45n
Robbins, Jerry H., 417n
Roblyer, M. D., 113n
Rodgers, Frederich A., 168, 171, 186n
Rosen, Sheri, 113n
Rosson, J., 446n
Rousseau, Jean Jacques, 85–86
Rubin, Louis, 139n, 165n
Rubinstein, Bonnie, 165n, 464n

Samler, Darel P., 282n
Sanford, Julie P., 254n
Sapon-Shevin, Mara, 139n
Sapp, Gary L., 417n
Schimmel, David, 282n, 394n
Schubert, Marsha, 373n
Schultz, Fred, 22n
Schultz, Jane B., 362, 373n
Schuster, Jack H., 70n
Schutz, Richard E., 100, 113n
Scribner, Jay D., 70n

Semler, Darel P., 394n
Senter, Joy, 97, 99, 113n
Shannon, Thomas A., 70n
Sharp, D. Louise, 165n
Shroyer, G., 446n
Smith, Frederick R., 45n
Smith, Robert M., 373n
Smith, Vernon, 139n
Sprinthall, Norman A., 23n, 351n
Sprinthall, Richard C., 23n, 351n
Staub, Frederick W., 395n
Stearns, Marian S., 373n
Stein, Harry, 446n
Stinnett, T. M., 325n
Stuart, Jesse, 165n, 233n, 464n

Toben, Carolyn, 417n
Travers, P., 446n
Travers, Robert M. W., 165n
Turnbull, Ann P., 362, 373n
Tweedy, Hewey, 408–410, 411n, 416n
Tyack, David G., 45n
Tyler, Ralph W., 9, 22n

Unruh, Glenys G., 91n

Valverde, Leonard A., 139n
Vitale, Michael, 254n

Wadsworth, Barry J., 23n, 351n
Weiner, Elizabeth Hunter, 255n
Wells, H. G., 6
Wesley, Edgar B., 303n
Williams, Dennis A., 113n
Wilson, Charles H., 325n
Wilson, Elizabeth C., 325n
Wingo, Max G., 208n
Wirt, Frederick M., 50, 56, 70n
Wolfgang, Charles L., 255n
Worsham, Murray E., 254n
Wright, Annette E., 99, 113n

Subject Index

Academic achievement, 6–9, 16–17, 40–
41, 76, 145–146, 160–162, 334,
341–348
Academies, 31–32
Administration of schools. *See*
educational management
AFL–CIO, 295, 298
American Federation of Teachers, 34,
284–300
concentration of members, 295–296
history, 296–299
proposed merger with N.E.A., 298
strike activity, 298
United Federation of Teachers
affiliate, 297
view of teaching profession, 286–288
Applications for teaching positions,
434–435
Auditorily handicapped learners, 360
Axiology, 196–197

Back-to-the-basics movement, 204
Baker v. Owens, 394n
Bandwagonism, 100
Behavioral objectives. *See* learning
objectives
Behaviorally handicapped learners, 362–
363
Bell, Terrel H., 130
Bilingual Education, 123–126, 333–336
See also civil rights
Binet, Albert, 36
Biological Science Curriculum Study, 77
Blind Learners, 360
*Blodgett v. Board of Trustees, Tamalpais
Union High School District,* 272,
282n

Board of Trustees v. Stubblefield, 269,
282n
Boston English Classical School, 32
Boston Latin Grammar School, 30–31
Brown v. Board of Education, 120–121
Brubaker v. Board of Education, 275, 282n
Burnout. *See* teacher burnout

"Cardinal Principles," 37–38
Carnegie Foundation Report, 132
Certification. *See* teachers' certification
Characteristics-of-learners curricula, 84–
88
strengths, 86–87
weaknesses, 87–88
Citizenship education, 14–15, 81–84,
145, 147–148, 157–159, 201
Civil rights, 41, 54, 63, 66, 119–128,
137, 263–264, 333–336, 353–373
bilingual education, 123–126, 333–
336
busing, 121
handicapped learners, 67, 126–128,
353–373
legislation and teacher hiring, 263–
264
magnet schools, 121
multicultural education, 123–126
poverty and children, 334
segregation issue, 120–123, 236
sex discrimination, 126, 392
Class size, 173
Classroom management, 176–177, 234–
254, 279–280
discipline, 242–251, 279–280, 380–
382
establishing rules and routines, 238

Classroom management (*Cont.*)
  lesson management, 239–242
  managing environments, 248–250
  preventing serious behavior problems, 243–246
  responding to inappropriate behavior, 246–248
  suspension and expulsion, 381–382
  teachers and significant misbehavior, 250–251
Closed file, 390
Cocurricular activities, 398–416
  barriers to learner involvement, 410–412
  claimed benefits, 406–408
  criticisms, 402–406
  elementary schools, 399–400
  high schools, 401–402
  learners' reasons for participating, 408–409
  middle schools and junior high schools, 400–401
  numbers of learners involved, 409–410
  teachers pay issue, 412–414
"Common school," 32
Competency testing, 60, 135–137, 264
  See also testing
Computer literacy, 95
Computers in schools, 94–115
  academic program applications, 101–103
  claimed advantages, 95–99
  concerns, 99–101
  program management applications, 103–106
  suggestions for teachers, 106–110
  terminology glossary, 113–115
Continuing contract, 265
Contracts. *See* teachers' contracts
Control of education, 29–30, 46–70, 259, 354–359
  federal influences, 49, 61–67, 354–359
  local influences, 50–55, 66–67
  state influences, 48–49, 55–60, 66–67, 259, 267
Counseling, 219–221, 250, 306
Counselors, 306–317
Curriculum. *See* school curricula

Daimler, George, 94
Deaf learners, 360
Deductive logic, 197
Demand for teachers. *See* supply of teachers
Developmental stages, 84–86, 337–340
Dewey, John, 6, 36, 39, 86, 199–200
Diagnosing learners, 216
Dillon's rule, 56–57
Directive counseling, 314–315
Discipline. *See* classroom management
Discipline-related instruction, 242–243
Dixon v. Alabama State Board of Education 378–379, 394n
Doe v. Renfroe, 394n
Doe, P. W. v. San Francisco Unified School District, 282n
Due process, 265–266, 268, 383–384, 394
  applied to teacher dismissal, 265–266, 268
  procedural component, 384
  substantive component, 383

Earth Science Curriculum Project, 77
Education for All Handicapped Act. *See* Public Law 94-142
Education Index, 225
Educational malpractice, 277–289, 392
Education professors, 306–311
Educational finance, 30–34, 41, 48, 133–137, 356, 369–370
  educating handicapped learners, 356, 369–370
  Horace Mann's views, 32
  taxpayers' views, 129, 133–137
Educational history, 3–45, 73–76, 123–128, 175–176, 354–356, 376–380
  academies, 31–32
  American education after World War II, 39–41
  American Federation of Teachers, 295–298
  bilingual education, 123–126
  changes in schools' legal relationship to learners, 376–380
  changing learner characteristics, 175–176
  early colonial period, 28–30, 75
  from 1800 to the Civil War, 32–34

"Great Society" proposals, 123–124
handicapped learners, 126–128, 354–356
high schools, 32, 34–35
late colonial period and Revolutionary
War period, 31–32
life adjustment education, 39
multicultural education, 123–126
National Education Association, 288–295
origins of subject-centered curricula, 76
progressive education movement, 39
sex descrimination, 126
Sputnik I's impact, 40, 61, 77
tradition of local control, 51
tradition of state control, 48
Educational innovations, 92–115
Educational malpractice, 277–288, 392
Educational management, 26, 28–30,
103–106, 234–254
See also control of education
classroom management and discipline,
234–254
computer applications, 103–106
program for handicapped learners,
368–372
Puritans' views, 28–30
relationships between teachers and
administrators, 311–314
teachers' roles, 221–223
U.S. versus foreign practices, 26
Educational purposes, 6, 11–18, 28–42,
71–88, 187–233
academic achievement, 16–17, 76,
145–146, 160–162
axiology, 196–197
citizenship, 14–15, 81–84, 145, 147–148, 157–159
Committee on College Entrance
Requirements' views, 34
epistemology, 193–195
essentialism, 200–201
existentialism, 202–204
hedonism, 196
individual development, 17–18, 36,
84–88, 148–149, 157–159, 356–359
logic, 197
metaphysics, 192–193

N.E.A. Committee of Ten's Views, 34
perennialism, 198–199
progressivism, 199
Puritan's views, 11–12, 75
reactions to *Sputnik I*, 61, 77, 291
reconstructionism, 200–201
social problem-solving, 13, 129
vocational preparation, 16
Educational quality, 6–9, 8–19, 40–41,
129–137, 277–278, 364–367
See also philosophies of education
Emotionally disturbed learners, 362–363
Epistemology, 193–195
Essentialism, 200–201
Evaluating learning outcomes, 217–218,
357, 389.
See also testing
Exceptional learners, 67, 126–128, 336,
353–373
auditorily handicapped and deaf, 360
behaviorally handicapped, 362–363
emotionally disturbed, 362–363
mentally retarded, 363–364
orthopedically handicapped, 360
visually handicapped and blind, 360
Existentialism, 202–204
Expulsion, 382
Extracurricular activities, 398–416
barriers to involvement, 410–412
claimed benefits, 406–408
criticisms, 402–406
elementary schools, 399–400
high schools, 401–402
learners' reasons for participating,
409–412
middle schools and junior high
schools, 400–401
numbers of learners involved, 409–410
teacher pay issue, 412–414

Family Educational Rights and Privacy
Act, 389
Federal control of education. *See* control
of education
Ford, Henry, 94
Franklin, Benjamin, 31, 201
Franklin Academy, 31
Freedom of speech and expression,
386–387

Gallup Poll, 10, 236
Givhan v. Western Line Consolidated School District, 273, 282n
Goss v. Lopez, 282n
Governance issue, 295
Guidance counselors. *See* counselors

Handicapped learners, 67, 126–128, 353–373
  auditorily handicapped and deaf, 360
  behaviorally handicapped, 362–363
  emotionally disturbed, 362–363
  mentally retarded, 363–364
  orthopedically handicapped, 360
  visually handicapped and blind, 360
"Hard" subjects, 195.
  See also "soft" subjects
Hedonism, 196
Hiring of teachers, 263–268, 423–446
  applications, 434–435
  choosing a grade level, 457–460
  credentials files, 436–438
  interviews, 438–442
  letters of inquiry, 427–431
  locating openings, 424–427
  placement centers, 424–427, 435–438
  résumés, 431–434
History of education. *See* educational history
Hitler, Adolf, 196
Hutchins, Robert, 17

"Imaginary audience," 347
Implementing instruction, 217
In loco parentis, 376–378, 394
Individualized programs, 17–18, 84–88, 148–149, 157–159, 199–200, 357
Inductive logic, 197
Ingraham v. Wright, 279, 283n
Instructional activities, 216–217
Instructional managers, 214
Instructional objectives. *See* learning objectives
Instructional planning, 213–219, 357–359
  determining objectives, 214–215
  diagnosing learners, 216
  evaluating learning outcomes, 217–218
  implementing instruction, 217
  planning instructional activities, 216–217
  requirements of Public Law 94–142, 357–359
Intermediate Science Curriculum Study, 77
International Mathematics Olympiad, 9
Interviews, 263–265, 438–442
IQ score, 37

Jefferson, Thomas, 6, 31–32
Job-seeking procedures. *See* hiring of teachers
Johnson, Lyndon, 123

Kalamazoo case, 34
Kennedy, John F., 6
Kingsville Independent School District v. Cooper, 274, 283n

Lau v. Nichols, 125
Lavassor, Émile, 94
Learners' characteristics, 84–88, 97–98, 153–156, 175–176, 331–351, 359–368
  bilingual children, 123–126, 333–334
  changing patterns in the classroom, 331–332
  children of poverty, 334
  defining *normal*, 340
  exceptional learners, 359–368
  grades one to three, 342–343, 457–458
  grades four to six, 343–344, 458–459
  grades seven to nine, 344–346, 459
  grades ten to twelve, 346–348, 459–460
  handicapped learners, 359–368
  motivation, 97–98, 153–156
  physiological development, 84–85
  Piaget's developmental stages, 84–85, 337–340
  preschool and kindergarten, 341–342
  Rousseau's views, 85–86
Learners' cocurricular activities, 398–416
Learners' extracurricular activities, 398–416

Learners' performance, 6–9, 16–17,
    40–41, 76, 145–146, 160–162,
    334, 341–348, 392
  U.S. and foreign nations, 9
Learners' rights, 376–392
  curriculum and instruction, 390–392
  discipline issue, 380–382
  Family Educational Rights and Privacy
    Act, 389
  freedom of speech and expression,
    386–387
  grades, diplomas, and graduation,
    389
  historical changes, 376–380
  in loco parentis, 376–378, 394
  marriage and pregnancy, 384–486
  privacy, 389
  search and seizure, 387–389
Learning objectives, 214–215, 357
Least restrictive environment, 354, 357–
    359, 372
  See also Public Law 94-142
Legal liability. *See* teachers' legal liability
Lesson planning, 239–242
Liability. *See* teachers' legal liability
Liberty rights, 268
Life-adjustment education, 39
Local control of education. *See* control
  of education
Logic, 197

Magnet schools, 121
Mainframe computer, 94
Mainstreaming, 128, 355–359
  See also Public Law 94-142
Mann, Horace, 32–34
Married learners, 384–386
Massachusetts School Law of 1642, 30
Mentally retarded learners, 363–364
Metaphysics, 192–193
Meyer v. Nebraska, 268, 283n
Minicomputers, 94
Minimum competency testing. *See*
  competency testing
Morrison v. State Board of Education, 270,
    283n
Motivation, 97–98, 153–156, 216
  computers, 97–98
Multicultural education, 123–126
  See also civil rights

"A Nation at Risk," 131
National Assessment of Educational
    Progress, 334
National Commission on Excellence in
    Education, 130–131
National Defense Education Act, 40, 61
National Department of Education, 34
National Education Association, 34, 37,
    284–300
  changing views of strikes, 290–293
  governance issue, 295
  history, 288–295
  sanctions tool, 293–294
  UniServ, 294
  view of teaching profesion, 286–288
NEA Reporter, 293
Needs-of-society curricula, 81–84, 202
  strengths, 82
  weaknesses, 82–84
Negotiations. *See* professional
  negotiation acts
Nondirective counseling, 315
Normal schools, 33–34
Nurses. *See* school nurses

"Old Deluder Satan Act," 30
Open records, 389–391
Oral contracts, 268
Orthopedically handicapped learners,
    360

Panhard, René, 94
Paraprofessionals, 177
Parducci v. Rutland, 274, 283n
Parent-teacher organizations, 226–228
Perennialism, 198–199
Performance objectives. *See* learning
  objectives
Personal computers. *See* microcomputers
"Personal fable," 347–348
Pettit v. State Board of Education, 271,
    283n
Phillips Academy, 31
Phillips Exeter Academy, 31
Philosophies of education, 187–233
  axiology, 196–197
  epistemology, 193–195
  essentialism, 200–201
  existentialism, 202–204
  logic, 197

Philosophies of education (*Cont.*)
  metaphysics, 192–193
  perennialism, 198–199
  progressivism, 199–200
  reconstructionism, 202
  See also educational purposes
Physical Science Study Committee, 77
Piaget, Jean, 84–85, 337–340, 351
Pickering v. Board of Education of
    Township High School District 205,
    273, 283n
Placement services, 424–427, 435–
    438
Plessy v. Ferguson, 120
Poverty and children 334
Pregnant learners, 384–386
Probable cause, 388
Professional development of teachers.
    See teachers' professional
    development
Professional negotiation acts, 291–292
Professional review board, 261–262
Program approval pattern, 261–262
Progressive education movement, 39
Progressivism, 199–200
Property rights, 268
Proposals Relating to the Youth of
    Pennsylvania, 31
Psychiatrists. *See* school psychiatrists
Psychologists. *See* school psychologists
Psychometrists. *See* school
    psychometrists
Public Law 94–142, 67, 127–128, 353–
    373
Pupil personnel services, 321
Pupils. *See* learners

Quality of education. *See* educational
    quality

Reagan, Ronald, 42
Reasonable suspicion, 388
Reconstructionism, 202
Rousseau, Jean Jacques, 85–86

Sanctions, 293–294
Sarac v. State Board of Education, 270,
    283n
Scholastic Aptitude Test, 9, 134

School calendar, 27
School counselors, 306–317
School curricula, 30, 41, 56, 71–91,
    318–320, 391–392
  academics, 31
  Boston Latin Grammar School, 30
  characteristics of learners, 84–88
  colonial period, 30
  curriculum specialists, 318–320
  early high schools, 32
  influence of "cardinal principles,"
    37–38
  late 19th century high schools, 34
  life adjustment education, 39
  needs of society, 81–84
  progressive education movement,
    39
  Public Law, 94–142, 346–359
  after *Sputnik I,* 40
  subject-centered, 73–81
  teachers' curriculum development
    roles, 223–224
School enrollments, 8, 30–31, 33–34,
    35
School history. *See* educational history
School management. *See* educational
    management
School nurses, 306, 321
School psychiatrists, 321
School psychologists, 317–318
School psychometrists, 321
School purposes. *See* educational
    purposes
Segregation. *See* civil rights
Serrano v. Priest, 134
Sex discrimination, 126, 392
Social promotion, 135
"Soft" subjects, 195
  See also "hard" subjects
Sputnik I, 40, 61, 77, 291
State control of education. *See* control
    of education
State v. McKinnon, 395n
State of Washington Administrative
    Code, 276
Strikes. *See* teachers' strikes
Structure of the discipline, 77
Students, *See* learners
Suspension, 381–382

Subject-centered curricula, 73–81
  advantages, 78–79
  broad fields, 80–81
  disadvantages, 79–80
Supply of teachers, 172–183
  general trends, 182
  related to teaching specialty, 183

Taxpayers' revolt, 133–135
  See also educational finance
Teacher burnout, 229
Teacher Education and Professional
  Standards Commission, 291
Teachers' aides, 177
Teachers' certification, 56, 158, 224,
  258–263
Teachers' competency testing, 264
Teachers' contracts, 265–268
Teachers' credentials files, 436–438
Teachers' employment situations, 172–
  175, 177, 258–268
Teachers' exceptional learners, 359–368
Teachers' family backgrounds, 168–171
Teachers' general characteristics, 166–
  172
  See also philosophies of education
Teachers' handicapped learners, 359–
  368
Teachers' interactions with other
  professionals, 305–324
  administrators, 311–314
  counselors, 314–317
  curriculum specialists, 318–320
  education professors, 307–311
  school nurses, 321
  school psychiatrists, 321
  school psychologists, 317–318
  school psychometrists, 321
Teachers' job searches. *See* hiring of
  teachers
Teachers' legal liability, 275–280, 392
  criminal liability, 275
  educational malpractice, 277–278,
    392
  malfeasance, 275–277
  misfeasance, 275, 277
  negligence, 275–278
  nonfeasance, 275, 277
  tort liability, 275

Teachers' nonteaching duties, 178–179
Teachers' organizations, 34, 37
  See also National Education
  Association and American Federation
  of Teachers
Teachers' philosophies. *See* philosophies
  of education
Teachers' professional development,
  224–226
Teachers' racial characteristics, 171
Teachers' reasons for teaching, 143–
  165, 449–461
  autonomy argument, 454
  contribution to society argument,
    456–457
  default argument, 450–451
  enjoyment of young people argument,
    454–456
  excitement of learning, 145–149,
    160–162
  importance of teaching, 145–149,
    157–159
  intellectually easy argument, 451–
    453
  lack of routine, 145–149, 152–157
  nice working conditions, 150–152
  relatives who teach argument, 453
Teachers' résumés, 431–434
Teachers' rights, 269–275
  academic freedom, 274–275
  freedom of expression, 273
  private lives, 269–273
Teachers' roles, 209–233
  administrative and supervisory duties,
    221–223
  cocurricular activities, 412–414
  counseling, 219–221, 250
  curriculum development
    responsibilities, 223–224
  extracurricular activities, 412–414
  instructional planning, 211–219
  professional development
    responsibilities, 224–226
  public relations, 226–228
Teachers' status, 10–11, 129, 157–159
Teachers' strikes, 290–293, 296, 298
Teachers' tenure, 265–266
Teachers' values, 158–159, 168, 176,
  187–233

Teaching techniques. *See* instructional
    activities
Tenure, 265–266
Tenure contract, 265
Term contract, 265
Testing, 36–37, 135–137, 188–190,
        217–218, 264, 357
    bias issue, 37, 137
    competency testing, 60, 135–137, 264
    instructional planning role, 217–218
    intelligence testing, 36–37
    Public Law 94–142 requirements, 357
    Scholastic Aptitude Test, 9, 134
Thompson v. Southwest School District,
        272, 283n
*Tinker v. Des Moines Independent
    Community School District,* 379, 387,
        395n

Title VII of the Civil Rights Act of 1964,
        263–264
Title IX of Public Law 92-318, 136
Today's Education, 293
Twentieth Century Fund Report, 125,
        131

Unification issue, 294
UniServ, 294
United Federation of Teachers, 297–298

Visually handicapped learners, 360
Vocational programs, 16, 31, 38, 201

Washington State Law Against
    Discrimination, 263
Williams, Roger, 28
Woods Hole Conference, 77